Conflict and Compromise
Volume II

CONFLICT AND COMPROMISE

VOLUME II
POST-CONFEDERATION CANADA

Raymond B. Blake

Jeffrey A. Keshen

Norman J. Knowles

Barbara J. Messamore

UNIVERSITY OF TORONTO PRESS

Library and Archives Canada Cataloguing in Publication
Blake, Raymond B. (Raymond Benjamin), author
Conflict and compromise / Raymond B. Blake, Jeffrey Keshen, Norman Knowles, Barbara Messamore.
Includes index.
Contents: v. 2. Post-confederation Canada.
Issued in print and electronic formats.

ISBN 978-1-4426-3557-9 (volume 2: paperback).—ISBN 978-1-4426-3558-6 (volume 2: hardback). —ISBN 978-1-4426-3559-3 (volume 2: html). —ISBN 978-1-4426-3560-9 (volume 2: pdf).
1. Canada—History. 2. Cultural pluralism—Canada—History. I. Keshen, Jeff, 1962–, author II. Knowles, Norman James, 1963–, author III. Messamore, Barbara Jane, 1959–, author IV. Title.

FC165.B54 2017 971 C2016-905201-X   C2016-905202-8

We welcome comments and suggestions regarding any aspect of our publications—please feel free to contact us at news@utphighereducation.com or visit our Internet site at www.utppublishing.com.

North America
5201 Dufferin Street
North York, Ontario, Canada, M3H 5T8

2250 Military Road
Tonawanda, New York, USA, 14150
ORDERS PHONE: 1–800–565–9523
ORDERS FAX: 1–800–221–9985
ORDERS E-MAIL: utpbooks@utpress.utoronto.ca

UK, Ireland, and continental Europe
NBN International
Estover Road, Plymouth, PL6 7PY, UK
ORDERS PHONE: 44 (0) 1752 202301
ORDERS FAX: 44 (0) 1752 202333
ORDERS E-MAIL: enquiries@nbninternational.com

Every effort has been made to contact copyright holders; in the event of an error or omission, please notify the publisher.

This book is printed on paper containing 100% post-consumer fibre.

The University of Toronto Press acknowledges the financial support for its publishing activities of the Government of Canada through the Canada Book Fund.

Printed in Canada

CONTENTS

PREFACE

Shortly after the Truth and Reconciliation Commission (TRC) released its final report in 2015, two professors from the University of Winnipeg wrote in an op-ed for the *National Post* that the Commission's report lacked "robust evidence gathering, comparative or contextual data, and cause-effect relationships."[1] While the professors did not deny the obvious harm that residential schools had done to Indigenous peoples, they pointed out that the report opted for a particular way of gathering the "truth." The TRC report was flawed, they suggested, when judged by contemporary Western juridical and objective social science standards.

The reaction from some in the academic community was swift and strident. A group of academics at the University of Manitoba, also in Winnipeg, expressed "concern and embarrassment" with their fellow scholars, claiming that the perspective offered in the op-ed was not "consistent with the views of the vast majority of our colleagues at the University of Manitoba." They further insisted that it did not reflect the "main currents of thought in those disciplines devoted to understanding genocide and settler-Indigenous relations."[2] Others considered the op-ed an example of "colonial

---

1 Rodney E. Clifton and Hymie Rubenstein, "Debunking the Half-Truths and Exaggerations in the Truth and Reconciliation Report," *National Post*, June 4, 2015, http://news.nationalpost.com/full-comment/clifton-rubenstein-debunking-the-half-truths-and-exaggerations-in-the-truth-and-reconciliation-report; and Rodney E. Clifton and Hymie Rubenstein, "Truth and Reconciliation Report Tells a 'Skewed and Partial Story' of Residential Schools," *National Post*, June 22, 2015, http://news.nationalpost.com/full-comment/rubenstein-clifton-truth-and-reconciliation-report-tells-a-skewed-and-partial-story-of-residential-schools.

2 Centre for Human Rights Research, University of Manitoba, "Petition Supports TRC Report," http://chrr.info/images/stories/Clifton_and_Rubenstein.79_signatures.pdf.

nostalgia" and hostile to Indigenous peoples. It was an unusual and very public exchange between professors who held different views on how to search for "truth" on a particular subject where history and the art of remembering play important roles.

This brief exchange between scholars shows that the search to understand the past is contested vigorously. That is nothing new, of course, but such exchanges have moved from classrooms and seminars on university campuses and from academic publications to the public space. In this instance, the exchange was carried out in Canada's national newspapers, through open letters and petitions. The exchange attracted the attention of mainstream media outlets and generated considerable traffic on social media. The exchange also hints that there is increasingly little room for debate among scholars in the search to understand the past. The presentation of the past has become politicized, and with the Truth and Reconciliation Commission it became particularly emotive and controversial, because there has been actual harm done by a privileged group toward a less fortunate people. The history of all nations contains controversial and sensitive issues, and those issues more than ever seem to enrage historians as they argue about what happened, why it happened, and the significance of such events.

Good history helps people know and understand the world in which they live. History is not simply a study of the past; it is a continual process of understanding the changes and challenges that we face as a society. The privileging of some subjects over others in the writing of history and the uneven remembering of the past has long been a fundamental component of the historian's work. Canadian history, of course, has been no exception. Over the past few decades, biography, working-class history, women's history, military history, and French-English relations have all been privileged at various times. At the moment, Indigenous-centred history, the politics of decolonization, and the history of dispossession are privileged, but that, too, will change as the next generation of scholars and students reinterprets and recalibrates Canada's past in new and different ways. The primary duty of historians, as Oscar Wilde suggested, is to rewrite history. That process of the writing and re-writing of history reflects the needs and ideas of the moment and the predilections, prejudices, and ambitions of each generation, but the past did happen and it cannot be unlived, nor can it be erased.

It is Canada's past and the challenges and opportunities that Canadians faced that this book attempts to understand. We acknowledge, though, that all writing of history tells a particular version of what human society has done. It is our hope that this history of Canada provides not only an account of events and challenges, but also an explanation of the factors that influenced their unfolding and an assessment of their consequences. Such an approach, we believe, can help to not only provide a richer understanding of the past but also help to build a better future. We seek to understand the dynamics that motivate the past by examining, for instance, changes in social practice, shifts in power, development of new institutions, and public and private morality. History tries to grasp the nature, causes, and results of change; it might even be said that history is a study of the human response to changing conditions and circumstances. In the writing and studying of Canadian history we realize that we must be sensitive to the current politics and mores that inform us as historians.

It is essential to question received versions of the past and debate, respectfully, with those who offer different interpretations. All interpretations of events are coloured by our own biases—our nationality, our gender, our social class, even our faith, and the very age in which we live. Additionally, we have come to recognize that the very selection of which events are studied is in itself a subjective decision. Any national history will include enormous gaps where historians have leapt across substantial geographical and chronological divides to focus on the next significant upheaval. History is no longer past politics as it once was, but encompasses all aspects of life in the past—social, economic, ideological, environmental, and cultural as well as political. Our approach here is to move chronologically, focusing on a narrative developing over time. The chronological approach is meant to help students make sense of events, to ground their knowledge of past societies—in all their social, economic, and ideological complexity—in a clear political context, with the necessary sense of linkages and causality that is the bedrock of historical understanding. Narratives about the past are a basic function of historical inquiry, and they help students focus on the events that are significant historical benchmarks or turning points. We also seek to address the different interpretations that historians and citizens have debated, and which politicize the study of Canadian history. There is more than one story to tell about the past.

We understand, too, that nations emerge from a people's needs, fears, understandings, and hopes. Of course, external conditions also come into play. In the 1860s, the architects of Canada had to deal with imperial control as well as the ambitions of their southern neighbours. In 1867, Canadians sought to preserve the integrity of some ethnic and religious communities and not others—a kind of recognition of factionalism that set boundaries on the national common interest. The Confederation project was conceived to preserve the French- and English-speaking communities in British North America more than it was to build a strong national identity. The search for justice for those—and now other—communities, including Canada's Indigenous communities, still preoccupies the Canadian political ethic. Our hope is that we have provided a vast and complex history tamed by assiduous research and scrupulous exposition. History is mostly granular—it can be narrow or vast, and we trust we have captured the latter perspective.

We believe that every period of Canadian history has been marked by cleavages and conflict—among Indigenous peoples, between newcomers and Indigenous peoples, between French and English, elites and rebels, workers and employers, rural and urban domains, immigrants and host society, region and centre; and ever-changing attitudes about women's rights, fundamental economic trends, and conflicts about culture and values. Those cleavages constantly challenge the idea of a single unified nation. Yet, Canadian history has also been marked by a process of negotiation and compromise that has enabled Canada to develop into one of the most successful, pluralistic countries in the world, especially when compared to many other countries. Within that framework, however, there have been winners and losers and less-than-contented compromisers. Some in Canada have not embraced difference and diversity, but rather demonized the "other," sometimes as a political lever; at various times, the country has drifted from negotiation and compromise toward a pattern of wedge politics.

We have sought to provide a coherent political framework in this book, but also to provide voice and agency to those whose stories have been brought to life by social and cultural historians. We aim to capture the best of both worlds—the narrative tradition that has always been integral to the study of history and a more all-inclusive history that students will recognize as their own.

Not all will agree with our interpretation, but notions of conflict and compromise permeate the book. We believe they provide a basis for discussion and, we anticipate, vigorous debate. Our aim is to tell a story and to demonstrate causation to students, as opposed to adopting a thematic approach, which does not treat time in a linear fashion and leaves students struggling to understand how one event connects to and sometimes causes another. We are mindful that the story of Canada is often messy and certainly never as neat as it might appear in the pages of this book.

We believe Canadians want a clear and compelling account to their country's past. They want to understand its triumphs and setbacks, visionaries and villains, giants of industry and champions of social welfare and civic rights. It is instructive, for example, to reflect on how truly flawed some of our great Canadians have been. In the academic context, history is not an exercise for promoting pride in citizenship or glorifying some meta-narrative imposing false order on a diverse and complicated past. There are dark aspects of our history: too many people have been marginalized and persecuted, often on the bases of religion, race, ethnicity, or gender. Canada remains a work in progress, a continuing project that began as a constitutional compromise, with much still to be done. We need only witness urban homelessness; First Nations reserves struggling with teen suicide, inadequate housing, and unsafe drinking water; regional inequities and alienation; gender discrimination and violence against women; and the lingering questions over religion and religious symbols in public spaces.

These deep-seated problems in need of urgent redress do not undercut the fact that Canada's story is fundamentally one of reasonable success when compared to many other nation-states that make up the international community—a point that is too often overlooked. Canada is one of the world's most prosperous and welcoming countries, where the rule of law protects people and property and where citizens have access to a rich array of social programs. It is a beacon to many in the world with growing evidence of opportunity, diversity, and social inclusion. In 2015–16, it welcomed 25,000 Syrian refugees with much fanfare. Nearly 20 per cent of Canada's population was born outside the country. The dream of a diverse nation has a long history in Canada and can be traced to George-Étienne Cartier, one of the very important proponents of Confederation, and others who insisted upon a Canada that recognized diversity in 1867.

The field of Canadian history has grown enormously in recent years, and scholarly output has been immense. A brief survey of Canada's history can never hope to cover all aspects of that past nor do justice to every approach taken by our colleagues. We continue to enjoy working in an environment of lively and varied, but civil and respectful, historical controversy. And we hope that some of the ideas raised in this book will inspire students to explore further the wonderful work of Canada's many engaging historians.

1 CREATING A NATION IN AN ERA OF CHANGE AND ANXIETY: CANADA 1864–1873

INTRODUCTION

When several colonies in British North America came together in 1867 to create Canada, there was no popular uprising against a tyrannical oppressor. Canada emerged in the era of nation building in the middle of the nineteenth century that saw a host of new countries emerge throughout the world. Nation building was then, as it is today, a challenging and complex process, propelled by local dynamisms and a variety of internal and external contingencies. Canada's nation-building efforts were largely liberal as Canadian politicians created a self-determining community and overcame the sectionalism and regionalism that had marred the previous decades in British North America. The British North Americans believed that larger political entities were economically and militarily advantageous, but they also felt threatened by a potential American invasion and were propelled toward statehood by a Great Britain eager for the colonies to assume greater control over their own affairs.

Leaders in British North America understood that their nation building project was primarily political and economic rather than cultural or ethnic. Canada was no primordial nation, but the colonial leaders believed that it could be a modern creation,

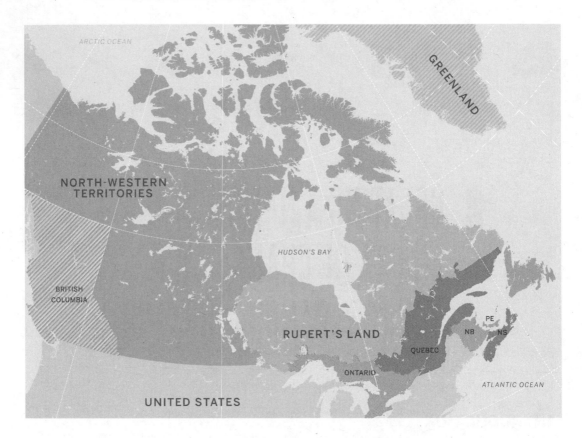

Map 1.1 Canada, 1867.

and it could rise above differences created by religion, region, and ethnicity.[1] They believed they could unite into a single geopolitical space several cultural, regional, and ethnic communities that had emerged in Canada's colonial past and then share a common citizenship. George Brown, one of the major proponents of Confederation and proprietor of *The Globe*, lauded the architects of union for their "earnest large-minded willingness to subordinate all party interests to the attainment of a larger project."[2] "We are endeavouring to adjust harmoniously great difficulties that have plunged other countries into all the horrors of civil war," he said, noting particularly the descent of the United States into civil war to settle internal differences.[3] George-Étienne Cartier, another leading figure in the Confederation

1 · Benedict Anderson, *Imagined Communities: Reflections on the Origins and Spread of Nationalism* (London: Verso, 1991).

2   *The Globe*, July 1, 1867, http://heritage.theglobeandmail.com.libproxy.uregina.ca:2048/PageView.asp. A complete run of *The Globe and Mail* newspaper is available online.

3   Peter B. Waite, *The Confederation Debates in the Province of Canada 1865*, 2nd ed. (Toronto: University of Toronto Press, 2006), 27–29, 36, 48, 54.

movement, agreed: "we were of different races, not for the purpose of warring against each other, but in order to compete and emulate for the general welfare." In the grandiose political rhetoric of the day, the proponents of union had great hopes for the northern half of North America, even if John A. Macdonald, the leading figure of the movement for Confederation, saw Canada as the first daughter of the British Empire, whose loyalty to the Crown was steadfast. In 1864, when the project of Canada was launched, Canada was simply "an empire of the mind" for colonial politicians.[4]

Some historians have downplayed the significance of the Confederation project, dismissing it as a practical and pragmatic business deal, conducted in a largely undemocratic manner by elite white men who were bigoted, divisive, and often misguided. Those critics cannot be dismissed, especially when viewed from our own time. Those behind Confederation, known for more than a century and half as the Fathers of Confederation—a term itself which has become problematic—were not democrats in our sense of the word; in fact, they were worried about the democratic excesses that had contributed to the bloody American Civil War, which had left 620,000 dead. The electoral system in the mid-nineteenth century was restrictive, excluding women—disenfranchised simply because of their gender—as well as many males. Others, such as Indigenous peoples, were excluded because of their race, while large minorities, such as the Acadians and Catholics, were underrepresented. In fact, Canada's nation-building project came with an attempt to marginalize, remake and, indeed, erase the Indigenous nations as they had existed in North America for millennia, as Canada moved to settle and develop lands in the west. One state's nation building frequently succeeds in destroying another; recently, Canada has been accused of cultural genocide for its treatment of Indigenous peoples.

What cannot be denied is that the period from 1864 to 1873 was a momentous decade in Canada's history. It saw the emergence of Canada as a new nation when the four colonies of Nova Scotia, New Brunswick, Canada East (Quebec), and Canada West (Ontario) launched Confederation in 1867 and were soon joined by three others: Manitoba (Red River) in 1870, British Columbia in 1871, and Prince Edward Island in 1873. Newfoundland refused to join during this period and would remain outside Canada until 1949. Yet, the period was marked by conflict, disunity, political instability, and the lack of inclusion. However, while it is tempting to accentuate the divisions and discord among the colonists and dismiss the politics of compromise and negotiation that made Confederation possible, it remains important to recognize that there was enough unity and common purpose among diverse groups to come together. Despite their differences and anxieties about each other, they were able to create a new

---

4　Alastair C.F. Gillespie, "Dispatches from 1865—Our National Ideal," *National Post*, February 7, 2015.

state and hold it together, even if the architects took each other "not by the hand but rather by the throat."[5]

The process was cynical, messy, and complicated, but colonial leaders negotiated constitutional arrangements and national institutions to satisfy their particular interests, consolidate the disparate parts into a single political entity, and forge a new country that spanned the continent by 1873. Their accomplishment cannot be dismissed even if, in the pursuit of national interests thought progressive at the time, they embarked upon their own corrosive policies of long-term colonialism toward Indigenous peoples that continue to create havoc in the country. They were dreamers and they were nationalists, even if they were not inclusive and their negotiations and compromises left many disappointed and marginalized. By the early twenty-first century, what they created has become one of the world's oldest and most successful federations.

PRESSURE FOR UNION

A number of factors propelled the colonies in British North America toward union, but the changing economic realities from the late 1840s through to the 1860s were primary. The colonies had recovered from major shocks in the 1840s when preferential treatment for their products—particularly wheat, flour, and timber in the British markets—started to unravel and the colonists felt abandoned. The search for a new economic order began, and in 1854, British North America (BNA) secured free trade in natural resources with the Americans. The impact of the Reciprocity Agreement and the American Civil War was enormous for the export trade of BNA, and when the Americans did not renew the trade arrangement in 1864, the colonies experienced another economic setback.

With assured markets in the United States and Britain gone, colonial leaders turned to the idea of integrating their colonial economies into a single east–west network. By the 1860s, the colonies had also begun a process of industrialization and urbanization, had developed banking systems, had launched themselves into the railway era, and had grand schemes of annexing the interior of the continent and building a railway to link all territory in British North America. The province of Canada was most aggressive in encouraging its manufacturing sector. In what would become Quebec, for instance, the value of manufacturing increased from $600,000 in 1851 to more than $15 million a decade later, and $104.5 million by 1881. In 1859,

---

5   Ged Martin, *Britain and the Origins of the Canadian Confederation, 1837–67* (Vancouver: University of British Columbia Press, 1995), 5.

Alexander Galt, a leader in the Montreal business community as well as minister of finance, increased the general tariff rate on most imports from 8.54% to 12.11% and from 15% to 20% for finished goods. The tariff was essential in raising revenues to cover public expenditures, especially those associated with railway construction, but the revised tariff schedule also provided protection for Canada's nascent industries. A newly emerging economic order required a new regulatory regime, even though staple production in wheat, lumber, and fish remained important, and much of the population remained dependent on farming.

The emerging middle classes from the commercial and industrial sectors in the larger urban centres were quickly replacing agrarian interests as the dominant group in British North America, and they were at the centre of the Canadian nation-building movement. They believed that larger nation-states were necessary to capitalize on the technological advances of the era, best symbolized by the increasing use of the steam engine and the transformative changes occurring in the production of textiles and in metallurgy. The Industrial Revolution was changing the way economies operated, and it placed new demands on the state. Even with rapid expansion in the transportation sector, particularly with a spate of railroad construction, the middle classes believed larger states, with a new kind of authority to provide new fiscal and legal structures, were necessary to facilitate the development of efficient economies and successful nations. Nation building allowed the middle classes to further their political and economic goals.

The growing middle class and their commercial interests promoted the importance of railways and all the colonies became engaged in ambitious programs of railway construction. This mode of transport was especially expensive in North America, where great distances and a rugged environment were the norm. With only 3.5 million people in British North America, it soon became apparent that governments had to be involved in railway construction. While governments eschewed direct public ownership, they certainly went out of their way to support the private, primarily British investment that spurred a railway boom lasting for much of the 1850s, when nearly 3,000 kilometres of track were laid in the Canadas. The Maritimes dreamed of capturing the trade from the interior of North America bound for Europe and embarked on their own railway projects; more than 600 kilometres of track were laid in the region. Like United Canada, the Maritime colonies also amassed a considerable debt in railways, and by the early 1860s, they, too, were finding it difficult to manage their debt load, let alone continue to build new lines. All colonial governments required a larger financial base to meet their obligations and to fulfill their hopes for intercolonial and transcontinental rail expansion.

British bankers who had funded the initial railway craze in BNA lost interest in constructing local lines. They had sunk about $100 million into the Canadas, and by the early 1860s the Grand Trunk Railway (one of the major railway firms) missed interest payments on its bonds and faced bankruptcy. Barings Bank of London, one of the key investors in the railway, dispatched Edward Watkin, an influential British railway executive, to Canada to investigate. The only solution to the Grand Trunk problem was further expansion: he proposed a line from Halifax to Quebec, followed with a transcontinental line to the Pacific to link all the colonies. Watkins and other businessmen came to the conclusion that political unification of the colonies was the best alternative for recouping their investments. In 1862, they created the British North American Association to promote colonial union and worked assiduously to promote the notion of union within the British Colonial Office in London that oversaw the affairs of the colonies. Without the support of a small but influential group of British investors, Confederation might not have occurred in 1867, if at all.

The general insecurity of British North America was heightened during the American Civil War. Britain had favoured the southern Confederacy and was worried about American retaliation when the Northern armies prevailed in 1865. Moreover, the boisterous rhetoric coming from the Americans contributed to the anxiety throughout British North America. William Seward, the US Secretary of State, spoke often of marching on Canada, and Charles Sumner, the chair of the Senate Committee on Foreign Relations, even talked of letting the American South secede from the Union and taking Canada instead. Newspaper articles of the time added to the nervousness in British North America; the *New York Times* commented regularly on the inevitability of the United States annexing Canada. In July 1866, a bill introduced into the US House of Representatives paved the way for the admission of all the British North American colonies and the western territories into the union, adding to the tension, even though the legislation never moved beyond the committee stage. As tensions mounted between Britain and the United States at the end of the Civil War, many in the British colonies believed that they were in peril. London dispatched 15,000 combat troops to Canada, and the colonies themselves made plans to bring their militias to 40,000. Some colonial leaders insisted that Confederation would strengthen the resolve of the colonies to remain under the British flag. It might also strengthen the colonial defences.

As concerns about an American threat mounted and the economy of British North America was being transformed, the colonies turned their thoughts to political consolidation, encouraged along the way by the British government. The year 1864 would prove to be momentous: the Maritime colonies of Nova Scotia, Prince Edward Island, and New Brunswick agreed to gather in Charlottetown to discuss a Maritime union. Most Maritime politicians saw little hope for their small colonies, and they believed that union could strengthen their colonies politically, economically, and militarily. They "equated consolidation with material progress and modernization" and shared with other British North Americans "an enthusiasm for railways, for expanded and more centralized school systems, for improved social services and for governments with enhanced access to credit."[6] In Prince Edward Island, there was growing realization that a union between the island colony and the others might be necessary to break the control that a group of largely absentee landowners had over their island. Arthur Hamilton Gordon, the recently appointed lieutenant governor of New Brunswick, was sent from London to promote a union of either the Maritime colonies or all of British North America. He became a strong advocate of union, and by 1864, "whether for good or ill, there was a national spirit stirring in the Maritime Provinces."[7] The Maritime colonies scheduled their conference to discuss union in Charlottetown for the beginning of September 1864.

At the same time, those in the United Canadas came together in a coalition determined to find a way out of a political system that had grown increasingly dysfunctional. In 1840, the *Act of Union* had created a single apparatus of government for the colonies of Canada East (population 650,000) and Canada West (population 450,000), each with an equal number of seats in the legislative assembly—an arrangement designed to reduce the influence of primarily French-speaking Canada East. Political leaders such as Louis-Hippolyte LaFontaine and Robert Baldwin were able to forge workable coalitions that spanned the cultural and linguistic divide, but changing demographics in the Canadas in the 1850s—the population of Canada West (953,000) surpassed that of Canada East (890,000)—led to further tensions between the two sections, notably on the issue of representation proportional to population. From 1862 to 1864, the legislature struggled to pass even significant legislation: both attempts to pass a Militia Bill, for instance, collapsed even in the face of heightened concerns about American aggression. Moreover, French-Canadian members of the legislature were becoming increasingly worried about the growing demands in Canada West for representation by population, which would place control of the assembly in the hands of the English-speaking Protestant majority. During that period, two elections had failed to produce a workable majority: four successive governments were sworn in, with each defeated in turn.

In late spring 1864, the government of John A. Macdonald and Étienne-Paschal Taché was defeated on a vote of confidence. Macdonald adjourned the legislature and asked the governor general, Lord Monck, for dissolution and new elections. Monck did not disagree, but first asked Macdonald to meet George Brown to consider constitutional options; Brown had earlier chaired a legislative committee that had proposed

---

6   Phillip Buckner, "CHR Dialogue: The Maritimes and Confederation: A Reassessment," *Canadian Historical Review* 71, no. 1 (March 1990): 1–45.

7   P.B. Waite, *The Life and Times of Confederation, 1864–1867: Politics, Newspapers and the Union of British North America* (Toronto: University of Toronto Press, 1962), 72.

Figure 1.1 Convention at Charlottetown, PEI, of delegates from the legislatures of Canada, New Brunswick, Nova Scotia, and Prince Edward Island to consider the union of the British North American colonies.

a federal system of either Canada East and Canada West or all of British North America. Macdonald and Brown agreed that a federal union was the only way forward, and the Great Coalition was born. Brown joined with Macdonald and Cartier to work for a federal union of all BNA colonies.

Cartier and others from Canada East realized that their long-term interests might be best served if they were rid of those in Canada West who seemed to harbour opposition to Roman Catholic separate schools and other cultural issues that French-speaking people believed important. Cartier knew that Quebec's best hope lay in winning control of important areas, such as education and its own legal system, that would safeguard his people from the English-speaking majority. The only political group not included in the coalition was Antoine-Aimé Dorion's radical *parti rouge*, but Dorion had suggested in the legislature in 1861 that he might accept representation by population if the parties agreed to a federation of the two provinces with a limited central government.

Many in the Canadas were also looking east and west in the 1860s. Brown's *The Globe* had declared that Canada West was "looking for new worlds to conquer," and the western prairie was the great prize for Canadian economic interests. However, Canada West had neither the financial resources nor sufficient credit to acquire Rupert's Land and the North-West Territory—the vast region that today extends from northern Quebec and Ontario to the Arctic Circle, south to the US border, and west to British Columbia—from the Hudson's Bay Company, which had been granted most of that territory in the seventeenth century. The Maritimes would provide new markets for Canadian manufactured goods, and the ice-free ports on the Atlantic Ocean were necessary for year-found shipping. That type of expansion could only come with a larger union of all the British colonies.

When the Canadians learned of the conference planned for Charlottetown in September 1864, they asked to be invited, and in late August 1864, they boarded the *Queen Victoria* for Charlottetown to sell the idea of a transcontinental union. The delegates became acquainted at the various dinners and galas in Charlottetown as well as in their more formal meetings, and once they got down to business, the Maritime delegates agreed to set aside their discussion on the smaller union to hear first from the Canadians. Over a few days, Cartier, Brown, Galt, and Macdonald made their case; then the Maritimers considered their options. As Brown reported to his wife, the Maritime politicians "were unanimous in regarding Federation of all the Provinces to be highly desirable—*if the terms of union could be made satisfactory*."[8] The Canadians and Maritimers agreed to meet again in Quebec City in October to hammer out the basis of a constitution for a new nation, but before the Canadians returned home, they toured the region and everywhere received a warm welcome. The Halifax *Morning Chronicle* noted a positive desire for union.

QUEBEC CONFERENCE AND THE PLANS FOR UNION

The Quebec Conference began amid much optimism on October 10, 1864, despite the obstacles that stood in the way of a union of British North America. Delegates were divided by geography, language, and histories, all of which they had to reconcile in order to create a nationally integrated economic union amid fears in the colonies of surrendering control of local affairs to a distant national government. The smaller colonies on the Atlantic Ocean were worried about protecting their interests against the larger inland colonies of the United Canadas. Canada East was particularly worried about a growing English-speaking Protestant majority in Canada West. Losing control over local issues, such as education and the administration of justice, was no trifling matter.

The dilemma facing the delegates at the Quebec Conference is encapsulated in the dreams of two of the leading delegates, Macdonald and Cartier, who held different conceptions of what Canada should be. Cartier realized that the geopolitical, cultural, and historical realities meant the new country had to recognize the differences that would exist in the new political community. For him, diversity was a virtue. He insisted on a

---

8   Quoted in Richard Gwyn, *John A.: The Man Who Made Us* (Toronto: Vintage Press, 2008), 305. Italics in original.

Canada that would provide constant accommodation of distinct minorities, declaring that "the idea of unity of races was utopian—it was impossible. Distinction of this kind would always appear....In our own federation we should have Catholics and Protestant, French, English, Irish and Scotch, and each by his efforts and his success would increase the prosperity and glory of the new confederacy."[9] For Cartier, the Canadian nation could thrive if it created a "political nationality" rather than an ethnically based one, "with which neither the national origin, nor the religion of any individual, would interfere."[10] The strength of the new nation was its diversity. Macdonald's dream for Canada, on the other hand, was a system of governance that fostered a central government that could manage a national economy. While Cartier insisted on sectarian recognition, language recognition, and Quebec's unique legal system, Macdonald insisted on general powers, appointing powers, overarching authorities, supervisory roles, and declaratory mechanisms that would foster economic growth and development and lead to the national self-sufficiency that was necessary for effective nationhood.[11]

The delegates at Quebec agreed upon a text of 72 resolutions that incorporated the competing visions of Macdonald and Cartier. It would provide the basis of the Canadian constitution, known as the *British North America Act* until 1982 when it was renamed the *Constitution Act, 1867*. Canada was to be a federation, dividing power, jurisdiction, and authority between two orders of government: federal and provincial. The federal principle was essential for a union among colonies so different. The federal government had responsibility for defence and creating a nationally integrated economy through its control of currency, weights and measures, and other economic regulatory measures, such as taxation. It was also given jurisdiction over international trade and commerce, and responsibility for developing national transportation and communication systems. Section 121 of the BNA *Act* provided for a common market: "all articles of the growth, produce or manufacture of any one of the Provinces...shall be admitted free into each of the other Provinces." The constitution also empowered the federal government to make laws for the Peace, Order and Good Government of Canada (POGG), an idea first used in New Zealand in 1852. That article of Confederation has been important for two reasons: first, it gave the federal government the authority to meet national needs and govern for the good of the nation, as Macdonald wanted; and, second, it provided the federal government with general and wide-ranging powers to become involved in areas of policy outside its enumerated

9 Quoted in Christopher Moore, *1867: How the Fathers Made a Deal* (Toronto: McClelland & Stewart, 1997), 233.

10 Quoted in Alastair C.F. Gillespie, "Dispatches from 1865—'Only Justice Can Appeal to All'," *National Post*, February 5, 2015.

11 On this point, see John D. Whyte, "Federalism Dreams," *Queen's Law Journal*, 34, no. 1 (Fall 2008): 1–28.

powers. The provinces retained the responsible government earned decades earlier and were given autonomy over education, religious and civil institutions, property and civil rights, and social welfare, though the latter at the time of Confederation meant public and reformatory prisons, hospitals, asylums, and charities. Authority to protect and promote the interests of the French-speaking community and culture in Quebec passed to the province, along with control over municipal affairs, ownership of public lands, and mines and minerals. The provinces could levy direct taxation, and as an equivalent to the POGG clause, the provinces had residual power over all matters of a merely local or private nature not assigned to the federal government.

In a classic federal system, the power to legislate is limited to that allocated in the constitution, and because each order of government is assigned exclusive powers, neither level of government could encroach upon the powers or jurisdiction of the other. The Canadian variant of federalism differed as the federal government was awarded supervisory powers that allowed it to encroach on provincial jurisdiction. Ottawa had authority to disallow and reserve any bill from the provincial legislatures— a feature seen as providing a supervisory or dominant role for the federal government over the provinces. The federal government also had the constitutional authority to protect the educational rights of religious minorities that existed by legislation at the time of Confederation. The delegates in Quebec were concerned about the place of some minorities in 1867. Although Canada has had less than a stellar record in its treatment of its minority groups, the politicians who created Canada recognized the importance of religious minority rights nonetheless. If a provincial majority imposed tyrannical measures against a provincial minority, section 93 of the BNA Act authorized the federal government to intervene to protect minority education rights in the provinces. The delegates also agreed upon an appointed Senate in a bicameral Parliament to represent the regional nature of the new country but, ironically, it was not empowered to resolve regional tensions that might emerge. The rights of the Indigenous peoples throughout British North America attracted little attention, largely because most delegates believed Indigenous peoples were quickly disappearing or adopting a European lifestyle; none of the Indigenous nations were present. They were considered wards of the state, and authority for "Indians and lands reserved for Indians" was given to the federal government.

DEBATING THE QUEBEC RESOLUTIONS AND CONFEDERATION

It must seem peculiar today that there was so little consultation with the public about the Quebec Resolutions. Even some resort to direct democracy would have been unlikely to meet our modern benchmark for democracy, as less than 20 per cent of

Figure 1.2 George-Étienne Cartier established a political partnership with John A. Macdonald and welcomed Confederation, promoting it as a union of diverse peoples who could overcome their differences to become a unified country.

all adults had the right to participate (because of restrictive property and gender-based qualifications regarding voting rights). Some historians have argued that the "people" were excluded from Canada's nation-building project: "the Fathers [of Confederation] were convinced that they did not need to attain the approval of the mere human beings for the political order they were designing for individuals."[12] Others disagree, and have suggested that the debates in the colonial legislatures were not over whether to consult the people, but over how they should be consulted.[13] At the time of Confederation there was widespread acceptance of the notion of representative democracy—that an elected representative was expected to make decisions for the people who had elected him, and that is what politicians did. None of the colonies was "yanked into Confederation by the British Government or by ambitious local elite." Confederation was debated in all of the legislative assemblies that represented the people. Macdonald insisted that Confederation was a democratic exercise: "We in this house," he said, "are representatives of the people, not mere delegates, and to pass such a law [as to have a referendum on the Quebec proposal] would be robbing ourselves of the character of representatives." He argued further that the elected members "represent the people of Canada and we are here to pass laws for the peace, welfare and good government of the country."[14] Macdonald and the other colonial politicians agreed on the supremacy of Parliament to give consent to Confederation, and no country can be created and survive without the people's consent.

In Ontario there was widespread support for Confederation, but it was hotly debated in Quebec where the French-Canadian majority worried about the loss of provincial autonomy. As the *Gazette de Sorel* commented on January 14, 1865, "We must never forget that French Canadians need

12 Ian McKay, "The Liberal Order Framework," *Canadian Historical Review*, 81, no. 4 (December 2000); Peter Russell, *Constitutional Odyssey: Can Canadians Become a Sovereign People?* (Toronto: University of Toronto Press, 2004).

13 Janet Ajzenstat, Ian Gentles, and Paul Romney (eds.), *Canada's Founding Debates* (Toronto: University of Toronto Press, 2003), chapters 11 and 12; and *Débats sur la fondation du Canada*, Édition français préparée par Stéphane Kelly et Guy Laforest (Quebec: Les Presses de l'Université Laval, 2003).

14 Quoted in Gwyn, *John A.*, 351.

more reassurance than the other provinces for their civil and religious immunities."[15] Dorion and the *parti rouge* saw Confederation as a direct threat to the powers of Quebec if Ottawa emerged as the dominant power in the new nation. Moreover, they also feared that a national government with an English-speaking majority might embark upon a policy designed to assimilate French-speaking Canada into an English-dominated nationality. Still, Dorion's motion in the legislature calling on members to repudiate all notions of a new nationality was defeated, earning the support of only 25 French-Canadian members.

The *parti bleu* represented an alternative element in Quebec politics, although it shared some of Dorion's fears. Led by Cartier and supported by the Catholic Church and the Protestant English-speaking minority, it argued that Confederation would undo the *Act of Union* and liberate Canada East from Canada West, giving it autonomy over the issues that were important to the province in a new Canada. All issues dealing with the French-Canadian nationality would fall within the jurisdiction of the provincial government in Quebec City. Cartier realized that there had to be some form of association with the English-speaking provinces for reasons of economic development and defence against the United States. But, as he said when he returned from helping to write the Canadian constitution in London, "That is why I was careful to make sure that the federal government would receive only that amount of power which was strictly necessary to serve the general interests of the Confederation."[16] *La Minerve* quoted with approval Cartier's views on Confederation: "As a distinct and separate nationality, we form a state within a state. We enjoy the full exercise of our rights and the formal recognition of our national independence."[17] Moreover, many in Canada East welcomed the prospect that Confederation afforded an opportunity to restore the economic might of the business community in Montreal. The vote on the proposed union, taken in the legislature at 4:30 AM on Saturday, March 11, 1865, carried easily at 99 to 33. Nineteen French Canadians voted against—six fewer than had supported Dorion's motion opposing the concept of a new nationality for the new nation.

There was much greater opposition to the Quebec Resolutions in the Atlantic region, though the debate centred on whether the Quebec Resolutions met their needs, not on the desirability of union. Many feared that the Quebec arrangements would produce a powerful and distant central government, leaving them with little influence; some demanded another conference to renegotiate the terms of union. As the *Woodstock Times* in New Brunswick opined, "Union is one thing and the Quebec

---

15 Quoted in A.I. Silver, *The French-Canadian Idea of Confederation, 1864–1900*, 2nd ed. (Toronto: University of Toronto Press, 1997), 34.

16 Quoted in ibid., 48.

17 Quoted in ibid., 41.

scheme is quite another."[18] Such views were particularly true of Newfoundland and Prince Edward Island. In Newfoundland, whose delegates had been at Quebec in 1864, the initial enthusiasm for union quickly dissipated. First, the strong Catholic community, with its deep attachment to Ireland, feared any alliance led by a British majority—as Confederation surely was. Second, merchants saw little benefit to a union that they believed would lead to higher tariff rates and favour economic development on the continent. Confederation had its proponents, though, and they argued that Canada was the best hope that Newfoundland had to deal with its depressing isolation, rampant poverty, reliance on a single staple commodity (fish), and spur its economic diversification. Prince Edward Island believed that union ignored its special circumstances, such as the lingering problem with absentee landowners; like Newfoundland, it opted to remain out in 1867. However, PEI joined six years later in 1873, when Canada offered most of what it had demanded in 1864, suggesting that the particular resolutions agreed upon in Quebec were the primary obstacle to its joining, rather than any inherent opposition to the principle of Confederation. After the pro-Confederation candidates were soundly trounced in the 1869 Newfoundland election, the issue periodically crept back into the political debate, but Britain's oldest colony did not join Canada until 1949.

There was also considerable opposition in New Brunswick and Nova Scotia, but the two colonies chose to deal differently with the ratification process and approving the Quebec Resolutions. When he returned to Fredericton and found that his cabinet opposed the Quebec Resolutions, Leonard Tilley took the debate on Confederation to the people in a general election. His chief opponent, Albert Smith, routed the supporters of Confederation: only 11 of the candidates supporting the Quebec Resolutions were returned to office. Charles Tupper faced similar opposition in Nova Scotia, led, ironically, by Joseph Howe, an earlier proponent of union, who vehemently opposed Tupper's refusal to consult the people in a general election. Howe saw little gain for Nova Scotia in a Canadian federation. When he already had London as his capital, he asked, why should he trade it for one in the backwoods of Canada? "Take a [Nova Scotian] to Ottawa, above the tidewater, freeze him up for five months, where he cannot view the Atlantic, smell salt water, or see the sail of a ship, and the man will pine and die."[19] His 18,000-signature petition asking London to stop the union was dismissed, and Tupper's supporters in the Nova Scotia legislature voted to join the union in 1865. However, in the ensuing federal election, Tupper was the only supporter of Confederation to win his federal seat; 18 of the 19 Nova Scotia members of Parliament went to Ottawa to undo the union.

---

18 Quoted in Buckner, "CHR Dialogue: The Maritimes and Confederation," 32.

19 Quoted in J. Murray Beck, *Joseph Howe*, vol. 2, *The Briton Become Canadian, 1848–1873* (Montreal and Kingston: McGill-Queen's University Press, 1983), 201.

Figure 1.3 The Conference at Quebec in 1864, intended to settle the basics of a union of the British North American colonies.

In the meantime, Smith's coalition in New Brunswick unravelled over patronage, religious disputes, financial support for the railways, and internal confusion, and it failed to present any alternative to Confederation. The British-appointed lieutenant governor, Arthur Hamilton Gordon, was no friend of Smith's and worked assiduously to promote Confederation in New Brunswick. The antics of a group of Irish nationalists, the Fenian Brotherhood, who harassed the British colonies from their base in the United States, created a panic in New Brunswick and, indeed, throughout all the colonies. The Fenian Brotherhood, created in 1858 for the purpose of liberating Ireland by holding Britain's North American colonies hostage, proved convenient for those favouring Confederation because it heightened issues of insecurity throughout British North America. Thousands of Irish Americans had joined the US Army during the Civil War, and when it ended, many in British North America feared that the Fenians would try to occupy Canada to achieve their objectives for Ireland. The Fenians did not represent a really serious threat to British North America, but the 1860s were a decade of increasing insecurity amidst fear among many that the Americans were intent on controlling all of North America. In the face of the Fenian scare, Smith's coalition collapsed and new elections were held in New Brunswick. The campaign—like most campaigns in British North America at the time—was swayed by patronage, money, and liquor. Tilley was re-elected to bring New Brunswick into Confederation.

After the Quebec Resolutions were approved in the colonial legislatures, they were passed by the House of Commons in London, England, and received royal assent on March 29, 1867. Canada was created by an act of the British Parliament, would remain very much tied to the British Empire for another six decades, and had "a constitution similar in Principle to that of the United Kingdom," but it was nevertheless Canadians themselves who had created the new country. The Parliament in London knew best not to interfere with the plans of the colonies where the principle of responsible government had been long established. As Thomas D'Arcy McGee noted in the debate on Confederation, it was a "scheme not suggested by others, or imposed upon us, but one the work of ourselves, the creation of our intellect and of our free, unbiased, and untrammelled will."[20]

BIG DREAMS, LIMITED CAPACITY: CANADA IN 1867

Sir John A. Macdonald, recently knighted for his role in Confederation, became Canada's first prime minister on July 1, 1867, and would remain so—except for a brief period from 1874 to 1879—until his death in 1891. He looked to the United Canadas for much of the foundation for governing, establishing a trend that has held since that time. With Confederation, Ontario and Quebec not only won control of their own provinces but also of national politics and economics. The civil service was recruited primarily from Ontario and Quebec, and the tariff rate for the new nation was adopted from the United Canadas. Ontario had the richest economy, with per capita commodity incomes 20 per cent above the national average. Quebec's per capita commodity income was only 86 per cent of the national average, while New Brunswick and Nova Scotia lagged at 83 per cent and 75 per cent, respectively. Regional economic disparity, then, was already a feature of Canada in 1867. Ontario was already the most populous province: in 1851, it accounted for 39 per cent of British North America's people, slightly ahead of Quebec's 36 percent; a decade later, it had 43 per cent of the population, and Quebec had 34 per cent; by 1871, Ontario had 44 per cent while Quebec had dropped further to 32 per cent. The Maritime share had dropped from 22 per cent in 1851 to 20 per cent in 1871.

Canada was diverse in many ways. It had several large cities: Montreal ranked first with 100,000 people, followed by Quebec City at 60,000. Toronto, at 50,000, was the largest urban centre in Ontario, and Halifax and Saint John each had a population of around 30,000. Yet more than 80 per cent of Canada's 3.5 million inhabitants lived in rural areas and were engaged in staple production in agriculture, forestry,

---

20 Quoted in Moore, *1867. How the Fathers Made a Deal*, 236.

mining, and fishing. Agriculture was, by far, the dominant sector, accounting for 54 per cent of commodity incomes across Canada; manufacturing accounted for 33 per cent of commodity incomes. New Brunswick and Quebec, two economies that depended heavily on the forestry sector, were the most dependent on manufacturing. The service sector, including construction, transportation, governmental services, and retail, accounted for one-third of the nation's gross national product in 1870. More than 55 per cent of Canadians were Protestants and 44 per cent were of the Roman Catholic faith. At Confederation, the Indigenous population constituted only 23,000 (North American Indian and Inuit), but this number rose to more than 100,000 when Rupert's Land and British Columbia were included. More than half the entire Canadian population was of British origin (England, Ireland, Scotland, and Wales). Those whose roots were in Europe (predominantly France and Germany) numbered more than a million, but those with Asian backgrounds were uncounted in the general surveys.

With slightly more than half of all working Canadians engaged in the agricultural sector, Canada was a rural nation in 1867, but the rural areas were far from homogenous. Clear distinctions existed between those who owned a piece of land and those that did not. The dominant group in any rural village or town was the professional class—lawyers and notaries, doctors, priests, and local merchants. Merchants continued to be substantial creditors, and farmers, lumbermen, and fishers were usually indebted to them. Most towns had several skilled craftspeople and large numbers of unskilled labourers engaged in production for a local economy. Yet, not all workers were equal. In the transition to industrialization then underway, skilled workers, those with a trade learned over a long period of time, were at the top of the working class with wages well above average. They were also the leaders of the nascent labour movement, mainly to protect their privileged position in society.

Life for women in Canada had never been easy. This did not change with Confederation. For those whose families were engaged in staple production, women played an important role alongside their husbands. Domestic chores such as washing, hauling water, cooking and cleaning, making the clothes that the family needed, caring for the children, and tending the vegetable gardens remained the preserve of women, even with the introduction of industrial production. Yet new modes of production significantly altered both the gender and the age of the formal labour force. Women moved increasingly into wage labour after 1850, and at Confederation, together with children, they accounted for 42 per cent of the industrial workforce in Montreal and 34 per cent in Toronto; about a quarter of all children between the ages of 11 and 14 worked in factories. Women also performed many tasks in the informal economy, such as taking in boarders, making clothes, and maintaining garden plots, and women were recruited to work at home on a piecework basis, especially in the garment trade. A few entered such professions as teaching and nursing, but the most important paid employment for women remained domestic service, one sector of the economy in which Indigenous women were encouraged to participate.

Many women were anxious, though, to escape the drudgery and exploitation of such menial work. *The Globe* reported in 1868 that "our working women dread household service, and hundreds would rather famish than apply at a servants' agency."[21] Life as a domestic servant not only meant long hours of hard labour, but also the risk of sexual exploitation: many of the young girls employed as domestic labour became pregnant by their employers. The case of Reverend Corbett, an Anglican priest who drugged, raped, and then attempted to perform an abortion on his servant Maria Thomas, was not unusual. Corbett served only six months for his crimes.[22]

Even when they were active participants in managing and providing for the needs of daily life, women had few legal claims to family property: the husband, for instance, could sell the family farm without any consultation with his wife, and if a wife outlived her husband, the family farm passed to the eldest son upon his father's death. Working-class life was not easy for many at Confederation. It meant harsh and often unsafe working conditions, and pollution and filth were commonplace. Crime, prostitution, excessive drinking, and labour unrest marked life in most cities. Crimes associated with heavy drinking were common. Of the 11,135 arrests in Montreal in 1870, 5,358 (4,313 men, 1,045 women) were linked to public drunkenness.[23]

Many in the working classes did not have the right to vote in 1867, as voting was a privilege rather than the right it is today. Voters had to meet three basic conditions— to be male, at least 21 years of age, and a British subject by birth or naturalization—in addition to whatever rules fell under the jurisdiction of the electoral laws of each province. Because of property-based qualifications, many Canadians could not vote, while others were excluded for various reasons: employment in government; receipt of social assistance or any help from charitable organizations; Indigenous ancestry; and in British Columbia, Chinese origin. All of the British North American colonies had disenfranchised women, and with provincial laws governing the voting rights, the exclusion of women was entrenched in the new Canadian constitution. In the 1870s, a women's suffrage movement emerged in all of the provinces to seek social, economic, and political equality with men.

---

21 Alison Prentice et al., *Canadian Women. A History* (Toronto: Harcourt Brace, 1996), 128.

22 Ibid., 128–29.

23 John Dickinson and Brian Young, *A Short History of Quebec* (Montreal and Kingston: McGill-Queen's University Press, 2008), 148.

CONSOLIDATION EAST AND EXPANSION WEST

In the federal election in 1867, which stretched over six weeks, approximately 73 per cent of eligible voters cast a ballot, giving Macdonald and his supporters 100 of the 180 seats in the House of Commons. Macdonald was well prepared to lead the new nation, as he had learned much about holding fractious elements together in the United Canadas (where he had governed for more than a decade). He may have been no philosopher-king, but he was pragmatic in governing the new country, which was still divided along regional, ethnic, and partisan lines. He had convinced many of those who had held leadership roles at Charlottetown and Quebec to join him in a Liberal-Conservative coalition.

The first manifestations of regional cleavages and strong provincial governments determined to achieve a better deal for their provinces—a common theme in Canadian history—emerged in Nova Scotia where, as noted above, the supporters of Confederation were soundly trounced in the 1867 election. Nova Scotia members of Parliament first went to Ottawa to take their province out of Confederation. Joseph Howe was their nominal leader, and

Figure 1.4 Joseph Howe, a Nova Scotian, opposed Confederation until Macdonald offered better terms to Nova Scotia and convinced Howe to join his government.

although his choices had narrowed considerably by the time he arrived in Ottawa after the first federal election in 1867, Macdonald realized that he had to deal with the Nova Scotian and others opposed to the union. He offered Howe a cabinet post, and using the federal spending power, he increased the annual federal subsidy for Nova Scotia. Through brokerage politics—the reconciling of the various regional, political, economic, and cultural interests—Macdonald further demonstrated his penchant for coalition building and convinced the Nova Scotians to take a leap of faith that Confederation could actually work. In the 1872 election, Macdonald's party won 13 of the 21 federal seats there, even though many in the province continued to harbour resentment toward Ottawa. On July 1, 1875, the rail line linking Nova Scotia to Quebec was completed—at a cost of more than $34 million—fulfilling one of the promises of Confederation.

In addition to addressing the anti-Confederation sentiments in Nova Scotia, Macdonald and his government quickly extended Canada's dominion over the rest of British North America, all the way to the Pacific Ocean. An important step in that process was the acquisition of the vast territory to the west and north known as Rupert's Land. For many, especially those in Ontario in search of new arable land, the destiny of Canada was one of expansion, especially to this territory. The West would provide not only arable land for the sons and daughters of Ontario farmers, but also a source of raw materials and an important market for eastern manufacturers. Thomas D'Arcy McGee, Canada's most fervent post-Confederation nationalist, captured the expansionist sentiment in 1868 when he said that "the future of the Dominion depends on our early occupation of the rich prairie land."[24] At the same time, Canada was increasingly worried that the Americans—who were developing their own western lands—would attempt to occupy the northern prairies. Canada acquired Rupert's Land and the North-West Territory from the British government and the Hudson's Bay Company for £300,000 and large swathes of agricultural land in March 1869.

The Canadian government failed to realize that it was not acquiring an empty land, and neither HBC nor the British and Canadian officials communicated with the inhabitants of the North-West about the impending transfer of their land. The chief settlement was at Red River, and over 80 per cent of the 12,000 persons resident there were Métis, the descendants of fur traders (Scots and French Canadians) and their Indigenous wives; more than 50 per cent of them were French-speaking and Roman Catholic. They had divided the land along the Red River in long narrow lots, a necessity for travel and food, and they had their own government, the Council of Assiniboia, established in 1835, as well as their own system of local courts. They had created their own economic and cultural society and had developed a strong sense of identity that they were prepared to defend.

A feeling of discontent and anxiety existed in the Red River Settlement in the late 1860s, after successive crop failures had resulted in widespread hunger and hardship. The situation was further aggravated by the disappearance of buffalo from the eastern plains: the herds were indiscriminately slaughtered in the wake of advancing settlers and American military operations against the Indigenous population. The Canadian government appointed William McDougall as the first lieutenant governor to the

---

24 Quoted in Doug Owram, *Promise of Eden. The Canadian Expansionist Movement and the Idea of the West, 1856–1900* (Toronto: University of Toronto Press, 1980), 77.

colony in late November 1869. McDougall was to lead the colonial administration until the colony was ready to become a province, but both he and his superiors in Ottawa quickly discovered that the right of self-determination was also important to the Métis. Canada would fumble its way through the initial period of occupation.

Led by 25-year-old Louis Riel, a bright, young Métis recently returned to Red River from Montreal where he had been training for the priesthood, the Red River settlers took great exception to the Canadians, who arrived to make the region a Canadian hinterland with their surveyors' chains, English language and cultural mores, Protestant religion, and superior attitude. Riel felt he had a special mission to defend his people from the threat of impending change. He believed the Métis represented a new nation, and he felt fully justified in stopping its transfer to Canada. He even expounded on the Settlement's own nation-building aspirations. On October 18, 1869, he led the formation of the National Committee of the Métis to decide how to protect their interests and their land. A few weeks later he established a provisional government including both Francophones and Anglophones. Riel and the Métis were not opposed to joining Canada, but they wanted union on their terms, and any constitutional arrangement had to guarantee the Métis their land, language, and religion.

Figure 1.5 Signed calling card of Louis Riel, showing a photograph taken in Ottawa after Riel was elected the member of Parliament for Provencher, Manitoba, in 1873.

The Canadians in Red River, largely from middle-class Protestant Ontario families, were also young and well educated. They organized as the "Canadian party" under such individuals as Dr. John Schultz, a medical doctor and merchant who had arrived in 1859, and Charles Mair, a poet and columnist in Red River for *The Globe*. They dismissed any notion of Métis nationalism—when they paid any attention at all to the Red River settlers. In January 1867, they had initiated a petition asking to be united with Canada and they largely shaped Macdonald's image of the colony.[25] They did little to cultivate support among the Indigenous population and saw the manoeuvrings of Riel and the provisional government as acts of lawlessness, not the manifestations of a self-determining people. The Canadians were arrested when they attempted to unseat the provisional government, but Riel released those who promised to leave the territory or abide by Métis law. Schultz and a few others refused, later escaping and again attacking the provisional government at Fort Garry. The Métis suppressed the uprising, recapturing several of the insurgents, including Thomas Scott, a 28-year-old Irishman, a member of the Orange Order, and a vehement anti-Catholic. Scott had arrived in Red River in 1869, worked as a labourer on the road from Red River to Lake Superior, and drifted toward the Canadian party. The provisional government sentenced the leader of the insurgents, Major Charles Arkoll Boulton, to death for treason for his role in the attack on Fort Garry. Riel intervened to save Boulton's life, but Scott was not so fortunate. He tormented his guards with insults and contempt and was court-martialed and sentenced to death for treason. "We must make Canada respect us," Riel said of the execution.[26]

Macdonald was sympathetic to the people of Red River, and he understood their anger. He wrote Cartier on November 27, 1870: "They are handed over like a flock of sheep to us; and they are told that they lose their lands....Under these circumstances it is not to be wondered at that they should be dissatisfied, and should show their discontent."[27] As he had with Nova Scotia, he opted initially for accommodation. He asked the influential Catholic bishop of the Red River Settlement, Alexandre Taché, to leave the Vatican Council in Rome and join with Donald A. Smith of the Hudson's Bay Company, who Macdonald had appointed as a special commissioner, to help defuse the growing tensions. The negotiations with Riel in early 1870 prepared the way for a delegation from Red River to negotiate the Settlement's entry into Confederation. In May 1870, they agreed on the *Manitoba Act*, by which Red River could enter Confederation as the province of Manitoba.

The Act satisfied most of the demands of Riel and the Métis. It assured tenure to the river lots already occupied and allotted a reserve of 1.4 million acres (566,580 hectares) for the next generation of Métis. The remaining land in Manitoba and Rupert's Land was deemed Dominion Land to be used for national purposes and, therefore, beyond the jurisdiction of the Manitoba legislature. The *Manitoba Act* also provided

25 Ibid., 81–82.

26 Thomas Flanagan, *Louis "David" Riel. Prophet of the New World* (Toronto: University of Toronto Press, 1979), 29–30.

27 Quoted in "John A. Macdonald," *Dictionary of Canadian Biography* (*DCB*), http://www.biographi.ca/009004-119.01-e.php?BioId=40370.

for denominational schools and the use of French as a language of record as well as debate in the provincial assembly. French-Canadian leaders in Quebec were extremely pleased with these developments, as they fulfilled the promise of the French–English duality of Canada.

Manitoba's entry into Confederation caused much resentment in Ontario, however, and accentuated the racial and religious divisions within the new nation. Ontario seethed at Riel's actions for standing in the way of its grand design for Canada. Moreover, Protestant and English-speaking Ontario harboured great distrust toward Catholicism, and it saw Riel and the Métis as little more than puppets of the Catholic Church. When Schultz and Mair escaped Red River for Toronto, they were met by a crowd of 5,000 supporters, who hailed them as Canadian and British patriots defending Crown and country against the Métis "rebels." Scott's execution added fuel to the nationalist fire raging in Ontario, particularly among the Orange Order—at the time one of the most powerful organizations in English-speaking Canada. It demanded retribution. In Quebec, relations between French-Canadian Catholics and the Orange Order were much better and, in many ways, they had found some semblance of political accommodation with each other. Not so in Ontario, where a resolution from Toronto Orangemen on April 13, 1870, called upon the government to avenge Scott's "murder," and pledged themselves "to assist in rescuing Red River Territory from those who have turned it over to Popery, and bring to justice the murderers of our countrymen."[28] Despite the earlier negotiations with Riel and his supporters, Macdonald hoped a display of military force in the West might satisfy Ontario. French Canada saw such actions and the inflammatory rhetoric in Ontario as a threat not only against the Métis but against all who might defend the Catholic faith and French culture in Canada. The events of Red River caused a deep emotional divide in Canada.

Macdonald understood the divisions between Quebec and Ontario perfectly. In Ontario, Riel was denounced; in Quebec, he was a hero. With Quebec and the Métis happy with the *Manitoba Act*, Macdonald hoped to appease Ontario with his dispatch of troops to Red River in July 1870 on the pretext of preventing further trouble. At the same time, Macdonald promised an amnesty to those engaged in the Red River Resistance and encouraged Riel to flee to the United States. There were rumours that Macdonald offered him money to remain there. Riel was twice elected to the House of Commons, but he was prevented from attending. In 1875, he was offered an amnesty on condition of five years' banishment from Canada, which he took. At the time, the Métis had achieved their objectives: Canada had been dissuaded from annexing their

28 "Thomas Scott," (*DCB*), http://www.biographi.ca/009004-119.01-e.php?BioId=38817.

land without consultation, and they had won entry into Canada as a province. They had achieved legislative guarantees that their land, religion, and language would be secure within the new Canadian regime. Within a few years, though, the Métis would call upon Riel to defend their interests again.

TREATIES WITH FIRST NATIONS: NATION BUILDING AND COLONIZING THE WEST

After the Canadian government acquired the North-West, it recognized that Indigenous peoples had rights to the land and continued the process initiated by the British government in the eighteenth century of dealing with Aboriginal title through treaty. The federal government followed the practice established by Britain since the Royal Proclamation of 1763, which prohibited settlers from occupying lands not ceded by First Nations in formal treaties. Ottawa subsequently negotiated 11 "numbered treaties" with Canada's Indigenous peoples, covering the territory from much of present-day northwest Ontario to the foothills of the Rockies and some of the Canadian North (this will be considered fully in the next chapter). These treaties followed practices established decades earlier in Upper Canada and provided for the cession of land by the First Nations to allow expansion of settlement into Western Canada. In addition to the promise of reserve land separate from newcomer settlement, and annual cash payments, Canada promised hunting and fishing rights, gratuities, the provision of agricultural implements and livestock, schools, and a variety of other benefits to protect the First Nations peoples from hunger and disease and enable them to embrace the agricultural economy.

There is ample evidence that in many cases on the plains this did not happen, and the reserve system led to the widespread hunger, starvation, and disease that the federal government had promised to prevent. Canada never regarded the treaties as being signed between sovereign nations, but as real estate transactions that extinguished Indigenous title and rights. Indigenous peoples, on the other hand, generally believed that they were sharing, not surrendering, their land and that these deals were taking place between autonomous communities. Furthermore, they believed that the elaborate ceremonies accompanying the negotiations were an indication of covenants between themselves, the Crown, and the deity and represented the highest order of diplomacy and law making within their communities. Today, the treaties are constitutionally recognized as binding agreements between Indigenous peoples and the Crown, but their interpretation has fallen to the courts. Over the decade of the 1870s, most of the Indigenous lands between Manitoba and the Rocky Mountains were transferred from the First Nations to the Government of Canada at almost no immediate cost to the Dominion. Yet, this transfer of vast areas in certain parts of Canada has never been formally negotiated by the two parties.

Two other nation-building developments were of significance in the West. First, the government created the North-West Mounted Police—now the Royal Canadian Mounted Police—in 1873 as an agent of the Canadian state to maintain peace in the region, protect the Indigenous peoples, particularly from whiskey traders, and to secure the North-West for Canada and keep the Americans out. Their scarlet tunic uniform was intended to take advantage of the respect that Indigenous groups had for the British Army. Second, and with no more than a few thousand European settlers in the West, the government passed the *Dominion Lands Act* in 1872 to facilitate white Anglo-European settlement of the West and to initiate a dominion settlement policy. The Act provided to each head of family, or male 21 years of age, 160 acres (64 hectares) free if he paid a $10 registration fee, resided on the land for 3 years, cultivated 30 acres (12 hectares), and built a permanent dwelling. If these conditions were met on the first quarter-section, it was his, and for a small fee he could add a second quarter-section. The government believed that even free land would pay for itself by bringing in immigrants who would need consumer goods, which, in turn, would generate manufacturing and trade in the new Dominion. Despite the offer of free land after 1872, few people ventured into the Canadian West until the 1890s, by which time the American West had largely been settled.

REACHING THE PACIFIC OCEAN: *A MARI USQUE AD MARE*

With the prairie west reasonably secure, Macdonald turned to British Columbia, hoping to fulfill the original dream of a transcontinental nation. The European population of the colony had grown rapidly following the 1857 gold rush, although Indigenous peoples remained the majority. There was also a great concern that the Americans would extend their influence in the colony. After all, on March 30, 1867, one day after the passage of the Canadian constitution, the United States purchased Alaska from Russia, effectively squeezing British Columbia on both sides. There was considerable talk—and fear—of annexation. The Americans had completed their first transcontinental railway in 1869 and were planning a second that would run near the Canadian border. In August 1869, American Secretary of State William Seward visited Victoria and left with the impression that British Columbians were eager to join the United States.

With its Pacific fleet based at Esquimalt, Britain did not want to lose British Columbia, and it worked after 1867 to have the colony join Canada. Anthony

Musgrave was sent to British Columbia as governor to promote union. British Columbia was seen as a natural extension of Canada and was necessary for the development of the transcontinental nation. When the Canadian government promised a rail link within a decade, assumed the colony's debt, and offered the usual subsidies, British Columbia joined. When the legislation passed the House of Commons in 1871, Cartier, who played a key role in the expansion to the Pacific, shouted "All aboard for the West!"[29]

While the boundaries of Manitoba had been limited to the settled portions of the territory, this was not the case with British Columbia. Although Aboriginal title to the lands in the colony had not been extinguished by treaty as it had been in much of Eastern Canada, British Columbia entered Confederation with the same boundaries it has today. As a result, resolving Aboriginal title would prove to be a difficult and protracted issue in the province.

CANADA AND FOREIGN RELATIONS

Nationhood for Canada did not mean independence. The *British North America Act* was silent on the conduct of international relations, except to note that Canada remained a part of the British Empire and was obliged to uphold any treaties the Empire had with other countries. Although foreign policy was largely left to the British, the federal government believed that it needed representation abroad, especially in London, to promote its interests. In 1869, Macdonald appointed Sir John Rose, a former finance minister and, at the time, a London banker, to informally promote Canada. Rose often lobbied British officials on Canada's behalf and promoted emigration to Canada. He was Macdonald's eyes and ears in London.

Canada's primary concern in international affairs, however, was with the neighbouring United States, and here it had two objectives: first, to maintain cordial relations; and second, to renegotiate a free trade agreement. The British withdrawal of their military forces from Canada (with the exception of the naval base at Halifax) in 1871 was an important step in achieving the first goal, and the Canadian government hoped that providing American access to Canadian waters would help achieve the second. American fishers wanted access to the waters of British North America, and American incursions into Canadian waters had been a point of contention between the Canadian and American fishers for more than a generation. In 1869, Canada dispatched cruisers to patrol the inshore waters and keep American vessels from

---

29 "George-Étienne Cartier," (*DCB*), http://www.biographi.ca/009004-119.01-e.php?BioId=39006.

trespassing on Canadian fishing grounds. In 1870, 16 vessels were arrested for illegal fishing. President Ulysses S. Grant was not amused. In his annual address to Congress he said (in a veiled threat to the British and Canadians) that "the time is not probably far distant when, in the natural course of events, the European political connection with this continent will cease." Then, ominously, he warned, "The course pursued by the Canadian authorities towards the fishermen of the United States during the past season has not been marked by a friendly feeling....Vessels have been seized without notice or warning, in violation of the custom previously prevailing." Grant wanted a resolution to the vexing problem, which became one of the important issues facing the British and Canadian negotiators who met in Washington in 1871 to resolve a number of pressing matters in Anglo–American relations, some of them dating back to the American Civil War.

Macdonald, the newly minted Canadian prime minister, acted as one of the British commissioners. In some respects, the presence of a Canadian represented a step forward in Canadian autonomy. Yet Macdonald would bear the political cost in Canada for failing to win some important diplomatic objectives. Macdonald believed that Canada could offer access to the fisheries in an attempt to force the US government to consider some form of reciprocal trade with Canada. As Macdonald saw it, "the fisheries are our trump card," but the Maritimes disagreed vehemently: they had no interest in sharing the waters off their coasts with the Americans. Still, the Treaty of Washington, signed on May 8, 1871, granted Americans the right to fish in the territorial waters off Quebec, Nova Scotia, New Brunswick, and Prince Edward Island, while British subjects were granted the same rights in American waters north of the 39th parallel. Moreover, fish and fish oil produced in Canada, Prince Edward Island, and the United States were to be traded on a reciprocal basis. Other contentious issues were sent to arbitration. Because it was gaining the most from these arrangements, the US government provided financial compensation to Canada for access to Canadian fisheries.

Macdonald realized the damage inflicted on the Maritime fishing industry, but he agreed to the treaty because the British government had promised to guarantee a loan for the construction of railways and canals in Canada if the treaty were adopted. With such a promise, Macdonald had Parliament ratify the Treaty of Washington—itself an act of symbolic importance—knowing that he had sacrificed Maritime fisheries for the perceived national good. Macdonald later discovered that the treaty had not just offended the Maritimes, but had also disappointed many in Ontario and Quebec who wanted free access for their agricultural products in American markets. Macdonald would eventually abandon hopes for reciprocity and become a vocal champion of protective tariffs.

CONCLUSION

Canada did not emerge from revolution, nor was it even a process driven by democratic impulses. Confederation was an exercise in continuity rather than a rupture, as it preserved the British connection. It was also driven by forces operating in Britain and the United States. This does not mean that Confederation was not debated among British North Americans or completed against their wishes. It emerged out of negotiations between the political leaders of the various colonies in the 1860s that took account of the some of the regional, economic, ethnic, and cultural dimensions of the people and colonies that were party to the negotiations in the period from 1864 to 1874. Many of those involved understood the complexities surrounding national identity, and some insisted that Canada's identity should be a shared one—the rights of minorities had to be respected, and no one identity could be hegemonic. Negotiations and compromise did not mean that all people were winners, however. Canada quickly expanded its boundaries beyond the original colonies to reach across the continent. Manitoba negotiated French language and Catholic education rights and its unique land-holding system as a condition of its entry into the federation. Prince Edward Island negotiated a deal to solve the problem of its absentee landowners; and British Columbia negotiated a transcontinental link to the east. The government was less generous, though, in its negotiations with, and accommodations of, Indigenous peoples. Yet, out of conflict, disunity, and political instability, and amid the fears of local communities, political leaders were able to come together in spite of the multitude of divisions—including the English–French conflict, a provincial rights' struggle, and Métis resistance to imperial expansion—that constantly pulled at its fabric. The proponents of Confederation moved Canadians beyond their local patriotism to create a nation. It was an arrangement designed to recognize the differences that existed in British North America at the time, and it provided an economic framework for growth and prosperity as well as an apparatus to give the new nation a chance. Canada had survived its first years of union, but difficult times lay ahead.

2 CHALLENGES, REALITIES, AND PROMISES: THE NATIONAL DREAM AND COLONIZATION, 1874–1896

INTRODUCTION

Understanding and making sense of the messy and diffuse events that together create Canada's national narrative is no easy task, especially when that narrative has been shaped by contingencies and ideas both contemporary and historical. Recent consideration of Canada's policies toward its minorities in the latter part of the nineteenth century, which is discussed in this chapter, illustrates the difficulty of trying to make sense of the past. For more than four decades, historians have known that the Canadian state relied on callous and sometimes inhumane measures, including the use of food as a weapon to subjugate the Plains Cree, Blackfoot, and other Indigenous peoples. Historians have long known the impact of disease on Indigenous peoples, even if recent historians have provided a vast amount of detail on those aspects of Canada's history.[1] The belief that Canada has always been just and

---

1 James Daschuk, *Clearing the Plains: Disease, Politics of Starvation and the Loss of Aboriginal Life* (Regina: University of Regina Press, 2013).

honourable in its dealings with its citizens was long ago shown to be a myth. Canada followed coercive policies toward its Indigenous peoples and used the brute force of the state later against First Nations as well as other ethnic groups such as the Chinese, Japanese, and Ukrainians to achieve its policy objectives.

Figure 2.1 Sir John A. Macdonald, 1868.

In today's Canada there is, rightfully, a growing concern about conditions facing Canada's Indigenous peoples. However, historical events are increasingly been interpreted without historical context and through the lens of modernity. Historians call this approach "presentism." Lynn Hunt, president of the American Historical Association, recently warned that presentism encourages a kind of moral complacency that usually leads us to find ourselves morally superior. The past, she laments, "becomes the short-term history of various kinds of identity politics defined by present concerns," adding that when we interpret the past in terms of the present, "Our forbears [*sic*] constantly fail to measure up to our present-day standards."[2]

We must be just toward all in our own time, but reading history through today's sensibilities and concerns, and without historical context, is about as enlightening as name-calling. Historical context, of course, is not used to justify the actions of those that lived in an earlier time, but it does mean that history can be instructive as we discuss issues of race and gender, among others. When we view history without context, John A. Macdonald is interpreted as a zealous and racist bigot, committed to genocide and the promotion of the Aryan race, and placed in the same category as Slobodan Milosevic, Leopold II of Belgium, and Adolf Hitler. In such an interpretation, Canada becomes an instrument of evil no different from Hitler's Germany. That is a difficult argument to defend.

---

2 Lynn Hunt, "Against Presentism," in *Perspective on History*, American Historical Association, May 2002, https://www.historians.org/publications-and-directories/perspectives-on-history/may-2002/against-presentism.

Macdonald has always been a complex figure. In some quarters today he is interpreted in ways that leave students of history—who are searching for an understanding of the past—simply shaking their heads in disbelief. Earlier generations of historians noted his binge drinking, but now it is intellectually fashionable to focus on Macdonald's allegedly "criminal" past. Some have taken to labelling him Canada's first "crime" minister because of devastation created by the Indian residential schools, which were instituted after Confederation, and by his policies toward Asian immigration. Even the Supreme Court Chief Justice Beverley McLachlin joined in, claiming in 2015 that Canada developed an "ethos of exclusion and cultural annihilation" against its Indigenous peoples, policies, she added, that represent nothing less than an attempt to commit "cultural genocide." The 2015 federal Royal Commission reached similar conclusions on the legacy of residential schools. Some historians now see Canada and its history as shaped only by a process of settler colonialism and the dispossession of Indigenous peoples.

Macdonald had his flaws, but many of the recent interpretations are inflammatory and narrow. As this chapter will show, Canada in the final decades of the nineteenth century experienced considerable turmoil and unrest, and it had to deal with a myriad of difficult issues, including those associated with race. Wrong decisions were made in many cases, and actions pursued that were misguided, improper, and now considered intolerable and criminal. After Confederation, Canada developed the habits of empire, and Macdonald and others did not consider the corrosive impact of the state's colonial policies on Indigenous peoples. Yet, there was no plan to eradicate First Nations under Macdonald and there was no genocide; Macdonald at one point even attempted to extend the vote to all adult Indigenous men who met the property qualifications, and he relented only in the face of vociferous Opposition attacks in Parliament to such a liberal policy. Macdonald was the Superintendent General of Indian Affairs, the longest serving in that role in Canadian history, but Indian Affairs was only one of the files on his desk. He relied on others to manage the day-to-day operations of the department. It should be noted, however, that Macdonald realized—as did First Nations' leaders themselves—that First Nations and all Canadians had to adapt to a changing world. The education and the medicine that First Nations leaders sought were not their traditional educational or health practices but those brought by Europeans to Canada; they, like Macdonald, were ready to accept many of the ways and knowledge of the settler society. The fact that Macdonald went through considerable expense to promote schooling suggests that his goals were not those of the genocide or ethnic cleansing of which he has recently being accused. Labelling Macdonald's policies of the 1880s and 1890s genocidal is a misreading of the historical record. His decision to turn education over to religious orders, who perpetrated unspeakable abuse at residential schools, was clearly a mistake he must own. As we study this period of Canada's history, it is important to understand the political context in which Macdonald and others, including Indigenous leaders, functioned. In Macdonald's case, the opposition Liberals constantly and viciously attacked any expenditure for First Nations. He operated as all prime ministers have—and do—in a distressingly real political world. The political climate in which Macdonald governed was far less tolerant than he was, and as students of history we must never rush to conflate outcomes with intentions.

Alexander Mackenzie, who was prime minister from 1873 to 1878, acknowledged in his final days in office the difficulty inherent in governing Canada: "We have a country vast in extent, vast in its territorial magnitude, vast in respect to its sectional views, and in its diversity of creed and race," he said. "It is a task which any statesman may feel great difficulty in accomplishing, to harmonize all those interests, and bring a genuine feeling of union to bear upon the prosperity of the country which he has to govern."[3] Neither Mackenzie nor Macdonald could bring harmony to Canada, but both managed to keep the country together. That task was never easy, and this chapter highlights the challenges, strains, and sometimes tragedies, associated with Canada's growth and maturation from 1873 to 1896. It examines relations between First Nations and Métis people and the Canadian government, and between French-speaking and English-speaking Canadians. It also considers the difficulties that Canada faced in developing a coherent national economic strategy, sustaining an effective federal–provincial relationship, and Canada's role within the British Empire. This is a chapter about managing political, ethnic, and class divisions in Canada, finding the accommodation necessary to maintain consent for the Canada project designed at Charlottetown and Quebec in 1864, and providing some normative balance in the new country as citizens, institutions, and governments dealt with the tensions inherent within.

THE PACIFIC SCANDAL AND A NEW GOVERNMENT

The Conservatives won a narrow victory in the second general election after Confederation in 1872, but some very damaging allegations were soon raised. The Liberal Party discovered that Macdonald had accepted large political contributions from Sir Hugh Allan, who had been awarded a lucrative contract to build Canada's first transcontinental railway. Macdonald attempted to dismiss the allegations, but with evidence mounting that Allan had given more than $350,000 to the Conservative

---

3　*The Pic-Nic Speeches Delivered in the Province of Ontario during the Summer of 1877.* Published by the Reform Association of the Province of Ontario, and prepared for the Press by the Secretary, Mr. G.R. Pattullo, of the Woodstock *Sentinel* (Toronto: Globe Printing and Publishing, 1878).

campaign, he was rightly worried. Particularly damning was Macdonald's telegram to Allan, published in a Liberal newspaper: "I must have another ten thousand; will be the last time of calling; do not fail me; answer today." Desperate to stave off defeat, Macdonald convinced the governor general, Lord Dufferin, to prorogue Parliament, prompting George Brown's *Globe* to charge that the Crown had shielded the guilty. The Liberals bided their time until a new session began in late October, but rather than face a vote of confidence in the House of Commons, Macdonald resigned on November 5, 1873. He left office in disgrace, finding refuge in the bottle, and Alexander Mackenzie became the new prime minister. When he sought his own mandate in January 1874, he chose morality as the major campaign theme—an issue that has served many opposition leaders well since Confederation. During the 20-day campaign, the shortest in Canadian history, he promised "to elevate the standard of public morality...and...conduct public affairs upon principles of which honest men can approve." The Liberals garnered 53.8 per cent of the popular vote and 133 of the 206 seats.

Figure 2.2 The Honourable Alexander Mackenzie, Prime Minister of Canada, 1873–1878.

Although Mackenzie led a party united primarily in its opposition to Macdonald, many in the new government had been associated with the reform politics of pre-Confederation Canada. Steeped in a liberal-democratic tradition and largely rural and agrarian, Mackenzie's party adhered to the principles of nineteenth-century liberalism: minimalist government, free trade, low taxes and fiscal restraint, democratic reform and egalitarianism, and provincial autonomy. In his first parliamentary session, Mackenzie introduced measures to improve the democratic process: general elections on the same day in all constituencies across Canada, outlawing the distribution of alcohol by candidates, closing pubs on polling day, and requiring all candidates to submit election expenses within two months of the vote to control campaign expenditures. He introduced the secret ballot to eliminate all sorts of abuse and intimidation that came with the open voting system. The franchise was extended beyond property owners, but women were not given the right to vote, although support for the cause was starting to build.

Mackenzie's belief in a minimalist role for the state collided with the expansionist and costly commitments he inherited from the Conservative government. The largest came in fulfilling Macdonald's promise of a transcontinental railway. Liberals did not believe, as Macdonald had, that if Canada did not exercise its control over the West it would be lost to the Americans. They had vehemently opposed subsidies to the Canadian Pacific Railway, and Mackenzie attempted to renegotiate the agreement. British Columbia Premier George Anthony Walkem had already complained to Macdonald that he had needlessly delayed construction of the railway, and when Mackenzie attempted to delay construction even further, Walkem appealed to the British authorities in London, who were sympathetic. Lord Carnarvon, the colonial secretary, recommended that Canada extend the completion date for the CPR to 1890 and build the Esquimalt–Nanaimo line in British Columbia as compensation for the delay. Mackenzie reluctantly accepted Lord Carnarvon's recommendation because anything less would have alienated British Columbia and threatened the unity of Canada.

THE STRUGGLE FOR GREATER AUTONOMY

Mackenzie also ran into trouble with London when he created the Supreme Court of Canada in 1875. It was to become the final judicial body of appeal rather than the Judicial Committee of the Privy Council (JCPC) in London. For Mackenzie, the Court was a symbol of Canadian nationalism and one that he hoped would instill pride in Canadians. His initiative did not sit well with Britain's law lords, who worried that ending appeals to the JCPC would curtail the important traditional right of every British subject—and, at the time, that meant all Canadians—to seek redress at the foot of the throne. Dufferin had already given the bill establishing the Court royal assent, and disallowing it after the fact was apt to be especially provocative to Mackenzie's government, even though British authorities still enjoyed the right after Confederation to disallow Canadian legislation. In this instance a compromise was found. The law was allowed to stand, but Canada's Supreme Court was supreme in name only: appeals could still be made to the JCPC, despite the wording of the legislation. Criminal appeals to London were abolished in 1888, but civil appeals not until 1949.

One way of limiting British interference in Canada's domestic affairs was to clarify the role of the governor general, whom the British government used as their agent in Canada. The *British North America Act* had been largely silent on the role of the governor general, whose appointment was decided by the British cabinet, not Queen Victoria. As such, the governor general was in a difficult dual role, required to accept advice from two sets of ministers. Beyond his role as resident head of state, advised by his Canadian ministers, he was a kind of colonial administrator and imperial watchdog, answerable to the Colonial Office in London. Lord Dufferin's interference was not limited to the construction of the railway to British Columbia and the establishment of the Canadian Supreme Court, however. One of the governor general's traditional prerogatives was that of mercy—the commutation of a death sentence to condemned prisoners. Mackenzie's administration, and notably his minister of justice, Edward Blake, believed that Dufferin should only exercise this prerogative according to ministerial advice. The governor general's official written instructions said otherwise, even if these instructions were out of date and did not reflect how Canada had evolved constitutionally after 1867. Although the Liberals were only too glad to have Dufferin's commutation of the sentence of Ambroise Lépine for his part in the execution of Thomas Scott in 1869 to two years' imprisonment, Blake wanted the instructions for the vice-regal office clarified in order to limit his power. During the turmoil over the delay in building the railway to British Columbia, Mackenzie wrote Dufferin that Canada was "not a Crown Colony (or a Colony at all in the normal acceptation of the term)" and that it "would not be dealt with as small communities."[4] The Canadian government could not do much about Dufferin, but it was determined to rein in his successor and ensure his role was not an activist one. When Dufferin's successor, the Marquess of Lorne, was named, the instructions issued to him eliminated those vice-regal powers that had become constitutionally obsolete. He was to avoid becoming involved in internal matters and he was to act according to the advice of his privy council in Canada.[5]

Blake was intensely nationalistic, and limiting the powers of the British-appointed governor general was only one of his goals in the pursuit of a strongly nationalistic Canada that would be more independent of London. Blake had been a contender for the Liberal leadership when Mackenzie was invited to be prime minister in 1873, and some have maintained that he was terribly disappointed that he was passed over for the top job. It seems more likely, however, that Blake himself shrank from the responsibility of leadership. He was acutely sensitive, prone to bouts of depression, disinclined to compromise, and perhaps better suited to opposition. Blake served sporadically in Mackenzie's cabinet, but was apt to resign whenever conflict arose:

4   Quoted in Ben Forster, "Frederick Temple Blackwood, Marquess of Dufferin," *Dictionary of Canadian Biography* (*DCB*), http://www.biographi.ca/009004-119.01-e.php?BioId=40683.

5   Barbara J. Messamore, *Canada's Governors General, 1847–1878. Biography and Constitutional Evolution* (Toronto: University of Toronto Press, 2006), especially pp. 177–213.

Mackenzie's archival papers contain no fewer than a dozen letters of resignation penned by Blake during the years the Liberals were in power.

The Liberals saw the necessity of promoting national patriotism in addition to building Canada's infrastructure, extending its territorial boundaries, and providing effective governance. In a speech in Aurora, Ontario, in 1874, Blake acknowledged the difficult task of governing Canada when the seven provinces were frequently divided by isolation, local interests, and petty jealousies. Can there be real union, he asked, by the government "giving sop now to one, now to another"? The future of Canada, he said, depended upon the cultivation of a national spirit. He stressed the importance of Canada's independence and its constitutional autonomy within the British Empire. "We are four millions of Britons who are not free," he told the gathering.[6] He then made the case for the reorganization of the Empire upon the basis of an imperial federation, presumably one in which Canada would enhance its sovereignty and independence. Blake was associated with the Canada First movement, a small group of young, English-speaking Canadians who believed it was important to foster a patriotic spirit among their fellow citizens. He had criticized the Treaty of Washington in 1871 because he believed Britain had sacrificed Canada's interests for favour with the United States. Five days after Blake's Aurora speech, Canada Firsters established the National Club in Toronto and launched a periodical, *The Nation*, as the organization's mouthpiece. *The Nation* promoted a national tariff (or tax on imported goods) to protect Canadian industry, an idea that Macdonald subsequently adopted.

Mackenzie's government embraced the liberal philosophy of free trade, however. Even before he met Parliament after the 1874 election, Mackenzie dispatched newly appointed Senator George Brown to Washington to push for a new free trade agreement. Brown convinced the Americans to sign a comprehensive free trade agreement in natural products and a wide range of manufactured goods. To the Liberals' surprise, many in Canada, especially manufacturers, wanted higher tariffs, not free trade. Mackenzie's government was saved from a quarrel with Canada's growing and increasingly protectionist manufacturing sector when US President Ulysses S. Grant decided not to push the draft treaty through a protectionist Congress.

THE NATIONAL POLICY

After the Conservatives' defeat, Macdonald contemplated resigning as leader and only slowly recovered his interest in politics. The Liberals struggled in office from the

---

6   Quoted in W.S. Wallace, "The Growth of Canadian National Feeling," *Canadian Historical Review* 1, no. 2 (June 1920): 143–50.

beginning, and a persistent economic crisis, which saw food riots in Montreal, internal party dissension, delays in railway construction, and temperance legislation added to the Liberal woes. Meanwhile, the Conservatives reorganized their local party organization and embraced new policies, including a new tariff policy that Macdonald boasted would benefit manufacturers, labourers, and farmers—the beginnings of a National Policy that would also include settlement of the West and a transcontinental railway across Canada. Riding a wave of rising protectionism across the globe, Macdonald announced in 1876 that, if elected, the Conservatives would raise the tariff to help Canada develop its economy. When the campaign began, he told supporters "there has risen in this country a Canadian Party, which declares we have Canada for the Canadians….You cannot get anything by kissing the feet of the people of the United States."[7] Anti-Americanism, the view that too close a relationship with the United States would undermine Canada's ability to act independently, plays well in Canada. The free trade

Figure 2.3 Macdonald presented the National Policy as good for Canada and as a way to keep American manufacturers out.

ideology of the Liberal Party had little appeal among voters, despite claims that the tariff was a tax on 95 per cent of the people to benefit the top 5 per cent. The 5 per cent had the ear of Macdonald, particularly the manufacturers, who lobbied hard for the tariff in the 1878 campaign. Protectionism and high tariffs made good politics, and voters opted for Macdonald's plan, forgave him for his earlier indiscretions, and returned the Conservatives to power in 1878. The election marked a fundamental shift in Canada.

---

7   Quoted in P.B. Waite, *Canada 1874–1896. Arduous Destiny* (Toronto, McClelland & Stewart, 1971), 91.

In their first budget following the election, the Conservatives raised the tariff on a variety of imports, including on some agricultural products, wanting farmers to believe that protection was in their interest too. The average tariff rate was set at 25 per cent, but when one manufacturer's output was another's input, compromise was necessary. What was not in doubt, however, was that the Conservatives considered tariff protection permanent—even if it annoyed the British, who favoured free trade. Canada would create its own east–west industrial economy that, after all, was one of the objectives of Confederation.

The National Policy was an important step toward Canadian sovereignty, and Macdonald's initiative of economic nationalism would remain in place for more than half a century. Its objectives were simple: create an integrated east–west economy by fostering the growth of the manufacturing sector in Central and Eastern Canada, settle the West, and secure the country with a transcontinental railway system. Within a short time, the industrial strategy appeared to be working. The Maritime provinces that had joined Confederation, in part, for access to the larger Canadian market, appeared to be well on their way to economic success. Throughout the 1880s and early 1890s, the region's staple production in agriculture, fishing, and timber enjoyed only modest growth, but the rate of industrial expansion surpassed that of Quebec and Ontario. The rise of the manufacturing sector, particularly in cotton cloth, refined sugars, rope and twine, and iron and steel, accounted for nearly half of the region's value of production in 1890; however, the success would be fleeting. Most of the secondary manufacturers were small, community-based, family-oriented enterprises that depended on loans from chartered banks, and they struggled against the larger and better-financed firms in Quebec and Ontario when overproduction of many products led to a period of industrial mergers and consolidation early in the twentieth century.

The growing metropolitan centres of Montreal and Toronto, meanwhile, quickly added to their economic clout. Within a decade of the introduction of the tariff, Ontario increased the value-added of its manufacturing sector by nearly 65 per cent. The new tariff structure did not keep foreign capital out of Canada, but that was never the objective. The Conservatives wanted economic development and jobs for Canadians; they were happy American corporations established brand-plants in Canada. Concerns of foreign ownership of the economy lay well into the future.

LINKING CANADA BY RAIL

A transcontinental railway was the second plank in Macdonald's National Policy. Without it, large-scale inter-provincial trade was not possible. Macdonald had not lost any of his enthusiasm for railways when he returned as prime minister, even if he approached railway expenditures and railway promoters with a little more caution. Macdonald believed that the railway had to be constructed in advance of settlement—the third pillar of his policy—to stake Canada's claim to the substantial territory in the West and build an east–west economy. In 1882, a Macdonald-appointed Royal Commission to consider the government's role in building the railway to the Pacific recommended that such schemes be left to the private sector. Macdonald agreed, although he realized that private companies would have to be amply rewarded for their risk in building a railway through the parts of Canada that in the early 1880s had relatively few European settlers.

The government signed a contract with the Canadian Pacific Railway on October 21, 1882, to complete a railway link from Montreal to British Columbia. George Stephen, the president of the Bank of Montreal, and his cousin Donald Smith, the chief commissioner of the Hudson's Bay Company, headed the syndicate. For the new sections of the transcontinental railway, the government provided the CPR $25 million and 25 million acres (10 million hectares) of arable land along the proposed route through the Northwest Territories. The sections of railway that the government had already built—estimated to be approximately 800 miles (1,300 kilometres) and valued at $31.5 million—were turned over to the company. The CPR would operate the railway once complete, its property and capital stock free from taxation in perpetuity, and its landholdings had tax-free status for 20 years, an attempt by the government to encourage the railway to participate in attracting European and American settlers to the Prairies. The government also promised that no lines would be permitted south of the CPR in the West.

There was considerable opposition to the CPR contract. The Liberals suggested that the government build the railway itself if it were funding the project. The Conservative caucus had to be persuaded that the contract was reasonable. The Toronto business community complained that its interests were sacrificed to those of Montreal, and the West criticized the government for ignoring its interests. The *Edmonton Bulletin* wrote that the contract had been negotiated and signed by people who knew nothing about the West and believed that "the sun rises in Halifax, shines all day straight over Montreal and Ottawa, and sets in Toronto."[8] Manitoba objected because the same capitalists who controlled the all-Canadian route also owned the American route to the south. When the federal government loaned Stephen and his group an additional $30 million in 1883, Charles Tupper, the minister of finance, had to grant subsidies for railway lines in Quebec and Manitoba to secure the support of his own MPs. A year later, when Stephen returned for another handout, only Macdonald's threatened

8 Ibid., 112.

resignation and the beginnings of an uprising in the West saved the CPR from bankruptcy. The line to Vancouver was completed in 1885.

IMMIGRANTS: DIFFICULTIES, DESIRABLES, AND "UNDESIRABLES"

Settling the West became an important aspect of nation building. The government had hoped that its version of the American homestead legislation—the *Dominion Lands Act* introduced in 1872—would attract massive immigration by giving away free land. It did not: only 1.5 million immigrants chose Canada, while more than 8 million flocked to the United States and nearly 3 million to Australia during the same period. Moreover, more than 2 million people left Canada, primarily from Quebec and the Maritime provinces, for the better economic prospects of the United States.

Canada's lacklustre performance in attracting settlers did not fail for lack of effort. Shortly after Confederation, the federal Department of Agriculture, which was responsible for attracting settlers, began a massive advertising campaign to sell potential immigrants and Canadians alike on the virtues of the West. The government opened immigration agencies in some Canadian cities, in Britain, and throughout Europe. It also encouraged particular groups, such as Icelanders, Mennonites from Russia, and others, to establish their own homogeneous communities on the Prairies, but the federal efforts only resulted in modest gains until the 1890s, when the railway provided easier access for getting to the western frontier and a means for farmers to market their produce. By then, the return of economic prosperity, rising grain prices, innovations in prairie farming, including new agricultural machinery and hardier strains of wheat, and the closure of the American frontier meant that Canada, finally, became attractive to immigrants from the British Isles, Europe, and even the United States.

Immigration to the West did not mean just homesteading. Many came to work in the coalmines opening up around Lethbridge and Banff in the 1880s and the new factories opening up across the country, but not all peoples were welcome. One group that found Canada a particularly unwelcoming place were Chinese migrant workers who were initially recruited to build the CPR. Eager to flee the crushing poverty in their homeland, more than 15,000 Chinese labourers were lured by politicians and businessmen seeking cheap labour to lay the CPR tracks through the mountains. Paid less than half what white workers earned, they often performed the most dangerous work, including the handling of explosives needed to blast through the mountains. While estimates vary, most agree that at least 10 per cent succumbed to smallpox or cholera or died in work-related accidents.

Chinese labourers were never desired as immigrants. Many Canadians—politicians and workers alike—complained that Chinese immigration presented a problem for Canada, especially as the railway was nearing completion. Labour groups protested that they depressed wage rates and took jobs from white Canadians; others were simply racists and asserted that because the Chinese could not be assimilated they would alter the character of Canada. A Royal Commission investigating the implications of Chinese immigration recommended restrictions and a head tax on each new Chinese immigrant. After considering the report, Macdonald, who once referred to Canada as an "Aryan" nation, told Parliament in 1885 that the Chinese worker "has no common interest with us, and while he gives us labour he is paid for, and is valuable, the same as a threshing machine or any other agricultural implement which we may borrow from the United States on hire and return it to the owner on the south side of the line…he has no British instincts or British feelings or aspirations, and therefore ought not to have a vote." Macdonald imposed a head tax of $50, increased on several occasions and in place until 1923, when Chinese immigration was banned altogether. In 2006, Prime Minister Stephen Harper offered an apology and compensation for the head tax on behalf of the Government of Canada.

LIFE IN THE WORKPLACE

Chinese workers were only one group that endured difficult working conditions in the 1880s and 1890s. These were years of hardship for most workers as factories emerged throughout the country under the auspices of the National Policy. Most workers were at the mercy of their employers, and such benefits as job security and continued wages in the event of injury and serious illness simply did not exist. Female cotton mill workers in Halifax, who appeared before the Royal Commission on the Relations of Capital and Labour that the federal government had appointed in 1888 to investigate the plight of workers, described a harsh life marked by low wages (between three and four dollars a week—about half what men earned), long hours standing in suffocating heat and dust performing repetitive tasks, strict discipline with fines for lateness and shoddy work, and an unpredictable work schedule. In Ontario knitting mills in 1881, women and children worked for nearly 60 hours for $1.65 a week. This was not unusual for factory work, which was heavily dependent on the labour of women and children.

Early labour unions were for the elite of the workforce—skilled craftsmen—and were not particularly interested in organizing women, children, or the unskilled. After Confederation, as the lines between labour and capital became more pronounced, this began to change, and it was reflected in the concerted efforts of labour for the Nine Hour Movement in the 1870s. Although the movement failed, it led to

Figure 2.4 Domestic service was the most common paid employment for women in Canada before 1900. The tasks varied depending on whether there were just one or several servants in the household. A servant working alone was often responsible for the cleaning, cooking, errands, kitchen, garden, and children. Her workday could be 15 hours; some days the domestic worked for 18 hours, as the upper classes began their fashionable late dinners around seven or eight o'clock at night.

the creation of the Canadian Labour Union in 1873, though it, too, collapsed a few years later. One major development was an import from the United States, the Holy and Noble Order of the Knights of Labor that organized more than 20,000 workers across Canada into an industrial union. The Knights wanted to organize all workers regardless of skill level, gender, or race (though they excluded Chinese workers), but the union would disappear—with the exception of a few chapters in Quebec—by the turn of the twentieth century. In Nova Scotia, the Protective Workman's Association organized most of the workers in the province's coal industries. Organized labour spread across Canada, but in 1890, many of the 240 established unions were located in Ontario and Quebec. The Trade and Labour Congress of Canada began in Ontario in 1883, and by 1900 its reach extended across the country.

Treaty Making and Preparing the West for European Settlers

After Confederation, Canada continued the British colonial practice of negotiating treaties with First Nations in advance of settlement. The Royal Proclamation of 1763 established the principle that Indigenous lands could not be alienated except by treaty with the Crown. Policy makers of the 1870s had the dual goal of acquiring those lands and helping Indigenous peoples adapt to changing conditions. They believed that First Peoples had to be protected from the pernicious influence of unscrupulous newcomers so they might ultimately participate in European-Canadian society. This meant bringing Christianity to them, settling them on agricultural lands to become farmers, and providing education. This general policy had been set out in pre-Confederation Canada with the 1857 *Act for the Gradual Civilization of Indian Tribes*, legislation that laid the groundwork for a series of Indian Acts in the post-Confederation era. This was without a doubt a process of subjugation and colonization, but the Canadian government hoped it would provide First Nations with a secure future. However, the results of such a process and a superior attitude turned out quite differently than was anticipated.

The series of treaties negotiated in the Northwest Territories after 1870 were designed to find some accommodation with Indigenous peoples before large numbers of settlers arrived. Joseph Howe, the secretary of state responsible for Indian Affairs, told his officials that they should "endeavour to secure the cession of the lands [from the Indigenous peoples] upon terms as favourable as possible to the Government." Most First Nations also wanted treaties, as treaty making was a way to assert their sovereignty over the land and to deal with the changing realities of the time. Most pressing for them was the depletion of the bison herds that were rapidly approaching extinction on the North American plains, declining from as many as 30 million in the mid-seventeenth century to a few hundred by the end of the nineteenth. It was one of the worst ecological and environmental disasters of all time. Overexploitation, drought, and environmental change, as well as advances in Indigenous hunting technology, contributed to the demise of the bison.[9]

The destruction of the bison herds was a catastrophe of enormous proportions, changing the way of life of Indigenous peoples. Starvation and hunger became common. Missionaries pressed Indigenous leaders to negotiate with the government, and the leaders themselves knew well the fate of their peoples in the United States. Throughout the entire treaty-making process, Indigenous leaders maintained that the survival and well-being of their people would be assured if they established a good, working relationship with the government, thereby facilitating the transition from a traditional to a "modern" way of life. Many saw agriculture and education as necessary for the future. Seven large-scale treaties, known as the Numbered Treaties, were signed in the 1870s. Treaty 1, covering much of southern Manitoba, was finalized on August 3, 1871; six others were negotiated by 1877, as the federal government prepared the way for European settlement and economic development.[10]

In the negotiations, First Nations made a number of demands on the state to protect their interests. They believed that the negotiations themselves implied recognition of their title to the territory they occupied, even though the federal

---

9 Andrew C. Isenburg, *The Destruction of the Bison. An Environmental History 1750–1920* (New York: Cambridge University Press, 2000), 1–9.

10 The text of the treaties are available at http://www.ainc-inac.gc.ca/pr/trts/hti/site/trindex_e.html.

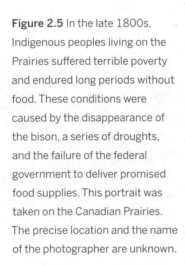

Figure 2.5 In the late 1800s, Indigenous peoples living on the Prairies suffered terrible poverty and endured long periods without food. These conditions were caused by the disappearance of the bison, a series of droughts, and the failure of the federal government to deliver promised food supplies. This portrait was taken on the Canadian Prairies. The precise location and the name of the photographer are unknown.

government wished to extinguish Indigenous title. Each treaty usually set aside a reserve large enough in area to provide 160 acres (64 hectares) for each family of five. The federal government agreed to provide and maintain a school on each reserve. Every man, woman, and child was given a gratuity of $5.00 and an annuity of $5.00. The treaties prohibited the introduction and sale of alcohol on the reserves. First Nations agreed to "cede, release, surrender and yield up to the Government of the Dominion of Canada, for Her Majesty the Queen and her successors forever, all the lands" included in each treaty and maintain peaceful relations with Her Majesty's white subjects.

The negotiations leading to Treaty 6, which covers the area of present-day central Saskatchewan and Alberta, are particularly instructive. In 1871, with the First Nations facing starvation from dwindling bison herds and suffering from a major outbreak of smallpox, chiefs of the Plains Cree, Woodland Cree, and Assiniboine nations approached the government to negotiate a treaty. The Canadian government, however, had decided to make treaties only when the territory was required for settlement; as settlers had not yet reached that far west, the government chose to wait. The treaty was finally signed in 1876 at Fort Carlton and included terms similar to those of the other Numbered Treaties across Western Canada. For the Cree, a promise of assistance from the Dominion government in the case of pestilence or famine had been a decisive factor; traditional medicine was powerless against the horrible smallpox plague. The treaty included a clause that the Indian Agent maintain a medicine chest to protect the health of First Nations. With this clause, health care became a treaty right. Later, in two separate rulings, including *Regina v. Johnston* in 1966, Canadian courts held that "the Indians are entitled to receive all medical services including medicine, drugs, medical supplies, and hospital care free of charge."[11]

Another important principle included in Treaty 6 was peace. By the 1870s, a strong peace movement had developed among Indigenous leaders. This was largely because they recognized the threat posed to their societies from inter-tribal conflicts as well as from disease. In one conflict between the Cree and the Blackfoot on the Oldman River in 1870, several hundred warriors were killed. First Nations had never been at war with European newcomers in the Northwest, and promised in Treaty 6 to keep that peace between Native nations: "They will maintain peace and good order between each other, and also between themselves and others of Her Majesty's subjects."[12]

Given the two different cultures and two different worldviews of the Indigenous peoples and the Canadian negotiators, there has been considerable dispute about what the treaties mean for Canada today. There is the general question of interpretation: are the treaties to be interpreted literally, or should the whole culture and history of treaty making be considered? For the Canadian government, the treaties meant that the First Peoples in Western Canada had surrendered title to the land in exchange for reserves and annual payments. However, Indigenous leadership saw the negotiations differently. They could not surrender the land as they did not own it. To them, the treaties were pacts of friendship, whereby they received gifts in exchange for permitting settlers to occupy certain sections of land. In fact, the treaties included provisions for the continued Indigenous use of the land for the purposes of hunting and fishing. Further, the chiefs did not see themselves as subservient to the Canadian government. When the First Peoples referred to the Queen as their great mother and called themselves "her Indian children," such language had different connotations than what the Canadian negotiators imagined. To the First Nations' chiefs, such phrases signified freedom—freedom that came from being a child—rather than being a dependant. Of course, the two sides spoke different languages and the interpreters were not always fully conversant in both.

---

11 *Regina v. Johnston*, Saskatchewan Court of Appeal, March 17, 1966. http://library2.usask.ca/native/cnlc/vol06/447.html.

12 The text of Treaty 6 can be viewed at http://www.indianclaims.ca/pdf/authorities/6%20eng.pdf. See also, A. Blair Stonechild, "The Indian View of the 1885 Uprising," in J.R. Miller (ed.), *Sweet Promises. A Reader on Indian-White Relations in Canada* (Toronto: University of Toronto Press, 1991).

HUDSON'S BAY

Treaties 1–5 (1871–1875)

UNITED STATES

Map 2.1 After Confederation, the Canadian government signed treaties with many First Nations. This map shows the treaties signed in Western Canada between 1871 and 1875.

The Numbered Treaties remain a point of contention, but what is important about them is that Canada and its citizens have too often forgotten the original promises made in treaties and have for too long ignored the well-being of one of its minority communities. This has resulted in the instability and disorder that are now upon us: the crime and social dysfunction in too many First Nations communities; the bitter relations between First Nations and Canada's governments and between First Nations and resource developers; the protracted struggle over land claims; the attempted cultural degradation of First Nations communities; and the failure to deliver on the promise of Indigenous self-government. It is necessary for Canada to "recall and re-institute the original promises based on respect for, and recognition of, entitlements to cultural integrity and economic sufficiency that flowed from the Indigenous presence" and from the treaty process.[13] The Canadian state must give all people the capacity to enjoy social and economic justice.

The Dominion government's notions of Indigenous–state relations in Canada are reflected in the *Indian Act, 1876*. This was an attempt to bring laws and regulations governing Canada's First Peoples under a single statute and continued the overall philosophy of the 1857 *Gradual Civilization Act* and subsequent legislation in 1869—much of which smacks of colonialism. The Act reflected a view that Indigenous peoples were essentially wards of the state, as government policy became steadily more interventionist and more controlling in the life of Indigenous peoples. The Act set out conditions for the sale of reserve lands and mandated elections for band councils in spite of traditional practices of governance. It effectively decides who could and who could not be considered an "Indian" under the law. Any woman who married

---

13 These points are discussed more fully in John D. Whyte, "Federal Dreams," *Queen's Law Journal* 34 (2008–2009): 1–24.

an Indigenous person would be considered an "Indian," but any Indigenous woman who married a non-Indigenous man lost her status and all privileges under the law. Indigenous peoples of mixed ancestry, such as the Métis, had to choose either an Indian identity and become part of a treaty, or scrip (land certificates) and remain outside the treaty arrangements and away from reserve lands. Métis scrip could be used only to acquire land from the Dominion Lands Office; many of the land vouchers were purchased by land agents and financial institutions, a process that left many Métis landless and without a community base. The *Indian Act* provided for the establishment of residential schools for Indigenous children between the ages of 5 and 16; attendance became compulsory in 1895. The use of brute force by the state to take children from their families can never be justified.

RIEL AND THE NORTHWEST RESISTANCE

By the early 1880s, there was considerable unrest in the Northwest Territories, and the 1885 Northwest Resistance, led by Louis Riel, was a remarkable exception to the notion of a peaceable Canadian West. First Nations were struggling on their reserve lands, much of which was marginal farmland at best. Many of the Indian Agents appointed by Ottawa were unsympathetic to their plight, and their leaders complained that Ottawa was not fulfilling its treaty obligations. Métis who had settled in the Qu'Appelle Valley of Saskatchewan after the 1870 uprising in Red River were also struggling, as the traditional buffalo-hunting and freighting life seemed impossible. Among the obvious threats were the new square grid settlement lots that were being surveyed in the Northwest Territories according to the Canadian township system. The Métis feared the loss of their valuable river lots along the Saskatchewan River.

European settlers were also disappointed with Ottawa. William Henry Jackson, the secretary of the North-West Settlers Union, outlined their grievances, including the lack of representation in the House of Commons, in several petitions to Ottawa throughout the early 1880s. The Northwest Territories did not have any form of self-government, something the settlers maintained was needed to deal with the lack of schools, roads, and other infrastructure in the territories. They complained, too, that land speculators and officials connected with the federal Conservative Party wielded too much power in the region. Compounding the problem was a series of severe winters, particularly in 1884 and 1885, that worsened conditions for all in the region. By that time, the whole region was seething with discontent.

By 1884, Jackson agreed that the North-West Settlers Union should pursue a common strategy with the Métis to win redress of their grievances: they turned to Louis Riel and hoped that he could repeat his winning formula in the Northwest. However, much had changed since 1870, not least Riel himself. In the intervening years since the Red River Rebellion, he had spent some time in a Montreal asylum, increasingly obsessed with religious visions. He had drifted south to Montana, married, had two children, and had become an American citizen. The four-man delegation that travelled to Montana in 1884 to seek out Riel's help might well have had early inklings that he was not the same man he had once been. Riel assured them that he had proof that God approved of the path they were taking. He had earlier adopted the name "David" in imitation of the biblical poet-king and believed that, as a "prophet of the New World," he had a divine mission to prepare for the second coming of Christ. Part of his mission was to transfer the papacy from its corrupt state in Rome to Manitoba. Riel renamed the days of the week and declared that Saturday, rather than Sunday, would be the Lord's Day, in keeping with the Law of Moses. While Riel's ardent Roman Catholicism was a central—perhaps even *the* central—part of his identity, his iconoclastic position toward the institutional church ensured that as the Métis of the Northwest moved toward armed resistance in 1885, they would not have the support of Roman Catholic authorities that had been so vital to the Red River Métis 15 years earlier. Most of the white farmers also quickly moved to distance themselves from Riel, but Jackson embraced the cause of the Métis and became Riel's secretary, converted to Roman Catholicism, and adopted the name Honouré Joseph Jaxon.

On March 19, 1885, shortly after the federal government finally announced the appointment of a commission to examine Métis grievances, Riel proclaimed a provisional government at Batoche (in what is now Saskatchewan). This strategy echoed the approach taken at Red River in 1869, when there was arguably a power vacuum between the ending of the Hudson's Bay Company authority and the transfer of Rupert's Land to Canada. There was no such power vacuum in the Northwest Territories in 1885; the region had no provincial status, but was firmly under Canada's jurisdiction. The declaration of a provisional government was an open act of treason. Further, the presence of the North-West Mounted Police on the plains made a quick military response to the uprising much easier than it had been in 1869.

The Métis military commander was Gabriel Dumont, and he sought support for his cause. Stores were ransacked and ammunition seized, telegraph lines were cut, and prisoners taken. When the Métis demanded the surrender of the North-West Mounted Police detachment at Fort Carlton, the Mounties retreated. On March 26, the Métis defeated the NWMP in a skirmish near Duck Lake, where 12 of the force died along with 6 Métis warriors, including Dumont's brother Isadore. Faced with the crisis of an armed insurrection, the Canadian government dispatched a large military force to the Northwest. Macdonald feared that First Nations and Métis might band together in a rebellious alliance, but there was no alliance between the Cree Nation and the

Métis, despite the multiplication of grievances among the First Nations. Promises made in the treaties were only slowly—if at all—honoured, and the federal government seemed deaf to the Native petitioning. The Indigenous population on the Prairies declined from approximately 33,000 in 1880 to slightly more than 20,000 in 1885, an annual death rate of 10 per cent. Beyond complaints to Ottawa about inadequate rations, Indigenous leaders also cited the lack of agricultural implements, of schools, and of medical provisions; even the location of reserves had not been settled. Yet, they preferred diplomacy and had planned a Grand Council for 1885 to send a delegation to Ottawa to deal directly with the government, confident that a strategy of concerted political action would yield results. When the Métis uprising began, they notified government authorities of their loyalty to the Crown.[14]

Despite the refusal of Indigenous leaders to embrace military action, First Nations on the Prairies became drawn into events of the Northwest Resistance just the same. Just after the NWMP had been routed at Duck Lake, Cree Chief Pītikwahanapiwīyin (Poundmaker) set out on foot for Battleford. He led a delegation of some 60 people, including women and children, and planned to remonstrate with the Indian Agent there about the need to supply rations to his starving band. He sent a messenger ahead to let the agent know they were coming. Other bands, including the Stoney people, joined him en route, swelling the numbers to over a hundred. When the group reached Battleford on March 30, the 500 residents of the town were alarmed, took up a defensive position in the fort, and prepared for a siege. The Indian Agent refused to meet Poundmaker, although the Hudson's Bay Company factor agreed to release food from the company stores. Neither Poundmaker nor Minahikosis (Little Pine), Chief of the Stoney, was able to restrain their frustrated people, who ransacked and burned Battleford homes. Little Pine himself had gone blind from the effects of starvation, and he and Poundmaker began to make their way back to their reserves. A few miles short of his objective, Little Pine died.

Meanwhile, another First Nations Chief, Mistahimaskwa (Big Bear of the Plains Cree), was having considerable difficulty keeping the younger men in his camp under control. They were impatient with negotiations and believed violence would produce a better outcome. When they learned of the Métis triumph at Duck Lake, Ayimâsis, Big Bear's son, and a number of younger Cree warriors, including Big Bear's war chief Wandering Spirit, rose up and on April 2, 1885, attacked the settlement of Frog Lake (in what is now Alberta). The Cree had already been driven past the point of reason, and the seizure of wine, spirits, and painkillers from the Hudson's Bay Company stores

---

14 Maureen K. Lux, *Medicine that Walks: Disease, Medicine and Canadian Plains Native People, 1880–1940* (Toronto: University of Toronto Press, 2001).

Figure 2.6 Chief Piapot and warriors on display, 1885.

caused the situation to escalate further. The Cree killed nine people at Frog Lake, including Thomas Quinn, the Indian Agent, a farming instructor, and two Catholic priests. Some 70 people were taken prisoner and brought to Big Bear's camp. A few days later, the Frog Lake Cree laid siege to Fort Pitt on the North Saskatchewan River.

Canada's military response was swift, with mobilization beginning on the day before the clash at Duck Lake. In contrast to the three months it had taken to respond to the 1869 crisis at Red River, some 3,000 men were whisked to the Northwest in under a month. No transcontinental railway existed in 1869, but by the spring of 1885, the railway spanned the plains, and CPR manager William Van Horne oversaw the transport of troops over the uncompleted sections north of Lake Superior. Militia units from Ontario, Quebec, and Nova Scotia joined western units and brought the total force available to resist the uprising to about 5,000. Major-General Frederick Middleton, an accomplished British military officer who had earlier been appointed General Officer Commanding (GOC) the Canadian Militia, led the operation. In addition to the columns led by Lieutenant Colonel William Otter from the rail station at Swift Current and Middleton himself moving from Qu'Appelle, Major-General Thomas Bland Strange led a third column from the railhead at Calgary.

At Fish Creek, Dumont succeeded in stopping Middleton's advance in an ambush on April 24, in which 6 militiamen were killed and 49 wounded, but the swiftness of the Canadian government's response and the quantity of forces sent doomed the Métis resistance. Their last stand came at Batoche on May 9, 1885, and lasted until the Métis ran out of ammunition three days later. Riel surrendered a few days later. Middleton dispatched a letter to Big Bear, warning of the consequences of continued resistance. Both Big Bear and Poundmaker surrendered in July, and each received three-year sentences for their role in the uprising. Another 50 First Nations were convicted on various offences, and 8 were executed. Honouré Jaxon was arrested by the Canadian forces for his role in the resistance but he was found not guilty by reason of insanity. It is Louis Riel, however, who has attracted much of the attention in the aftermath of the failed resistance.

Riel was found guilty for treason before a magistrate and a jury of six English-speaking Protestants in Regina. Much of the debate about his guilt has focused on his mental health: was he insane? Riel had twice been institutionalized in the 1870s, and his lawyers prepared a defence based on insanity, but Riel would have none of it, arguing that such a plea would nullify both his religious mission as well as Métis grievances. The jury seemed to understand Riel's mental state and, although they found him guilty, they recommended that Judge Hugh Richardson show mercy in his sentencing. The law was clear, however: treason was punishable by death. The verdict was appealed to the Court of Queen's Bench of Manitoba (which had jurisdiction over the Territories), and then to the Judicial Committee of the Privy Council. Both appeals were dismissed. His defence seemed to ignore the fact that Riel was an American citizen. Many have argued that his trial was a miscarriage of justice and have demanded a pardon from the Canadian government, to no avail.

Macdonald knew better than anyone the cleavages that existed within Canada and the dilemma Riel created for the new nation. Ontario continued to demand punishment for the Métis court-martial that had convicted Thomas Scott of insubordination and treason on March 3, 1870, and had him executed by firing squad the following day. With Riel finally in custody, English-speaking Protestants throughout Ontario demanded that Macdonald let him hang. On the other hand, Quebec demanded clemency for the Catholic and French-speaking Riel. French-speaking cabinet ministers convinced Macdonald that an independent medical team be permitted to examine Riel's state of mind. Two of the three doctors found Riel sane, and Macdonald let the law take its course: Riel was hanged in Regina on November 16, 1885, prompting outrage in Quebec and jubilation in Ontario. In time, Riel became an important symbol as a martyred leader who fought for the rights of Canada's First Nations and Métis peoples. The seeds of a major political realignment in national politics were also sown as French Canada began to reject Macdonald's Conservative Party following Riel's execution.

RECONCILING DIVERSITIES: SCHOOLING AND EDUCATION

It was understood in 1867 that Confederation would not obliterate the religious and ethnic differences that existed in the new nation. It was hoped, however, that within the federation, regional and provincial differences, and differences of ethnicity and religion, might not only be reconciled but embraced to increase the prosperity and glory of the new nation. George-Étienne Cartier, one of the Fathers of Confederation, had said in the Confederation debates in 1865 that he hoped Confederation would create "a political nationality with which neither the national origin nor the religion of any individual would interfere." That proved difficult, and the furor created between French- and English-speaking Canadians over Riel's hanging was only one of a series of incidents that tested the strength of the new political nationality in the generation after Confederation. Schooling and education soon became others. Exclusive responsibility for education had been left with the provinces at Confederation, and Ottawa had authority only to protect denominational rights in the provinces that existed before Confederation. As Catholic education came under attack in several provinces between 1874 and 1896, education and schooling proved to be nearly as divisive as the hanging of Riel.

In the nineteenth century, education was an important agent of social and cultural change, critical to inculcating particular values in young Canadians. All peoples, including First Nations, recognized the importance of education. While there was general consensus that the state should fund education, there was little agreement on who should provide for its delivery. Most children between the ages of 7 and 12 attended school for several months each year even before the introduction of compulsory education later in the nineteenth century. Catholics maintained that education was inseparable from religion and many, especially Protestants, saw the educational system as the best way to create young people in Canada schooled in the English language and British customs and traditions.

Most of the post-Confederation controversies over education involved Francophone minorities outside of Quebec. Quebec itself had established separate Catholic and Protestant systems of education, and this system satisfied both religious groups. When New Brunswick opted in 1871 for a single, tax-supported, non-sectarian public school system in the *Common Schools Act*, Catholics in that province were outraged. They appealed to Ottawa and the courts, but because their religious schools had existed by practice and tradition rather than by any legislative authority, Ottawa was powerless to intervene. The issue created a maelstrom of protest, with bishops and priests encouraging parents to keep their children home. When they encouraged parents not to pay their local taxes, several parish priests were jailed. The militia was dispatched to Caraquet in northern New Brunswick in 1875 to quell the growing protest, and in the ensuing clashes with local Catholics, Louis Mailloux, a 19-year-old Acadian, and Constable John Gifford were killed. Nine Acadians were charged with murder but none was convicted. Soon after, a compromise was reached that allowed all Catholic children in more populated school districts to attend the same school, thus providing by default for Catholic schools. Members of the clergy were allowed to teach in the schools, but only if they completed the same examinations as all other teachers. Religious instruction would be permitted in Catholic schools after the end of the regular teaching day.

The ethnic and linguistic quarrels revealed a growing divide between Quebec, which increasingly saw itself under attack from English-speaking Canadians, and the rest of Canada. Although most of Quebec had condemned the violent resistance in the Northwest in 1885, it was angered by Riel's hanging and the changes to Catholic education in New Brunswick: both were seen as an assault on Roman Catholic Canada. Honouré Mercier, a leading member of the Quebec Liberal Party, created a coalition—or *parti national*—to protect and strengthen the position of Quebec within Confederation; his party won the provincial election of 1887. When he sought the advice of Pope Leo XIII on how to divide the funds given to the Jesuit Order for its land and properties, which had been confiscated after the British Conquest in 1763, Ontario reacted angrily. It saw the Pope's involvement as evidence of clerical control of Quebec and the subjection of the state to the church. Many Protestants demanded the absolute separation of church and state and called on the federal government to disallow the Quebec legislation. However, a motion introduced in the House of Commons providing for the disallowance of the *Jesuit Estates Act* was defeated 188 to 13.

At the same time, radicals mounted an aggressive campaign to promote a Canada that was Protestant and British. At the forefront was the Equal Rights Association (ERA), created in Toronto in June 1889, which demanded equal rights for all Canadians, but was anti-French Canadian and anti-Catholic. D'Alton McCarthy, a close colleague of Macdonald, became one of its primary spokespersons, though the prime minister went to great lengths to distance himself and the Conservative Party from McCarthy's antics. The ERA saw the French language, especially outside of Quebec, as one of the greatest threats to the development of Canadian nationalism and the creation of a British Canada. McCarthy tried, unsuccessfully, to abolish the use of French throughout the Northwest Territories, where it had been given equal status with English in the territorial councils and courts in 1877. Although McCarthy's campaign attracted little support across Canada, his rhetoric worried Quebec, and Premier Mercier called upon French-speaking Canadians at the 1889 Saint-Jean-Baptiste Day celebration to unite to keep Quebec French-speaking and Catholic. One Quebec MLA suggested that a militia be kept at the ready "to defend French Canadian institutions and laws against Anglo-Saxon aggression."[15]

Although McCarthy played a minor role in rallying Manitobans against French and Catholic education, one of the great struggles for Cartier's vision of duality played out there. Manitoba entered Confederation as a bilingual and bicultural province in 1870, but its cultural and linguistic duality had been threatened by the arrival of English-speaking farmers primarily from Ontario throughout the 1870s and 1880s. In 1890, Manitoba eliminated official bilingualism (the legislation doing so would be declared unconstitutional in 1979) and created a single public school system funded by the province. The new education system ceased the funding for both Protestant and Catholic schools, which had been guaranteed in 1870, in favour of public, non-sectarian ones. The language of education in the new public schools was to be English. The same process was at work in the Northwest Territories, where legislation in 1892 ended French-language education after the third grade and removed French as one of the official languages in the legislature.

The issue was the loss of French-Canadian and Catholic rights in Western Canada, but the controversy played out primarily outside the region, especially between politicians in Quebec and Ontario. Catholic bishops demanded that the Government of Canada protect the minority rights of Catholics as they were guaranteed in the BNA Act. However, even a petition signed by most of the Catholic bishops in Canada calling for federal disallowance of the Manitoba legislation had little impact, even though both the Conservatives and the Liberals in Parliament were embarrassed by the treatment of minorities by the provinces. Each party agreed that the best recourse was through the courts, as it generally is with any contentious and divisive issue. The Supreme Court of Canada and the JCPC upheld the validity of the Manitoba legislation but agreed, nonetheless, that Ottawa had the right to restore through remedial legislation the rights that the Catholic minority had enjoyed in Manitoba since 1870. Once the courts ruled, Ottawa was forced to act. It proposed remedial legislation calling for the restoration of separate (religious) schools, but the Manitoba government refused to comply. The province asserted that its new schooling legislation was not based on any

15 Larry L. Kulisek, "McCarthy, D'Alton," in *Dictionary of Canadian Biography*, vol. 12, University of Toronto/Université Laval, 2003, accessed November 16, 2016. http://www.biographi.ca/en/bio/mccarthy_d_alton_12E.html.

religious preference: it was simply improving the quality of schooling for all children without any regard for their faith.

The best hope for a solution lay with compromise and accommodation. Macdonald had managed the issue fairly well, as he had with other religious and cultural matters that threatened national unity. Unfortunately, Macdonald died on June 6, 1891, and his party—and the Government of Canada—were in disarray for its remaining years in office. Ontario Conservatives did not want the restoration of Catholic schools in Manitoba; Quebec members wanted the Manitoba legislation disallowed. Canada had four different prime ministers in the last five years of Conservative rule. John Abbott (1891–92), previously the minister of justice, became the first politician from Quebec to be prime minister but resigned because of ill health. John S. Thompson (1892–94), from Halifax, was the first Roman Catholic to be prime minister, but he died of a heart attack while visiting Queen Victoria at Windsor Castle. Mackenzie Bowell, former Grand-Master of the Orange Lodges of Canada, followed, but he was forced to resign in 1896 amidst a cabinet revolt after he introduced remedial legislation in the House of Commons, promising redress to Manitoba Catholics. Charles Tupper, who replaced Bowell as prime minister on May 1, 1896, also supported remedial legislation, believing that the promise made to the Catholic minority at Confederation had to be honoured. However, extreme Protestants like D'Alton McCarthy and the Liberals under Wilfrid Laurier ensured that the legislation would not be passed before the 1896 federal election. Although Tupper's Conservatives won more votes than the Liberals, and carried half the seats in English Canada, the Liberal landslide in Quebec elected Laurier as the first French-speaking prime minister. Tupper earned the ignominy of being the shortest-serving Canadian prime minister to date. Laurier maintained throughout the crisis that a solution had to be found that balanced Manitoba's right to determine its own education system as provided for in the constitution and Ottawa's obligation to protect religious minorities.

PROVINCIAL RIGHTS AND THE MEANING OF CONFEDERATION

Relations were also strained between the national government in Ottawa and other provinces immediately after Confederation. Oliver Mowat, the premier and attorney general of Ontario from 1872 to 1896, was at the centre of many of the federal–provincial disputes. He had attended the Quebec Conference in 1864, but he later withdrew briefly from politics for a career as a judge. As premier, Mowat oversaw a period of rapid urbanization and industrialization, but it was his fight with the Macdonald government in Ottawa that earned him an important place in Canadian history.

Known as the "Father of Provincial Rights," Mowat believed that the BNA *Act* was an agreement between the provinces. He insisted that in the Confederation agreement, the provinces had retained the sovereignty and jurisdiction they had prior to union, except for the specific responsibilities surrendered to the federal government in 1867. His interpretation gave rise to the "compact theory" of Confederation, meaning that Confederation arose as an agreement among the provinces and that the Constitution could only be amended with the unanimous consent of all the provinces. Macdonald, by contrast, believed that the provinces had limited sovereignty, while the legislative powers of the federal government were extensive. In the early years of Confederation, the federal government used its power of disallowance over provincial legislation quite capriciously. Mowat was adamant about protecting the jurisdiction and sovereignty of the provinces.

The disputes over the distribution of legislative jurisdiction and power between Ottawa and Ontario in this period should be seen as an attempt by the provincial and the federal governments to interpret exactly what the delegates thought they had agreed upon at Confederation. However, the courts would have the final say in the constitutional disagreements over the division of powers between the provincial and federal governments. The Supreme Court of Canada routinely ruled against Mowat in his attempts to establish provincial sovereignty, but the highest court, the Judicial Committee of the Privy Council in London, England, ruled with the provinces. It awarded jurisdiction to the provinces on a number of key issues such as the appointment of the Queen's Counsel—an honorific title bestowed on lawyers to recognize meritorious service in the legal profession—the regulation of private property and civil rights, and the control over natural resources on all lands reserved for First Nations' occupation.[16] The JCPC's interpretation of the constitution created a decentralized Canada.

Mowat, of course, was not the only premier to confront Ottawa during this period. In Nova Scotia, Premier W.S. Fielding attributed his province's deteriorating financial position to unfavourable terms of union in 1867. Because 70 per cent of provincial revenues came from Ottawa, Nova Scotia demanded a new financial arrangement with the federal government. When Macdonald dismissed the grievances, the provincial legislature passed a motion asking Ottawa to release the province from Confederation. Fielding never pushed the issue of secession because sections of Nova Scotia were benefiting from the tariff provided under the National Policy and had no interest in leaving Confederation. Neither did Fielding, really, who later went to Ottawa to join the new Liberal government in 1896.

---

16 *St. Catherines Milling and Lumber Company v. The Queen (Ontario)* [1888] UKPC 70 (12 December 1888). The Judicial Committee of the Privy Council Decisions, http://www.bailii.org/uk/cases/UKPC/1888/1888_70.html.

Premier Mercier invited all of the premiers to meet in Quebec City in October 1887 to discuss their lingering grievances against the federal government. This was the country's first inter-provincial conference, and the timing and venue almost seemed to suggest a revisiting of the terms of Confederation after 20 years. Fielding's attendance implied he would attempt to work within Confederation rather than try to get out of it. Prince Edward Island and British Columbia (both with Conservative governments) refused to attend. Mowat chaired the meetings, and the premiers agreed upon several resolutions to strengthen the provinces and, foremost, to end Ottawa's power of disallowance of provincial legislation. On the face of it, the conference had no real significance; Macdonald dismissed it as the machinations of his political foes. Yet, because the federal government had lost a number of constitutional battles at the JCPC, Macdonald had already become more cautious about using the federal veto power.

DEFENDING CANADIAN INTERESTS ABROAD AND AT HOME

Even after 1867 Canada was still very much a part of the British Empire, and Britain controlled Canada's foreign relations. Canada depended upon Britain for defence, and the British Royal Navy maintained its naval bases at Halifax and Esquimalt. The understanding was that with the withdrawal of Britain's army from Canada, Canadian militia would fill the gap, although Canada's lack of attention to military matters was a perennial irritation to British authorities and a frequent source of frustration to those British officers who presided over Canada's neglected militia. While Macdonald recognized the subordinate position of Canada within the Empire, he hoped the relationship would change over time and the colonial system would be "less a case of dependence on our part, and of over-ruling protection of the part of the Mother Country, and more a case of healthy and cordial alliance. Instead of looking upon us as a merely dependent colony, England will have in us a friendly nation, a subordinate but still a powerful people to stand by her in North America in peace or in war."[17]

Macdonald realized Canada needed permanent representation in London, and in 1880, he formalized the role of the Canadian representative first appointed in 1869, establishing the office of High Commissioner and a "resident minister." This appointment marked the beginning of Canadian permanent representation abroad—a position was soon added to Paris, France—but the British government was worried that Canada's diplomatic presence in London might threaten the unity of the Empire

---

17 Quoted in C.P. Stacey, *Canada and the Age of Conflict. A History of Canadian External Policies, 1867–1921* (Toronto: University of Toronto Press, 1992), 1–2.

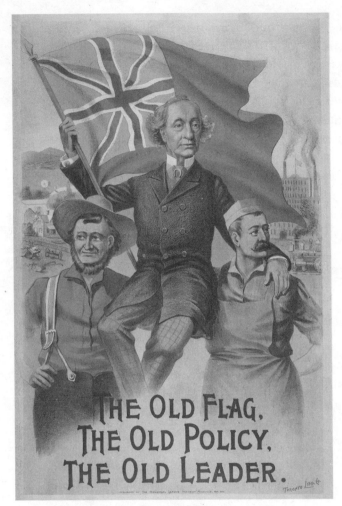

Figure 2.7 The Old Flag—The Old Leader, Conservative campaign poster, 1891.

in matters of foreign policy. They relented on the office, but did not want any title that suggested a diplomatic role for Canada. Later, when Sir Charles Tupper became the first High Commissioner to Britain he subsequently negotiated a trade deal with France, though officially it was an economic arrangement between France and Britain. Still, it represented an important step in Canada managing its own international affairs. In 1894, Canada appointed its first resident commercial agent abroad when John Short Larke was named the Canadian Trade Commissioner to Australia. This appointment came after the creation of the Department of Trade and Commerce in 1892, and Mackenzie Bowell, the first minister of the new department, led a trade mission to Australia.

Economic considerations, particularly with the United States, remained the basis of much of Canada's foreign relations between the 1870s and 1896. The Conservatives' National Policy was a response to the growing wave of protectionism in the United States and around the world, and a desire to develop the Canadian economy. In 1888, the Liberal Party adopted a platform that favoured unrestricted reciprocity, or complete free trade, with the Americans and made it the dominant plank in their 1891 election campaign. Macdonald and his Conservatives responded to the Liberal challenge calling free trade "veiled treason" that would lead to the destruction of Canada and annexation to the United States. The campaign, Macdonald's last, saw his party triumph at the polls with an even larger share of the popular vote than it had garnered in 1887. His campaign poster, "The Old Flag, The Old Policy, The Old Leader" proved most effective. Shortly after their defeat, the Liberals quietly dropped their commitment to free trade and embraced the National Policy in time for the 1896 campaign.

While Macdonald was eager to demonstrate his loyalty to the Crown at election time, he was determined to keep his distance from those in Britain who wanted dominions like Canada to assume a greater role in defending the Empire. By the 1880s, with the acceleration of economic and territorial rivalries on a massive global scale, London renewed its interest in the dominions, marking the end of British apathy toward Canada and the other territories within the Empire that began in the 1830s. Macdonald wanted nothing to do with any imperial military adventures, however, and he reminded a British Royal Commission on the Defence of British Possessions and Commerce Abroad in 1880 that he was opposed to a general system of imperial defence. Still, he left little doubt that if Great Britain needed help, Canada would not disappoint.

In 1884, General Garnet Wolseley was dispatched to the Sudan in Africa to rescue a British mission led by General Charles Gordon, a British military hero in the Crimean War (1853–56), who had encountered stiff resistance from local Sudanese insurgents in the region. Wolseley, who recalled how adept the Canadians had been in assisting the British forces during the 1870 expedition to Red River, asked that Canadian "voyageurs" be part of his contingent to the Nile River. When the request arrived through Governor General Lord Lansdowne, Macdonald did not have any objection, as a Canadian voyageur contingent would be an imperial initiative and undertaken without any Canadian involvement or support. In fact, Canada's *Militia Act* forbade the dispatch of Canadian militia units outside of Canada. When the 386 men in the contingent set sail for Africa, it was Canada's first contribution to a British overseas military operation, but these men were all civilians under six-month contracts for non-combat duties. When the situation escalated after the death of General Gordon, Macdonald refused to offer Canadian troops (as the territory of New South Wales in southern Australia had) because he believed the conflict was not in the Canadian national interest. For Macdonald, there would be no automatic Canadian participation in minor imperial conflicts.

Shortly after the incident in the Sudan, the British called the first colonial or imperial conference for 1887 on the occasion of Queen Victoria's Golden Jubilee. Macdonald sent Sir Alexander Campbell, the postmaster general and newly appointed lieutenant governor of Ontario, and Sandford Fleming, who would give the world standardized time. The British were interested in an imperial system of defence; Macdonald was not, and he attempted to focus on postal and telegraphic communications. At the Jubilee conference and the one that followed in 1894 in Ottawa, the Marquess of Ripon, the British colonial secretary, made it clear that in commercial and all other treaties, Britain did not see the need for Canadian autonomy. That view would change in a generation when Canada and the rest of the world became embroiled in the first of two major wars.

CONCLUSION

Creating Canada in 1867 might have been the easiest part of nation-building. As this chapter shows, the nation that was built on accommodation, diversity, and tolerance of minorities was not working as many had hoped. Canada was proving difficult to govern, as Prime Minister Mackenzie acknowledged in 1878. Minority communities were threatened in New Brunswick, Manitoba, and the Northwest Territories, as the majority was not particularly accommodating on matters such as French-language and Catholic education. As Riel and the First Nations and Métis communities discovered, the tolerance of minorities did not extend very far toward them in this period either. Similarly, some immigrant groups, such as the Chinese, learned that there would be no accommodation for them in Canada. In politics, as provincial rights emerged as an important issue, the federal and provincial governments quarrelled over the meaning of the Confederation agreement and the respective powers of each order of government. Many of these matters frequently became the focus of party politics in the period from 1874 to 1896.

This was also a period of consolidation. The National Policy that combined tariffs, railways, and settlement of the West was launched, not merely as an economic objective but also as a nation-building project that would integrate the various regions of the country. This period saw the emergence of embryonic national institutions such as the Supreme Court of Canada and the National Art Gallery of Canada. Canada was also showing signs of change as a process of industrialization and urbanization began to alter the national fabric. The nation would soon discover that it was the destination of choice for many people seeking a new life in North America, and this would bring even more profound and lasting change as Canada entered the twentieth century.

3 DEVELOPMENT AND DISSONANCE, 1896–1914

INTRODUCTION

While a faltering economy and self-doubt marred Canada's early years, the end of the nineteenth century ushered in a period of rapid growth and increasing optimism. Between 1896 and 1914, Canada's population increased from 5.1 to 7.9 million. Immigration and internal migration transformed the West. Between 1891 and 1911, the population of Manitoba grew from 152,000 to 461,000, and British Columbia's from 98,000 to 392,000, while in Saskatchewan and Alberta, where the first census occurred in 1901, the population had grown from 91,000 to 492,000 and 73,000 to 374,000 respectively by 1911.

In Central Canada, cities, industry, retail establishments, and financial institutions expanded and modernized. Accompanying such trends, however, was rising concern over resource depletion, urban slums, corporate concentration, class conflict, and moral and social degeneration. Captains of industry were regarded as both heroes and robber barons. Increasingly mechanized farms achieved record output, but anxiety mounted over rural depopulation and the rising power of industrial and financial interests. The young dominion took in new provinces and further integrated with mass-circulation newspapers, more transcontinental railways, telegraphs, telephones, and the introduction of wireless communication in 1901. Yet, intense, defensive *clerico-nationalisme* dominated Quebec, and regional sentiment mounted in the West and the Maritimes. Imperialists gushed about Canada rising to premier status within the British Empire, but loyalty to Britain brought bitter division between French and English. Historians Ramsay Cook and Robert Craig Brown describe the Canada of this period as "A Nation Transformed."[1] It was a time that inspired many to imagine impending greatness, but also to fear intensified division. Ultimately, things held together, and Canada further coalesced, as leaders, most importantly Prime Minister Wilfrid Laurier, pursued the path of compromise and bridge building.

LAURIER AND THE NEW LIBERAL ERA

On June 23, 1896, nearly 20 years of consecutive federal Conservative governments ended when Liberal leader Wilfrid Laurier became Canada's first French-Canadian prime minister. Born in 1841 in Saint-Lin-Laurentides, Quebec, Laurier grew up in a family where politics was a staple. Convinced their son needed to know English, his parents sent him at age 11 to live with the family of John Murray, a Scottish Presbyterian, in New Glasgow, Quebec. Two years later, he was enrolled in the Jesuit-run Collège de l'Assomption and after went to McGill University, graduating with a law degree in 1864.

Laurier first aligned himself with the *parti rouge* and opposed Confederation. By 1871, however, he accepted Confederation as a *fait accompli*, joined the Liberals, and was elected provincially. Bored with provincial politics, he ran successfully for the federal Liberals in 1874. Three years later, in a defining moment of his political career, in a speech in Quebec City, he dissociated Liberalism—which the Catholic Church portrayed as heretical—from European revolutionaries and anti-clerical *rouges*. With Edward Blake losing the 1883 and 1887 elections, the Liberals turned to the young, charismatic, and fluently bilingual Laurier as their new leader.

Laurier benefited from a Conservative Party that had fallen into disarray following Macdonald's death. Laurier's opponent in the 1896 federal election was the 74-year-old Charles Tupper, who came across as yesterday's man. Laurier spoke of "sunny ways," such as in reaching a compromise on the still vexing Manitoba Schools Question. The Liberals triumphed with 117 seats compared to 86 for the Conservatives.

Laurier prioritized national unity. Although sympathetic to aggrieved French and Catholic minorities in Manitoba, he would not run roughshod over Anglophone opinion and provincial control over education. He sent two Quebec MPs—Minister of Public Works Israel Tarte and the 28-year-old Henri Bourassa—to negotiate with Manitoba's provincial Liberal government led by Thomas Greenway. The only

---

1   Robert Craig Brown and Ramsay Cook, *Canada, 1896–1921: A Nation Transformed* (Toronto: McClelland & Stewart, 1974).

concession Greenway offered was a half hour's optional Catholic education at the end of the regular school day. French Catholics were outraged, but Laurier received the offer as a step forward. He also requested that a papal delegate be sent to Canada, hoping an empathetic report would diffuse tensions. In March 1897, Monsignor Merry del Val arrived. Several conversations with Laurier and a trip west convinced him that Manitoba's offer was the only realistic option for the time being. Pope Leo XIII's encyclical, *Affari Vos*, soon followed in which he wrote that the settlement, though "defective," should not prevent Catholics from accepting "partial satisfaction."[2]

Laurier pursued compromise with trade policy. His policy of avoiding significant tariff adjustments was supported by business and organized labour, which feared freer trade with the United States would result in job losses. Laurier also received accolades in English Canada for announcing, in 1897, an imperial trade preference as high as 25 per cent.

Farmers hoping for free trade were disgruntled. Anger in agricultural areas also festered over the monopoly status still enjoyed by the Canadian Pacific Railway throughout large parts of Western Canada. In September 1897, Laurier's government provided the CPR with an annual subsidy of $600 per kilometre of track through more than 550 kilometres of mountainous terrain in exchange for the railway lowering, by 15 per cent, the price of transporting wheat east and a variety of settler goods shipped west. This arrangement became known as the Crow's Nest Pass rate.

Prohibition was another potential source of controversy. Powerful temperance groups like the Dominion Alliance argued that alcohol fuelled growing crime and immorality. During the election campaign, Laurier promised a referendum on prohibition. In September 1898, a razor-thin majority of 51.2 per cent supported its implementation. Anglophone provinces were in favour, but in Quebec, where temperance was viewed as Protestant-led, only 18.8 per cent voted yes. Laurier balked at taking action given the unclear results and the fact that only 44 per cent of eligible voters cast ballots.

IMPERIALISM, ALASKA, AND SOUTH AFRICA

To counter rising German military strength and expanding colonial ambitions, Britain's Colonial Secretary Joseph Chamberlain pursued the creation of an Imperial Federation that would speak and act as one. Imperialist sentiment was ascendant, especially with Queen Victoria's 1897 diamond jubilee celebration in London. Laurier basked in its splendour; his grandiloquent speeches heralding the glories of the Empire made him a favourite with the British press. However, he knew it would be economically and politically disastrous for Canada to commit to every imperial venture.

2   Joseph Schull, *Laurier: The First Canadian* (Toronto: Macmillan of Canada, 1965), 378.

The same year as the diamond jubilee, gold was discovered in the far off reaches of the Yukon at a place called Rabbit Creek. Thousands raced north to what became known as the Klondike Gold Rush. However, the area known as the panhandle stretching down the northwest coast that was the entry point into the gold fields remained disputed between Canada and the United States. In the fall of 1897, Laurier arrived in Washington with British representative Sir Louis Davies for talks with State Department officials and President William McKinley. This resulted in an Anglo–American joint commission. The British delegate, Lord Herschell, proved a strong and effective advocate for Canada. However, things profoundly changed with his death in 1899. Two years later President McKinley was assassinated and replaced by Theodore Roosevelt, who insisted that Canada did not have a legitimate claim.

The belief in Canada that Britain would support its claim on the panhandle reflected not only a long and close association between the two, but also rising imperialist sentiment. Led by prominent Anglo-Protestants, Canadian imperialists did not speak of Canada as a colony, but as a dominion that, because of its wide-open space for settlement, vast resources, and the vigour of its northern population, would eventually rise to leadership within the Empire. Imperialists naïvely cast French Canadians as loyal to the Crown because they appreciated the rights provided to them as far back as the *Quebec Act* in 1774.

Relations with the United States also shaped imperialist discourse. Bilateral trade was expanding, Canadians consumed American culture, and there were many friendly cross-border activities, such as sporting competitions. Nevertheless, there was also suspicion and fear. In 1895–96, there came the potential for armed conflict between America and Britain over the disputed British Guyana-Venezuelan border. While many Canadians admired America for its emerging economic and military power, others loathed it as aggressive, materialistic, and corrupt, believing that only Britain's imperial might prevented the United States from annexing Canada.

Yet, many Canadians were frustrated by being treated as a junior partner by Great Britain. In popular British literature, Canada was portrayed as a vast frontier populated by Indigenous savages, fur traders, cowboys, and Mounties. Perceived British arrogance was also manifested through the General Officer Commanding (GOC), a post created in 1880 to which a senior British officer was appointed to manage Canada's military. Most GOCs concluded that Canada's military was in a sad state and in need of major reform, a position that put several at loggerheads with Canada's minister of militia and defence and resulted in their early departure. Among the most contentious GOCs was Major-General Sir Edward Thomas Henry Hutton, who was sent to South Africa to command troops in the Boer War as a way of removing him from the position.

The roots of the 1899–1902 Boer War lay in Britain's attempts to consolidate its hold over mineral-rich southern Africa, a struggle that pitted them against the Dutch Afrikaners, or Boers (a Dutch word meaning "farmer"). A major mineral find in 1886 in the Boer-administered Transvaal region drew thousands of British prospectors from the neighbouring Cape Colony. Fearing a loss of control, the Boers denied British newcomers voting rights and more heavily taxed their mining operations, which London used as a pretext for war starting on October 11, 1899.

Laurier condemned Boer persecution of British settlers, but he would not commit troops. He employed a technical excuse, stating that Canada's *Militia Act* prohibited participation in a foreign war that did not involve the defence of Canada. Much of French-speaking Canada sympathized with the Boers because of their resistance to the British. Newspapers like the *Farmer's Weekly Sun* and labour newspapers like the *Voice* cast the British as motivated by greed. On the other hand, pro-war opinion—namely to save besieged Anglophone settlers and to stand by Britain—resonated loudly throughout much of English Canada.

Laurier faced a cabinet divided between French and English on the question of Canadian involvement. Ultimately, he offered a compromise: Canada would provide a battalion of 1,000 men commanded by a Canadian but financed by Britain once arriving in South Africa. Laurier also stated this would not set a precedent for Canadian involvement in future imperial wars. Still, only nine French-Canadian MPs—five Tories and four Liberals—supported the strategy.

Numerous Anglo-Canadians volunteered for military service, far more than needed. Those accepted formed the 2nd Battalion, Royal Canadian Regiment. They left Quebec City on October 30 for a month-long voyage to Cape Town. Once there, they spent the next two months training and coping with insects, extreme heat, and diseases like typhoid fever, which ultimately claimed more lives than enemy bullets.

With British casualties mounting against Boer guerilla fighters, the Canadians joined the fray. Their objective was Kimberley, a diamond-mining town. The Boers made their stand to the south at Paardeberg Drift. Green Canadian troops, after taking 80 casualties and faltering in the first day's fighting, launched a night-time advance. Holding hands so they would not stray from each other, at sunrise they found themselves with an excellent vantage point over the Boers, who then surrendered. News of the victory sparked celebrations across Canada.

Although the British force of 400,000 in South Africa eventually achieved victory, the war grew less popular. British dead reached 22,000, and they adopted controversial, brutal tactics such as a scorched earth policy and creating camps in which Boer civilians were concentrated, and where over 25,000 died, primarily from malnutrition and disease. Morale among Canadian troops declined; most men refused to extend their term of service beyond the one-year obligation. By the time the war ended in May 1902, 7,368 Canadians had volunteered, with 89 killed in action, 181 dying from disease, and 252 wounded.

Having forged a workable compromise on Canadian involvement in the Boer War, and with Canada's economy on the upswing, Laurier entered the November 1900 federal election in a strong position. His easy-going confidence, personal charm, and eloquence contrasted sharply with Tupper, who came across as old and blustering. The Liberals gained 11 seats over 1896, reaching 128 compared to 79 for the Conservatives.

In February 1901, Robert Borden replaced Tupper as Conservative leader. Born in 1854 in Grand Pré, Nova Scotia, Borden's unpretentious and reserved nature reflected the low-key agricultural community in which he grew up. He successfully ran for Parliament in Halifax in 1896 and quickly established a reputation for being hardworking and effective on parliamentary committees. As Conservative leader, he stayed clear of internal party strife and focused on rebuilding a weakened political organization.

Laurier, too, faced internal party challenges. In autumn 1902, upon returning from an imperial conference in London, he fired his powerful public works minister, Israel Tarte, for openly contradicting government trade policy. The imperial conference had also proven difficult because Joseph Chamberlain sought to tighten the bonds of the Empire. A coy Laurier said that Canada was ready to discuss imperial federation, but only if this meant obtaining a meaningful role in helping to shape Empire policy. He knew this was something Canadian imperialists wanted but that Britain would not deliver, thus letting him off the hook with respect to making commitments. Frustrated with Laurier's manoeuvring, Chamberlain, in private correspondence, called him "the damn dancin' master."[3]

The next year, with Theodore Roosevelt continuing to take a hard line on the Alaska panhandle, London concluded that supporting Canadian claims was not worth the risk of worsening relations with the United States. Lord Alverstone, a prominent jurist and member of the Alaskan Boundary Commission, received secret instructions to avoid deadlock, this being code to side with the Americans if he thought their claim was legitimate, which is what happened. Canada's two representatives symbolically resigned from the committee. Many Canadians spoke of betrayal, but the bonds of loyalty to the Mother Country enabled the imperialist cause to weather the storm.

CROSS-CURRENTS IN CANADA'S NEW CENTURY

Strong opposition to imperialism in Quebec reflected not only suspicion of Britain but also an inward-looking and devout Francophone society. The *ultramontaine* creed,

---

3 Ibid., 410.

which stressed the need for self-improvement through Catholicism, was a major force in Quebec. The Church struggled with the concept of modernization, seeing this as importing the supposed Anglo-Protestant values of individualism and an obsession with money. Most clergy supported rural colonization because farming was presented as godly work. Outside the Church, Jean-Paul Tardival, the American-born editor of the newspaper *La Verité*, advocated Quebec separatism to protect the French-Catholic "race." Henri Bourassa, who in 1903 formed the *Ligue nationaliste*, advocated for a bilingual Canada; in Quebec, however, he also emphasized the central role of the Catholic Church in providing moral strength and social stability. Quebec provincial governments—under Liberals Félix Marchand (1897–1900), Napoléon Parent (1900–05), and Lomer Gouin (1905–20)—sent mixed messages. They paid homage to the Catholic Church and rural values, but also courted foreign investment to create jobs, promote modernization, and build government revenue.

Across the country, accelerating economic growth generated excitement and optimism. In January 1904, Laurier, speaking at the Canadian Club in Ottawa, declared that "as the nineteenth century was that of the United States, so, I think, the twentieth century shall be filled by Canada." That year, his government revealed plans for a second transcontinental railway. The Grand Trunk was selected for the project, for which it created a subsidiary, the Grand Trunk Pacific. It received subsidies, tax breaks, and land grants. The federal government hoped that it would cooperate with the western-based Canadian Northern railway. However, the Canadian Northern responded by launching its own transcontinental railway, which eventually produced an overbuilt and money-losing transportation network.

With a federal election approaching, Borden sought to hammer Laurier on the railway deal. However, most Canadians perceived the new transcontinental lines as a sign of progress. That November, the Liberals received an increased majority of 137 seats compared to 70 for the Conservatives. During the election, Laurier spoke of how recent, accelerated growth in the Prairies had prepared the way for the creation of new provinces. The following year, the Autonomy Bills created Alberta and Saskatchewan. The process was not without controversy, though. One source of debate was the decision to create two provinces rather than one, a choice that, some charged, related to partisanship. F.W.G. Haultain, who ran the Northwest Territorial government, was a Conservative supporter. Some opined that Laurier did not want to place too much power in one large provincial government, very possibly under Haultain's direction. By splitting the territory, many thought the Liberals would control at least one province. Two Liberals, Walter Scott in Saskatchewan and Alexander Rutherford in Alberta, were asked to form governments that would call the first provincial elections. Both built political machines that would keep the Liberals in power in Alberta until 1921 and in Saskatchewan until 1929.

Further controversy erupted over state funding for separate and bilingual schools in the new provinces. Under the 1875 *Territories Act*, Protestants or Catholics could tax themselves to create their own government-supported schools. Things changed as more non-Francophones moved west. In 1893, funding for French education ended. Eight years later, the territorial government gained control over schools and continued the practice. Laurier sent his Irish Catholic justice minister, Charles Fitzpatrick, and Henri Bourassa, accompanied by papal delegate Monsignor Donato Sbaretti, to the West to negotiate the schools issue. The result appeared to return things to the situation under the 1875 legislation. Interior Minister Clifford Sifton, Laurier's most prominent Western Canadian MP, resigned upon learning of the deal, insisting that a common language was essential for building unity in this new territory. Although Laurier did not ask Sifton to rejoin his cabinet, he tasked him with making recommendations on redrafting the education rules. The result re-imposed the restrictions, whereupon an outraged Bourassa left federal politics.

Canada's continuing growth and modernization helped Laurier ride out such controversies. Urban expansion accelerated. Between 1891 and 1911, the number of Canadians living in communities of 1,000 or more rose from 35 to 42 per cent of the population. Between 1861 and 1901, Toronto's population went from 65,000 to 238,000, and between 1881 and 1901, the rise in Montreal was from 223,000 to 393,000. To many, cities were centres of progress, as epitomized by electric street lighting, giant department stores, public mass transportation, and universities. Entertainment and sport venues thrived in cities. By the turn of the century, Montreal was issuing nearly 8,000 bicycle licences annually. Communities constructed public swimming pools, gymnasiums, tennis courts, and golf courses.

Technological advances seemed to promise a better life to all. At Toronto's annual Canadian National Exhibition, the biggest draw was Manufacturers' Hall, where companies displayed their latest innovations. Business and industrial leaders were increasingly regarded as heroes. Industrial and manufacturing activity expanded at a record pace, though in 1910 industrial products still accounted for only 22.5 per cent of the value of Canada's total output. Between 1900 and 1912, the number of companies incorporated per year in Canada soared from 53 to 658, and total capitalization of Canadian industry from $12.9 million to $490.6 million. Overwhelmingly, such activity congregated in southern Ontario and southern Quebec because of their larger labour and capital pools, superior transportation networks, and closer proximity to major American markets. The late nineteenth and early twentieth centuries brought more investment and foreign ownership in Canada. Whereas British investment gravitated into bonds, a large percentage of American money went to establish Canadian-based branch plants of US firms to bypass Canada's steep tariffs.

Figure 3.1 Modernization in Montreal. An electric tram on St. Catharine Street, 1890s.

Larger urban markets, rising incomes, and better transportation reinforced the growing dominance of major department stores. Although many smaller operations were driven into bankruptcy, most Canadians welcomed these larger establishments for providing greater choice and lower prices. In 1905, Eaton's opened a five-storey store in Winnipeg that employed 1,250 when the city's total population was 90,000. That year, Eaton's printed 1.3 million catalogues that, like its merchandise, were distributed nationwide.

Although many in rural areas fretted over growing urban influence, farms were doing better than ever. Implements such as mechanized manure spreaders, cultivators, hay loaders, and disc harrows came into widespread use. Over the last two decades of the nineteenth century, the price of a self-binder (which increased wheat productivity 20-fold over manual techniques) was halved to $150. However, more expensive farmland and the pull of industrial jobs made rural depopulation a major concern. From 1891 to 1901, Ontario's agricultural districts lost 50,000 people. In Western Canada, farmers claimed that high Canadian tariffs denied farmers cheaper American products, particularly farm implements, in order to support inefficient Central Canadian industry. Many in the West accused Ottawa of providing sweetheart deals to Central Canadian railway moguls, while ignoring the argument that lower traffic in the Prairies translated into higher unit transportation costs. Grievances also multiplied over the price of grain storage, especially as railways owned many grain elevators. Laurier's government established a Board of Railway Commissioners in 1903 to monitor freight rates, but many viewed it as lacking power.

Prairie farmers, following the example of those in the American West, created cooperatives, especially for grain storage. In Alberta, the United Farmers of Alberta, an advocacy group that, by the end of World War I, had become a highly effective political organization, managed the cooperative movement. By no means did all Western Canadians feel aggrieved, though, as much of the region was booming. All three transcontinental railways went through Winnipeg, which in the early twentieth century trans-shipped more wheat by rail than Chicago.

Modernization was also strongly evident in British Columbia. This included in politics, which was moving away from factionalism toward more defined, and disciplined, parties. Between 1898 and 1903, British Columbia had five different premiers, but in 1903, Richard McBride, who was identified as a Conservative, was appointed premier and his opponents coalesced into a Liberal opposition. McBride proved an effective leader, remaining in power until 1915.

Besides coal on Vancouver Island and the southwestern BC mainland, discoveries of gold and silver occurred in the Kootnenays; copper, silver, lead, and zinc in Slocan; and copper in Phoenix. Lumber shipments to the Prairies for construction steadily increased. Dairy and beef cattle farms grew substantially and, with development of refrigerated rail cars, acreage devoted to fruit and vegetable farming expanded sixfold between 1881 and 1911. While resource development remained a priority, conservation also took on a larger role. New steam-powered machinery for cutting timber meant that forests could be quickly depleted. Conservation was motivated not only by the desire to preserve nature, but also from the self-interest of capital to manage resources. Conservationists were not opposed to development; many favoured larger corporate enterprises within the forestry sector because they were viewed as taking a longer-term approach to extraction and reforestation, as opposed to smaller companies under pressure to maximize profits as quickly as possible.

Some parts of the Maritimes experienced strong economic growth, such as Moncton and Amherst, which were located along the transcontinental railway. Markets for Maritime coal and timber remained robust. Apple orchards expanded in the Annapolis Valley. Still, some 100,000 people left the Maritimes during the 1890s, mainly for jobs in Central Canada. Maritimers who wanted the region to partake fully in industrial modernization often blamed the federal government for tariff policies that ignored Maritime industries and for providing poor regional rail subsidies. Yet such critics ignored the fact that compared to Central Canada, the Maritimes did not possess the capital, labour pool, or proximity to major North American markets to attract industry.

FIRST PEOPLES

First Peoples were left behind as Canada modernized. Those who sought to integrate into the white economy were typically employed in low-skilled and low-paying jobs, such as those in BC salmon-canning factories. Indian Agents remained arbitrary in directing band life, with the aim of breaking down traditional ways. Indigenous peoples in British Columbia continued to be arrested for partaking in the *potlatch*, a religious ceremony in which gifts were distributed. However, to maintain workable relations, law enforcement officials often ignored this activity, as well as the pass system, which required Indigenous Canadians to have government documentation for unfettered travel off reserves. With the arrival of more white settlers and resource development, they faced increased pressure to surrender reserve land. Desperate for cash, some bands sold their property, typically for well below its value—a process actively encouraged by Indian Agents.

In the summer of 1899, federal Treaty Commissioners met in what are now Alberta and northwest Saskatchewan with three First Nations—the Wood Cree, the Beaver, and the Chipewyan—to negotiate Treaty 8. Like other Numbered Treaties, Treaty 8 was designed to acquire land for European settlement on First Nations' territory. Once signed, Canadian criminal law was to apply to all members of society, including the First Nations. First Nations leaders came with their demands, insisting that their economic and cultural practices continue after the treaty-making process. They demanded, too, exemption from the most onerous obligations of citizenship (taxation and conscription), for receipt of social benefits, and for preservation of religious and cultural integrity. They sought, in other words, privileges on which to construct an inter-cultural accommodation between themselves, settlers, and the Canadian state.

The terms of Treaty 8 accommodated First Nations' demands, but the arrangement did not last. Frank Oliver, who took over as minister of the interior in 1905, had little concern for First Peoples. He considered them an obstacle to progress, especially those he viewed as not productively using all the land they were ceded. Between July 1, 1896 and March 31, 1909, nearly 300,000 hectares of prairie reserve land had been surrendered by First Peoples.

Many Indigenous children continued to be placed in church-run residential schools. Many of these were boarding institutions located far from families and

Figure 3.2 Cree dancing at treaty payment, Edmonton, Alberta, c. 1900.

bands; their aim was to root out First Peoples' culture. The schools were often overcrowded and the buildings wretched; malnourishment and disease flourished, as did mortality rates. Physical and sexual abuse was common. Many children ran away, which prompted authorities to move the schools further from families and bands. Some children fought back, and there were several cases of arson, such as at the Mohawk Institute in Brantford, which was destroyed in 1903.

White society also expanded to remote northern territories, bringing disease and disruption from alcohol. In 1902, on Southampton Island in Hudson Bay, an entire band of 68 people perished. Missionaries arrived to educate and to convert and sought to end Inuit practices like wife swapping. The federal government maintained it had no financial responsibility to the Inuit, and there was little desire to establish treaties. The Inuit were portrayed as too nomadic to have bona fide claims on particular domains. This gave Ottawa greater latitude to promote resource development.

WANT AND REFORM

To the south, rapidly expanding urban centres brought not only excitement and optimism, but also hardship and despair. Rudimentary social services were overwhelmed,
squalour became more prevalent, and social unrest intensified. Working-class homes
were commonly less than 50 square metres. Many lacked internal heating and indoor
plumbing. Urban sewerage systems and sanitation collection fell far short of need. In
Montreal, Herbert Brown Ames, a shoe manufacturer, philanthropist, and municipal
politician, organized a statistical survey in 1897 that documented a horrid state of
affairs for the city's working classes, who lived in an area called the "City Below the
Hill." Some neighbourhoods had an infant mortality rate of 20 per cent—then the
highest recorded in North America.

The late nineteenth and early twentieth centuries brought a "City Beautiful"
movement to North America, emphasizing the need for more parks, tree-lined streets,
and the decoration of urban landscapes with statues, arches, and fountains. Still, many
of those with money fled the city core for suburbs such as Etobicoke outside Toronto,
Elmwood outside Winnipeg, and Uplands outside Victoria. Expanding streetcar
service aided suburbanization, as did the mass production and increasing affordability
of automobiles. With cheaper land, suburbs became affordable for the middle classes.
There, one could purchase a semi-rural estate, feel closer to nature, and live in neighbourhoods shielded by discriminatory housing covenants that excluded less favoured
ethnic and racial minorities.

The urban workplace was typically growing larger. This meant a less personal
relationship between employer and employees. Factories mechanized, increasing output
and decreasing unit costs, thus providing consumers with better prices. However, these
trends also meant less reliance on skilled workers and the disappearance of many
well-paid jobs. Workplace tasks were increasingly broken down into smaller, simpler
components accompanied by tighter managerial control and intensified pressure to
accelerate production. Government regulations to protect workers were minimal, largely
due to the fear of hurting or driving away business. Women and children worked for a
third to a half of what men earned. Not until 1907 did Ontario's government pass a law
stipulating that children under 16 be limited to a maximum workday of 11 hours.

Social legislation was weak or non-existent. Governments claimed welfare bred
dependency, though they also lacked revenue to fund social services (income taxes
did not appear until World War I). In 1901, Toronto's city council budgeted only 5¢
per capita for relief. Able-bodied men were often compelled to perform work, such
as cleaning parks, to receive food vouchers or other assistance. Working-class wages
remained low, and companies often paid little heed to safety. Between 1904 and 1911,

there were 9,340 on-the-job fatalities in Canada. Employers were hostile to unions, claiming they undermined efforts to run cost-effective operations and were controlled by radicals intent upon fomenting revolution. In 1902, the Toronto Employers' Association was founded; its members pledged to provide assistance to one another, such as by firing and refusing to hire union leaders.

Growing numbers of Canadians spoke out against want, suffering, and stark inequities. They worried about the disenchanted turning to radicalism. Several religious leaders responded by promoting the ideals of the Social Gospel movement, which advanced Christian activism as a means of addressing social challenges and ills. Most prominent in Protestant churches, particularly the Baptist and Methodist, which reflected their less hierarchical structure, Social Gospellers spoke of creating the Kingdom of God on earth. This led them to promote things like public housing and the abolition of child labour.

Demands for social reform also came from an array of urban professionals, academics, and others regarded as progressives. They stressed the need for greater order and efficiency and urged that more rigorous analysis of problems be undertaken in order to better understand their roots and the best means of responding. In part, the rise of progressivism reflected a shift within universities to empirical-based social sciences and natural sciences, and growing faith in professions such as engineering to solve the problems of an increasingly complex urban-industrial society. Progressives became involved in a kaleidoscope of causes, such as the need to improve urban housing, regulate utilities, pursue urban beautification, and improve public health.

Reformers also prioritized the need to improve labour relations, as industrialization brought increasing friction between capital and labour. Among the most prominent figures in this area was William Lyon Mackenzie King, who would go on to become Canada's longest-serving prime minister. Born in 1874 in Berlin (now Kitchener), Ontario, King was the second of four children to John King, a lawyer, and Isabel Mackenzie, the daughter of rebel leader William Lyon Mackenzie, whom King often cited as an inspiration for his reformism. At the University of Toronto, where King majored in political economy, he became enthralled with the writings of the British economic historian Arnold Toynbee, who advocated Christian-inspired social reform and established the first university settlement house in London's East End, where students volunteered to help educate the poor. While at the University of Toronto, King frequently visited the city's red-light district in order to—as he insisted—help save prostitutes. In 1896, he left to do post-graduate work, first in Chicago and then at Harvard, eventually earning a PhD. While in Chicago, he volunteered at Hull House. Situated in the city's notorious 19th Ward slum, Hull House provided a day nursery, free lectures and classes, and emergency assistance.

Returning to Toronto in 1897, King, then a reporter for the *Mail and Empire*, wrote on the city's social problems. Demonstrating political shrewdness by holding back a story on the post office purchasing uniforms from companies using sweated labour, King ingratiated himself to Postmaster General William Mulock. This resulted in King being appointed to manage the federal government's new publication, the *Labour Gazette*.

King expressed support for "responsible unions,"[4] meaning those that rejected radicalism. He insisted that compulsion would not produce effective labour agreements. This philosophy appeared in the 1907 *Industrial Disputes and Investigation Act* (*IDIA*) that King helped prepare. Under its provisions, the employer or employees involved in a labour dispute could apply for state assistance to help achieve a settlement. Once receiving the request, the government prohibited strikes and lockouts pending investigation and conciliation and the issuing of a non-binding report by a tripartite board with both labour and corporate representation. However, Canada's Trades and Labour Congress soon dismissed the *IDIA* as ineffective because it contained no means to force employers to engage in collective bargaining.

Unions were becoming more prominent in industrializing Canada, though in 1911 they still only comprised 5 per cent of the workforce. There were some large and violent strikes, such as the 1906 Winnipeg streetcar workers' strike over wages that saw widespread destruction of property and clashes of workers with police, private detectives, and militia. More workers joined international unions affiliated with the American Federation of Labour (AFL), seeking the resources and strength of this large US labour body. The AFL prioritized the organization of skilled labour into what were called craft unions, rather than joining skilled and unskilled workers into what were called industrial unions. AFL unions focused on issues like pay and working conditions, including controlling the impact of mechanization and managerial shop-floor control, principally to protect better-paid craft workers. They shunned political radicalism—but not strikes—to achieve a better deal for their members.

Politically radical unions gained strength in areas where resource extraction dominated, with the most significant concentration being in Western Canada. British Columbia had the highest strike rate in Canada, with those working in coalmines leading the way. In this setting, class divisions were particularly stark. Men received abysmal pay, often lived in tents or crude bunkhouses, and, being physically isolated, were often forced to purchase provisions at overpriced company stores.

Socialists became more significant in Canada's labour movement and political landscape. In 1906, Toronto's socialist mayoralty candidate garnered an impressive

---

4 Charlotte Gray, *Mrs. King: The Life & Times of Isabel Mackenzie King* (Toronto: Penguin, 1997), 138.

8,600 votes in a second-place finish. Historian Ian McKay classified the mining district of Springhill, Nova Scotia, as "possibly the *reddest* spot on the map of Canada's liberal order."[5] Socialists enjoyed their greatest electoral success in Western Canada, particularly in British Columbia. In 1901, the Socialist Party of British Columbia emerged in the province's coalmining districts, and two years later won two provincial seats. In 1907, socialists were elected provincially in Nanaimo and Newcastle, British Columbia, and in the coalmining areas of Grand Forks and Rocky Mountain House, Alberta.

Hostility developed between the TLC and radical Western Canadian industrial unions. In 1903, the TLC ordered back on the job its members participating in sympathy strikes in support of a Western Canadian-based walkout by workers seeking membership in the radical United Brotherhood of Railway Employees. Responding, BC-based labour trade councils in Nanaimo, Phoenix, Fernie, and Victoria withdrew from the TLC.

Western Canadian workers in particular joined the militant Industrial Workers of the World (IWW). Established in 1905 in Chicago, the IWW advocated socialism and the use of general strikes to destroy capitalism. Besides tapping into worker frustration, the IWW's appeal also derived from providing practical services such as mail drops and medical depots to itinerant labourers. Also important was that the IWW produced printed material in several languages, as its potential clientele came from many backgrounds. The federal government deported IWW organizers coming from the United States and banned IWW meetings. The TLC leadership tacitly endorsed such actions through its silence.

IMMIGRATION

Xenophobia reinforced hostility to unions. Many longer-settled Canadians feared immigrants. Slavs were seen as steeped in radicalism because of strong socialist movements in their homelands. Immigrants also generated concerns over job security and that their presence would drive down wages. The union movement supported immigration restriction. Still, Canada needed immigrants to fill the West, as well as for industrial jobs and its growing resource sector. In 1896, Canada's population stood at 5.074 million; between that year and 1914, some 3 million newcomers arrived. Such migration was encouraged by falling international shipping rates, rising wheat prices, land shortages in Europe, the closing of the American frontier, improved rail access to the West, and more job opportunities.

---

5 Ian McKay, *Reasoning Otherwise: Leftists and the People's Enlightenment in Canada* (Toronto: Between the Lines, 2008), 129.

Although changed by immigration, Canada's population remained overwhelmingly white, Anglo, French, and Western European. The 1901 census indicated that Canada was 96.2 per cent Caucasian. Most Canadians expressed a clear preference for white, Protestant British and American newcomers, viewing them as easiest to assimilate, followed by northwest Europeans and Scandinavians. The least favoured were Slavs, Southern Europeans, Jews, and visible minorities.

Canada's Department of the Interior managed immigration, reflecting its oversight of Western Canadian land for settlement. From 1896 to 1905, Clifford Sifton served as minister of the interior. Under his direction, Canada focused on attracting agriculturalists by advertising free land and establishing an immigration office in central London. Land in Britain was increasingly expensive, many wanted to escape England's rigid class structure, and people had family, relatives, and friends in Canada. Whereas 1,200 people settled in Canada from Britain in 1900, in 1912–13, this number peaked at 150,000. American migration to Canada increased from 19,000 in 1900 to 139,000 in 1912–13.

Requiring more immigrants to support Canada's growing economy, Sifton turned to the Ukraine and Russia.

Figure 3.3 Advertising cheap land to Americans in the Canadian West.

Between 1891 and 1911, half a million people arrived in Canada from continental Europe. The largest numbers were from parts of the Ukraine known as Galicia and Ruthenia. These people fled from poverty, authoritarianism, and, for many, persecution, such as Jews, thousands of whom were killed in state-tolerated or sanctioned *pogroms*.

Sifton regarded Central Europeans, particularly Ukrainians, as tough and highly motivated. Many others stereotyped them as unkempt, wild, violent, thieving, and drunkards. Sifton's successor, Frank Oliver, expressed concern about the impact of such immigrants. "It is not merely a question of filling the country with people who will produce wheat and buy manufactured goods," he said. "It is a question of the

Figure 3.4 Slavic settlers at the Crowsnest Pass, Alberta, c. 1900–20.

ultimate results of the efforts being put forward for the building up of a Canadian nationality so that our children may form one of the great civilized nations of the world, and be one of the greatest forces in that civilization."[6]

In 1909, Methodist minister J.S. Woodsworth published a landmark study on immigration, *Strangers Within Our Gates*. As superintendent of the Methodist church's All People's Mission in Winnipeg's north-end slum, Woodsworth, whose ideas had much in common with socialism, arranged for English classes, religious instruction, and emergency assistance for newcomers. Still, Woodsworth shared the dominant view that for immigrants to succeed they had to adopt Anglo-Protestant norms. Among the groups he highlighted in his book were Russian Jews. He wrote of a Jewish migrant who arrived in Fort Qu'Appelle, in what is now Saskatchewan, in 1903. The rest of the family, eight in all, followed in 1905. They initially survived on $4 weekly, roughly equivalent to one-third of that earned by an average urban labourer. However, within a couple of years they had all learned English and boasted a two-storey home. Most Jewish immigrants had few opportunities outside of the lowest

6 Ibid., 106–7.

paying jobs, like in the textile sector. Montreal housed Canada's largest Jewish population. There, in 1913, several hundred Jewish children, with parental support, went on strike from their classes at the Aberdeen School—which was part of the province's Protestant school system Jews were compelled to attend—because teachers referred to them as dirty and refused to apologize.

Visible minorities experienced the most intense prejudice. They were considered impossible to assimilate and culturally, morally, and genetically inferior to whites. Although Canada sought immigrants from the United States, this did not include African Americans. Black men were portrayed as savage and with voracious sexual appetites that endangered white women. Rumours in 1911 that a sizable number of blacks were leaving Oklahoma, bound for Alberta, generated a petition bearing the names of 14 per cent of the province's population demanding that the federal government stop this movement.

On Canada's west coast, whites raised alarm over being overrun by hordes of Asians. Even with the 1885 implementation of a $50 head tax on each Chinese migrant to Canada, by World War I, Canada's Chinese population had reached some 30,000. Typical stereotypes of the Chinese were that they were dirty and diseased; responsible for gambling and opium dens; and spread prostitution. Sikhs and Hindus solicited comments about being unkempt and heathen. The Japanese were cast as warlike, as demonstrated by Japan's military incursions into China in the mid-1890s and defeat of Russia in 1904–05, a disquieting event for many whites as it was the first military victory by an Asian country over a European one.

With BC politicians lobbying for Asian exclusion and a federal election approaching, the federal Liberals increased the head tax against the Chinese in June 1900 to $100. British Columbia politicians demanded $500, which was equivalent to the average annual salary of a labourer. Laurier initially resisted, hoping to expand Canadian trade with China, but caved by 1903. The following year, only eight Chinese officially entered Canada.

In 1907, an economic downturn coincident with the arrival of more East Asians triggered a riot in Vancouver that destroyed much of the city's Chinese district, the most prominent Asian target. The federal government responded by punishing the victims: in 1908, it barred Asian immigrants who did not arrive via continuous voyage. At the time, no direct scheduled crossings existed between Asia and Canada. Also in 1908, Mackenzie King travelled to Japan to negotiate an unofficial "Gentleman's Agreement" on immigration because Britain's treaties with Japan and its authority over Canadian foreign policy technically made Japan exempt from the continuous voyage rule. Japan promised to keep annual migration to Canada to a maximum of 400 to avoid the public dishonour of a Canadian quota against its people.

WOMEN

Several women's groups were among the critics of increased immigration. Partly this was because male newcomers, and not women, could gain the right to the vote. Led by middle- and upper-class Anglo- and French-Canadian women, they argued that through the vote, females, as defenders of families and a higher standard of virtue, would exert a civilizing and nurturing influence on society. At that time, the most widely accepted goals for women were marriage and motherhood. While most women had children, talk circulated about Anglo-Protestant race suicide because non-Anglo immigrants and Francophones had higher fertility rates. Playing on the theme of women being weak and delicate, the medical profession gained a greater presence in the process of childbirth by advancing the idea that they could remove its pain by administering anesthetics. The addition of section 179C to the Criminal Code in 1892 added to pressure to have children by imposing up to two years' imprisonment for anyone who offered, sold, or advertised medicine or devices to prevent conception or cause an abortion.

Both under Quebec's Civil Code and English common law, wives received similar rights as children and the insane. They could not obtain credit on their own or exert any legal control over joint property. While adultery by a wife was grounds for the husband to demand a divorce, if the wife demanded it the husband's adultery had to be accompanied by desertion, incest, bigamy, or raping another woman.

At home, much of the wife's day consisted of toil and drudgery. Certainly, there were improvements; the early twentieth century saw the appearance of hand-powered washing machines, for instance. Most city homes had running water, though working-class ones usually had just one tap. In rural areas, where more than half of Canadians lived, things were far more basic. In rural Manitoba, two-thirds of homes had no running water and coal lamps lighted most.

Economic necessity compelled numerous women to take paid work. In 1901, women made up approximately 15 per cent of Canada's labour force. Wives and mothers often performed home-based piecework, such as making clothes, for which they earned a pittance, especially since they had to provide their own equipment and material. Popular attitudes did not favour female work outside the home because it was seen as threatening the breadwinner status of men and taking women away from domestic duties. In the early twentieth century, some 90 per cent of women who worked outside the home were single or widowed. Moreover, women were confined to low-paying jobs often perceived as an extension of housekeeping or nurturing. Their most common job before World War I was as domestic workers. Many women worked in textile and boot and shoe factories, given their presumed skill at sewing. Those in clerical jobs increased from one-sixth to two-fifths of the total in this occupation between 1891 and 1911. Many firms viewed women as brightening up the office. Moreover, male office generalists were phased out as administrative work was broken down into lower-paid and more repetitive tasks, particularly with the appearance of typewriters.

Some women pursued public activities through religion. A notable number in English Canada became involved in overseas missions, such as to India and China, where they taught children and administered health care. Closely connected to Protestant churches was the Women's Christian Temperance Union. Determined to uplift Canadian society, its 10,000 members championed prohibition, the stamping out of prostitution and obscene literature, the sterilization of criminals, the provision of assistance to deserted wives, and women's suffrage, so they could use their influence to better protect families and prevent social and moral decay.

Dr. Emily Howard Stowe, the second woman licensed by the Ontario College of Physicians and Surgeons (after graduating from medical school in New York), was the first major leader in Canada's suffrage campaign. As head of the Dominion Women's Enfranchisement Association (DWEA), she and her supporters achieved a breakthrough in 1883, when Ontario provided the municipal franchise to widows and unmarried women who owned property. In 1903, her daughter, Dr. Augusta Stowe-Gullen, took over the DWEA. Known for aggressive tactics, in 1909 she organized a march of 1,000 women on the provincial legislature. In 1911, Flora MacDonald Denison replaced her, and the DWEA was renamed the Canadian Suffrage Association. Denison was even more controversial, having separated from her husband and advocating easier divorce laws and legalized birth control. In 1912, a rival and conservative Equal Franchise League was formed. It insisted that women would use the ballot to achieve a "purifying, civilizing, and stabilizing influence,"[7] not to challenge male authority. While women assumed more public roles and lobbied for the vote, many constructed their arguments for greater involvement based upon being "mothers of the nation." The strategy indicated acceptance of existing attitudes and structures, but also advanced longer-term progressive change.

CULTURE AND STATE ENTERPRISE

Friction between traditionalism and modernism was evident in other areas, including events designed to build cohesion. Such was the case with the 300th anniversary celebration of Champlain's founding of Quebec City in 1608. Quebec nationalists insisted it commemorate the birth of a French-Catholic nation. Laurier's government offered

7   Robert Craig Brown, *Robert Borden: A Biography. Vol. 1, 1854–1914* (Toronto: Macmillan, 1975), 122.

$300,000 for the celebration, but only if the message was that Champlain established the roots of Canada. The re-enactment of the September 1759 battle on the Plains of Abraham demonstrated the utilization of history for contemporary political goals. Actors in the uniforms of the two sides marched and countermarched, but rather than engaging in a mock battle, they eventually came together in a show of mutual triumph.

The Quebec tercentenary spoke to the belief that a sense of shared identity was possible. This was also a challenge because cultural institutions were in their infancy and overwhelmingly dependent upon private philanthropy. Not until 1910 did Canada's National Gallery obtain its first full-time director who emphasized the acquisition of Canadian art—in part because European works were too expensive. In theatre, British and American touring companies were most popular. Of the books cited by the British trade journal *Bookseller and Stationer* as top sellers in Canada between 1899 and 1918, 44 per cent were American, 36 per cent were British, and just 20 per cent were Canadian. Only a few Canadian authors obtained a sizable following, such as Ralph Connor for *The Man from Glengarry* (1901) and Lucy Maude Montgomery for *Anne of Green Gables* (1908). Rather than conveying a Canadian identity, both were localist, describing distinct cultures in the Ottawa Valley and Prince Edward Island respectively. Regionalism remained strong in Canada. In 1909, farmer organizations, primarily in the Prairies, formed the Canadian Council of Agriculture to lobby for greater equity by demanding lower tariffs, railway, and grain storage rates.

The concentration of power also fuelled resentment. In 1910, there occurred a record 32 corporate mergers worth $157 million. The federal government responded with *An Act to Provide for the Investigation of Combines, Monopolies and Mergers*. However, with numerous loopholes, and no prosecutions, critics soon dismissed it as toothless. Yet, support grew for stricter regulation and public ownership of utilities. Several local governments sought to establish maximum rates. In Ontario, pressure grew for shifting hydroelectric power from private to public control. Far from being radical, the Waterloo Board of Trade spearheaded the campaign, charging that private ownership resulted in too much energy being sent to the United States and Toronto because such markets brought greater profits. In 1906, Ontario's Conservative government created the Hydro-Electric Power Commission, which began signing contracts with municipalities to deliver energy over publicly owned transmission lines.

CHANGING THE GUARD

Robert Borden anticipated a major breakthrough in the autumn 1908 federal election. The previous year, he called a national Conservative convention in Halifax that produced a platform revolving around the theme of "purity in politics," promising, for example, implementation of exams and meritocracy in appointing civil servants. The approach was designed to contrast with supposed Liberal corruption, such as massive tax breaks provided to the two new transcontinental railways and because of rumoured graft in the Department of the Interior. Yet, once again, Canadians gave the Liberals a majority government, with 133 seats compared to 82 for the Tories.

Soon after the election, however, the government faced a potentially explosive situation over naval defence. Britain announced a program to construct massive dreadnought battleships to counter a German naval build-up. Laurier refused Britain's request to help fund construction of the vessels. Instead, he promised to create a Canadian navy, which he argued would help Britain by freeing up its Royal Navy from Canadian coastal defence activities. Initially, Borden supported Laurier. Things changed the next year when Reginald McKenna, Britain's First Lord of the Admiralty, announced that Germany's aggressive shipbuilding program threatened to overtake the Royal Navy. Australia promised Britain money to construct a dreadnought. Anglo-Canadian opinion turned decisively toward doing the same, as did Borden.

Figure 3.5 Wilfrid Laurier during his last trip to Western Canada as Prime Minister, 1910.

Laurier responded with the Naval Service Bill. Once passed by Parliament in May 1910, it established the Royal Canadian Navy. Canada was to create a force of five cruisers and six destroyers. Laurier maintained that in times of emergency Parliament could make these ships available to Britain. This time, the attempt at compromise flopped. In English Canada, the "tin-pot navy," as it came to be called, was portrayed as useless to Britain. In Quebec, Bourassa mobilized opposition by arguing that the Naval Service Bill would drag Canada into imperial wars, a view he hammered home in a newspaper he founded that year called *Le Devoir*. There, Borden remained silent on the naval controversy, leaving matters to Frederick Monk, who ran the Quebec wing of the federal Conservative Party. Monk formed an alliance with Bourassa's *nationalistes* to condemn the Naval Service Bill and to defeat Laurier.

French–English relations deteriorated further over French-language education in Ontario. A 1908 report by F.W. Merchant, Ontario's chief inspector of public and separate schools, claimed that Francophone children were failing to learn English. In January 1910, Howard Fergusson, the provincial Conservative member representing Kemptville, introduced a resolution into the Ontario Legislature declaring that English should be the sole language in public education. An *Association canadien-française d'éducation de l'Ontario* (ACFÉO) appeared the same month to defend bilingual and French schools. Premier J.P. Whitney ordered another report by Merchant, seeking to delay matters until after a provincial election.

In 1911, the issue of trade catapulted to the political forefront. The US Congress was buckling under pressure to bring down consumer prices by lowering tariffs. Canada was offered an attractive deal that would eliminate duties on a wide range of primary products and open American markets further to Canadian manufactured goods, while not obliging Canada to immediately reciprocate on duties applied against American products. Finance Minister W.S. Fielding triumphantly announced the proposed deal to the House of Commons on January 26. The Conservatives were dejected. Several Liberals urged Laurier to call an election, but instead he left Canada to attend the coronation of George V as England's new King.

This provided time for Canadian industrial and manufacturing interests to mobilize opposition. The mantra became that the United States would soon demand Canada lower its tariffs, with the result being US economic domination and perhaps even the political absorption of Canada. A group of prominent men of business and finance (calling themselves the *Toronto 18*), who were well-known Liberal supporters, announced they would vote Conservative to derail the free trade agreement.

When the actual agreement came before Canada's Parliament, the Conservatives initiated a filibuster to extend debate interminably as a means of preventing its passage. Convinced that he could sell the free trade deal to Canadians, Laurier dissolved Parliament and called an election for September. He opened his campaign in Trois-Rivières, declaring: "I am branded in Quebec as a traitor to the French and in Ontario as a traitor to the English…I am neither. I am a Canadian."[8] Monk, in alliance with the *nationalistes*, siphoned off support in what had been rock-solid Liberal Quebec. In English Canada, Laurier's stand on free trade and the navy hurt him, especially among

---

8 Robert Choquette, *Language and Religion: A History of English–French Conflict in Ontario* (Ottawa: University of Ottawa Press, 1975), 163.

imperialists, industrialists, and urban workers. The popular vote actually remained close, favouring the Tories 51.6 to 48.4 per cent, but the seat count was decisive with 135 Conservatives compared to 85 Liberals.

While remaining relatively quiet about the naval issue during the election campaign, Borden was forced to confront it soon after becoming prime minister. In March 1912, Winston Churchill, Britain's staunchly imperialist First Lord of the Admiralty, presented an alarming picture of German naval strength. In June, Borden left for England to discuss the situation. Upon returning home, he introduced the Naval Aid Bill to contribute $35 million to Britain to construct three dreadnoughts. Monk resigned as minister of public works, believing himself betrayed. In December 1912, the Naval Aid Bill came before Parliament. The Liberals raised various procedural points to stall the legislation. After five months of deadlock, Borden invoked closure for the first time in Canadian history to end debate and to force a vote on the bill, which the government won by a majority of 33. It was all for nought, however, as two weeks later the Liberal-dominated Senate overturned the legislation.

Meanwhile, with Whitney's re-election as Ontario's premier, Merchant submitted his second report. It maintained that French and bilingual schools were failing to properly teach English. The result, passed in June 1912, was Regulation 17. It severely restricted instruction in French past grade one and phased it out completely by grade four in all schools receiving provincial funding. The ACFÉO condemned Regulation 17 as a "cruel, arbitrary, unjust, and sweeping denial of…elementary natural, as well as constitutional rights."[9]

Compounding matters was that the economy, after more than a decade of generally strong growth, retracted swiftly and sharply. In Edmonton, jobless protestors occupied several churches frequented by the upper classes. Economic troubles also fed xenophobia, as cheap immigrant labour was portrayed as stealing jobs or driving down wages. Determined to enforce the continuous voyage rule against Asians, in May 1914 Canadian authorities prevented the Japanese steamer *Komagata Maru* from docking in Vancouver with its passenger manifest of 340 Sikhs, 24 Punjabi Muslims, and 12 Hindus because the vessel had arrived from Calcutta via Hong Kong. The ship remained anchored in the harbour with its crammed human cargo forced to endure sweltering heat and eventually food shortages. After five weeks, the RCN, in its first official assignment, forced the *Komagata Maru* out of Canadian waters.

In late July, Borden travelled to the Muskokas for a vacation. His rest was brief. Simmering tensions were coming to a head in the Balkans after a Serb nationalist

---

9   Robert Choquette, *Language and Religion: A History of English–French Conflict in Ontario* (Ottawa: University of Ottawa Press, 1975), 163.

assassinated the Archduke of Austria and his wife in Sarajevo on June 28. On July 28, Borden read in the newspaper that Austria had declared war on Serbia. That evening, after getting in a round of golf, he received a telegram advising him to return to Ottawa immediately. Europe was cascading toward conflict.

CONCLUSION

Between 1896 and 1914, Canada became more urban, industrial, and interconnected. Farms mechanized, food production boomed, millions settled in the Prairies, and three railways traversed the nation. Expressions of Canadian culture grew more evident, and Canada stepped more boldly onto the world stage. With seeds planted by the Social Gospel and progressive movements, Canada's social welfare system began to take root, as did more regulation to contain abuses within the capitalist economy. Organized labour emerged as a force, Canada became more multicultural, and women assumed public roles and sought expanded rights. A young country was coming of age. However, such tumultuous change revealed, created, or exacerbated conflict. These years also witnessed worry and protest over corporate concentration, urban blight, class conflict, and political radicalism. Regionalism remained potent; mass immigration intensified xenophobia; and imperialism arguably did more to divide than to unite Canadians.

In his 15 years as prime minister, Wilfrid Laurier prioritized unity and pursued compromise. Still, he was eventually overwhelmed by competing interests—namely those of imperialists, nationalists, and *nationalistes*—over his solution to the naval dispute and the proposed free trade deal with the United States. Robert Borden, the outwardly unassuming Halifax lawyer whom many wrote off as too dull for politics, had proven his critics wrong. His first years as prime minister were rough as he faltered on the naval issue and faced an economy that went into a tailspin. However, his greatest challenge lay ahead, as on August 4, 1914, he led Canada into "the war to end all wars."

4 NATION IN CRISIS: RESPONDING TO WAR AND UPHEAVAL, 1914–1919

INTRODUCTION

World War I is still widely regarded as the most brutal conflict in modern history. It conjures images of muddy, rat-infested trenches, the killing ground of No-Man's Land, masses of men hurled into storms of shell and machine-gun fire, and the legacy of lost idealism and the death of romanticism. The spark that set it off came on June 28, 1914, when a Serb nationalist assassinated the heir to the Austrian throne, Archduke Franz Ferdinand. His murder challenged Austria-Hungary's aim to control the Balkans.

The manner by which Austria demanded that the perpetrators be brought to justice would have destroyed Serbia's sovereignty; the real purpose of the Austrian ultimatum was to provoke war so that Austria-Hungary could reassert dominance in the region. Germany backed Austria, despite the possibility of war with Serbia's ally and protector, Russia. Germany believed France and Britain would not come to Russia's aid despite their alliance, known as the Triple Entente. On July 28, Austria-Hungary declared war on Serbia. Russia mobilized its forces, and on August 1, Germany went to war against Russia. France followed two days later by declaring war against Germany. Germany invaded Belgium to bypass and encircle French forces.

This act violated Belgian neutrality, which Britain had pledged to defend, thus bringing it into the war on August 4. By the time it all ended on November 11, 1918, the war had claimed 10 million military and 6 million civilian lives. Canada's 66,000 dead and 172,000 wounded represented 2.5 per cent of its population.

In August 1914, Canada was still a colony. When Britain declared war, Canada was committed. The war transformed Canada. Its fledgling industrial base flourished and social change accelerated. From a nation of some 8 million came tremendous outpourings of patriotism. Some 630,000 Canadians, or nearly 8 per cent of the country's population, donned a military uniform, and more than 80 per cent of them were volunteers. Millions of Canadians united to back Britain and defend freedom from German militarism. The sale of Victory Bonds raised billions of dollars, at a time when the overwhelming number of Canadians earned less than $1,000 annually. However, the war also tore deep into the national fabric, pitting much of French- against English-Canada, heightening regionalism and class strife, and precipitating unprecedented assaults on freedoms. Robert Borden led Canada through arguably its most turbulent period. To many, he was a strong and decisive leader. By the end of the war, Canada was far more of a nation than a colony. Yet, contrasting with the collective pride shared among millions were the deep and bitter divisions that reverberated long after the guns fell silent. Many Canadians blamed these on Borden's unwillingness to waver or compromise.

A GLORIOUS ADVENTURE

News of Britain's declaration of war reached Canada on the morning of a Monday bank holiday. Large crowds gathered outside newspaper offices to hear the latest developments. Reports described enthusiastic, celebratory crowds breaking into renditions of "O Canada" and "God Save the King." Harold Innis of Otterville, Ontario, who went on to become one of Canada's most renowned scholars, said of his decision to enlist: "It is because if the Christian religion is worth anything, it is the only thing I can do." Not everyone looked upon the coming of war with great anticipation. "This war is the suicide of civilization,"[1] Prime Minister Robert Borden wrote privately, even as he prepared to lead Canadians into it. Although it was known that people died in wars, not since the American Civil War a half century earlier had North America suffered mass casualties in battle, and Canadian memories of that earlier conflict were dim. Also, with a severe economic downturn persisting well into 1915, military service meant a job paying at least $1.10 a day and the means to support one's family,

---

1 Christopher Moore, "Before the Fall," in Mark Colin Reid (ed.), *Canada's Great War Album: Our Memories of the World War* (Toronto: HarperCollins, 2015), 1, 11.

especially as the money soldiers sent home was supplemented by a government separation allowance and support from the privately run Canadian Patriotic Fund.

At the outset of the war, Canada's permanent army was a paltry 3,000 men, and its militia of some 70,000 was poorly equipped and trained. The country moved quickly to mobilize. Canada's Parliament approved an overseas contingent of 25,000 and a war appropriation of $50 million. Ottawa also armed itself with new, and unprecedented, powers. On August 22, the Conservative majority passed the *War Measures Act*, which permitted Ottawa to impose a command economy—that is, one run by the government and not market forces—to intern suspected dissenters, and to censor all means of communication.

Two days after Canada went to war, Sam Hughes, the minister of militia and defence, dispatched telegrams to the commanders of the country's 226 militia units. He instructed them to send between 125 and 250 men each to a new military base he had ordered constructed at Valcartier, 30 kilometres north of Quebec City, on land he had the government purchase in 1912 to train militia units. The facility was close to good rail connections and a major port, but it was only designed to accommodate 5,000 men, not the more than 30,000 who would soon congregate at the site. Additional land was acquired, and construction proceeded at a frenetic pace; in just two weeks, "2.5 miles of rifle ranges…twelve miles of water mains; fifteen miles of drains; railway sidings; 200 baths; buildings; electric lights; telephones; and tents for over 30,000 men"[2] appeared.

Hughes sought to create an army of citizen soldiers whom he hoped to lead into battle. The British, recalling difficulties with Hughes in the Boer War, informed Borden they preferred Hughes's military role be confined to Canada. Hughes did spot and promote good militia commanders, such as Lieutenant-Colonel Arthur Currie, whom he put in charge of the 2nd Brigade. However, Hughes also championed less competent friends and supporters, including his son Garnet, whom he made second-in-command in the 3rd Brigade. Initially, the number of volunteers overwhelmed Canadian recruiting centres; numerous men were turned away because there was no room. However, two-thirds of the 1st Division were British born, men who, as it turned out, had a strong attachment to the mother country.

Other expressions of patriotism were widespread. By the end of August 1914, the Imperial Order Daughters of the Empire (IODE) raised $100,000 to establish a hospital ship. That same month, the first nationwide appeal for the Canadian Patriotic Fund, which was to provide money to the dependants of servicemen, quickly exceeded its $6 million target.

---

2   Jonathan Vance, *Maple Leaf Empire, Canada, Britain and the Two World Wars* (Toronto: Oxford, 2012), 46.

In early October, 25,000 men were loaded onto 30 converted passenger liners and steamers for a 12-day journey to Britain. Arriving at Plymouth, England, to cheering crowds, they were placed under the command of Lieutenant General Edwin Alderson, a 36-year veteran of the British army, who had commanded Canadians in the Boer War.

THE ENEMY WITHIN

Many Canadians, with no previous experience of total war, worried about spies and saboteurs, especially with the neutral United States containing millions of German-Americans. Newspaper accounts of nefarious schemes afoot stoked fears. The February 1916 fire that demolished the House of Commons, caused by careless smoking, was initially blamed on German-American saboteurs in screaming headlines. One thing most German-Canadians had going for them was that their long-settled status in Canada made them British subjects. This was not the case with some 60,000 more recently arrived Ukrainians from the Austrian-controlled province of Galicia, who were classified as enemy aliens. Within a month of the war starting, Sir William Otter, the first Canadian-born General Officer Commanding, was convinced to come out of retirement to become the director of internment operations.

Canada interned 8,579 individuals: some 3,100 German reservists, 800 prisoners-of-war sent to Canada by the British, and nearly 4,700 enemy aliens. Twenty-four internment stations were established in British Columbia, Alberta, Ontario, Quebec, and Nova Scotia. Living facilities included tents, railway cars, bunkhouses, armouries, barracks, forts, exhibition buildings, and factories. Internees were sent to remote places, such as Kapuskasing in northern Ontario, as well as to Canada's emerging national parks, such as Banff, where they built roads with picks and shovels, setting the groundwork for what politicians predicted would be a post-war tourist boom. In violation of the Hague Convention, men who refused to work were denied food and subjected to corporal punishment. Some 100 prisoners died from illness and 6 were killed, including some who tried to escape.

INTO THE BREACH

In the first month of the war, German forces advanced rapidly, all the way to the outskirts of Paris. In early September, they were turned back at the Battle of the Marne. Both sides dug in, constructing a trench network stretching some 700 kilometres from Nieupoort, by Belgium's northern coast, to the Swiss frontier. In England, Canada's 1st Division was assigned to train at Salisbury Plain, near Stonehenge. Acquired by Britain's War Office during the Boer War, it was entirely inadequate to accommodate the number of incoming Canadians. Weeks of rain produced massive flooding as the terrain consisted of a thin layer of soil over impervious chalk. Tents leaked, uniforms became sodden, defective Canadian-made boots disintegrated and a massive influenza rate and an outbreak of cerebrospinal meningitis ensued. British instructors provided effective training but were resented by many Canadians for the harsh discipline they imposed.

In December 1914, the Princess Patricia's became the first Canadian formation to cross the English Channel into France. The following February, the 1st Division followed. Two months later Canadians joined the Second Battle of Ypres, defending the only section of Belgium the Allies still held. The enemy enjoyed superior firepower, surrounded the Allies on three sides, and was determined to make a breakthrough. April 22 dawned warm and sunny, but things soon

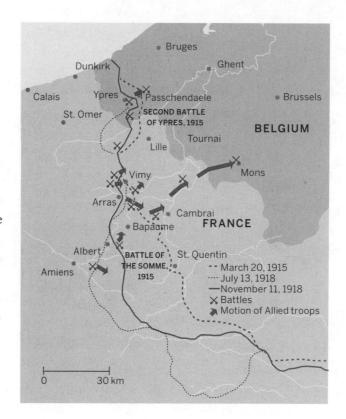

Map 4.1 The Western Front, 1914–18.

turned ghastly as the Canadians confronted French territorial soldiers from Algeria retreating in panic, some literally turning green from the first large-scale use of chlorine gas. A six-kilometre breach opened up in the allied lines, and only the Canadians stood in the way of a major German breakthrough. On April 24, cylinders released a toxic cloud directed at Canadian lines. As the eerie green mist approached, Canadian soldiers, without gas masks, were ordered to urinate onto a cloth and hold it over their mouth and nose, as the ammonia would help neutralize the gas. To make matters worse, the Ross rifle, the standard issue for Canadians, jammed during rapid-fire due to its "straight pullback bolt" that "did not provide enough leverage to remove spent casings."[3] Many men grabbed Lee-Enfield rifles from dead British or Mausers from slain German soldiers. Over the course of 16 days, the Canadians took 6,000 casualties, one-third of their fighting force, though they remained well-disciplined and held their position.

3   Tim Cook, *At the Sharp End: Canadians Fighting the Great War, 1914–1916* (Toronto: Viking, 2007), 131.

Life at the front was often vile. Men frequently went for weeks without bathing; trenches were often waterlogged; rotting food, wet uniforms, open-pit latrines, and sometimes decomposing bodies produced an indescribable stench; rats fed off corpses and army rations; lice infested uniforms; and enemy shelling often seemed relentless. Men dared not look over trench parapets, lest a sniper pick them off. Thousands were immobilized with shell shock, the tell-tale signs of which included "trembling hands…twitching lips…[and] bloodshot, hollow eyes."[4] Many doctors tried to provide rest and relaxation, but hospital records indicate that some 70 per cent of those afflicted were quickly sent back into action. Some, despite a possible death penalty, fled from the fight. A total of 216 death sentences were imposed on Canadian soldiers, mostly for desertion or cowardice; 25 executions were carried out.

Figure 4.1 Funds provided by Canada's then retailing giant, the T. Eaton Company, also helped provide for the creation of a Machine Gun Battery in 1915.

To cope, men adopted a fatalistic attitude, turned to religion, sometimes put faith in superstitions and lucky charms, and developed a sardonic sense of humour, as expressed in songs and regimental and battalion newspapers that poked fun at authority figures and the sorry predicament of the "poor bloody infantry." Only when rotated to the rear, or on their annual two-week leave, could troops relax. Desiring to let loose and live for the day, drunkenness was a continual problem. Men also hungered for sex, and devastated Europe provided desperate women and legal brothels. With epidemic venereal disease rates, Canadian troops were eventually provided with condoms and prophylactic kits, though principally by the YMCA as the military did not want to be perceived as encouraging loose sexual behaviour.

Compounding difficulties for Canadian forces in the first half of the war was German air superiority. Canada had no air force at the war's outset because its leaders did not view the country as prone to aerial attack. Canadian men with a taste for flight joined British air services. In 1915, British authorities approached the Canadian government in search of qualified pilots to enlist in Britain's Royal Flying Corps,

---

4 Tim Cook, *Shock Troops: Canadians Fighting the Great War, 1917–1918* (Toronto: Viking, 2008), 201.

but few recruits resulted because of a stipulation that they had to hold an aviation certificate earned at the applicant's expense. In 1917, the British established the Royal Flying Corps Canada to recruit and train pilots. That year, air-training facilities were established at Camp Borden, Deseronto, and North Toronto, Ontario, and Canadians were also sent to Fort Worth, Texas, to prepare, as it had capacity and weather highly conducive to air training.

Flight training lasted between four and six months, and recruits were allowed to retake exams. There was only a 4.9 per cent wastage rate in training, compared to 33 per cent in World War II, so the capabilities of some graduates were questionable. The aim was to get men to solo after a maximum of six hours; sometimes, this occurred after one. The training fatality rate was 1 for every 1,902 hours of flying time, far higher than in World War II, but it did drop to 1 in 5,800 hours by October 1918.

The navy was no better. Canada went to war with a handful of small Fisheries Protection Service vessels, the HMCS *Rainbow* on the Pacific and HMCS *Niobe* on the Atlantic coast. The *Rainbow* was a light cruiser, made for a crew of 300, while the *Niobe* was a dated heavy cruiser requiring 700 personnel. However, in August 1914, Canada's navy had only 350 regular personnel and 250 reservists, meaning both vessels used sailors loaned by Britain's Royal Navy.

With Canada's coasts so vulnerable, British Columbia's premier, Richard McBride, paid $1.5 million—double the

Figure 4.2 Recruitment propaganda seeks to attract volunteers for the 5th Royal Highlanders of Canada Black Watch 2nd Reinforcing Company.

1913–14 Canadian naval budget—for two small diesel-powered submarines manufactured in Seattle. However, the vessels were soon relegated to anti-submarine training exercises on Nova Scotia's Bras d'Or Lakes.

The early phases of the war on the east coast saw the Canadians dependent on the British. The *Niobe* was assigned to watch German vessels leaving New York City's harbour, but ran aground early in the war and was thereafter confined to dockside duties.

In February 1915, the German navy implemented a policy of unrestricted submarine warfare, which meant U-boats could attack any ship, including commercial vessels and those of non-belligerents, without warning. Britain asked Canada to provide more ships, but Ottawa balked given the costs of its rapidly growing army. Admiral Charles Kingsmill, the Director of the Royal Canadian Navy, turned to private sources, enlisting small vessels into service to protect Canada's coastline. These became known as the Motor Craft Reserve. Newly commissioned armed yachts, such as two donated by John Eaton, the owner of Eaton's department stores, joined with Fisheries Protection Service vessels to form the St. Lawrence Patrol.

RALLYING THE HOME FRONT

In Canada, inspirational press coverage sought to counter long casualty lists. Soon after the Second Battle of Ypres, the federal government created the position of chief press censor, who received authority to prohibit sources "preventing, embarrassing, or hindering the successful prosecution of the war."[5] The chief censor banned 253 printed sources, 222 of which came from the neutral United States; the Americans did not enter the war until April 1917. In Canadian churches, Britain and its allies were portrayed as providing "Christ's soldiers." New books assigned in high schools included *How Britain Strove for Peace* and *Germany's Swelled Head*. Cadet units emerged at virtually every high school, with the Ministry of Militia and Defence covering the costs. Some 20,000 underage boys managed to enlist in the Canadian Expeditionary Force.

Volunteer initiatives to support the war effort enveloped communities, with women leading numerous campaigns. The IODE, whose membership grew by one-third—to 40,000—during the war, sent millions of books, magazines, and cigarettes to soldiers. The Women's Canadian Club started tea shops and second-hand stores to raise money for various war charities.

By early 1915, Canada had raised the 2nd Division and by September, 69 of 71 infantry battalions authorized by Ottawa attained full strength. Appeals often emphasized ethnic heritage, such as for Scottish or Irish battalions. "Chums" battalions were established among men who knew one another from work or local communities, while "Sportsmen's" battalions promoted themselves as composed of men of athletic ability.

---

5   Ottawa, Government of Canada, *Order in Council, PC 1330*, 10 June 1915.

However, as the war dragged on, recruiting problems mounted. Many Francophones saw World War I as Britain's conflict. Native-born Anglo-Canadians demonstrated less inclination to enlist compared to British expatriates. Lower recruitment in the Maritimes reflected less enthusiasm among Acadians, a long-settled Anglophone population, and an economic boom in port cities that meant well-paying jobs. In rural Canada, young men were increasingly needed on farms to meet the growing demand for food. By the end of 1915, Canada had recruited nearly a quarter million volunteers for military service, but rising casualties demanded more. On New Year's Day 1916, Robert Borden publicly committed Canada to the ambitious and symbolic (but many military leaders said unrealistic) goal of raising a voluntary army of half a million men. Citizen recruiting committees visited employers to identify men eligible for military service. Patriotic rallies turned into recruiting drives. At one massive gathering in Toronto's Riverdale Park, where the crowd was estimated at 200,000, women placed chicken feathers on men in civilian clothes to shame them into service.

Quebec was the greatest challenge. Hughes, confident to the point of delusion, said his Huguenot ancestry would help rally Québécois—despite his membership in the Orange Order and support for Regulation 17, which a 1916 petition to repeal gathered 600,000 names in Quebec. With French Canada initially demonstrating support for the war, enough Québécois volunteered for the 1st Division to start a French-speaking regiment. However, Hughes dispersed them into Anglo-dominated battalions. Only with considerable pressure from prominent French-Canadian politicians, and a $50,000 donation from the Montreal doctor and militarist Arthur Mignault, was the French-commanded and -speaking 22nd Battalion created within Canada's 2nd Division. To fill its ranks, it was necessary to recruit Francophones from across Canada.

ECONOMIC EXPANSION

The expanding war effort brought both economic opportunities and challenges. Rising demand for food, both for Canada's growing cities and to feed troops and civilians overseas, resulted in a major upsurge in agriculture. Between 1914 and 1919, the price of wheat tripled; yet, problems emerged through overexpansion (to take advantage of high prices) and the federal government's encouragement of Western farmers to over-specialize in wheat. Canadian farms had to cope with growing labour shortages as young men joined the military or took better-paying urban war jobs.

By March 1915, 200 Canadian firms were involved in war production, overwhelmingly in southern Ontario and Quebec. Initially, the federal government's Shell Committee arranged war contracts. However, it was grossly mismanaged and corrupt. Complaints multiplied over defective products, including an abnormally high proportion of shells that were duds. Accusations multiplied about war profiteering and committee members taking kickbacks. By the end of 1915, the British government threatened not to purchase any more Canadian shells.

In December 1915, the Imperial Munitions Board (IMB) replaced the Shell Committee. The IMB was an arm of the British government, but in Canada it was run by a Canadian, Joseph Flavelle, president of the massive William Davies meat-packing company. Under the IMB's direction, Canada became a significant arms producer, and did so with contracts that established strict quality control, delivery deadlines, and maximum profits. Some 600 factories and 25,000 workers became linked to the IMB, which emerged as Canada's largest corporate enterprise. It established Canadian Aeroplanes Limited, which produced some 2,600 JN-4 trainers and 30 F-5 flying boats—one of the largest airplanes at the time—and shipbuilding facilities in Toronto, Welland, and Midland, Ontario.

The IMB was not free from controversy. It had strained relations with labour as Flavelle, fearing additional costs that could hurt war production, rejected a "fair-wage clause." It was accused of favouritism by directing nearly all contracts to firms in urban Ontario and Quebec, though when it came to shipbuilding, British Columbia received the most business. The IMB suffered a public relations disaster when Canada's cost-of-living commissioner reported that William Davies made an 85 per cent profit in 1916. Flavelle became an object of scorn, sarcastically nicknamed "the "Baron of Bacon.""

INCREASING PROFESSIONALISM OVERSEAS

In September 1915, when the 2nd Division arrived at the front, the Canadians formed their own corps under Lieutenant General Alderson's command. The following March, these still mostly untested troops arrived at St. Eloi, just to the south of Ypres. Prior to an offensive, massive mines were set off underneath German trenches. The ground was transformed, leaving no identifying markers for advancing troops, and they had to traverse massive craters, the largest measuring 55 metres across and 20 metres deep. Failure here cost Alderson his command.

Alderson's replacement was British Lieutenant-General Julian Byng. A strict disciplinarian and "cool and effective field commander,"[6] Byng was determined to improve Canada's battlefield performance. However, his first tests in June at Sanctuary Woods and Mount Sorrel were disappointments. The Canadians fell back 700 metres,

---

6   J.L. Granatstein and Desmond Morton, *Marching to Armageddon: Canadians and the Great War, 1914–1919* (Toronto: Lester & Orpen Dennys, 1989), 112.

8 battalion commanders were immobilized with shell shock, and General Malcolm Mercer, commander of the newly formed 3rd Division, was killed.

For the allies, the war reached a low point in mid-1916. Convinced that German defences could be broken, Britain's Commander-in-Chief, Douglas Haig, prepared for a massive attack at the Somme. Nearly 2 million shells were fired in advance, but they failed to destroy enemy defences. On July 1, British troops, many over-laden with equipment and slowly advancing toward German lines, were slaughtered, suffering over 55,000 casualties. Also decimated was the Newfoundland Regiment. In just half an hour at Beaumont Hamel, more than 700 of the 830 who went over the top became casualties.

Still, the Canadians learned and improved. Strategy and leadership became more effective. General Arthur Currie, who had risen to command the 1st Division, incorporated "bite and hold" infantry tactics in coordination with rolling artillery barrages. Canadian troops were acquiring a reputation for trench raiding. These nighttime operations involved a group of riflemen, bombers, and wire-cutters attacking a portion of enemy lines to create fear, inflict damage, and gather information.

LOOMING CRISIS AND SOCIAL CHANGE

Borden's announcement of a half-million man military initially inspired more enlistments: 29,185 in January, 26,658 in February, and 34,913 in March 1916. However, this quickly waned, and in no month after June 1916 did more than 10,000 men volunteer. Hughes's political stock plummeted with waning recruitment and allegations of corruption involving the Shell Committee, confirmed by a 1916 Royal Commission. Hughes also openly denounced Borden's decision to establish the Ministry of Overseas Military Forces in England, which he saw as challenging his authority. Convinced he could bully Borden into reversing his decision, the gamble backfired and, on November 9, Hughes was fired and replaced by the more low-key parliamentary veteran Edward Kemp.

The increasing demands of war created conditions for social change. In August 1914, the Red Cross established 100 spots for Canadian women to go overseas as nurses. Nurses were typically portrayed in terms that denied their professionalism by tapping into traditional notions of womanhood: the belief that they were selfless, self-sacrificing "angels of mercy" was even reflected in their quasi-religious uniform of a white, nun-like dress. All told, 2,504 Canadian nurses, and roughly 2,000 less-trained women with Voluntary Aid Detachments who performed supporting medical, clerical, and driving duties, served in England, France, and the Eastern Mediterranean. Many nurses worked at casualty clearing stations, performing triage and administering

Figure 4.3 Playing on racial stereotypes, the loyalty of Indigenous peoples is stressed to build support for the Canadian Patriotic Fund. In fact, a large percentage of this financial support came from the diversion of government funding for reserve bands.

care, sometimes within range of enemy artillery. Thirty-six Canadian nursing sisters died during World War I—15 at sea, 15 from disease, and 6 from enemy fire.

In Canada, women performed an array of jobs to release men for overseas service and to meet growing demands. Some 35,000 women were hired in munitions plants, almost all in Ontario. There were far more applicants than jobs available as women sought to escape traditional employment such as domestic service. In Toronto, in 1918, of 6,000 women who applied to work in munitions factories, only 2,000 were placed. They were overwhelmingly young and single, as it was considered undesirable that married women and mothers work. Women were paid less than men doing comparable jobs, confined to lower-status positions, and, in factories, often kept under watch by female inspectors to ensure that their behaviour not be morally compromised.

The war also had an impact on race relations. Initially, Indigenous peoples were kept out of uniform because it was said that the enemy would not accord "savages" civilized treatment. The ban was never fully enforced, and in December 1915 it was formally removed. Ultimately, some 3,500 Aboriginals enlisted. Some sought to escape poverty on reserves, to recapture a warrior tradition, to earn respect and better treatment for their people, and to express allegiance to the Crown, which had accorded treaty rights. The federal government, and particularly its Indian Branch, spoke of Indigenous enlistment as demonstrating their increasing assimilation into Canadian society. Yet, of 600 First Nations communities in Canada, only 100 contributed to the Canadian Patriotic Fund. Two Indigenous military formations were created: the 107th based in Winnipeg and the 114th in Ontario, but neither attained full strength. By 1916, only 4 of 70 chiefs from the Six Nations openly supported enlistment, and nearly all vigorously opposed conscription and emphasized First Peoples' legal exemption from compulsory service. In Canada, the *Indian Act* was amended to make it easier for the federal government to take over reserve land for war needs. Those who hoped that loyal service would produce greater rights were disappointed. Indigenous veterans were denied equal access to veteran programs; for instance, they were refused loans under the Soldier Settlement program to purchase land because it was said that they were not responsible enough to cope with debt. Fred Loft, a Mohawk veteran, started the Pan-Canadian League of Natives, an initiative that spoke to growing frustration. Its principles, drawn up in December 1918, stated: "Not in vain did our young men die in a strange land; not in vain are our Indian bones mingled with the soil of a foreign land for the first time since the world began; not in vain did the Indian fathers and mothers see their sons march away to face what to them were unknown dangers."[7]

Black Canadians also sought to enlist, with the expectation that it would bring greater equality. Some were accepted into combat units, like the Black Watch of Montreal, but many more were rejected. In April 1916, the No. 2 Construction Battalion was created, an all-black—but white-commanded—Nova-Scotia-based formation. Eventually attached to the Forestry Corps in France, its members worked as loggers and in lumber mills and performed construction and shipping work, including building and repairing trenches. Although serving alongside white soldiers, they remained strictly segregated, including when not working.

By the time Canada's forces reached four divisions in 1916, 75,000 recruits annually were required to maintain its fighting strength. To this end, a married man no longer required his wife's written permission to enlist, and the minimum height, chest size, and eyesight requirements for the infantry were lowered. The growing crisis with enlistment led to more finger pointing from English to French Canada. By mid-1916, 27 per cent of Canadians lived in Quebec, but only 14 per cent of recruits came from the province, and a large number of those were from Quebec's Anglophone minority. In April 1916, the civilian-run Hamilton Recruiting League became the first of its type to formally demand the implementation of conscription, a call soon loudly echoed throughout English Canada.

With options narrowing to reach enlistment targets, the government moved closer to conscription. During the last week of 1916, a new National Service Board launched a nationwide survey of available labour. When pressed, Borden refused to promise

---

7   Timothy Winegard, *For King and Kanata: Canadian Indians and the First World War* (Winnipeg: University of Manitoba Press, 2012), 182, 184.

that the survey would not be used to identify conscripts, but the board's director, R.B. Bennett, made such a pledge, especially in Quebec.

EXTERNAL RELATIONS AND MILITARY SUCCESS

From 1915 onward, Canada was borrowing more from US money markets to help finance the war. When the United States entered the war in April 1917, the two nations coordinated naval patrols for the purposes of hemispheric defence. Also in 1917, Canada sent its own representative to Washington, who worked out of Britain's embassy, to better plan resource allocation to maximize military production, and in February 1918, created the Washington-based Canadian War Mission.

Although unquestionably loyal to Britain, Canada's government grew frustrated over lack of consultation, including on the use of Canadian troops. Borden was furious when British Prime Minister Herbert Asquith told him that sharing too much information could result in security breaches. However, in December 1916, over 100 British Liberals, frustrated by Britain's lack of success against Germany, deserted Asquith and made War Minister David Lloyd George prime minister. Seeking greater mobilization of empire resources, Lloyd George established an Imperial War Cabinet to involve the dominions in consultation. Borden arrived in London in March 1917 and the next month—with Canada's prime minister claiming much of the credit—the Imperial War Cabinet passed Resolution IX, declaring the dominions as "autonomous members of the Empire."

The trend toward greater recognition was bolstered by success on the battlefield, particularly at Vimy Ridge, where Canada's four divisions fought together for the first time, capturing a position the Germans had held since October 1914. Byng and Currie, the two key commanders, incorporated lessons from the French, such as the benefits of giving greater autonomy to junior officers and men on the ground to make decisions. Units were prepared for specific objectives, and platoons comprised of bombers, gunners, and other specialists became the key fighting formation. Scientific methods were used to locate enemy artillery by mathematically comparing light flashes to the sound the artillery produced, an innovation developed by the former McGill University engineering professor Colonel Andrew McNaughton. Tramways and plank roads were built to points near the front to supply as much as 800 tonnes of ammunition, rations, and equipment daily. Practice fields, including a full-scale mock-up of Vimy Ridge, were created behind the lines.

At 5:30 AM on April 9, 1,000 large Canadian guns opened fire and 40,000 Canadians went over the top in precisely timed sequence, following behind an intense, but well-executed, creeping barrage. The ridge was captured the first day, and over the next three days the Canadians surged forward 4,000 metres, the longest sustained

Figure 4.4 The British war artist Richard Jack provides a romanticized rendering of the Battle of Vimy Ridge.

advance by the allies to that point in the war. News of the victory was carried on the front page of major newspapers, including the *Times* of London and the *New York Times*.

In Canada, Vimy quickly took on the status of a nation-building event. One newspaper, under the headline "Makers of Canada," printed an illustration of Canadian troops charging up the ridge, while underneath was the well-known painting of the Fathers of Confederation at the 1864 Charlottetown conference.[8] However, the costs were steep, as German artillery, though softened, was by no means neutralized. The clash produced 10,602 Canadian casualties, including 3,598 dead, losses that pushed the country closer to implementing the very divisive policy of conscription.

Victory at Vimy resulted in Byng's promotion to command Britain's 3rd Army. Command of the Canadian Corps went to a Canadian, Arthur Currie, whom Byng had groomed for the position. On August 15, Currie had the Corps attack Hill 70, near Vimy. Artillery barrages and the release of chlorine and phosgene gas preceded the offensive, which was launched at 4:25 AM, securing the high ground that morning and the remaining objectives the next day. Over the following three days, the Germans counter-attacked 21 times, using mustard gas shells, before conceding defeat.

8 Ottawa, June 30, 1917, 5.

Figure 4.5
Canadian at an abandoned German pill-box at Passchendaele, November 1917.

Field Marshall Haig next focused on Passchendaele, about 10 kilometres northeast of Ypres. Millions of shells were directed against German lines to prepare for the advance. However, this destroyed the irrigation system on the low-lying ground; that and heavy rainfall turned the terrain into sludge where, in many parts, the muddy water was waist deep. Haig tasked the Canadians with capturing the village of Passchendaele and the surrounding ridge. Currie resisted, viewing the battleground as a death trap, but Haig, his superior, insisted. The Canadians built corduroy roads to transport supplies and artillery across the mud-soaked terrain. They attacked on October 26, and over the 12-day battle, suffered 15,654 casualties, some drowning in the muck. Some called Currie a butcher, though Canada's casualty rate was one-third lower than at the Second Battle of Ypres. However, the gap between battlefield losses and new enlistments continued widening, a trend that moved Borden and his government toward implementing conscription.

While the ground campaign remained the focus of Canada's military effort, its contributions to air combat expanded. The pace of aerial recruitment increased, helped along by the fact that many young men did not want to be conscripted into the army. In all, 22,812 Canadians served with Britain's flying services. Of the 13,160 who were aircrew, 1,388 were killed, 1,130 were wounded, and 377 became prisoners of war.

Whereas Canadians comprised 6 per cent of British flying casualties in 1915, that figure reached 16.8 per cent by 1918.

Aviators were romanticized as "knights of the sky." For many, the airplane was the epitome of the new modern age, but as Jonathan Vance writes, it was also used in an ironic, anti-modern way, in reasserting the primacy of the individual (the pilot) in a war that, on the Western Front, had turned into mechanized industrial slaughter.[9] Ignored was the fact that the life expectancy of a pilot was lower than for a member of the infantry.

The best-known aviators were called aces, pilots who shot or forced down five or more enemy aircraft. By the end of the war, 10 of the 27 top aces in the British service were Canadians. Among those, Major W.A. "Billy" Bishop was Canada's highest-scoring ace, with 72 victories. Historian Brereton Greenhous insists that Bishop exaggerated his record, as many of his kills were not witnessed.[10] However, this mattered little to a public eager for good news; Bishop's exploits fit the bill and he achieved unrivalled fame and status as a hero, eventually having a mountain peak in the Canadian Rockies and, in 2009, Toronto Island Airport named for him.

With increasing numbers of Canadian fighter pilots in Britain's Royal Flying Corps, pressure grew for separate Canadian squadrons. Edward Kemp, Canada's minister of militia and defence, considered it shameful that Canada had managed to build a separate Army Corps but had not, like Australia, produced its own flying corps. The British considered separate Canadian squadrons too difficult and impractical to implement during the war. Instead, initially, distinct badges were approved for Canadian aviators. But with continued pressure, including from Borden, a separate Canadian section, semi-Canadian commanded, appeared in the final stages of the war—the beginning of the Canadian Air Force (which added the designation "Royal" in 1924).

The war at sea also became more significant to Canada. In October 1916, Germany's *U-53* arrived at Newport, Rhode Island, demonstrating that armed submarines could now cross the Atlantic. After leaving Rhode Island, it sank five allied steamers in international waters, thus raising fears over similar activity off Canada's Maritime coast and in the mouth of the St. Lawrence. In February 1917, Germany renewed its strategy of unrestricted submarine warfare to starve out Britain and force it to the peace table before this renewed strategy would draw the United States into the war. The Borden government ordered a dozen anti-submarine Battle Class trawlers, which began appearing in late 1917. However, it proved difficult to produce adequate

---

9 Jonathan Vance, *High Flight: Aviation and the Canadian Imagination* (Toronto: Penguin, 2002).

10 Brereton Greenhous, *The Making of Billy Bishop: The First World War Exploits of Billy Bishop, VC* (Toronto: Dundurn, 2002).

arms for the ships. Canadian vessels engaged in detection and avoided engagement. Much more effective were commercial convoys protected by American and British naval vessels organized from several Maritime ports, especially Halifax.

However, in Halifax, rapidly increased port activity, combined with slipshod procedures for handling extra traffic, resulted in disaster. On the morning of December 6, 1917, the Belgian relief ship *Imo* collided with the *Mont Blanc*, a French munitions vessel carrying 600 barrels of aviation fuel and over 2,700 tonnes of TNT. The result was the greatest human-made explosion to that point in history. Out of a population of 45,000, 2,000 Haligonians were killed, 9,000 were injured, 10,000 were left homeless, and the city's north end and large parts of Dartmouth were levelled.

INTENSIFYING DEMANDS AT HOME

By the winter of 1916–17, fuel shortages emerged as a result of soaring demand from war industry and labour shortages in coalmines. In June 1917, the federal government appointed a fuel controller empowered to enforce cuts in public consumption. Buildings deemed non-essential, such as theatres, were forced to close an extra day per week. Also in June, Ottawa appointed a food controller due to increased overseas and urban Canadian demand and shortages of domestic farm labour. Canadians faced meatless days in restaurants and fines for hoarding. Many in urban areas grew "war gardens" in their yards or in designated city lots.

Financing the war became more challenging. Defence expenditures rose from $13 million in 1913 to $311 million in 1916 and continued climbing. Adding to costs was the federal government's 1917 buyout of the heavily indebted Grand Trunk, Grand Trunk Pacific, and Canadian Northern railways to create the Canadian National Railway. Finance Minister Thomas White was advised to borrow from Canadians. In November 1915, the federal government tested the waters by seeking $50 million through the sale of war bonds, offering 5 per cent interest. The goal was exceeded by nearly fourfold. In February 1916, another war bond drive topped its target of $250 million, which was 10 times more than what was raised by a modest Business Profits Tax introduced that same year. In 1917, Ottawa added a "temporary" tax on personal incomes. At a time when the average income was $800 per year, only single people making over $2,000 annually and families earning over $5,000 would pay income tax.

A National Executive Committee based in the Department of Finance arranged for banks and stock and bond houses to receive a 0.5 per cent commission on each war bond sold. A Dominion Publicity Committee, also operating through the Department of Finance, organized public appeals. Commencing six weeks before the 4th Victory Bond issue date in November 1917, and especially during the three-week purchasing period, it became virtually impossible for Canadians to open a newspaper or magazine or walk down the street without confronting posters and advertisements telling them that duty, honour, and loyalty compelled them to purchase a bond. Propaganda also reminded them that at 5 per cent interest, war bonds constituted a better investment than putting one's money in the bank. The results were extraordinary: In November 1917, 820,000 Canadians loaned Ottawa $398 million, and in November 1918, over 1 million people provided $660 million.

MORAL AND SOCIAL REFORM

To numerous Canadians, the spirit of duty and self-sacrifice manifested by millions was regarded as proof that the war was divinely guided: good was vanquishing evil and civilization was moving forward. Many saw the adoption of prohibition as further evidence of that process. Abstinence was linked to patriotism, as prohibition would save grain, allow distilleries to convert to war production (to make shell propellants and disinfectants), and better enable people to commit their full abilities to the war effort. Wartime prohibition started in Manitoba with the 1915 election of the Liberals. The new government, as promised, undertook a referendum, and with strong public endorsement adopted prohibition on June 1, 1916. Soon after, Saskatchewan and Alberta followed suit, as did Nova Scotia in late 1916, with the exception of Halifax, which had long enjoyed a lucrative liquor trade to serve garrisoned military personnel. In 1917, New Brunswick went dry, and Prince Edward Island strengthened its 1901 prohibition legislation. That same year, the Ontario *Temperance Act* was passed shortly after the provincial government received a petition with 825,000 signatures demanding prohibition. Quebec moved more slowly, reflecting suspicion of the Protestant led temperance movement. In early 1918, its legislature abolished retail sales of spirits, but still allowed wine, light beer, and cider. On April 1, 1918, the federal government declared Canada dry for at least one year after the war ended.

Growing support for female suffrage was also partly premised on a perceived link between the war and social uplift. Given women's many contributions to the war effort, more Canadians concluded they would use the vote to produce a better post-war world. Adding momentum was the argument that it was unacceptable in wartime that women of British background be denied the vote while male immigrants, including those from enemy countries, enjoyed this privilege. Nellie McClung, Manitoba's most prominent suffragist, worked tirelessly for both the war and the vote. In January 1916, Premier T.C. Norris made good on an election campaign promise, and Manitoba became the first province to extend the vote to women. Alberta's Emily Murphy, another prominent suffragist whose province followed Manitoba later in

1916, played a leading role in registering women for war-related volunteer campaigns. Saskatchewan, which also came on board in 1916, saw a petition signed by 11,000 supporting female enfranchisement on the basis that they had "raised patriotic funds, knitted socks, rolled bandages, cared for the wounded…and surrendered husbands, fathers, and sons to the battlefields."[11] British Columbia and Ontario followed in 1917, where governments acted to offset endorsements of female suffrage by their opponents.

In September 1917, two months before a federal election, the Borden government forced the *Military Voters Act* and the *Wartime Elections Act* through Parliament. The first provided nursing sisters with the vote, and the latter did the same for service-men's wives, widows, mothers, sisters, and daughters who were 21 years of age or older. The government enfranchised women who, it believed, would support conscription. Soon after being re-elected, Borden's government passed the *Women's Franchise Act* that extended the vote to all female British subjects 21 years of age and older (though Asian and Indigenous Canadian women had to wait until after World War II before receiving the vote).

CONSCRIPTION

While women's suffrage was controversial, the campaign to implement conscription that provided them with the federal vote was more divisive. While in London in the spring of 1917 to participate in meetings of the Imperial War Cabinet, Borden confronted a gloomy situation. In March, Russian Czar Nicholas II abdicated follow-ing widespread rioting. Social Democrats under Alexander Kerensky established a provisional government and agreed to back the allies, but Russia's military was in disarray, with many defecting to the Bolsheviks, who were rapidly gaining control. Italy's army was collapsing before Austrian and German forces, and mutinies were spreading among French soldiers. America's entry into the war on April 2 offered great hope, but its mobilization would take months.

Canada remained well short of its target of a 500,000-man army. The National Service Board survey identified some 300,000 men still available for military service. Upon returning to Canada in May 1917, Borden instructed Solicitor-General Arthur Meighen to prepare a *Military Service Act (MSA)*. Presented to Parliament on May 18, it decreed that all single men and childless widowers aged 20 to 32 register for possible compulsory service.

---

11 James Pitsula, *For All We Have and Are: Regina and the Experience of the Great War* (Winnipeg: University of Manitoba Press, 2008), 94.

Borden appealed for national unity and bipartisan support of the MSA. He offered to form a coalition government with Laurier, who rejected the idea. Besides his personal opposition to conscription, Laurier feared that if he joined Borden, this would hand Quebec over to Henri Bourassa's supporters, with the distinct possibility of violent French–English discord. When the MSA came before Parliament, Quebec Liberals unanimously opposed the bill, and were joined by nine Quebec Conservatives. By contrast, Ontario Liberals supported the MSA 10–2. It became law on August 28, but its implementation was delayed until after the December federal election.

Before dropping the election writ, Borden's government imposed closure on Parliament to ensure passage of the *Military Voters Act* and the *Wartime Elections Act*. The former, besides enfranchising nurses, empowered the government to determine the distribution of military votes where servicemen did not indicate their riding. The latter stripped the vote from conscientious objectors and those of enemy background naturalized after March 31, 1902. As nearly all these immigrants came to Canada while Laurier governed, they, like conscientious objectors who opposed conscription, were assumed to be Liberal supporters.

Numerous Liberal MPs in English Canada agonized over whether to stand by Laurier, as they supported conscription or believed their constituents favoured it. Realizing that many Liberals were primed to defect, Borden reconstituted his Conservatives into the Union Party just before Parliament dissolved, a change he cast as encouraging political non-partisanship. By November, many Liberals became Union candidates, including Manitoba's former premier Arthur Sifton and Ontario's Opposition leader Newton Rowell.

The election was arguably the nastiest and most divisive in Canadian history, and also the greatest failure of finding accommodation and compromise since 1867. The Unionists set the tone, even portraying Laurier as a friend of the German Kaiser. To solidify its hold on English Canada, Unionists promised that conscription would not apply to families that already had a man in uniform. Seeking to improve prospects in rural areas, Borden pledged that those needed on farms would also be exempt. The Unionists won 151 seats to the Liberals' 82. The Liberals took 62 of 65 seats and nearly 73 per cent of the popular vote in Quebec. In the Maritimes, Liberal support remained strongest in ridings with a significant Acadian presence, like Restigouche-Madawaka in New Brunswick. In Ontario, the Unionists won 74 of 82 seats, with 63 per cent of the vote. The Liberals retained some strength in parts of eastern Ontario, like Prescott and Russell, where Franco-Ontarians were concentrated. In Western Canada, 54 of 56 seats and 71 per cent of ballots went Union.

Ultimately, some 125,000 men were conscripted; 47,049 went overseas, and 24,132 joined Canadian forces in France. Only 23 per cent of those conscripted were

French-speaking, as most Québécois, particularly those from agricultural areas, convinced conscription tribunals of their need to remain at home. On January 19, 1918, the day after the first conscripts reported for duty, representative J-N. Francoeur proposed to the Quebec Legislature that the province secede from Canada. Of those conscripted, 6.7 per cent in the West, 9.3 per cent in Ontario, and an astonishing 40.8 per cent in Quebec did not report for duty, despite a possible five-year jail term. Federal authorities raided places like theatres, dance halls, pool halls, and roller-skating rinks, arresting young men without exemption papers. The most serious incident occurred over the Easter weekend in Quebec City. The trigger was the arrest by two federal Dominion police officers of a young man unable to provide military exemption papers. A mob went to the police station, ransacking it despite the man's release. A couple of days later, protestors destroyed the offices of the pro-conscription newspapers, the *Quebec Chronicle* and *L'Événement*. After two days of rioting, Borden imposed martial law. Troops arrived from Ontario and Western Canada, as the federal government feared that French-Canadian soldiers would not act against the local population. The major clash came on April 1 after soldiers were fired upon; the result left 4 civilians dead and some 70 wounded, as well as 32 soldiers injured.

In March 1918, Germany launched its last major offensive. Within three days, it had recaptured virtually all of its losses on the Somme and again threatened to take Paris. However, over the course of two weeks, German casualties reached some 250,000; also, with their supply lines badly overstretched, the offensive collapsed. Initially, the thrust generated alarm among the allies, so much so that Borden's government cancelled conscription exemptions, including for farm labourers, a decision that prompted thousands from rural Ontario and Quebec to march on Parliament in protest.

Anxieties also mounted over the growing strength of Bolshevism. In October 1917, socialists seized power in Petrograd, and on March 3, 1918, signed the treaty of Brest-Litovsk with Germany, taking Russia out of the war. Canada became involved in supporting anti-Communist forces, first in early 1918 by sending 40 officers and men to Archangel, near Murmansk, as military trainers. In October, Canada contributed some 4,000 soldiers to a larger allied intervention in Siberia to back the Czech Legion, which had seized control of the Trans-Siberian railway and had set out for Vladivostok where anti-Communists remained in control. The Canadians saw very limited action. In late 1918, two Canadians were killed along the Dvina River near Archangel. There was little popular support for the intervention in Canada, especially after the war in Europe ended. In April 1919, Borden pulled the plug, and by June, the troops were home.

The decision to get involved drew strength from fears over the export of Bolshevism to Canada. Communists held important positions in many unions, particularly in Western Canada. Galloping wartime inflation fed labour militancy;

between 1916 and 1918, Canada's cost of living rose 42 per cent. The labour movement demanded that wealth be conscripted before men. Strikes grew in scope. In April 1918, there occurred an illegal walkout by Winnipeg civic employees, and in the summer there was a nationwide strike by letter carriers. The federal government moved to clamp down on radicalism. In autumn 1918, an Order in Council banned more than a dozen socialist organizations.

In the final months of the war, Canada's home front faced a different but deadly foe in the Spanish influenza epidemic. In this pre-antibiotic period, the flu killed an estimated 25 million people worldwide, including an estimated 50,000 in Canada. Theatres and other public venues closed down, and church services were cancelled. The flu impacted particularly hard on Indigenous peoples. In Norway House, a largely Cree and Métis community in northern Manitoba, one-fifth of the population died within six weeks.

TRIUMPH AND NEW TRIALS

Overseas, Canadian troops played a decisive role in the final push to victory. In July 1918, French and American forces defeated the Germans in the Second Battle of the Marne. Four months of heavy fighting had destroyed Germany's remaining offensive capacity. By summer 1918, Canadian forces in Europe reached peak wartime strength of 150,000, and their last major action had occurred at Passchendaele. Consequently, they were strong and rested when the time came for the Allies to launch an offensive. The Corps was also exceptionally well organized and armed and, with Currie at the helm, skillfully led. Nevertheless, the German army remained a formidable foe, especially since it was now fighting to defend its homeland. Canada's leadership in what came to be called the Final Hundred Days resulted in more than 45,000 casualties, but the Corps reclaimed 1,300 square kilometres; liberated 228 villages, towns, and cities; and captured 623 heavy guns, 2,842 machine guns, 336 trench mortars, and 31,537 Germans.

Canadians awoke on November 11 to news of the Armistice. Celebrations continued throughout the day and into the night with fireworks, street dancing, and burning effigies of the Kaiser. Befitting its accomplishments and sacrifices, Borden demanded that Canada have a separate signature on the Treaty of Versailles that formally ended World War I and a separate seat at the new League of Nations. Britain opposed separate Canadian status, arguing that the Empire should speak with one voice. The United States was also opposed, claiming that separate Canadian representation would mean an extra voice for British interests. Borden shot back by saying that, proportionately, Canada had done more than the United States to defeat Germany. Canada,

Australia, and South Africa were each permitted two representatives—the same as Belgium—and New Zealand one at the Versailles conference's plenary sessions and a signature on the treaty. However, the leaders of the four principal powers—Great Britain, the United States, Italy, and France—privately made the important decisions. Canada also obtained its own seat at the League of Nations, along with other self-governing dominions like Australia and New Zealand.

Despite nearly a quarter-million dead and wounded, upbeat and romanticized notions of the war persisted. Millions of Canadians flocked to post-war battle trophy shows to see items captured by Canadian soldiers. At Toronto's Canadian National Exhibition, the best-attended pavilion, attracting over 200,000 people in 10 days, was a war trophy display billed by the *Toronto Star* as "living evidence of Canadian valour in France and Flanders."[12] Stained glass memorial church windows conveyed the themes of heroic and saintly sacrifice: one example represented the Canadian soldier as a medieval knight vanquishing the German infidel. Communities across Canada raised money to build memorials to commemorate those who had died defending freedom. Many were quite elaborate and uplifting, showing, for example, soldiers with "arms raised in victory, or marching forward, their duty done nobly in the Great War for Civilization."[13]

Yet, Canada faced formidable challenges in reintegrating some 400,000 veterans. Tens of millions of dollars were spent on veterans' programs but it was not enough. Canada's government operated with minimal tax revenues, was wary of adding significantly to a war debt of $1.3 billion, and still harboured a view of welfare as encouraging dependency. In 1915, the federal government created the Military Hospitals Commission to provide medical care and pensions for wounded veterans. In early 1918, this became part of a new Department of Soldiers' Civil Re-establishment, which administered a broader range of programs. On paper, Canada provided the most generous pensions for the wounded among allied countries, but only 5 per cent of claimants obtained the top-paying category compared to more than 50 per cent who received remuneration in the bottom 20 per cent of the award structure. Pension commissioners, most of whom were not veterans, tended to approach their job as guardians of the public purse. Veterans were also disqualified from retraining programs if it was felt they could return to their pre-war line of work. Under the Soldier Settlement scheme, some 25,000 veterans received assistance to buy a farm. However, their eventual failure rate was very high because of declining crop prices, government unwillingness to ease repayment terms, and men being assigned land in remote areas with poor access to markets.

---

12 *Toronto Star*, September 3, 1919, 3.
13 Cook, *Shock Troops*, 623.

Discord continued to reverberate in rural Canada. The war brought record demand for numerous commodity and good prices, but many farmers remained angry over the government's decision to cancel conscription exemptions for agricultural labour. The nationalization of bankrupt railways resulted in suspension of the Crow's Nest Pass rate as a cost-saving measure. Also rankling was the federal government's regulation of wheat prices. Toward the end of the war, as the price of wheat reached a record high, the federal government created a Board of Grain Supervisors to control prices and oversee distribution. Soon after the conflict, this became the Canada Wheat Board, but it was dismantled as grain prices tumbled. To no avail, farmers demanded that the Wheat Board be reimplemented and set a minimum price. Following a Union government budget in June 1919 that failed to deliver tariff concessions as previously promised, Manitoba's T.A. Crerar, the federal minister of agriculture, and eight other Union MPs from Western Canada defected to sit as independents.

The trend among farmers toward creating their own political movement quickly gained momentum. In October 1919, the United Farmers of Ontario (UFO) decided to contest the provincial election. It won only 22 per cent of the popular vote, but this translated into 44 seats in a legislature of 111 because of rural over-representation. To form a government, the UFO joined with 11 Labour representatives, whose strong showing reflected yet another source of continuing discontent.

More workers were drawing motivation from the idea that a war fought to defend freedom and advance civilization should bring greater rights for labour. A growing segment of labour concluded that social justice would result only from the destruction of capitalism. Strikes spread across North America, in Canada claiming a record 2.1 million workdays in 1919. The largest started on May 1 when Winnipeg metal trade workers went on strike to achieve union recognition, something for which they had battled for more than a decade. The next day, building and construction trade workers who sought better wages joined them. On May 6, both groups appealed to the Winnipeg Trades and Labour Council for support. Influenced by the success of sympathy strikes to back Winnipeg municipal workers the previous year, the result, announced May 13, saw trade council members endorse a citywide general strike by an overwhelming margin of 11,000 to 500.

After five weeks, authorities arrested the eight principal strike leaders. Four days later, on June 21, came "Bloody Saturday." It started with a rally by strikers against the resumption of streetcar service. When the crowd failed to disperse as ordered, the mayor read the *Riot Act*. Mounties on horseback, with revolvers drawn, charged into the crowd, killing two strikers. Fearing another, and deadlier, confrontation, the strike committee ended the walkout on June 26. Seven of the eight arrested strike leaders were convicted of "seditious conspiracy" and received jail sentences ranging from six months to six years. The following month, section 98 was added to Canada's Criminal Code, the severity of which exceeded any wartime attack on free expression. It established a maximum penalty of 20 years' imprisonment against anyone who printed, published, wrote, edited, issued, or sold "any book, newspaper, periodical, pamphlet, picture, paper, circular, card, letter, writing, print, publication, or document of any kind in which it is taught, advocated, advised or defended…that the use of force, violence, terrorism or physical injury be used as a means of accomplishing any governmental, industrial, or economic change."[14]

NEW CONCILIATORY LEADERSHIP

On February 22, 1919, 50,000 people—half of Ottawa's population—lined city streets to pay their final respects to Sir Wilfrid Laurier, who had died five days earlier at the age of 78. The Liberals began a process of renewal by announcing a national leadership convention to take place in Ottawa in August. It was to convey a new democratic spirit, as some 1,000 delegates were to be selected from constituencies across Canada to choose the next leader, rather than the past practice of the party's parliamentary caucus making the selection behind closed doors.

The Liberals chose William Lyon Mackenzie King, a master political tactician with an astonishing ability to read the public mood, build coalitions, impress the right people, and demolish enemies. First elected in 1908, King served as minister of labour until defeated in the 1911 Conservative sweep of Ontario. He established himself as a labour relations expert, making a great deal of money working for the famous multi-millionaire John D. Rockefeller, Jr. He resurrected Rockefeller's image and established labour peace—though by creating a company-controlled workers' association—following the April 1914 Ludlow Massacre at the Rockefeller-owned Colorado Fuel and Iron Company, when privately paid guards killed 20 men, women, and children evicted from company housing.

Throughout his years in the United States, King maintained ties with the Liberal Party, though the distance enabled him to evade public commentary on the contentious issue of conscription. As the 1917 election approached, he returned to the political fray. He considered joining the Union Party but stayed loyal to Laurier, whom he considered a political mentor. However, King tried to stake out a more nuanced position than Laurier, claiming that he did not reject conscription in principal, but for reasons not entirely clear, opposed the specific legislation advanced by Borden's

---

14 *Revised Statutes of Canada*, 10 George V, Chapter 146, 7 July 1919.

government. King lost the riding of North York, just outside Toronto, by 1,000 votes, but did better than most Liberals in the area.

At the Ottawa convention, English-Canadian members were determined that the party leadership should go to one of their own after 28 years of Laurier at the helm. King trumpeted his reform past—including his personal lineage to rebel leader William Lyon Mackenzie, his grandfather—and the fact that he was a labour relations expert, presenting himself as a conciliator who could build bridges between opposing forces. At 45 years old, he came across as youthful, at least when compared to the initial front-runner, 70-year-old William Fielding, the former Nova Scotia premier and federal finance minister, who many Liberals never forgave for supporting the Unionists on conscription.

CONCLUSION

The impact of World War I on Canada was profound and multi-faceted. Canada's annual defence budget soared from $72 million (29.3 per cent of total government expenditures) in 1914 to $439 million (59.3 per cent) in 1918. The government managed the lives of Canadians as never before, establishing new taxes, imposing compulsory military service, implementing food and fuel control, curtailing basic freedoms, and introducing the first nationwide social welfare program for veterans. Organized labour grew more powerful, aggressive, and to many, threatening. Women gained the vote. Prohibition triumphed. Patriotism and jingoism enveloped much of English Canada, and Canada's contributions to the war effort generated tremendous pride and nationalism and raised the country's profile and international status.

Yet, contrasting with the triumph at Vimy, Canada's decisive role in the Last Hundred Days, and innumerable contributions made on the home front were deep divisions caused by conscription, the persecution of ethnic minorities and political dissenters, and nearly a quarter-million Canadians killed or wounded with countless others psychologically scarred for life. Borden was decisive in what he felt was necessary to do in order to win the war and maintain social order. His determination would lead to a realignment of Canada's political party structure and a 1917 federal election that was essentially rigged. It has become almost axiomatic to state that during World War I Canada transformed from "colony to nation." And yet, despite national pride that emanated from Canada's role in the war, in many ways the road ahead did not seem as clear in 1919 as it had in the heady days of August 1914. Throughout the 1920s, legacies from World War I reverberated loudly in Canadian society, culture, politics, the economy, and international relations. There was much of which the country was rightfully proud, but also much to repair.

5 THE TURBULENT TWENTIES

INTRODUCTION

World War I supposedly shattered many beliefs, traditions, and restraints, convincing people to live for the day. The "Roaring 20s" were said to be a period when people cast aside the prudish and repressive strictures of Victorian and Edwardian times. They lived faster, looser, and with a sense of daring. It was a time of bootleggers, mobsters, and people who winked at the law to visit speakeasies. It was a period of prosperity and get-rich-quick schemes; of garish styles like long raccoon coats; of nonsensical sayings like "twenty-three skidoo"; of flappers who conveyed sexual liberation; of frenetic dances like the Charleston; and of fast-paced jazz.

There was change, to be certain, even transformational change, but also great anxiety and resistance accompanied that process. Many bemoaned what they saw as moral degradation and sought to establish greater controls. There was intolerance of newcomers and efforts to keep women firmly in domestic roles. Modernism clashed with traditionalism, and Canadian nationalism with regionalism, factionalism, North American integration, and internationalism. Political leadership faltered in the face of transition and frequently reflected and contributed to discord. New political movements and parties were born from linguistic, class, and regional discontent. Yet, for over 80 per cent of this often difficult, unstable, and divisive decade, William Lyon Mackenzie King remained at the helm. King demonstrated a masterful ability to broker and compromise, scheme and strategize, to move Canada forward, though often haltingly, to become an increasingly modern, urban, industrial, autonomous, and prosperous nation. In the process, he made himself and the Liberals into what many would come to view as the country's natural governing group.

DESCENT TO DIVISION, 1920–1921

Although he had led Canada to victory in war, Robert Borden was desperate to leave office shortly after the conflict ended. He was exhausted, physically and mentally. His government was despised in French Canada and was bleeding support among workers and farmers. In February 1919, Western Canadian MPs who had resigned from Borden's government the previous year organized themselves into a distinct parliamentary bloc called the Progressives.

In July 1920, Borden retired and was succeeded as prime minister by Arthur Meighen. Elected to Parliament in 1908 to represent Portage la Prairie, Manitoba, Meighen was appointed as solicitor-general in 1913. Before becoming prime minister, he also served as secretary of state, minister of the interior, minister of mines, minister of Indian affairs, and minister of justice. Known for his keen intellect and superior skills in political debate, Meighen also came across as aloof, cold, and uncompromising.

He became prime minister as the economy nose-dived. High wartime inflation continued into peacetime, totalling 27 per cent in 1919–20. Many firms overproduced, which then sparked rapid deflation, followed by a sharp contraction in production. Business bankruptcies in Canada climbed from 900 in 1919 to 2,451 in 1921, and unemployment reached 15 per cent. The federal government faced increased pressure to alleviate suffering. However, Meighen, a fiscal conservative, loathed adding to the public debt and viewed welfare as encouraging dependency. He responded cautiously, agreeing in December 1920 to have the federal government make $500,000 available for relief, but on a one-third cost-sharing basis with municipal and provincial governments, which produced little action.

Political discontent grew in many parts of the country. In July 1921, the United Farmers of Alberta (UFA) won power with 38 seats in a provincial assembly of 61. Anger also mounted in Atlantic Canada. With the recovery of European and Scandinavian fleets, employment in the Maritime fishing sector declined by 30 per cent to just over 12,000 by 1923. The completion of the Panama Canal in 1914 and its large-scale use after the war to transport west-coast timber to Europe hurt the Maritime forestry sector. The expansion of hydroelectric power in Central Canada, and new and more accessible coalmines in places like Pennsylvania, cut mining jobs in Cape Breton by 25 per cent.

Maritimers directed their discontent against the federal government. They griped over reduced tariff protection for Maritime coal and steel and Ottawa's decision at the end of the war to incorporate the Maritime-based and -managed intercolonial railway into a new national system that eliminated rail subsidies. Business interests formed a Maritime Board of Trade to campaign for better tariff and rail rates, improved port facilities, and increased subsidies. Meighen dismissed their demands as excessive.

A NEW DIRECTION

Meighen called an election for December 6, 1921. He attacked the Liberals as free traders who would bring about Canada's absorption into the United States and denounced the Progressives for promoting class warfare. Liberal leader Mackenzie King made vague references to tariff reform, as he was careful not to alienate strong protectionist forces in Quebec. He also reminded French Canadians of Meighen's close association with conscription. Anger in the agricultural West rose as the price of wheat plummeted from $2.78 a bushel in September 1920 to $1.76 in April 1921.

The Liberals captured 117 seats, one shy of a majority, while Meighen's Liberal and Conservative party (which changed its name to Conservative after the election) won just 50 seats. Canada's French–English divide was starkly evident, as the Liberals took all 65 seats in Quebec. The results also shattered Canada's two-party political tradition with the election of 65 Progressives: 38 (of 43 available seats) from the Prairies, 3 from British Columbia, 21 from Ontario, and 1 from New Brunswick.

The Progressives' breakthrough spoke to longstanding rural grievances, distrust of urban and financial power (especially in Toronto and Montreal), lingering wartime anger over conscription, and the post-war collapse of wheat prices. Their platform included tariff reductions, the nationalization of railways and utilities, progressive taxes, and more direct forms of political participation, such as referenda, to introduce and approve legislation and to recall representatives judged as failing to serve constituents.

King created a cabinet that balanced between region, religion, and language. Ontario and Quebec each received six cabinet posts, Nova Scotia two, and all the other provinces, except Manitoba, one. Francophones, Anglophones, Catholics, and Protestants were all represented. His government proceeded cautiously, initially pursuing a balanced budget. King courted the Progressives, classifying them as "Liberals in a hurry." He asked T.A. Crerar, the Progressives' leader, to consult with, or even to join, his cabinet.

King benefited from divisions within Progressive ranks. One faction, led by Crerar, that garnered most of its support from Manitoba and Saskatchewan, wanted to make the Progressives into a political party that could work effectively within Parliament

Delivering the Goods

Figure 5.1 A 1922 cartoon showing the Prairie provinces turning to the Progressive Party.

and broaden its base of support beyond farmers. A smaller, doctrinaire group, which had most appeal in Alberta and Ontario, countered them. Inspired by those such as UFA president Henry Wise Wood, they rejected the need for party unity and expansion, claiming it would dilute Progressive ideology and turn them into just another political party that placed power above principles. They advocated that MPs vote according to the wishes of their constituents and that "Group Government," based upon representation by broad occupational categories, replace the party system. Lack of cooperation between the two factions prevented the Progressives from assuming the role of official opposition. In November 1922, a frustrated Crerar resigned as leader and was replaced by Robert Forke, a former municipal politician from Brandon, Manitoba.

Political action by farmers at the provincial level had mixed results, with the less doctrinaire achieving greater success. The United Farmers of Manitoba, first elected in 1922, worked with the Liberals, with whom they formed a coalition in the 1930s. The UFA, in power until 1934, adopted orthodox economic policies, demanded party unity, and rejected Group Government. Rural depopulation and a faltering economy hurt the United Farmers of Ontario, but also damaging was division between Premier E.C. Drury, who favoured broadening the base, and those demanding Group Government. In 1923, Ontarians voted the Tories back into power with an overwhelming majority of 75 out of 110 seats.

The sense of things worsening was evident in the Maritimes. Out-migration increased, mainly to the northeastern United States and Western Canada. Through redistribution, the number of federal parliamentary seats held by the Maritimes declined from 33 to 30 in the elections of 1917 and 1925, respectively. The early 1920s saw a growing fascination in the region with traditional folk society and culture, a trend fed by a belief in a simpler and better past, and because the promotion of folk culture offered a means of attracting tourists.

Under the rallying cry of "Maritime Rights," sentiment grew for a Maritime union or even for secession from Canada. The Tories benefited from this anger, since many in the region believed King had deceived them by suggesting sympathy for their grievances when running for prime minister. In 1923, the Conservatives came to power in Prince Edward Island and won a federal by-election in Kent, New Brunswick, a riding the Liberals had held since 1896.

Canada's working classes also suffered. High unemployment made many workers fearful of trying to start or join a union lest they lose their job. The early 1920s saw a concerted effort by employers to roll back wages, bust unions, and blacklist union organizers. Union membership plummeted from 376,000 in 1919 to 240,000 in 1924. The political left fractured. The Trades and Labour Congress wanted nothing to do with radical groups, especially with the recent addition of Section 98 to Canada's Criminal Code threatening up to 20 years' imprisonment for those advocating, or even defending, violence as a means of accomplishing political or economic change. Strike activity plunged from 3.4 million days in 1919 to 800,000 the following year. The trend among labour was to seek measured and moderate adjustments. The post-war period witnessed success at the polls for worker candidates, with 11 elected to Ontario's legislature in 1919 and a similar number in Manitoba in 1920—emphasizing policies to improve labour rights and to introduce social welfare.

LINGUISTIC AND SOCIAL STRAINS

Canada's labour movement also experienced linguistic and religious division. In Quebec, resentment to English Canada from World War I as well as fears over initial post-war radicalism and alien values being inculcated by American-controlled international unions resulted in the clergy intensifying efforts to link with the Francophone working class by creating the *Confédération des travailleurs catholiques* in 1921. Soon with a membership of 18,000, its affiliates installed Catholic priests as counsellors and as the final authority in labour negotiations.

Quebec's Liberal government, whose control of the legislature stretched back to the turn of the century, sought to bridge modernization with respect for tradition. It tried to attract large-scale investment, which increasingly brought the provincial economy under Anglo-Canadian and American control. However, Premier Louis-Alexandre Taschereau also praised the Catholic Church's influence and that of agriculture for establishing a higher moral standard. His government increased funding to assist Francophones to take up farming. Conservative nationalism stressing *la survivance* of a Quebec steeped in a Catholic and rural heritage became more prominent. Leading in this crusade was Abbé Lionel Groulx, a cleric, historian, author, educator, and the central figure in establishing *L'Action française*, an intellectual movement transplanted from France. Its membership, though small, was influential, attracting prominent Francophones from law, education, journalism, and the Church. The group insisted that education infuse Catholic values; presented farming as instilling a higher ethical standard; and used history to buttress its cause by idealizing New France as a devout, ordered, and just society. Groulx embraced the idea of two solitudes existing between English and French; indeed, he presented Confederation as artificial and Canada's unravelling as inevitable.

Another source of discontent and division related to the ongoing mistreatment of Canada's First Peoples. They accused governments and businesses, such as timber enterprises, of seizing land never surrendered by treaty. Indigenous parents were still being coerced—by threats of cutting off government aid—to send their children to church-run boarding schools where they were forced to speak English and dress like whites, where physical and sexual abuse was common, and where deadly disease flourished in decrepit conditions. In some cases, tuberculosis produced a 50 per cent mortality rate among Native schoolchildren. An amendment in 1920 to the *Indian Act* provided the federal franchise only to First Nations peoples who moved off reserves, which removed them from the band list and any claims to reserve land. Canada's Indigenous peoples remained stereotyped by "lack of ambition, idleness, and unreliability."[1] Yet, with the fur industry in steep decline and more hunting areas denuded of stock, many First Peoples were being forced into the paid labour market, often as seasonal workers in the resource sector and as farm labourers with lower wages than whites. Some First Peoples earned a living by playing into caricatures, joining "wild west" and rodeo shows as "Indian" warriors. In the late 1920s, some 20 Cree and Ojibway men formed rival hockey teams that travelled throughout Ontario and the Northern United States where they "wore buckskin jerseys…ceremonial headdresses made of feathers," and provided "demonstrations of canoe paddling, bow-and-arrow whittling and shooting, birch-bark canoe construction, moose calling, and snowshoe making."[2]

---

1   Robin Jarvis Brownlie, "'A Better Citizen than Lots of White Men': First Nations Enfranchisement—An Ontario Case Study, 1918–1940," *Canadian Historical Review* 87 (2006): 48.

2   Andrew Holman, "Telling Stories about Indigeneity and Canadian Sport: The Spectacular Cree and Ojibway Indian Hockey Barnstorming Tour of North America, 1928," *Sport History Review*, 43 (2012): 183.

In the emerging discipline of anthropology, Canadian academics classified First Nations as being at the "bottom of a developmental hierarchy" on the basis of "agricultural proficiency, transportation infrastructure, [and] linguistic and cosmological sophistication." Duncan Campbell Scott, the Deputy Superintendent of Indian Affairs, presented assimilation as the best solution to the "Indian problem." Writing in 1920 in support of forced enfranchisement, and thus the loss of reserve rights, he stated: "our objective is to continue until there is not a single Indian in Canada that has not been absorbed into the body politic."[3] In 1923, the Ontario-based Six Nations, hoping to embarrass Canada's government into changing some of its policies toward Indigenous peoples, took their case for self-government to the League of Nations in Geneva. Some smaller countries that had battled for independence indicated support, but ultimately the League agreed this was an internal Canadian matter. In 1927, another amendment to the *Indian Act* barred First Peoples from hiring lawyers to pursue land claims against the government.

Government policy was determined that Canada remain a white, Christian, and British country, a trend reinforced by an initially weak post-war economy and the view that immigrants stole jobs. Lingering wartime anger had Germans, Austrians, and Hungarians barred from Canada until 1923. The same applied to Hutterites, Doukhobours, and Mennonites for having preached pacifism, and because many spoke a German dialect. In 1923, the Chinese head tax was replaced by changes to the *Immigration Act* that virtually barred Chinese migration to Canada. In the 1922–23 school year, Chinese parents in Victoria removed their children from classes because of the school board's decision to segregate them into separate institutions.

TURNING INWARD

Canadian foreign policy in the early post-war period could be viewed as a retreat from the high ideals and new, uplifted world order that many predicted would emerge from the war. Although Canada had fought to preserve democracy from what was portrayed as barbaric militarism, Canadian governments now recoiled from potentially risky international engagements, and the military was gutted soon after the war ended; in the 1922 federal budget, the government allocated the military a meagre $1.46 per capita. Sensitive to opinion in Quebec and seeking to build upon heightened Anglo-Canadian nationalism out of the war, Canada sought greater autonomy from the Empire. It rejected Article X of the League of Nations

---

3 Jonathan Peyton and Robert L.A. Hancock, "Anthropology, State Formation, and Hegemonic Representations of Indigenous Peoples in Canada, 1910–1939," *Native Studies Review* 17 (2008): 55, 63.

covenant, the provision providing for *collective security*, meaning that League members would commit militarily if necessary to prevent unwarranted aggression by one nation against another.

Canada took some 100 older surplus aircraft from Britain. Managed by the new Canadian Air Board, these were mainly used for civilian purposes such as surveying, supplying remote areas, and watching for forest fires. The Air Board also operated training courses for the Royal Canadian Air Force, but the federal government had sold off most of the country's training aircraft. In 1922, as a cost-cutting measure, the Department of Militia and Defence and the Air Board were amalgamated to create the Department of National Defence.

Mackenzie King was determined to avoid Canada's involvement in controversial foreign ventures, fearing the consequences for national unity. This was evident in the September 1922 Chanak Crisis. Located on the Turkish side of the Dardanelles, Chanak was guarded by a British garrison under the terms of the 1920 Treaty of Sèvres. Turk nationalists rejected the treaty and, 80,000 strong, approached Chanak, demanding its control. Britain sought a show of support from the Empire. Sensing the opportunity to make headway in English Canada, Meighen declared to a meeting of Toronto businessmen that when the "Mother Country" asked for help, the only proper response was "Ready, aye, ready, we stand by you." King believed that the massive casualties of World War I had made Anglo-Canadians less jingoistic. The Progressives, with their focus on domestic issues like the tariff, opposed participation, and nearly every Quebec MP rejected Canadian involvement. Still, wary of publicly snubbing the British and angering Anglo-Canadians, King said Canada's Parliament would decide the country's response, realizing that it would take time to recall MPs and debate the issue. The delay worked brilliantly, because before Parliament could address the matter, Britain and Turkey signed an armistice.

Closer to home, Canada further integrated with the United States, which surpassed Britain as Canada's most important trading partner. By 1921, 45.6 per cent of its exports and 69 per cent of its imports tied Canada to its southern neighbour. High tariffs encouraged the creation of more Canadian-based branch plants of American businesses in order to avoid paying duties. By 1930, American capital controlled 68 per cent of Canadian-based electrical factories, 42 per cent of machinery shops, and 41 per cent of chemical plants.

Reflecting the growing importance of the US–Canada relationship, King travelled to Washington in 1922 to meet American President Warren Harding, the first official summit between leaders of the two countries. The next year, Canada negotiated a foreign agreement for the first time without British involvement when Ernest Lapointe, Canada's fisheries minister, signed the Halibut Treaty with the United States to regulate Pacific fish stocks.

The overt anti-Americanism of Canada's earlier years dissipated. Political leaders on both sides of the border bragged of more than a century of bilateral peace, holding it up as an example to European nations. Still, Canada's "Defence Scheme #1," introduced in 1921, was designed to resist an American invasion. While most military officers thought this "a contingency too remote…to be considered," there were still many who believed "that…an Anglo-American conflict was not unthinkable," and, as such, Canadians should "keep our powder dry."[4]

Post-war Canada redeveloped its relationship with Britain to achieve greater equality. In 1923, King travelled to London to attend his first imperial conference. In the wake of the Chanak Crisis, Britain wanted to reassert leadership within the Empire. King viewed the Empire as a force for good and as a counterweight against excessive American influence, but he was also acutely aware that Canada's association with imperialism and British wars had produced dangerous internal division.

King brought Oscar Douglas (O.D.) Skelton to London as a key advisor. He first heard Skelton, the Dean of Arts at Queen's University, in a January 1922 speech at the Ottawa Canadian Club, where Skelton argued against a united Empire foreign policy. King found Skelton compelling and shared his views. Skelton saw Canada as a North American nation and was highly suspicious of Britain which, at the 1923 conference, he saw as "attempt[ing] to catch naïve colonials in the imperial web."[5]

King agreed, but did not want to appear anti-British. His goal was to replace the Empire with a "Co-operative Commonwealth" in which members would be linked by shared ideals, values, and histories, not by binding commitments. The conference dragged on for six weeks. An exasperated British Foreign Secretary, Lord Curzon, commented privately: "the obstacle has been Mackenzie King…who is obstinate, tiresome, and stupid."[6] South Africa's leader, Jan Smuts, came up with a compromise final communiqué, which advanced the idea of autonomy within the context of the Empire.

In 1924, Canada rejected the proposed Geneva Protocol to reinvigorate the principle of collective security at the League of Nations. Instead, Canada argued that a proviso should be added to Article x stating that no country could be compelled into an act of war without approval from its government. Senator Raoul Dandurand, Canada's representative at the League, compared the country to a "fireproof house," whose distance protected it from the flames of war that so often seemed to engulf Europe.

---

4   Galen Roger Perras and Katrina E. Kellner, "'A Perfectly Logical and Sensible Thing': Billy Mitchell Advocates a Canadian-American Aerial Alliance against Japan," *The Journal of Military History* 72 (2008): 798.

5   Norman Hillmer, *O.D. Skelton: A Portrait of Canadian Ambition* (Toronto: University of Toronto Press, 2015), 90.

6   R. MacGregor Dawson, *William Lyon Mackenzie King: A Political Biography, 1874–1923* (London: Methuen & Co Ltd., 1958), 477.

In other respects, Canada enhanced its presence abroad. In 1925, it spent an unprecedented $1.3 million to acquire a neoclassical mansion in Trafalgar Square to serve as the new home of its High Commissioner in Britain. Canada also began professionalizing the Department of External Affairs. The elderly Sir Joseph Pope, who had served as undersecretary since the creation of the department in 1909, had managed a small staff that focused on passport work and matters of protocol. King turned to Skelton to replace Pope in 1925. Determined to enhance departmental capacity and skill, and with a budget to recruit, Skelton insisted that those shaping Canada's foreign policy have a university degree, preferably in law, history, political science, or economics. Skelton personally marked exams and he interviewed the top prospects. The recruitment campaign attracted people like Rhodes Scholar Norman Robertson and future prime minister Lester Pearson, who also attended Oxford.

SOCIAL AND CULTURAL CROSSCURRENTS

By the early 1920s, the number of Canadians living in urban settings—communities of at least 1,000 people—surpassed the rural population. By mid-decade, at a time when the country's population stood at 9 million, Toronto reached 600,000 people, a 50 per cent increase from a generation earlier. Montreal, Canada's largest urban centre, grew from 750,000 to 1 million during the 1920s. Canadians moved to new suburban areas such as Outremont in Montreal, Rosedale in Toronto, and Point Grey in Vancouver. Land on the urban fringe was cheaper, more people could afford cars, and in many cities streetcar service extended to outlying areas. Suburbs were popular among the growing middle class. Many were inspired by the idea of a semi-rural estate. The suburbs also provided segregation from poorer Canadians and immigrants, who often faced restrictive housing covenants. In Westdale, a suburb of Hamilton, housing developers promised to keep out "Negroes, Asiatics, Russians, Serbs, Rumanians, Turks, Armenians…[and] Jews."[7]

Canadians were becoming more mobile. Between 1920 and 1924, the average price of a car dropped 38 per cent—dipping below $700—and dealers offered finance plans that brought vehicles within reach of many members of the working class. By the end of the decade, Canadians owned 1.2 million automobiles, resulting in burgeoning road construction to keep pace with demand. Cars made for a more fast-paced life, though they also gave urbanites greater means to seek tranquility in the surrounding countryside, something loathed by many farmers. Cars also provided more vacation options. In 1925, over half of the 104,000 visitors to Rocky Mountain Park—later renamed as Banff—arrived by car.

---

7   Richard Harris, *Creeping Conformity: How Canada Became Suburban, 1900–1960* (Toronto: University of Toronto Press, 2004), 88.

Increased mobility was also evident in the expansion of air travel, which built upon advancements in the sophistication and reliability of aircraft during World War I. In 1920, the Canadian Air Service Association was established, followed by the Commercial Air Pilots' Association of Canada the next year. The post office inaugurated air service in 1927, starting with Rimouski (where trans-Atlantic liners docked) to Montreal. Bush pilots served remote areas—mainly mining and timber operations—and surveyed land. By the end of the decade, the Ontario Provincial Air Service had 33 aircraft and patrolled 50 million hectares of forests. In 1926, Western Canada Airways was created, mostly serving remote communities in northern Manitoba and Ontario. In 1930, it was renamed as Canadian Airways Limited after purchasing some small eastern airlines and became a major carrier of freight and passengers.

Canadians embraced a stronger consumer ethos during the 1920s. Canada's major department stores, Eaton's and Simpson's, expanded their factories and, with improved transportation networks, their mail-order departments. Canadians became enamoured with American products, clamouring for the latest improvements and trends. They also embraced American cultural exports. For every homegrown magazine Canadians bought, eight were imported from the United States. By 1923, 98 per cent of the motion pictures seen by Canadians were American-made.

The advent of radio broke down the isolation of many Canadians, linking them to a broader, primarily American, mass culture. The first US radio station, KDKA in Pittsburgh, began broadcasting in November 1920. One month later in Montreal, the Marconi Company started station XWA. Canada had 30 radio stations by 1923, and that number doubled by the end of the decade. However, most Canadian stations had weak signals. Those living near the international border typically tuned in to American stations that carried slickly produced comedy, drama, and variety shows. By the end of the 1920s, about 80 per cent of programs broadcast on Canadian stations were American in origin.

The federal government appointed a Royal Commission on Broadcasting in 1928. Although chaired by a pillar of capitalism, Bank of Commerce president Sir John Aird, it recommended a public monopoly over broadcasting. However, soon after the commission reported, Canada entered the Great Depression and there was little appetite to spend large sums to create a public broadcasting network. The result was a hybrid system: the creation of a public broadcaster along with the maintenance of privately owned stations.

Americanization also affected Canadian sports. In 1924, the Boston millionaire Charles Adams paid $15,000 as a franchise fee to establish the Bruins, the first US-based National Hockey League (NHL) team. With the Bruins drawing as many as 10,000 spectators a game, others were enticed. In 1925, the Pittsburgh Pirates joined the league, and in New York City, the millionaire bootlegger William "Big Bill" Dwyer paid what was considered the astounding price of $75,000 to move Hamilton's NHL squad to the just-completed Madison Square Garden, where they became the New York Americans. Their success at the box office produced a second New York team in 1926, the Rangers. Before the decade ended, the Chicago Black Hawks and Detroit Cougars joined the NHL, thus making it a league of six American and four Canadian teams (the Montreal Canadiens, Montreal Maroons, Ottawa Senators, and Toronto Maple Leafs).

Canadian cultural nationalism manifested itself in other areas. The *Canadian Bookman*, a literary review founded in 1919, promoted domestic works, as did the Canadian Authors Association started two years later. Bestselling books expressed nationalistic and romanticized themes, such as Jean McIlwraith's *Kinsmen at War*, "a novel that depicts the star-crossed love of a Canadian and an American in the context of the War of 1812."[8] Canadian art began attracting more notice and respect with the appearance of the Group of Seven. Several members—Frank Varley, Arthur Lismer, and A.Y. Jackson—had recently been official Canadian war artists. The catalogue to their first show, held in May 1920 in Toronto, stated that their aim was to "paint Canada in a new way."[9] To do so, they applied the techniques of European impressionism and post-impressionism to present the harsh beauty of the Canadian Shield as symbolizing the country's strength, beauty, and grandeur.

MORALITY

Change in the 1920s generated concerns over declining moral standards. The decade witnessed the weakening of the church-based social gospel movement. More Canadians joined secular service clubs like the Rotarians and Foresters, through which, besides contributing to the community, they pursued professional contacts and obtained services like life insurance. To reinvigorate Protestantism, thousands of Methodist, Congregationalist, and Presbyterian churches merged to form the United Church, which was formally founded on June 10, 1925. With nearly 700,000 members, it became Canada's largest Protestant denomination. However, it was criticized in some quarters for its theological liberalism and active social agenda.

The collapse of prohibition generated consternation. Federal prohibition ended in early 1919. Before the year ended, Quebec legalized the sale of beer and light wine. Although charges for drunkenness dropped dramatically under prohibition, large numbers of Canadians ignored the legislation. Between 1920 and 1929, the annual

---

8 Jody Mason, "Anti-modernist Paradox in Canada: The Graphic Publishers (1925–32) and the Case of Madge Macbeth," *Journal of Canadian Studies* 45 (2011): 106.

9 Peter Mellen, *The Group of Seven* (Toronto: McClelland & Stewart, 1970), 98.

number of Canadians convicted under liquor control acts nearly doubled to 19,000. With the United States maintaining prohibition until 1933, many Canadians became involved in "rum running" to America. The Bronfman family made a fortune by creating a series of heavily guarded liquor warehouses near the Saskatchewan-American border that shipped as many as 10,000 cases of alcohol monthly to America.

Moderation leagues emerged in every province to promote government liquor sales, arguing that this would undercut criminal activities and massively raise public revenues. In an October 1920 plebiscite, two-thirds of Quebec voters approved government-owned liquor stores. The next year, voters in British Columbia and the Yukon followed, as did Manitoba in 1923, Alberta in 1924, and Saskatchewan and Newfoundland in 1925. Ontario's deeply religious attorney general, W.F. Nickle, remained steadfast for prohibition, but his more pragmatic boss, Conservative Premier Howard Ferguson, believed it was not working, wanted the revenue, and saw the issuance of liquor licences as an excellent means of establishing patronage-based loyalty. As the December 1926 provincial election approached, Ferguson said that if returned to office the Conservatives would approve government liquor sales. With another legislative majority, Ontario's first liquor store opened on June 1, 1927. Before the end of the decade, New Brunswick and Nova Scotia legalized liquor. Only Prince Edward Island remained dry, until 1948.

The American government accused Canada of making little effort to stem the flow of booze south. While most smugglers went to great lengths to hide their stash, poorly paid customs officials often took bribes to look the other way. Many people romanticized bootleggers, even as they turned to violence to protect and pursue their business. The potential profits were huge. A $16 case of liquor in Vancouver could fetch $80 in Seattle. Fleets of Maritime schooners set sail for the Caribbean or for French-owned St. Pierre and Miquelon to get cheap rum and whiskey. Then they anchored just outside the 12-mile (19-kilometre) limit of America's coastal waters. At night, they transferred their cargo onto small boats which would then sneak the liquor ashore. By the mid-1920s, an estimated 50 per cent of Maritime ships were involved in the liquor trade. This produced international disputes, as American coastal authorities searched, seized, and often shot at Canadian boats in international waters, sometimes with fatal consequences.

Moral qualms also focused upon adolescents. They were staying in school longer since, besides compulsory attendance laws—except Quebec until 1943—high school entrance exams and fees were waived. Keeping young people out of the labour force longer encouraged the appearance of a distinct youth culture. The press carried sensationalist accounts of girls wearing sexualized flapper-type dresses, bobbing their hair like starlets, and applying makeup to look older, and of boys joining gangs, drinking, and turning to crime. Seeking greater control, authorities applied the 1908

Figure 5.2 Destruction of illegally produced liquor at Elk Lake, Ontario, 1925.

Juvenile Delinquents Act more widely by creating more juvenile courts and probation programs.

For women, some changes seemed transformational, though less so when considered against the resistance they generated. Many women hoped to build upon obtaining the vote to establish greater equality. However, in the 1921 federal election, just five women ran for office and only one was successful, Agnes MacPhail, a schoolteacher who represented the Progressives in the Ontario constituency of South Grey by Georgian Bay. At the provincial level, women gained little political presence, and only in Western Canada. Louise McKinney was elected to the Alberta legislature in 1917 as part of the short-lived Non-Partisan League, for which Irene Parlby also won as a candidate in the 1919 provincial election. In British Columbia, Mary Ellen Smith, a Liberal, won a 1918 Vancouver by-election, succeeding her late husband in representing the riding. Nellie McClung sat as a Liberal member of the Alberta legislature from 1921 to 1926.

In Quebec, women were still trying to obtain the provincial vote. Opposition from the Catholic Church prompted the *Fédération nationale Saint-Jean-Baptiste* to officially end its support for women's suffrage in 1920. Two years later, Marie Gérin-Lajoie, president of the *Fédération*, formed the Provincial Franchise Committee, with one English-speaking and one French-speaking section. Archbishop Paul-Eugène Roy denounced the initiative, casting suffrage as an Anglo-led movement that would divert women from their primary roles as producers and protectors of the French-Canadian family. Gérin-Lajoie took her appeal to the International Union of Leagues of Catholic Women, but her efforts yielded nothing. Soon after, she resigned as president.

More young women were attending high school, but more classes in domestic science, typing, stenography, and bookkeeping accompanied this trend. Female university undergraduates nearly doubled over the decade to 7,500, or almost a quarter of Canada's university population. Over 80 per cent were enrolled in arts, compared to women making up less than 2 per cent of medical students and less than 0.25 per cent of those in law.

The decade conveyed liberalizing fashion trends for women. Corsets and bloomers went out of style. Skirts still went to the ankle, though the look was slimmer and more form fitting, suggestive of independent and active woman—or what became known as the "New Woman." The importance of beauty became more prominent with the rise of mass advertising, including for face creams, cosmetics, mouthwashes, and deodorants. Women also expanded their presence in sports, helped by changing clothing styles that gave them more freedom of movement. Lawn tennis and softball became more popular for women, and more university sporting teams included women. In 1920, Queen's University's women's basketball team played its first intercollegiate game at McGill. Fanny "Bobbie" Rosenfeld, whose nickname referred to her short, bobbed hair, became a widely celebrated top-ranked female athlete, capturing Canada's first Olympic track and field medals, a gold and a silver, in 1928. Yet, popular misconceptions continued—that athletic women were too masculine, risked their reproductive organs, and had puny babies.

The image of the "New Woman" was young, urban, white, slender, attractive, adventuresome, aggressive, and openly flirtatious. Hollywood presented women as more liberated and sexual, as personified by the fun-loving flapper. The 1920s also brought form-fitting one-piece bathing suits and the beginnings of beauty pageants. To some, the "New Woman" reflected a society that had turned away from prudish pre-war restraints, but to many others, she became an object of scorn—immoral, vain, and irresponsible.

Contrasting with the image of the 1920s as a period of female liberation was the expectation that unmarried women retain their purity. With the growing influence of Freudian psychology came greater recognition that women had strong sexual drives, but it was still felt that female sexuality had to remain within the confines of marriage, unlike the unstated notion of young men sowing their wild oats.

Consternation mounted over women having fewer children. Between 1921 and 1931, the fertility rate of women aged 15 to 49 dropped by a quarter to just under 100 per 1,000. This was primarily due to a declining infant mortality rate and the fact that in growing urban areas (as opposed to farms) children rarely contributed to, but nearly always drained, the family income. However, many people focused on careerism as the primary threat to women's commitment to the family. Between 1921 and 1931, the total number of working women grew by nearly half to reach 665,859, though this translated into only 16.9 per cent of Canada's labour force. Employment options for women overwhelmingly remained within gender-based stereotypes: secretaries, teachers, nurses, waitresses, textile workers, and domestics. Marriage and motherhood continued to be portrayed as the most important roles for women. In the early 1920s, *Maclean's* magazine started a Bride's Club section whose message was that true happiness was found in the home. Letters to magazine personnel columns showed that men desired wives who would tend to the domestic sphere; the "business girl" was portrayed as selfish and vain.

Mothers faced increased pressure to follow advice from a growing number of healthcare professionals. More women were delivering babies in hospitals, and those babies were more likely to survive. Between 1921 and 1929, Canada's infant mortality rate dropped from 135 to 76 per 1,000. Many women welcomed the professional guidance, though the dominant message was that no one should ignore it. The federal government encouraged the trend by creating the Division of Child Welfare in 1919. Placed under the direction of Dr. Helen MacMurchy, who the Ontario government had hired to develop strategies to reduce infant mortality a decade earlier, the Division disseminated information on household hygiene and achieving rapid success in everything from breastfeeding to baby bowel movements. Doctors appeared to have more to say about women's bodies. Medical professionals still commonly expressed the view that menstruating women required relaxation or that women with jobs outside the home suffered more stillbirths.

POLITICAL KING

While Canadians struggled with social change, controversies and the need for compromise continued to typify the political arena. To hold Quebec, Prime Minister King increasingly relied upon advice from Ernest Lapointe who, in 1924, moved from fisheries minister to justice minister. Until his death in 1941, Lapointe served as King's Quebec lieutenant, sitting next to the prime minister in Parliament.

Lapointe sought to increase French-Canadian representation in the cabinet and the civil service and to reduce the influence of those whom he regarded as harbouring anti-French attitudes. There was rampant speculation that he was responsible for derailing Justice Lyman Duff's bid to become Chief Justice of Canada's Supreme Court because he was regarded as insensitive to French Canada. In other areas, Lapointe, like King, was pragmatic rather than ideological. For example, to bolster the strength of the Liberal government outside of Quebec, particularly in the Prairies, Lapointe was flexible on the matter of tariff reductions.

In the 1924 Speech from the Throne, the Liberals promised fewer taxes, a balanced budget, and lower tariffs. Robert Forke, the new leader of the Progressive Party and later a member of King's cabinet, said he would work with the government to produce the details. Things became more complicated after Labour MP J.S. Woodsworth proposed an amendment to reduce tariffs on necessities of life and to make up for lost government revenue by implementing steeper taxes. These measures reflected Progressive policies. However, Forke and his supporters feared that if they backed Woodsworth, the Tories, despite favouring protectionism, would join them to defeat the Liberal budget and force an election.

Forke's decision to support the Liberals drew fire from more doctrinaire Progressives who accused him of placing politics above principle. Fourteen Progressives, almost all from Alberta, broke ranks, not just to support Woodsworth, but also to form a separate parliamentary bloc they called the "Ginger Group," named after Albert "Ginger" Goodwin, a perceived paragon of principle who was slain while resisting conscription.

With his budget approved and the Progressives imploding, King stepped up appeals to farmers by reintroducing the Crow's Nest Pass rate in 1925. He also promised Progressives who supported him that he would make good on a 1922 pledge to return land taken from the Prairie provinces in 1905 to entice railway developers and homesteaders.

King continued to face discontent in the Maritimes. In June 1925, the Liberals received a shock in Nova Scotia, a province they had governed for 43 years and where the Tories held only three seats. Running on a "provincial rights" platform, the Conservatives reversed the tally, winning 40 of 43 seats. In August, New Brunswick replaced a minority Liberal government with a strong Conservative majority.

Several advisors warned King to delay a federal election. However, he remained confident because the Liberals had won six recent federal by-elections. King stumbled on the campaign trail, presenting "blandly middle-of-the-road policies."[10] The economy remained weak, and Arthur Meighen appeared confident and definitive with his call for higher tariffs to protect Canadian jobs. On election night, October 29, the Conservatives took 116 seats compared to 99 for the Liberals. The badly fractured Progressives dropped to 24 seats. King lost his riding of North York, though he was soon re-elected to Parliament in a by-election in Prince Albert, Saskatchewan.

Responding to this seeming political disaster, King proved that beneath his rather dull exterior lay a "bold and...daring tactician."[11] Many, including some within his

---

10 Hillmer, *O.D. Skelton*, 139.
11 Dawson, *William Lyon Mackenzie King*, 77.

own party, called on him to resign. Initially, King said he intended to do so. However, he asked Governor General Julian Byng that, if Meighen could not command the confidence of Parliament, would the Liberals then be given a chance to govern. Upon further reflection and after consulting his caucus, King decided not to hand over power; instead, he would let Parliament decide the fate of his government. He counted on support from the Progressives and two Labour MPs, convinced they would not back the high-tariff, pro-business Tories.

Parliament convened on January 7, 1926. The Liberals' Speech from the Throne was a clear play for Progressive support. It promised to create a non-partisan Tariff Board, to reduce freight rates, and to speed construction of the Hudson Bay railway to provide Western Canada with better international trade outlets. For the Maritimes, the government said it would appoint a Royal Commission to investigate the region's grievances. King also sought to gain support from Parliament's two Labour MPs, J.S. Woodsworth and A.A. Heaps, by pledging to create an Old Age Pension scheme. King had declared support for Old Age Pensions at the 1919 Liberal Party convention, but ignored this after becoming prime minister. The situation for elderly Canadians without financial means was desperate. Many were forced to live at places like the Ontario County Refuge where, in the early 1940s, it was reported that 96 seniors slept in the attic, 9 in hallways, and 16 in the basement.

The challenges confronting King went beyond the need to build bridges with other parties. In January 1926, allegations surfaced that numerous customs officials, including several high-ranking ones, had been complicit in smuggling liquor to the United States. King bought time by authorizing a parliamentary committee to investigate the emerging scandal.

The April 1926 federal budget introduced tax cuts and tariff reductions. In spring, the Old Age Pension Bill passed through Parliament. As well, a Royal Commission on the Maritimes was appointed under the respected British jurist Sir Arthur Rae Duncan. There was also better news for King on the economy. By the first quarter of 1926, industrial employment had rebounded to its highest level in six years.

In June, the parliamentary committee examining the customs scandal issued a damning report, citing widespread graft. Realizing that Progressive support for his government was gone, King asked Byng to dissolve Parliament and to call an election. Byng refused, insisting that Meighen's Tories, who held the most seats in Parliament, be given a chance to govern—something that King himself had requested when he had considered relinquishing power following the election. King now said the decision was not Byng's to make; rather, his role was simply to execute the prime minister's wishes. To do otherwise, King argued, was to throw Canada back to the time when it was ruled by the decree of governors.

On June 28, King resigned and Byng asked Meighen to form a government. It lasted three days. Meighen then asked Byng to call an election. With no other possible government, the governor general agreed. To King, the sequence of events demonstrated Byng's contempt for Canada's Parliament and favouritism for the

Figure 5.3 Governor General Lord Byng

Tories. King rallied Canadians based upon criticism of British interference and protecting Canadian independence. The Liberals triumphed with a majority of 116 seats, compared to 91 Conservatives. A dejected Meighen asked the Tories to find a new leader, while the Progressives, left with just 11 seats, spiralled toward political oblivion.

The new Liberal government was sworn in on September 26. A week later, King travelled to London to attend another imperial conference. He approached the gathering with more confidence than he had three years earlier. Besides his new mandate from Canadians, Britain was no longer pressuring for a common imperial foreign policy or defence arrangements. The previous year, Mackenzie King's government said that Canada would not be bound by the Locarno Treaty, under which the signatories, including Britain, agreed to defend the borders of France, Belgium, and Germany.

O.D. Skelton, who accompanied King to the 1926 Imperial Conference, favoured an unequivocal statement of Canadian independence. King thought this would anger Britain's many staunch supporters in English Canada. Still, he worked to redefine the relationship between Britain and the dominions. The conference's *Balfour Report* (named for Britain's Colonial Secretary who chaired the conference) spoke of "communities within the British Empire…equal in status, in no way subordinate one to another in any aspect of their domestic or external affairs, though united by a common allegiance to the Crown."[12] King also convinced the British to establish a High Commission in Canada through which government-to-government correspondence would proceed, thus affirming the governor-general's role as ceremonial. However, "the umbilical cord with the mother country was not completely severed."[13] It would take another five years for Britain to provide Canada with complete control over its foreign policy in the Statute of Westminster.

In 1927, Canada was elected to the League of Nations Security Council for a two-year term, the first among the British Dominions. London was not pleased,

12 Hillmer, *O.D. Skelton*, 154.

13 Lita Rose Betcherman, *Ernest Lapointe: Mackenzie King's Great Quebec Lieutenant* (Toronto: University of Toronto Press, 2002), 127.

fearing public disagreements between the two countries, and King was leery, believing the role could place Canada in the forefront of contentious international disputes. However, Skelton helped convince King that Canada should be seen as supportive of the League and that being part of its inner decision-making circle would raise Canada's international profile. To King's relief, during Canada's term, the League did not deal with especially controversial matters.

That same year Canada established a diplomatic lega-tion in Washington. Although one rung below an embassy, this was nevertheless a major development for Canada. Befitting it, King's government spent $500,000 to acquire a mansion in the heart of Washington's diplomatic quarter. Soon after, the United States reciprocated by establishing a legation in Ottawa. The following April, Sir William Clark, formerly comptroller general of Britain's Department of Overseas Trade, became the first High Commissioner to Canada. To maintain balance between French and English Canada, in September, Canada's Office of the Commissioner General in Paris, which had been established in 1882, was upgraded to a legation. France then established the same level of representation in Ottawa. In 1929, Canada opened another legation in Tokyo; Japan was then Canada's fourth largest trading partner.

Figure 5.4 Canadian Prime Minister William Lyon Mackenzie King and British Prime Minister Stanley Baldwin leaving a memorial service at Westminster Abbey during the 1926 Imperial Conference.

Although expanding its presence, and perhaps prestige, abroad, Canada continued to reject collective security. The only international treaty the King government enthusiasti-cally endorsed was the 1928 Kellogg-Briand Pact that sought to outlaw war as an instrument for settling international disputes, an agreement many sarcastically labelled as a "big international kiss."

By the late 1920s, pacifism had gained a considerable following in Canada, coming to include many who belonged to farm, women's, students', church, and mainstream labour organizations. As in Britain and the United States, a number of books written by Canadian Great War veterans highlighted the gruesome and soul-destroying nature of the conflict, the most notable being *All Else Is Folly* in 1929 by Peregrine Acland and *Generals Die in Bed* in 1930 by Charles Yale Harrison. Yet, Canada's commemoration of the war throughout the 1920s in official memorials, service rolls, stained glass church windows, art, and most popular literature continued to convey reverence for those who sacrificed, pride in the country's battlefield accomplishments, and that the struggle to defeat Germany preserved freedom. In 1928, the Armistice Ceremonial Committee of Canada was formed. Led by prominent politicians, religious leaders, and other well-known public figures, it campaigned to give Armistice Day greater prominence (at the time it coincided with Thanksgiving). In 1931, the date was changed to November 11 to mark the end of the war, and the name was changed to Remembrance Day. The day brought prayers for peace, but was primarily about commemorating the efforts and sacrifices of those who fought, not to promote pacifism.

In Parliament, King faced new opposition. In late 1927, the Conservatives selected R.B. Bennett of Calgary as their new leader. First elected to the assembly of the Northwest Territories in 1908, seven years later, at age 35, Bennett became leader of Alberta's Conservative Party. Profoundly self-assured, often overbearing, and with an incredible capacity for work, Bennett was so determined to succeed that he even chose to eat six meals a day because he believed he required a more physically imposing presence for politics. Elected to the federal Parliament in 1911, five years later he assumed the position of director of the National Service Board. Passed over for a cabinet post by Meighen, he resigned in 1921. Before returning to Parliament four years later, he amassed a personal fortune through shrewd investments and by inheriting a principal share in the E.B. Eddy paper company. King dismissed his new opponent as inexperienced and bombastic.

Another political challenge was the persistence of campaigns for greater provincial rights. In Ontario and Quebec, there was growing concern that King was trying to grab control over hydroelectric power on international waterways, a lucrative source of revenue and engine of economic development. Ontario Premier Howard Ferguson and Quebec's Alexandre-Louis Taschereau formed an alliance to resist Ottawa. Although contributing to intergovernmental discord, this also created an incentive to eliminate a longstanding barrier to national unity: Ontario's Regulation 17. Ferguson realized the legislation complicated his ability to form a common front with Quebec. In 1925, he appointed a Commission of Inquiry to examine bilingual schools; its favourable report on their quality resulted in the repeal of Regulation 17 in 1927. This also hastened the end of *L'Action française* in 1928, because the most prominent symbol of Anglophone intransigence was removed. However, also contributing to the organization's demise were intense internal divisions and suspicions over a secessionist agenda.

King had other reasons for optimism. Besides enjoying a majority government, the economy continued to gain steam. By 1927, unemployment dipped below 3 per cent. A buying frenzy was emerging on Canadian stock markets, fuelled by rising employment and income and very low margin requirements for purchasing stock. Everyone with a little extra cash seemed to be dabbling in the stock market, oblivious to the fact that stocks were becoming increasingly overvalued.

The federal government achieved *rapprochement* with the Maritimes as a result of the Duncan Royal Commission, which reported in 1927. The commissioners agreed that the region was unduly suffering and recommended increases in federal subsidies, lower freight rates, and improvements to rail, ferry, and port services; still, King was happy that they did not personally blame his government for regional problems. The Liberals responded with some relief on rail rates, new subsidies for Maritime coking plants, port improvements in Halifax and Saint John, and money for a second ferry to Prince Edward Island.

The Liberals also presented themselves as responding to social need with the first distribution of Old Age Pension cheques in 1927. The number of state-supported pensioners grew from 2,712 in 1928 to 42,553 by 1930. However, the program was modest. Only British subjects aged 70 or older with an annual income of less than $125 qualified for the maximum $20 monthly pension, and in assessing assets, their children's income was counted.

NEW CANADIANS AND WOMEN AS PERSONS

In 1925, with Canada's economy starting to recover and requiring more labour, the federal government paid the country's major railways, which were also in the steam-ship business, to bring immigrants to Canada. The plan was to target people from Britain, but not enough could be attracted. As such, Canada's government once again turned to Central and Eastern Europe. Racism spiked in response, especially since a high proportion of these newcomers were Catholic.

The white-robed and hooded Ku Klux Klan, the racist American organization, set up shop in Canada. Its strongest presence was in southwestern Ontario (focused against Catholics and blacks), British Columbia (against Asians), and Alberta and Saskatchewan (against Eastern and Central European Catholics and Jews). In Oakville, some 40 kilometres west of Toronto, Klan members descended on a home where a black man cohabitated with a white woman. A cross was burned on the front lawn and the man was warned that if he was "ever seen walking down the street with a white girl again," the Klan "would attend to him."[14]

In Saskatchewan, Klan membership was estimated as high as 40,000 out of a population of 900,000. Liberal Premier James Gardiner attacked the organization as certain to bring violent racial discord, as it had in America. Saskatchewan members insisted they were different, loathe to use violence to keep Canada Protestant and

14 Constance Backhouse, *Colour-Coded: A Legal History of Racism in Canada, 1900–1950* (Toronto: The Osgoode Society for Canadian Legal History by the University of Toronto Press, 1999), 174.

British. Saskatchewan Conservative leader J.T.M. Anderson demanded that Ottawa cut immigration and worked closely with the Klan to rally support. Gardiner's opponents also gained ground, legitimately attacking his government's widespread use of patronage. Technically, the Liberals won the 1929 election with 28 seats and 45.5 per cent of the vote compared to 24 Tories with 36.5 per cent, but 11 Progressives and independents, determined to rid Saskatchewan of Liberal machine-style patronage politics, supported Anderson, who became premier.

For women, compared to immigrants, the late-1920s yielded better results, at least symbolically. Seeking to build on the election of women to the House of Commons and provincial legislatures, pressure grew for women to be declared as eligible to sit in Canada's appointed Senate. This had been denied because Section 24 of the BNA Act identified a qualified "person" for the Senate with the pronoun "he." Five prominent Alberta women—Emily Murphy, Nellie McClung, Louisa McKinney, Irene Parlby, and Henrietta Muir Edwards—launched the *Persons Case*, as it became known.

On five occasions between 1920 and 1927, the federal government refused demands to change eligibility for the Senate to include women, in large part because it feared a backlash from Quebec where the Taschereau government was on record as opposed. Murphy—who, in 1916, had become the first female magistrate in the British Empire—noted that under the *Supreme Court of Canada Act*, five people, acting as a unit, could petition the Court on interpretations of the constitution. Justice Minister Ernest Lapointe, who sympathized with these women (who became known as the Famous Five), backed their challenge to Section 24. In April 1928, Canada's Supreme Court ruled against the women. Adopting a strict interpretation of the BNA Act, it concluded that if the term "person" was meant to include women, the framers of the constitution would not have specifically linked it to the pronoun "he." The case was appealed to the Judicial Committee of the Privy Council in London, England. In October 1929, Lord Sankey, speaking for the Council, compared the BNA Act to "a living tree capable of growth and expansion within its natural limits,"[15] meaning that it considered the Supreme Court's interpretation of a "person" as too narrow and thus overruled it.

CONCLUSION

The 1920s often seem portrayed in terms of how the decade compared to what came before and after. Reacting to the horrific human costs of World War I, people seemed

---

15 John T. Saywell, *The Lawmakers: Judicial Power and the Shaping of Canadian Federalism* (Toronto: University of Toronto Press, 2002), 192.

Figure 5.5 Prime Minister Mackenzie King and guests unveiling a plaque commemorating the 10-year anniversary of the *Persons Case*.

to be cutting loose and living for the day; and when compared to the Great Depression that followed, the 1920s certainly "roared" economically. However, the roar can also be characterized as symbolizing the political and social turbulence of the decade, one in which the currents of change moved in different, and often contradictory, directions.

Canada grew more autonomous, urban, industrial, and North American in its economy, culture, and outlook. Consumerism, and eventually a stock market buying frenzy, took hold, though only later in the decade and after a deep recession. While often presented in popular memory as a period of freewheeling capitalism, the decade also saw important, though limited, breakthroughs with social welfare, such as Old Age Pensions.

Independent, active, and sexually liberated women became more prominent, though not until the end of the decade were Canadian women accepted as "persons" under the law. While Canadians celebrated the triumph of democracy with the defeat of Germany, the 1920s brought intense xenophobia and the busting of unions. Stronger expressions of Canadian nationalism contrasted against pronounced French–English discord, strong regionalism, the rise of third parties, and increased economic and cultural integration with the United States. While Canada became an independent actor on the world stage, it used its voice to weaken the League of Nations.

The decade began with Arthur Meighen as prime minister. Although unequalled as a parliamentary debater, his determination to steadfastly stand by principles often made him appear rigid and headstrong. He regarded King with contempt, as making policy according to the whims of public opinion. Yet, King remained prime minister for all but one year of the decade. By balancing between often competing interests, King effectively directed the ship of state through the turbulence of the post-war period. Nevertheless, even this master politician, who, in defying the odds, retained power after losing it in 1925, could not cope, at least initially, with the Great Depression that followed in the 1930s.

6 COLLAPSE, RETRENCHMENT, AND THE PROMISE OF REFORM, 1929–1939

INTRODUCTION

On October 29, 1929, the Wall Street stock market in New York crashed. Hundreds of millions of dollars in assets evaporated. The event rapidly spread to Canadian markets, given the close economic ties between the two countries. On Toronto's Mining Exchange, the value of shares plummeted from $710 million in 1929 to $140 million a year later, while in Vancouver over the same period, the drop in the annual number of shares traded went from $143 million to $9 million.

What became a decade-long economic catastrophe devastated millions of Canadians. The once gainfully employed turned to soup kitchens; hundreds of thousands abandoned their farms; bartering became common, as people had no cash; and the personal psychological toll was incalculable. Canada turned away from international engagement, even in the face of increasingly dire threats to world peace, to focus on the calamity at home. Worry grew over social disorder as violent clashes occurred. Doubts multiplied over the ability of the prevailing political structure to respond adequately to the economic collapse. Some political leaders turned reactionary and repressive. Desperate Canadians turned to saviours preaching unorthodox and sometimes radical ideas, people who often gained influence and power by condemning the federal government. However, a crisis of such magnitude also compelled more and more people to rethink assumptions that encouraged reform and conciliation, such as the fact that being unemployed did not indicate personal laziness or failure and that governments had to accept more responsibility for the welfare of Canadians.

ECONOMIC COLLAPSE

The stock market crash was symbolic of deeper structural problems. Over the latter half of the 1920s, rampant speculation grossly inflated the value of many company stocks. In the United States in 1929, new investment in companies totalled $3.2 billion, compared to an $87 billion increase in the value of their shares traded. Speculation and overvaluation also became prevalent on Canadian markets, with many brokerage houses knowingly selling hyper-inflated stocks and ratcheting up prices through insider trading. Soon after the crash, Ike Solloway, who ran Toronto's largest brokerage house, was fined $225,000 (approximately $4 million today) and sentenced to four months in jail for fraud.

Government policy exacerbated the downturn. In 1928, the United States raised interest rates to contract the money supply, hoping thereby to cool off the stock market and to get people to put their money into safer investments like bonds. Over the course of 1929, the tight money policy began to slow down activity in other areas, such as home construction. Consumer spending declined and unemployment moved upwards. When the stock market crashed, already skittish consumers reacted by retracting their spending significantly, thus magnifying the impact. The downturn also intensified due to the American Federal Reserve Board's decision not to re-inflate markets to keep credit flowing. To protect jobs, the United States Congress raised tariffs under the 1930 *Smoot-Hawley Act*. This sparked similar responses by other governments, including Canada's, producing a dramatic drop in global trade. Whereas the value of Canadian exports in 1928 was $1.3 billion, by 1932 it had fallen to $0.5 billion.

Governments were woefully unprepared to deal with the collapse. They provided few social services and those offered were miserly. This reflected limited state revenues, traditionally modest roles for government, and a determination to keep taxes low. Local governments still provided the bulk of welfare, mainly through modest make-work projects. The still-prevalent view was that the unemployed could find jobs if they truly wanted.

In January 1930, a gathering of Western Canadian mayors in Winnipeg made a collective plea to the federal government to provide money for public works. Prime Minister King believed that the decline was a temporary downturn in the normal business cycle, and that it was unnecessary for the government to assume additional costs.

In Ottawa, Canada's two Labour MPs, J.S. Woodsworth and A.A. Heaps, proposed that the federal government establish an unemployment insurance program. The Conservatives backed the proposal despite having opposed unemployment insurance in the recent past. Goaded in Parliament, King uncharacteristically lost his temper and declared that he would not give an extra nickel to any provincial Conservative government. Soon after making the remark, he confided in his diary that he likely went too far.

Still, as the July 1930 federal election approached, King felt optimistic about his chances against the new Conservative leader, Richard Bedford Bennett. However, King had not convinced enough Canadians that he had an effective strategy to turn the economy around. Bennett, a tremendously successful businessperson, said he knew how to create wealth and had a plan, namely to "blast" Canada out of the Depression by raising tariffs to protect Canadian markets and jobs. A powerful speaker, "Bonfire" Bennett as some called him (once clocked at more than 200 words per minute) boldly declared: "The Conservative party is going to find work for all who are willing to work, or perish in the attempt."[1]

Figure 6.1 Prime Minister Richard Bedford Bennett speaking in Toronto.

During the 6-week campaign, Bennett travelled over 22,000 kilometres by rail and road and delivered nearly 200 speeches. His rallies attracted thousands and were carried over radio. With mass production, the price of radios dropped by 75 per cent over the 1930s, and between 1924 and 1940, radio ownership in Canadian households grew eightfold to top 81 per cent. Bennett was well suited to this medium, especially compared to King, whose airtime performances were flat and scripted. Although the popular vote remained relatively close, favouring the Tories 48.8 to 45.2 per cent, the Conservatives triumphed decisively in parliamentary seats with 134 compared to 91 Liberals, 11 Progressives, and 2 Labour representatives

Hard(er) Times

Though an Albertan, Bennett selected an Ontario-centric cabinet. He gave only 5 junior portfolios to Quebecers despite the fact that 25 Conservatives were elected in the province. He also micro-managed, convinced that he knew best. Soon circulating among

1   Larry A. Glassford, *Reaction and Reform: The Politics of the Conservative Party under R.B. Bennett, 1927–1938* (Toronto: University of Toronto Press, 1992), 77.

the press corps was a joke about Bennett walking down the corridors of Parliament talking to himself, with the punch line being that he was holding a cabinet meeting.

In early 1931, Bennett left for England. Officially, the trip was to sign the Statute of Westminster. This formalized Canada's complete control, and that of the other self-governing dominions, over their foreign policy. Bennett sought to use the visit to try to achieve freer trade among Commonwealth members. However, no side was willing to make concessions for fear of giving others an advantage. Returning home, Bennett delivered on his promise to raise tariffs, ratcheting up rates by as much as 50 per cent. Rather than blasting Canada out of the Depression, this fuelled a protectionist trade war and the downward cycle of Canadian commerce. For example, in British Columbia, exports dropped from $238 million in 1929 to $100 million by 1934.

As a self-made multi-millionaire from humble roots in rural New Brunswick, Bennett believed in self-reliance, thrift, and hard work and that welfare bred dependency. He responded cautiously to demands for more federal government support of welfare, especially with modest state revenues. Ottawa largely kept out of direct taxation, then a shared jurisdiction with provincial governments. According to the *British North America Act*, social welfare was primarily a provincial responsibility.

In 1930, Bennett's government offered $20 million in emergency aid to the provinces, but on a shared-cost basis with federal funds capped at one-third of total relief expenditures. Keeping to economic orthodoxy, Bennett sought to minimize budget deficits. To that end, the federal government laid off thousands of civil servants, cut the salary of many more, and delayed public works projects. Bennett insisted that his government would not accept the dole—a direct payment to the unemployed—and that the able-bodied perform work to receive relief. Within a couple of years, however, he moderated that stance because make-work projects cost far more than a straight payment to the jobless. Some major public works projects were initiated; for example, the Saskatoon City Hospital was significantly upgraded. However, most publicly supported work involved basic manual labour, such as cleaning parks.

Cash-strapped provincial governments downloaded half or more of relief costs onto municipalities, even though property taxes, the major source of local government revenue, were generally exhausted, since few homeowners could absorb increased levies; many had already lost or were on the brink of losing their homes. To prevent people from starving, municipalities went into deep debt—and in some cases bankruptcy—to provide assistance. Even with the tight-fisted approach, Bennett's government ultimately spent an unprecedented $200 million through matching relief grants.

By 1931, over half a million Canadians were searching for work, and by 1933, unemployment peaked at 30 per cent. For many, being on welfare was humiliating, viewed as a personal failing and a disgrace. Numerous men refused assistance no matter their circumstances, often forcing their wives to apply, though some women pleaded with social workers to pressure their husbands to seek aid. Even with rapidly increasing numbers of unemployed, the idea persisted that the jobless were "dirty, lazy, incompetent, mentally and physically ill and lacking…individual initiative."[2] Convinced that there existed wastage in the distribution of relief, Bennett demanded that provincial and municipal governments work harder to cut off support to those deemed capable of finding work, otherwise Ottawa would reduce its matching financial contributions.

The process of applying for public assistance reinforced the sense of shame. People had to prove their need to local boards that, in many cases, demanded they sell all luxuries (car, radio, jewellery, or anything else deemed unnecessary). Relief often came in the form of vouchers for the cheapest basic food staples. No leeway was made for personal preferences or religious and cultural dietary laws and customs. Many found the vouchers embarrassing and difficult to use, as not all vendors accepted them because they did not want to wait, or go through bureaucratic hoops, to receive government reimbursement.

There was no standardization between locales as to who got what, reflecting a patchwork system of support. Relief payments often depended on the economic health of a locale, though a common denominator was sporadic and inadequate assistance, often less than a week per month. For example, in Amherst, Nova Scotia, support was set at $5.70 monthly, but in Sydney and Glace Bay, it was $4.00. Generally, when it came to relief, the married were favoured over the single, those with children over the childless, and British subjects over recent immigrants. Local relief boards often excluded those who had not lived in a community for a specified period. Across Canada, the needy queued at soup kitchens, often run by churches, where "heavy reliance was placed upon…hash and cereals."[3]

Lives were shattered and people lost hope. The recorded number of suicides increased from 593 in 1928 to 805 in 1931. Men went door-to-door seeking odd jobs. With Canadians cash-strapped and with no public health insurance, doctors were often forced to accept food for services. In Hamilton, one survey concluded that doctors did not receive traditional payment for half of the services performed. Doctors in several communities petitioned governments to establish public health insurance for low-income Canadians. In 1934, Winnipeg doctors, whose income fell by half during the first three years of the Depression, refused to provide all but essential services,

2 Michael Ekers, "Production of the Unemployed in Depression-era British Columbia," *Antipode* 44, no. 4 (2012): 1120.

3 James H. Gray, *The Winter Years: The Depression on the Prairies* (Toronto: McClelland & Stewart, 1966), 147.

prompting the local government to implement a relief program to help low-income patients pay for medical care.

Pressure built during the Depression to dismiss women from the paid workforce so that more men could perform the breadwinner role. To this, women's groups offered weak resistance and male-dominated unions typically none at all. Quebec's legislature nearly passed a measure that would have required a woman to show financial need to take a job other than as a farm cook or domestic servant. Overwhelmingly, working women remained in a narrow range of low-income jobs. In Toronto, early in the Depression, 27 per cent were in personal services (mainly as domestics and waitresses), 28 per cent in clerical work, 17 per cent in manufacturing (primarily in the textile sector), and 11 per cent in professional roles, primarily teaching and nursing. Generally, women received one-third to one-half of the pay that men earned in similar positions, with non-Anglo-Saxon women typically earning less. More women turned to home-based employment, but here too things became harder. One analysis concluded that whereas recompense received for sewing a dozen dresses in 1929 was $5.00, by 1934 it was just $1.35. Women also contributed to the family income by doing home repairs, tending to boarders, cooking with cheaper ingredients, and growing vegetables or raising small animals for food, including in urban areas.

Across the spectrum of society, things became harsher. Veterans renewed their campaign for a cash bonus. The 1930 *War Veterans Allowance Act* provided only marginally increased support for those whose injuries prevented them from working. The already sorry plight of Canada's First Peoples and Métis further deteriorated. By the end of the decade, their life expectancy was half that of non-Natives. In 1930, the federal government began funding some on-reserve nursing stations, but to save money, disbanded medical clinics in many remote First Nations communities. In 1931, Ottawa drastically cut medical assistance to the Inuit in the northern Quebec area of Ungava, claiming that this was a provincial responsibility. Quebec disagreed, arguing that the Inuit, like other Indigenous peoples, were wards of the federal government. While governments bickered, the Inuit waited, suffered, and starved, as their hunting grounds were slowly depleted of caribou, seal, and fox. Not until 1938 did the courts rule that responsibility for the Inuit fell to Ottawa.

Many Canadians looked for others to blame for their misery, and the Jews were a popular target. Anti-Semitism spiked, fuelled by the opposing stereotypes of Jews as wealthy manipulators of the money system, or as political radicals intent on exploiting the current economic catastrophe to create disorder. Fascism enjoyed growing support. In Quebec, its emphasis on the need for order and the defence of traditional moral values resonated with parts of the Catholic Church. In 1932, Quebec's Adrien Arcand, Canada's most prominent Fascist, founded *Le Goglu*, a publication that promoted

French-Canadian racial purity and the need to protect Quebec from excessive liberalism, materialism, and Communism, behind which, it said, was "the Jew." An *Achat chez nous* movement urged *Québécois* to boycott Jewish merchants. Swastika clubs emerged in Toronto during the early 1930s, comprised largely of jobless and disaffected young men. In August 1933, hundreds engaged in a pitched battle against Jewish youth near the Christie Pits baseball yard.

With rising unemployment, immigration declined to a trickle. Whereas Canada accepted 144,983 immigrants in 1929, by 1935 the total was merely 11,277. Many accused immigrants of stealing jobs. In 1931, Bennett's government banned immigrants, other than farmers, who were not of British stock. A concerted effort was made to deport immigrants who were suspected of supporting Bolshevism. When those who were politically suspect lost their jobs, they were arrested because it was relatively simple to deport newcomers for vagrancy. Over the first four years of the Depression, some 20,000 people were expelled from Canada.

Fear of foreigners was fuelled by the growing strength of the Communist Party of Canada (CPC). Seeking to harness growing anger and desperation, it provided relief services for, and organized demonstrations by, the unemployed. The Workers' Unity League, a union the CPC established in 1929, peaked at some 40,000 members by the early 1930s. Several of their street protests, such as in Ottawa and Windsor, sparked violent clashes with police, something many Communist leaders welcomed in the hopes of moving Canada closer to class warfare.

Prime Minister Bennett was determined to crush Communism. Working with Ontario's attorney general and local law enforcement authorities, on August 11, 1931, a raid was launched on Communist Party headquarters in Toronto. Eight men, including the party's leader, Tim Buck, were charged under Section 98 of the Criminal Code and received jail terms ranging up to ten years (though ultimately all were released within three). Most Communists went underground, though Bennett remained worried about them fomenting social turmoil. The following March, he ordered armoured cars to patrol at Parliament during a National Unemployment Conference.

RETRENCHMENT ABROAD

With the Depression preoccupying Canadians, there remained little appetite to become involved in international issues. As during the 1920s, Canadian foreign policy remained guided by the desire to avoid the possibility of costly and divisive engagements. This was evident in September 1931, when Japan invaded the Chinese territory of Manchuria to expand its access to minerals and influence throughout Asia. The League of Nations, increasingly viewed as toothless, met in emergency session. Bennett's government said nothing, reflecting the overwhelming view that Canada had no vital interests in this fight. Things became more complicated when Japan threatened Shanghai, which contained significant Western business interests. In March 1932, the League called for an immediate ceasefire. Canada criticized Japan, though, like Britain, in very temperate terms. Unfazed, Japan established the new puppet state of Manchukuo in what had been Manchuria and quit the League. Canada maintained cordial relations with Japan, continuing strong bilateral trade, and commented no further on events in Manchuria.

Canada commanded little notice internationally, especially given deep cuts to its military. During the early 1930s, the permanent army was capped at a few thousand personnel. Militia funding dropped from $11 million in 1929 to $1.6 million three years later. In 1932, the federal government proposed an annual budget of $422,000 for the navy, which was not even enough to cover its fixed costs. However, when Commodore Walter Hose, the navy's chief officer, threatened to resign, Ottawa backed down and returned funding to the 1931 budget figure of $2 million.

DEEPER INTO DESPAIR

In 1932, Bennett hosted a summit of Commonwealth leaders in Ottawa to try to rekindle efforts to create freer trade. There was plenty of pomp and press coverage, as Canada had never before hosted such a large and prestigious international gathering. A few export items were given a modest Commonwealth preference, but the overall results were negligible and behind-the-scenes exchanges became bitter. Bennett considered Britain's Prime Minister Stanley Baldwin condescending, while his British counterpart regarded Bennett as pigheaded.

The Depression united the country in misery. Between 1928 and 1933, Canadian manufacturing output plunged by 48 per cent, retail sales by 44 per cent, and investment in durable assets by an incredible 82 per cent. In the same period, Canada's gross national product—the total annual value of goods and services—contracted by 42 per cent. In Ontario and Quebec, manufacturing production dropped by half between 1929 and 1933. In British Columbia, production declined from $331 million in 1929 to $149 million in 1932. On the other side of the country, in the Maritimes between 1929 and 1933, timber production plunged by 75 per cent, fishing by 47 per cent, and coalmining by 45 per cent. Economic crisis in Newfoundland moved people there in 1934 to vote to end democratic self-government in favour of a British-run commission government, which imposed a severe austerity program to reduce a public debt that threatened bankruptcy.

Large areas of the Prairies were devastated. In 1932, the price of wheat bottomed out at 34¢ a bushel, less than 20 per cent of its 1928 value. Between 1931 and 1936,

14,000 farms comprising 1.2 million hectares were abandoned. An estimate the next year classified two-thirds of Saskatchewan's farm population as destitute. One-fifth of Saskatchewan's population left, thus ending its status as Canada's third most populous province. Drought in Alberta demolished cattle herds, so much so that in 1935 the federal government bought 15,000 half-starved livestock to prop up the market and prevent an exodus of ranchers to places like Edmonton and Vancouver, which could not cope with the unemployed already there. Across the Prairies, the scale of devastation was biblical, with droughts, high winds, and blinding dust storms destroying once fertile topsoil. The first such episode came in 1931. After a brutally cold winter with virtually no snow, a hot and dry summer reduced the soil to dust, a cycle that repeated itself every year in large parts of the southern Prairies until 1937. Hot, dry weather also brought plagues of grasshoppers. Clouds of 'hoppers would suddenly appear, blacken the sky, and descend to devour all vegetation. "The whole countryside appeared to be blowing away and there were drifts of grey dust over everything,"[4] wrote the governor general's wife, Lady Tweedsmuir, whose visit to the region in 1934 moved her to start a program to distribute tens of thousands of free books to uplift people's spirits.

As many as 100,000 men "rode the rods," hopping on rail cars and moving from place to place in search of work. They took up temporary residence in derisively named "hobo jungles" on the outskirts of cities and towns by the railway tracks, places composed of "crude huts made from tin sheets, packing crates, boxes, and other debris hauled from garbage dumps."[5] Bennett claimed many were swindling the system, spending relief money on "candy and beer."[6] Seeking to pressure the provinces to ferret out the fraudulently unemployed, in 1934 the federal government cut its matching grants to support relief by as much as a third.

As the Depression worsened, Prime Minister Bennett became an object of scorn. Canadians sarcastically spoke of "Bennett buggies" (a car pulled by a horse because its owner could not afford the gas), "Bennett barnyards" (abandoned farms), and "Bennett coffee" (boiled grain). Because Bennett considered charity a private matter, few Canadians realized that he sent thousands of dollars of his own money to people who wrote him about their hardships. What Canadians saw was Bennett's tough, external demeanour. Furthermore, his rotund physical appearance and wealthy background increasingly came to symbolize the image of an uncaring plutocrat.

---

4 Geoffrey Little, "'The People Must Have Plenty of Good Books': The Lady Tweedsmuir Prairie Library Scheme, 1936–40," *Library and Information History* 28, no. 2 (2012): 103.

5 Laura Sefton MacDowell, "Relief Camp Workers in Ontario during the Great Depression of the 1930s," *Canadian Historical Review* 76, no. 2 (1995): 208.

6 John Manley, "'Starve, Be Damned!' Communists and Canada's Urban Unemployed, 1929–1939," *Canadian Historical Review* 79, no. 3 (1998): 489.

Figure 6.2 A couple with their Bennett buggy in Viking, Alberta.

Bennett's government persisted in its campaign to crush radicalism. Communists were weakened not only by authorities who infiltrated leftist groups and militant unions, but also because those of Anglophone background looked disdainfully upon Communist organizations as being rife with foreigners. Communists also expressed frustration with the optimism most Canadians still harboured—even the unemployed—that things would eventually get better. Starting in 1933, Canada's Communist Party, seeking to expand its support, and following direction from the Soviet-based Comintern, adopted the policy of "broadening out" by pursuing alliances with social democrats, an overture that was not reciprocated.

Bennett remained concerned that the deepening economic crisis threatened the stability, and perhaps even the survival, of the capitalist system. He was especially worried about Canada's growing transient population, a group largely young, male, and single. With fewer responsibilities and often feeling themselves shunned by society, authorities feared that radical agitators could influence them.

To try to keep such men occupied and under control, Bennett latched onto an idea proposed by Charlotte Whitton, the conservative-minded head of a think-tank called the Canadian Welfare Council, and endorsed by General Andrew McNaughton, the chief of the general staff, that work camps administered by the Department of National Defence be established. There, transients could contribute to civilian infrastructure projects and rebuild crumbling military facilities. McNaughton's report, *Unemployment and Relief in Western Cites*, presented current programs as "fragmented, poorly administered, and overly costly."[7] He pointed to successful work camps

---

7   Ekers, "'The Dirty Scruff,'" 1131.

in Western Europe and the United States and presented outdoor labour as having a rehabilitative effect on the unemployed.

The first camp opened in October 1932, and by 1934, nearly 60 had emerged. The largest concentration was in British Columbia, to which many unemployed flocked due to its milder weather. Over 115,000 men participated in the work camp scheme. Several large projects were completed: by 1935 in Ontario, 4 aerodromes, 24 landing strips, 3 air stations, and 3 military barracks were built. Camp workers laboured on 40 highway projects across Canada, including in national parks like Banff, to make them more accessible for tourism.

Most camps were located in remote areas, often out of range of radio signals. This was intentional so that any radicalism among participants could be quarantined and to isolate camp workers from outside agitators. Many saw themselves as banished. They received food and shelter, though often in tents or dilapidated and overcrowded bunkhouses, and their pay of 20¢ daily was considered insulting. Their work was often backbreaking and purposefully assigned with primitive equipment to keep them occupied longer at the lowest possible cost.

Although staffed by civilians, men in the camps complained that they were run like military facilities; indeed, the *King's Orders and Regulations*, the military legal system, governed. Worker committees were prohibited, and anyone involved in a protest could be banished and forced to make his own way home. Anger festered and produced conflict. The camps experienced 359 strikes, and 17,391 men were dismissed for disciplinary breaches. As historian Pierre Berton concluded, "McNaughton's scheme for staving off revolution had the seeds of revolution inherit in it."[8]

NEW ANSWERS OR NEW THREATS?

More and more Canadians concluded that mainstream politicians had no answers to reverse the crippling effects of the Depression, and they began turning to others advocating sweeping change. In 1932, some 100 farmers, workers, academics, socialists, Labour Party representatives, and former Progressive Party members gathered in Calgary to form the Co-operative Commonwealth Federation (CCF). The CCF spoke of working toward implementing socialism through democratic means, while in the short term pursuing better social welfare. Its leader, former Methodist minister J.S. Woodsworth, had represented the largely working-class and immigrant federal riding of Winnipeg North since 1921. Although committed to parliamentary institutions and peaceful change, and rejecting overtures made from Communists to form a common front, the CCF was still portrayed as radical. This was largely due to its 1933 *Regina Manifesto*. In

---

8   Pierre Berton, *The Great Depression, 1929–1939* (Toronto: McClelland & Stewart, 1990), 159.

setting out the party's purpose and platform, not only did it advocate practical measures such as comprehensive crop insurance and a National Labour Code, but also declared that "no CCF government will rest content until it has eradicated capitalism and put into operation a full program of socialized planning."[9] Yet, as historian James Naylor writes, the CCF had difficulty making inroads among youth, partly because its leadership was viewed as too influenced by electoral ambitions at the expense of pursuing fundamental change.[10] Conversely, the CCF achieved virtually no presence in Quebec, where the Catholic Church condemned it as socialist, alien, and atheist.

Not until 1940 did the CCF win its first seat in the Maritimes. In the 1934 Ontario election, it won just one seat and 7 per cent of the popular vote. In British Columbia, where labour militancy in mining districts was more pronounced, the CCF won 31.5 per cent of the popular vote in the 1933 provincial election, though this translated into only 7 out of 47 seats. The next year in Saskatchewan, where the Depression arguably hit the hardest, the party took 24 per cent of the popular vote but only 5 of 55 seats. In its first federal election in 1935, the CCF attracted 9.3 per cent of popular support, but only 7 MPs in a Parliament of 245.

Between August 1933 and July 1935, five provincial Conservative governments lost power. In the Maritimes, Tory administrations fell to moderate reform Liberals in Nova Scotia, New Brunswick, and Prince Edward Island. The only provincial government to retain power throughout the Depression was Manitoba's centre-left Liberal-Progressive coalition under John Bracken, though it was reduced from majority to minority status in 1936.

In British Columbia, Fraser Tolmie's Conservative government, torn by internal dissent on how to respond to the Depression, faced Liberal T.C. "Duff" Pattullo. Drawn west by the Klondike gold rush, Pattullo settled in Prince Rupert, became a prominent businessman and mayor, and in 1930 provincial Liberal leader. "[I]mmensely self confident, dapper, even a bit flamboyant,"[11] he rebuilt the party organization, bought radio time with his own money, and gave as many as 20 speeches a day. Despite his business background, he championed "socialized capitalism," declaring his intent to launch public works projects and for the government to "recognize both the duty and the desirability of giving larger consideration to the needs and welfare of society generally,"[12] a message that brought him victory with 34 out of 47 seats.

9 "The Regina Manifesto," http://www.saskndp.com/documents/manifest.pdf.

10 James Naylor, "Socialism for a New Generation: CCF Youth in the Popular Front Era," *Canadian Historical Review* 94, no. 1 (2013): 79.

11 Jean Barman, *The West Beyond the West: A History of British Columbia* (Toronto: University of Toronto Press, 1991), 254.

12 Robin Fisher, *Duff Pattullo of British Columbia* (Toronto: University of Toronto Press, 1991), 215.

Pattullo delivered on some reforms. His government raised the minimum wage, introduced an eight-hour workday, increased support for education, and funded public works projects such as construction of a bridge over the Fraser River to connect Vancouver and New Westminster. The provincial debt rose, but expenditures were partially offset by increased royalties on rising mineral prices.

The politics of reform were also evident in Saskatchewan where, in June 1934, Liberal James Gardiner ousted the Tories by running on a platform advocating unemployment insurance, drought relief, and easier credit for farmers. That same month, Mitchell Hepburn brought the Liberals back to power in Ontario after a 28-year hiatus. An onion farmer by background, the hard-drinking and combative Hepburn sold himself as a champion of ordinary folks and the downtrodden, even though his property was valued at $150,000—50 times more than the average Ontario farm. The next year, his government passed the *Industrial Standards Act* enabling it to impose fair wages across sectors to offset a trend toward sweated labour. Rarely enacted, it was designed to address only the worst abuses, where downward pressure on wages among people desperate to keep their jobs even had many claiming public relief because their pay did not provide for subsistence. For instance, electricians in Toronto working as much as 50 hours a week were earning the same as the daily wage in 1929. Hepburn forged strong ties with the business community, particularly those involved in resource development, to which his government provided generous tax breaks. He argued that such risk takers represented the best hope to lift Ontario out of the Depression, but also from this source his Liberal Party received hefty donations.

In 1935, more radical change occurred in Alberta with the election of the Social Credit Party under William "Bible Bill" Aberhart, an event considered so unique that it made the front page of the *New York Times*. Born in Perth County, Ontario, in 1878, Aberhart initially trained as a teacher. After earning a BA through Queen's University correspondence courses, he moved to Calgary in 1910 and became a school principal. A devout Baptist, in 1927 he became dean of the Protestant fundamentalist Calgary Prophetic Bible Institute. A gifted speaker, he obtained widespread fame as a preacher, especially for his *Back to the Bible Hour* broadcast over CFCN, a Calgary radio station whose powerful signal blanketed the Prairies and the northwest United States, and from which Aberhart drew a weekly audience of as many as 350,000.

Aberhart spoke of his conversion to Social Credit after a former student committed suicide, a tragedy he blamed on the Depression. Conceived by the Scottish engineer, C.H. Douglas, social credit theory advocated greater state control over the monetary system to correct the problem of under-consumption, something that Douglas, a virulent anti-Semite, blamed on usurious Jewish financiers. Although anti-Semitism permeated Social Credit in Alberta, Aberhart publicly avoided the screed.

Figure 6.3 Alberta Premier William Aberhart speaking in Calgary, August 1936.

Also, to the dismay of Douglas, Aberhart advanced a highly simplified version of Social Credit theory, but it was easily understood by the masses, particularly the $A + B$ *Theorem* that spread like a prairie wildfire. With A being total salaries and wages, B being the other costs of production and profits, and C being the total price charged for goods, under-consumption was explained by the difference between the values of A and C. Aberhart's solution was to provide people with B so that when added to A, the total would equal C, thus solving under-consumption. Aberhart claimed this plan would be accomplished by the province distributing $25 monthly to every Albertan. Economists warned of hyper-inflation, jokes circulated about "funny money," and it was pointed out that the provincial government had no constitutional authority to print money. Nevertheless, Albertans took hope from Aberhart's message, believed in him as a man of God, and viewed his promise of free money as manna from heaven. During the election campaign against the United Farmers of Alberta, he relentlessly attacked the banks and promised to wrestle power from the "Fifty Big Shots" running the country, which Albertans understood to mean the barons of Toronto's Bay Street and Montreal's St. James Street, Canada's main financial districts. In August 1935, Social Credit swept into power with 56 out of 63 seats.

As premier, Aberhart initially adopted a cautious approach, fearing disinvestment if Social Credit monetary policy was immediately implemented. His government emphasized debt reduction and made modest improvements to health services and education. Several MLAs who considered themselves Social Credit purists threatened to resign. Aberhart responded in 1937 by introducing legislation authorizing the provincial government to print scrip, or promissory notes, while a companion piece of legislation denied court appeals by banks over currency production. However, the federal government challenged the measures, and in March 1938, Canada's Supreme Court quashed them. Aberhart blustered against federal intrusion but did not initiate an appeal. Instead, he demanded greater provincial powers and blamed Ottawa for Alberta's continuing economic woes. Seeking to contain attacks on his government, Aberhart introduced the *Accurate News and Information Act*. It provided the provincial government with the power to compel the publication or correction of a story and to force a reporter to reveal a source. Alberta newspapers fought back, overturned the legislation in court, and collectively received the prestigious Pulitzer Prize, the first time it was awarded to a non-American source.

BANISHING BENNETT AND RE-CROWNING KING

Although assailed as heartless, Bennett's government had spent more on public assistance than any previous one. Still, pressure for more government intervention to stimulate the economy magnified from many sources. British economist John Maynard Keynes's theory, that governments should spend their way out of a depression and then pay down the debt in better times, was gaining more adherents, including in university economics departments across Canada.

To deal with the crisis in prairie agriculture, Bennett's government introduced the 1934 *Prairie Farm Rehabilitation Act*, which provided funds for large-scale re-seeding, drought resistant grasses, and new methods of tillage to preserve moisture and to protect soil. The same year, in an effort to provide greater stability to the financial sector and more coordinated economic planning, the federal government created the Bank of Canada, which set interest rates and established minimum reserve requirements for all Canadian chartered banks. To promote public education, unity, and nationalism, and to counteract American influence, the federal government created the Canadian Radio Broadcasting Corporation in 1932, which four years later became the Canadian Broadcasting Corporation (CBC).

Overworked and nearing nervous exhaustion, Bennett contemplated retirement. His Conservative Party was showing internal divisions as Bennett and his well-known minister of trade and commerce, H.H. Stevens, had a very public political divorce. A small businessman by background, Stevens sometimes proved antagonistic toward major capitalists because he believed they abused their power to destroy competition. Aware of Stevens's growing popularity as a people's champion, Bennett appointed him to head up a parliamentary Price Spreads Commission. Many of its findings were shocking, such as the Eaton's department store paying a home-based female worker 9.5¢ for each dress she produced and then selling them for $1.59. Before releasing the report, Stevens publicly accused top executives at the retailing giant Simpson's of milking $10 million out of the firm. With Simpson's threatening legal action, Bennett ordered Stevens to apologize, but he refused. Bennett responded by changing the parliamentary commission into a Royal Commission and removed Stevens, who then resigned from the government to create the Reconstruction Party three months before the federal election. It attracted 8.7 per cent of the popular vote—and a single seat for Stevens—with most of those votes being siphoned from the Conservatives.

For a while, it seemed that Bennett might snatch victory from what appeared to be impending and certain defeat. In January 1935, without warning his caucus, he used national radio to announce a bold initiative: a Canadian version of US President Franklin Roosevelt's New Deal. Bennett promised a national minimum wage;

ON-TO-OTTAWA TREKKERS ARRESTED ON JULY 1st, 1935

FOR YOUTH
AND DEMOCRACY

SECTION 98

Figure 6.4 Canada's Communist Party condemns arrests made from the On-to-Ottawa trek. In 1936, fulfilling an election promise, Mackenzie King's government removed Section 98 from Canada's Criminal Code.

unemployment, health, and accident insurance; collective bargaining rights for labour; and better Old Age Pensions.

However, the program soon came across as ill-conceived and opportunistic, as a deathbed conversion to achieve re-election. The Tories placed these promises in the Throne Speech. Bennett expected a short debate in which the Liberals would oppose the plan for being fiscally irresponsible, thus allowing him to run as the voice of reform, but a wily King moved quickly past the Throne Speech to demand that the Tories table their legislative package. The only thing the Conservatives could provide was an unemployment insurance plan they quickly cobbled together that required massive provincial funding and provided meagre support for which little more than half of Canadian workers would qualify. With the Conservatives looking incompetent, disingenuous, and unable to reverse the crippling effects of the Depression, the Liberals were able to run an election campaign that made few specific promises and that presented the choice to Canadians as between "King or chaos."

The idea of chaos growing under Bennett became more prevalent as the election approached. Anger continued to mount in the work camps McNaughton had conceived. Starting in late 1934, in British Columbia's interior, about half of 7,000 camp workers organized by a new Relief Camp Workers' Union voted to go on strike. With no response from the federal government, they converged on Vancouver where they occupied several public buildings. Their leader was Arthur "Slim" Evans, a die-hard Communist and veteran of numerous violent strikes as part of the militant United Mine Workers.

Evans sought to organize the strikers for a pilgrimage to Ottawa. In April 1935, about 1,000 strikers departed by boarding railway boxcars for what became known as the "On-to-Ottawa trek." Initially, the federal government ignored them, believing their spirits and campaign would fade away in the cold and snow of the Rocky Mountains. However, the trek took on the aura of a crusade and its numbers grew as it moved through communities. By Medicine Hat, Alberta, it was 1,500 strong.

Figure 6.5 Protestors and police battle in the Regina Riot.

Bennett feared that if the trekkers reached Winnipeg, which was widely viewed as the "centre of western Canadian radicalism,"[13] they could become an uncontrollable mob. He instructed the country's two major railways, the Canadian National and Canadian Pacific, to complain that the trekkers were trespassing on their property. Responding to this, his government declared the trek illegal and halted it in Regina, where the RCMP directed the protesters to the local fair grounds. A delegation, led by Evans, was allowed to meet Bennett in Ottawa. When they arrived, Bennett was condescending and hostile, accusing them of fomenting revolution and warning that his government would do "whatever is necessary to maintain law." Evans shot back, telling Bennett he was not fit to be the "premier of a Hottentot village."[14]

Things started to come to a head on June 27, two weeks after the trekkers arrived in Regina. When they refused to relocate and began initiating plans to continue the trip east by truck, authorities took action to end things. The Relief Camp Workers' Union was declared an illegal organization, and arrest warrants were issued for the trek leaders. On Dominion Day, July 1, nearly 4,000 trekkers and their supporters gathered in Regina's Market Square. When the leaders started to address the crowd, tear gas canisters were released and police advanced with clubs. By the time the mêlée ended, one detective was dead, a dozen police were wounded, half a dozen civilians had been shot (one later died), and more than 100 trekkers were injured.

---

13 Bryan Palmer, *Working-Class Experience: Rethinking the History of Canadian Labour, 1800–1991* (Toronto: McClelland & Stewart 1992). 246.

14 Bill Waiser, *All Hell Can't Stop Us: The On-to-Ottawa Trek and Regina Riot* (Calgary: Fifth House, 2003), 134, 138.

In the immediate lead up to the federal election on October 14, 1935, Bennett also faced a foreign crisis that reflected badly on his government. On October 3, Fascist Italy, whose dictator, Benito Mussolini, spoke in terms of reviving the glory of ancient Rome, used a border dispute involving its colony in Somalia to invade neighbouring and resource-rich Abyssinia (Ethiopia today). The League of Nations met in emergency session to determine its response. Few considered military intervention, but economic sanctions were on the table. Bennett said that Canada's Parliament would decide the country's response once recalled after the election. King, better sensing the public mood, publicly rejected any possibility of Canadian involvement.

With reports of Italy using poison gas against the Abyssinians, Canada's representatives at the League of Nations convinced Bennett to give them some latitude in responding. In a League Economic Sub-Committee tasked with recommending on sanctions, Canadian representative W.A. Riddell, before checking with Ottawa, proposed that Italy be denied imports of coal, copper, iron, steel, and most crucial of all, oil, as estimates indicated Italy had about a three-month supply of petroleum to fight its war. Many expressed alarm over Canada's apparent willingness to take the lead against Italy, a position that further sealed Bennett's fate.

The election saw the Liberals crush the Tories, winning 173 out of 245 seats. A dejected Bennett offered to resign, but the Conservatives did not replace him as leader until 1938 with the 30-year parliamentary veteran Robert Manion.

Prime Minister King recalled Riddell from the League of Nations in Geneva and rejected sanctions. Rather, he pursued Canadian interests abroad by seeking freer trade with the United States, arguing that Bennett's policy of protectionism had been an economic disaster.

King proceeded cautiously in developing domestic economic policy. He appointed C.A. Dunning as finance minister, a fiscal conservative who opposed adding to the national debt. Initially, the Liberals trimmed relief grants to the provinces, justifying this based on a modestly improving economy. King announced the creation of a National Employment Commission (NEC), but made it solely an advisory body rather than one that would help with job creation or unemployment relief. He also referred Bennett's unemployment insurance legislation to the courts to test its constitutionality, a move some criticized as a way to avoid taking action.

In late 1935, King called a dominion–provincial conference to improve intergovernmental relations. However, recent federal cuts to relief payments soured the meeting. With Quebec, federal–provincial relations grew particularly strained with Maurice Duplessis's election. A lawyer from Trois Rivières, Duplessis was first elected to the provincial legislature in 1927 and six years later became leader of the province's Conservative Party. In 1935, he formed an alliance with *L'Action libérale nationale*

(*ALN*). Led by Paul Gouin, the son of former Quebec premier Lomer Gouin, *ALN* followers were renegade Liberals who broke ranks with Liberal Premier Alexandre Louis Taschereau, whom they cast as too close to the business community, too focused on attracting American investment, and as lacking commitment to protect Quebec's French-Catholic character. In the 1935 provincial election, the Conservative–*ALN* alliance promised to bust corporate monopolies, increase wages, provide state-run hydro, and create a progressive labour code. The Liberals, who had run Quebec since 1897, held on—but just barely—by a margin of 47 to 42 seats.

Over the ensuing months, Duplessis spearheaded a relentless attack on government mismanagement and corruption. He revealed that Taschereau's brother had deposited interest on public money into his personal bank account, a revelation that forced the premier to resign. Another election was called for August 1936. The *ALN*–Conservative alliance ran under the banner of the *Union Nationale*. However, Gouin had been squeezed out of the new party, and few *ALN* members were candidates. The *Union Nationale* triumphed with 76 out of 90 seats.

Duplessis largely abandoned social reform, allied with big business, and courted American investment. Still, he connected to French-Catholic Quebec. Charismatic and comfortingly paternalistic, he stressed the need to protect traditional Québécois culture and society. He backed continuing Church control over social services and the education of French Catholics (which also saved the government money); emphasized the need to strengthen the rural sector because of the strong moral values agricultural life supposedly inculcated; zealously protected Quebec's powers within the federation; and pursued an unrelenting campaign to crush "godless" radicals. In 1937, his government passed the *Padlock Act*, which gave it the power to close for up to one year any place used "to propagate communism or bolshevism by any means whatsoever."[15]

SOCIAL CHANGE

By the mid-1930s, the Depression had played an important role in advancing social change. In numerous provinces, school boards placed greater emphasis on practical subjects, including industrial arts, as well as on vocational guidance, to enhance employability.

Other changes were more controversial. One was to legalize the dissemination of birth control information and devices, which had carried a maximum penalty of two years' imprisonment. Legalizing artificial birth control faced strong opposition. Anglo-Saxon leaders warned of "race suicide" in the face of larger immigrant families.

---

15 See Government of Quebec, *An Act to Protect the Province Against Communistic Propaganda*, March 24, 1937

The Vatican continued to prohibit birth control for Catholics. Only the United Church of Canada accepted birth control, justifying it on the basis of fostering more stable marriages and families.

The Depression compelled more Canadians to limit family size. Law enforcement authorities increasingly ignored clinics that disseminated birth control information. Rising unemployment generated concern over parents being unable to care for their children, with the anticipated results being overwhelming strain on state resources and rising crime.

Among those subscribing to such ideas was Kitchener manufacturer A.R. Kaufman, who in 1932 founded the Canadian Birth Control League. Four years later, one of his employees, Dorothea Palmer, was arrested in the heavily French-Catholic community of Eastview, outside of Ottawa, for distributing League literature. She was acquitted in her initial trial and subsequently before the Ontario Court of Appeal, as the judges decided that in some circumstances birth control was a social good.

Pressure for change also mounted from organized labour, which grew more powerful over the course of the Depression, particularly in Ontario, where the American-based Congress of Industrial Organizations (CIO) focused its efforts. Since its creation in 1935, the CIO achieved strong results organizing American workers in major industries, such as auto, rubber, and steel. It adopted the strategy of the sit-down strike, meaning its members occupied a work site to prevent operations from continuing.

In December 1936, the CIO launched a campaign to organize General Motors (GM) autoworkers in Oshawa, Ontario. Mitchell Hepburn waded into the battle, casting the CIO as filled with Communists whose invasion from America would undermine Ontario's economic recovery. A union recognition strike began at GM on April 8, 1937. Hepburn wired federal justice minister Ernest Lapointe, warning of the potential for violence and demanding RCMP personnel be dispatched to augment local police. Lapointe authorized sending one detachment. However, Mackenzie King, a former labour negotiator who wanted to avoid inflaming matters, rejected Hepburn's demand for a second detachment. Hepburn accused the federal government of treachery and publicly stated he was "no longer a Mackenzie King Liberal." The premier ordered the Ontario Provincial Police to the GM plant and authorized the recruitment of a temporary constabulary force that the strikers nicknamed the "Sons of Mitches." After a few weeks, GM made it clear that it wanted the dispute settled. In a face-saving compromise for Hepburn, GM workers were allowed to organize a union as long as it was not accredited as part of the CIO. What resulted was CIO in all but name—a formality soon rectified—and the strikers won a 44-hour workweek and a seniority system.

When it came to unemployment insurance, it seemed Ottawa might be off the hook. In June 1936, Canada's Supreme Court rejected Bennett's unemployment insurance scheme, claiming that this fell under provincial jurisdiction. The federal government appealed the case to the Judicial Committee of the Privy Council, but that court upheld the verdict. Reacting, a growing number of commentators, including Canadian legal and constitutional scholars, recommended that federal powers be enhanced so the government could effectively deal with crises like the Depression. In 1937, the King government appointed a Royal Commission on Dominion–Provincial Relations (known as the Rowell-Sirois Commission, after its heads, Ontario Chief Justice Newton Rowell and Quebec notary Joseph Sirois) to analyze "the economic and financial basis of Confederation and the distribution of legislative powers in light of economic and social developments of the last seventy years."[16]

Some provincial governments, particularly those in the Maritimes, which were more dependent on federal largesse, indicated a willingness to consider a revised power-sharing structure. However, Pattullo and Aberhart were leery, and Duplessis and Hepburn were hostile. The Commissioners insisted their goal was to create more fairness within Confederation, such as by recommending a federally administered National Adjustment Grant to equalize revenue per capita among the provinces—an idea governments in Ontario and Quebec cast as a federal power grab. The public mood, however, demanded improvements and an end to political stalemate.

PURSUING PEACE AND APPEASING AGGRESSORS, 1936–1938

Tensions were mounting outside Canada. As Nazi Germany became more aggressive, Canadians began worrying about another world war. Recalling the massive losses and longstanding divisions, especially between French and English, from World War I, King stuck by his preferred approach to foreign policy—that it not foment disunity. As such, he stressed that every effort be made to retain peace.

In March 1936, King did not protest Germany's remilitarization of the Rhineland, despite this being a blatant violation of the 1925 Locarno Treaty. The next year, his government passed the *Foreign Enlistment Act* to prevent Canadians from joining the Spanish Civil War. Those who broke the law faced up to two years in jail. Still, some 1,500 Canadians fought in Spain. Nearly all joined the Mackenzie-Papineau battalion, Canada's contribution to the International Brigades composed of some 35,000 volunteers from 22 countries. Most were Communists, who fought alongside Spanish

---

16 "Dominion-Provincial Relations: Royal Commission on," http://www.thecanadianencyclopedia.com/index.cfm?PgNm=TCE&Params=A1ARTA0002349.

Republicans against Francisco Franco's Nazi-supported Nationalists. Ill-trained, ill-equipped, and poorly led, nearly 50 per cent of the Canadians were killed.

Like a labour negotiator, King believed he could help broker a lasting peace in Europe, and he arranged to meet Adolf Hitler in June 1937. Impressed or seduced, King in his diary described the Nazi dictator as "a calm, passive man" whose eyes had "a liquid quality...which indicates keen perception and profound sympathy."[17] He expressed willingness to consider German claims in Europe, but privately made it clear to Hitler that Canada would fight if the Nazis attacked Britain. While in Germany, King said nothing about the persecution of Jews, even though they had been forced to wear a prominent yellow Star of David in public since the 1935 Nuremberg Laws. Canada's government had also ignored calls from Jewish groups, leftist organizations, and several major newspapers to boycott the 1936 summer Olympics that were being held in Berlin, where the German team excluded Jews, and anti-Semitic propaganda was evident at venue sites. Although writing in his diary with sorrow about the desperate plight of German Jews, ultimately for King the question of whether or not to help the Jews, by accepting more into Canada, was a political one. He concluded that opening the doors, even just a little wider, would gain him few and likely cost him many votes. Between 1933 and 1939, 4,000 European Jews were permitted into Canada compared to 200,000 taken into the United States, 70,000 into Britain, and 50,000 into Argentina.

King remained committed to appeasing Hitler. He was silent over the *Anschluss*, Germany's 1938 military occupation of Austria. Soon after, the majority German-speaking population in the Czechoslovak region of Sudetenland demanded incorporation into Germany. Britain's Prime Minister Neville Chamberlain urged the Czech government to negotiate with the Nazis, a stance King supported. In September, Chamberlain, following meetings with Hitler in Munich, triumphantly returned to London declaring that he had achieved "peace for our time" by agreeing to cede Sudetenland to Germany. King wired Chamberlain his "unbounded admiration at the service you have rendered mankind."[18]

King moved slowly on rearming Canada, fearful of sending a message that he was preparing the country for war. In 1936, he rejected a British request to create a Canadian-based Commonwealth air training scheme. The next year, Canada's defence budget increased from $20 million to $36 million, though military leaders estimated that a minimum of $57 million would be needed to achieve a decent level of preparedness. Assessing King's foreign and defence policies, James Eayrs used the

17 J.L. Granatstein and Norman Hillmer, *For Better or for Worse: Canada and the United States to the 1990s* (Toronto: Copp Clark Pitman, 1991), 142.

18 H. Blair Neatby, *William Lyon Mackenzie King, 1932–1939: The Prism of Unity* (Toronto: University of Toronto Press), 293.

terms "low" and "dishonest," accusing the prime minister of placing narrow political interests, particularly his desire to retain support in Quebec, over properly preparing Canada for a war that any reasonable person would have known was coming. However, J.L. Granatstein and Robert Bothwell portrayed King's strategy in a more positive light: as pursuing peace until every possible avenue was exhausted, thus enabling him to bring a relatively united country into World War II.[19]

MOVING TO A NEW ORDER

As the decade closed, some 900,000 Canadians, out of a workforce of 3.8 million, remained registered with public agencies as unemployed. However, the length and scope of the Depression would moderate views of the unemployed as being lazy. Practically everyone knew people who had lost their jobs and that it was not easy to obtain another.

At the end of 1937, a member of the NEC informed King that it would soon issue a report recommending that the federal government create an unemployment insurance program. King instructed Minister of Labour Norman Rogers to pressure the NEC's chair to quash the recommendation, claiming it was not financially feasible. Rogers resisted because he believed that Ottawa had to do more. King accepted a recommendation to hand over the question of unemployment insurance to the Royal Commission on Dominion–Provincial Relations. In the short term, he agreed to establish a parliamentary committee under Rogers to recommend on increases to public welfare. Rogers soon advised spending an extra $75 million. Opposed, however, was Finance Minister Dunning, who remained wedded to the need for a balanced budget, which meant no extra spending. King compromised, splitting the difference by authorizing an additional $40 million for public relief in the 1938 budget. That budget also allocated an extra $60 million to the military, though to many this was only a down payment on what was needed after years of neglect. The Royal Canadian Navy, which had seen modest upgrades to its fleet over the previous two years, lobbied for the purchase of large modern Tribal Class Destroyers, but this would not come until four years into World War II.

On January 16, 1939, the opening day of the parliamentary session, King, seeking to prepare people for the possibility of conflict, quoted Laurier's comment made at the outset of World War I, that "when Britain is at war, Canada is at war." It drew widespread criticism from Quebec and prompted King to pledge that if war did come he would not implement conscription. Three months later, Germany effectively tore

19 James Eayrs, "'A Low Dishonest Decade': Aspects of Canadian External Policy, 1931–1939," in H.L. Keenleyside (ed.), *The Growth of Canadian Policies in External Affairs* (Durham: Duke University Press, 1960), 14–34; J.L. Granatstein and Robert Bothwell, "'A Self-Evident National Duty': Canadian Foreign Policy, 1935–1939," *Journal of Imperial and Commonwealth History* 3 (1976): 212–33.

up the Munich agreement by expanding its occupation of Sudetenland into the rest of Czechoslovakia. Britain abandoned the policy of appeasement and provided defence guarantees to Poland and Romania. King urged continued negotiations with Hitler and privately criticized Chamberlain for drawing a line in the sand.

King sent Hitler correspondence pleading for renewed discussions. He received a reply on July 21, proposing some friendly student and officer exchanges, and the possibility of another private meeting. Plans were soon made for King to visit Germany in November, but it was not to be. On September 1, Germany invaded Poland.

CONCLUSION

In 1939, Canada's federal government spent $317.2 million on social assistance, $100 million more than in 1926. When considered as a percentage of the country's gross national product, both years produce a figure of around 6 per cent. Government support may have consistently failed to meet need, but this does not mean that things remained static. Over the course of the decade-long and devastating Depression, a growing number of Canadians from all walks of life grew ready, and indeed eager, for change—and often radical change—to reverse the economic collapse. Fewer people were blaming economic hardship on personal failure or indolence. Governments spent record sums on welfare and assumed unprecedented and often crippling debts; by the end of the decade, Prime Minister King, the champion of strategic compromise, was moving toward Keynesian economic planning.

Canadian foreign policy reflected a population willing to fight a *just* war, but also one that had shed much of the militarist and romanticist perspective on combat that had been prevalent before World War I. There was fear of Canada being dragged into another conflict not in keeping with its interests. Like most of the free world, Canada initially recoiled in the face of Nazi aggression. Yet, King's strategy of pursuing peace until the last possible moment, while also slowly rearming, would bring a mostly united, and at least marginally prepared, country into World War II.

Responses to the Great Depression laid significant groundwork for important changes in the roles and responsibilities of governments. The 1930s also saw Canada take a long journey from isolationism and appeasement to help confront the scourge of Fascism, with King, in particular, skillfully, though perhaps also amorally, managing affairs to minimize internal strife along the way. However, the changes that came to Canada's political, social, cultural, and economic landscape during these years would pale in comparison to the transformative impact and legacy of the coming war.

7 MANAGING THE NATION: THE STRUGGLE FOR UNITY, 1939–1945

INTRODUCTION

World War II remains the largest conflict in human history. It claimed some 60 million lives, or 3 per cent of the world's population. Millions perished in Nazi concentration camps, incendiary bombs turned cities into raging infernos, and the atomic bomb obliterated Hiroshima and Nagasaki. The war radically changed the geopolitical balance of power, ending the status of Britain, France, Germany, and Japan as leading powers, and leaving the United States and the Soviet Union as unrivalled and antagonistic global superpowers.

In Canada, from a population of 11.5 million, over 950,000 men and 50,000 women donned a military uniform. Canada created the Allies' third largest navy and fourth largest air force. The modern interventionist federal government emerged, as did the basis of Canada's welfare state. New rights appeared for labour, as did new opportunities for women. The country's economic and military ties to the United States grew far tighter; Canada's Far North was accessed as never before; and the stage was set for Newfoundland to become Canada's tenth province.

Prime Minister Mackenzie King knew that he could not keep Canada out of the conflict should Britain declare war. Yet, he had been "scarred by the terrible slaughter of the Great War"[1] by how it almost tore apart French and English Canada and brought heightened discord based on class and region. For this reason, he had worked desperately—though irresponsibly, insisted his critics—to resist rearming Canada and to champion appeasement until Germany invaded Poland. Once the die was truly cast, however, and there was no way to maintain peace, Canada mobilized for total war, ultimately on a scale far exceeding that of World War I. In doing so, King maintained his determination to contain internal conflict and retain unity and consensus by avoiding missteps he saw as having occurred during World War I, with respect to recruitment, conscription, and managing social and economic policy. In meeting this challenge, he demonstrated, arguably better than any other Canadian leader, uncanny skills as a conciliator and political manager.

GEARING UP, 1939–1940

On September 1, 1939, Germany invaded Poland. Two days later, Britain declared war on Germany. Canada did not join for another week, a nod to its recently acquired control over foreign affairs. This also provided a brief window to obtain war-related goods from the United States, whose *Neutrality Act* prevented it from supplying arms to nations at war. Although not yet at war, the federal government declared the *War Measures Act* in effect. Under its provisions, it introduced the Defence of Canada Regulations enabling it to intern enemy aliens, prohibit organizations deemed subversive, imprison those "mak[ing] statements intended or likely to prejudice the recruiting, training, discipline, or administration of any of His Majesty's forces," and to censor all media.[2] By 1941, 35 associations were banned, including the Communist Party, as it supported the August 1939 Nazi-Soviet Non-Aggression Pact and Russia's invasion of Finland, and denounced the Allies for waging an imperialist war of aggression. The federal government refused to legalize it even after the Soviet Union became an ally following the June 22, 1941, Nazi invasion of Russia, only permitting it to re-emerge as the Labour Progressive Party in 1943.

Parliament convened on September 8, 1939, to vote on Canada's entry into the war. Only two Quebec MPs expressed opposition, as did the leader of the CCF, J.S. Woodsworth, a committed pacifist. On September 10, 1939, Canada joined the fight against the Nazis. King wanted Canada to fight a war of limited liability, meaning one where the contribution of materiel, not manpower for combat, would dominate. His goal was to minimize casualties and to prevent the need for conscription, something

---

1   Tim Cook, *The Necessary War: Canadians Fighting the Second World War* (Toronto: Allen Lane, 2014), 239.

2   Canada, *Order in Council*, PC 882, October 13, 1942.

he had pledged to Quebec that his government would not implement. He bristled at the army leadership's initial proposal to send over a 60,000-strong expeditionary force; he even wanted to avoid dispatching a division of 20,000. King was more prepared to involve the navy and air force because he saw this as bringing fewer casualties.

There were no celebrations in Canada accompanying the declaration of war. It had only been a generation since the country endured a quarter-million casualties. Having resisted rearmament, Canada was woefully unprepared. Its army of just 5,000 permanent force members and 46,000 poorly trained militia had only a "handful of machine guns"[3] and two light tanks.

Nevertheless, a deluge of young men, including a not insignificant number of World War I veterans, immediately sought to enlist. Some wished to escape the still crippling effects of the Depression; others enlisted to escape a bad marriage, a poor job, or out of general boredom; others still were moved to support Britain, which was still regarded as the mother country. The military paid $1.30 a day, while the federal government provided a dependents' allowance initially set at $35 monthly for a wife and $12 each for a maximum of two children (this time, there was no Canadian Patriotic Fund reliant on donations). By the end of September, Canada's army had ballooned from 5,000 to 61,000.

Canada's earliest major contribution was to help to provide for the air war by hosting the British Commonwealth Air Training Plan (BCATP). Aviation had become increasingly important in World War I, and during the interwar years, planes made huge advances in speed, range, reliability, and the destructive payload they could deliver.

Yet, given King's hesitation about making it look as if Canada was ready to commit to war, negotiations to produce the BCATP were long and, especially for Britain, exceedingly frustrating. Britain had first proposed a Commonwealth air training scheme in 1936. Canada was considered an ideal location because of its vast open spaces, access to America's large air industry, relative safety from enemy attack, and closer proximity than Australia for ferrying planes to England. Canadian negotiators pushed Britain to bear most of the costs despite Canada reaping the lasting benefits through the construction of airfields. After protracted negotiations, which stretched into November 1939, Canada agreed to contribute $313 million, Australia $97.4 million, New Zealand $21.6 million, and Britain $218 million. The impact of the program was huge. Whereas before the war Canada graduated about 125 pilots annually, under the BCATP that number rose to 1,500 aircrew monthly.

King's fear that the war had the potential to split the nation along French–English lines was stoked early in the conflict. Quebec Premier Maurice Duplessis called a snap election in autumn 1939, looking to obtain a mandate to resist what he predicted

---

3 Cook, *Necessary War*, 24.

would be a wartime power grab by the federal government. Faced with the probability that the war would soon heat up, and that Ottawa would require more powers, King wanted Duplessis removed from office. The government poured money into close ridings to support provincial Liberal candidates. King's key cabinet ministers from Quebec—Justice Minister Ernest Lapointe, Public Works Minister P.J.A. Cardin, and Minister of Pensions and Health Charles Power—publicly threatened to resign if Duplessis was re-elected, the implication being that this would produce greater Anglophone control in Ottawa and increase the likelihood of conscription. Duplessis also underestimated support in Quebec for what was deemed a just war against the Nazis. On October 25, Liberal Adélard Godbout became premier with a whopping 54 per cent of the popular vote and 70 of 85 seats in the Quebec legislature.

King, though entering the fifth year of his mandate as prime minister, obtained agreement from Conservative leader Robert Manion to delay a federal election until late 1940. However, King believed that, given his opposition to conscription, his electoral prospects were better if the vote occurred earlier, before the war in Europe started to intensify. His opportunity came on January 18, 1940, when George Drew, leader of the Ontario Conservative Party, made a speech to the provincial legislature that was highly critical of Ottawa's limited war effort. Premier Mitchell Hepburn, whose relationship with King was one of mutual loathing, introduced a motion into the legislature regretting that "the Federal Government…ha[d] made so little effort to prosecute Canada's duty in the war."[4] King seized upon this statement to call an election as a referendum on his war leadership.

Manion advocated a coalition government to back a more concerted war effort. However, the Conservatives, politically decimated during the Depression, appeared short on talent. In Quebec, Manion's strategy conjured memories of Robert Borden's Union government (where Manion got his start), which was created in large part to ensure the passage of conscription. The result on March 26 was the most lopsided to date in a federal election, with the Liberals winning 181 of 245 seats. Manion retired and was replaced by R.B. Hanson, formerly the trade and commerce minister under Bennett, as interim leader.

GEARING UP AT HOME, 1940–1942

After the 1940 election, the lull in combat known as the Phoney War—following Germany's brutal month-long campaign to conquer Poland—abruptly ended. On April 9,

---

4   J.L. Granatstein, *Canada's War: The Politics of the Mackenzie King Government* (Toronto: University of Toronto Press, 1990), 76.

1940, the Nazis invaded Norway and Denmark using *blitzkrieg*, or lightning quick, offensive tactics. The next month, they sliced through the European low countries—Belgium, the Netherlands, and Luxembourg—and by June 23, they had conquered France. In August, the Battle of Britain commenced with the *Luftwaffe* pummelling England from the air in preparation for *Operation Sea Lion*, the planned invasion of England.

In Canada, the war now became serious and frightening. In mid-1940, air raid blackout drills, initially confined to coastal areas, moved inland as far as Calgary and Toronto. Canadians backed myriad volunteer activities to support the war effort. Also in 1940, the federal government declared the YMCA, Salvation Army, Knights of Columbus, and Canadian Legion as official auxiliaries for Canada's military, providing them collectively with as much as $13 million annually to help provide sporting equipment, recreational huts, and educational services. Canadians also heavily invested in eventual victory as 10 wartime and 1 post-war Victory Bond drives raised a total of $12.5 billion.

With the fall of France, Canada's federal government passed the *National Resources Mobilization Act* (*NRMA*). It took a census of all available labour, both male and female, 16 years of age and older, and established conscription for home defence for single men, aged 19 to 45, initially for one month, but increased to four months in February 1941. In April, the length of service was extended indeterminately—possibly for the entire war.

Canada moved closer to the United States, which reflected both Canadian defence needs and concern in Washington over North American security. The prime minister and the American president, Franklin Roosevelt, with whom King viewed himself as having a close relationship, had first discussed coastal defence in March 1937. With Britain possibly facing defeat, King had to think of hemispheric defence. In August 1940, Roosevelt invited King to Ogdensburg, New York, where the president was inspecting troops as part of his re-election campaign. The result was the creation of the Permanent Joint Board on Defence. With equal representation from both countries, and chaired by civilians, it was the first-ever bilateral defence pact to provide for the security of North America. Many worried that it would become a permanent institution, continuing long after the wartime emergency.

Within Canada, the growing demands of World War II redefined the division of powers between the federal and provincial governments. Ottawa needed more money. Where the cost of fighting World War I peaked at around a million dollars a day, this more mechanized conflict was already claiming nearly 80 per cent more by the end of 1940. Taxation was an obvious funding source but was a joint constitutional jurisdiction with the provinces. To address this situation, the Liberals turned to the Report of the Royal Commission on Dominion-Provincial Relations, the release of which occurred shortly after the 1940 federal election. Given its mandate to examine the failings of governments to combat the Depression, the Royal Commission did not actually refer to the war. It outlined how, over the previous generation, social welfare demands had increased well beyond the capacity of municipal and provincial governments. Its answer was to provide the federal government with control over income, corporate, and inheritance taxes in exchange for Ottawa creating a national unemployment insurance scheme, a national adjustment grant to ensure all parts of the country met minimum standards in areas like education and health, and to assume up to 40 per cent of the combined municipal–provincial debt.

Momentum to implement the report was buttressed by the need to empower the federal government to meet the rising demands of the war. In July 1940, the federal government introduced an unemployment insurance fund into which employers, employees, and the federal government would contribute. The provinces agreed to a constitutional amendment to allow the new scheme to proceed, though with the jobless rate plummeting in wartime, the unemployment fund quickly accumulated a large surplus.

The King government called a dominion–provincial conference for January 1941. Hepburn attended under protest and tried to rally Alberta's William Aberhart and BC's Duff Pattullo to form an oppositional front. Finance Minister J.L. Ilsley threatened unilaterally to raise income and corporate taxes as a wartime emergency measure. Hepburn remained rigid, claiming that power redistribution was unnecessary to fight the war and would permanently weaken Ontario. However, he found himself increasingly isolated and portrayed as hurting the war effort. Forced to relent, Hepburn was humiliated and soon resigned as premier. The ultimate result was the 1942 *Dominion–Provincial Taxation Agreement Act* under which the provinces rented their tax fields to Ottawa, at least for the war's duration.

To run Canada's expanding war effort, cabinet ministers increasingly relied on the senior civil service—the so-called "mandarins"—many of whom had been educated at elite institutions like the London School of Economics and Oxford University. There, they became familiar with, and generally supportive of, the theories of John Maynard Keynes, the British economist whose advocacy of government intervention to smooth out business cycles had gained much popularity during the Depression.

Canada moved toward a command economy partly to avoid repeating problems that emerged during World War I. Such was evident with the creation of the Wartime Prices and Trade Board (WPTB). With high inflation causing severe economic and social strain during World War I, in autumn 1941 the WPTB imposed a freeze on wages and prices. Most came to regard this as a resounding success, for whereas the cost of living had risen by 17.8 per cent from August 1, 1939, to October 1, 1941, it decreased to 2.8 per cent between October 1, 1941, and April 1, 1945.

While the WPTB focused on controls, the Department of Munitions and Supply concentrated on production. Between 1940 and 1942, the value of war production in Canada increased nearly eightfold, to $2.6 billion. Canada produced an astounding 400 naval and 391 cargo ships, 50,000 tanks, 16,000 military aircraft, and 850,000 military vehicles. The minister of munitions and supply, C.D. Howe, cut through red tape, sending letters of intent to firms so they could get moving on war production, and then quickly following up with formal contracts. Munitions and Supply ensured that firms producing for the war effort acquired needed raw material and technical expertise. Howe recruited "dollar a year" men—experts from industry whose salary continued to be paid by their companies—to advise on war production.

Not everyone was happy. Organized labour expressed anger at being excluded from advisory roles. There were charges of conflict of interest as advisors were drawn from the same sector they were asked to regulate, such as BC lumber baron H.R. Macmillan, who was made timber controller. Complaints were made about Munitions and Supply favouring firms in southern Ontario and Quebec—for instance, the Maritimes received only 3.7 per cent of war contracts. However, Howe believed that larger firms, situated in areas with bigger labour markets, more capital, and superior transportation links, were best equipped to deliver as needed, and he was ready to act against those that failed to do so. National Steel Car in Malton, Ontario, which Howe considered inefficient, was taken over by Munitions and Supply in October 1942 and run as a Crown corporation (a government-owned enterprise) called Victory Aircraft. In all, Munitions and Supply created 28 Crown corporations such as Polymer (that produced synthetic rubber), Defence Industries Incorporated (armaments), and Research Enterprises Limited (optics, radar, and other technologically advanced items with a military application). Moreover, Munitions and Supply controlled profits on war contracts, typically to 5 per cent.

Even with war production concentrated in Central Canada, the war-generated economic boom spread nationwide. In British Columbia, some 39,000 persons obtained jobs in shipbuilding. A large proportion of the 137 BCATP facilities to train pilots, navigators, bombardiers, gunners, and wireless operators were located in the Prairies. The Northwest Staging Route opened up remote areas in northern Alberta and British Columbia and in the Yukon. Established in late 1941 in cooperation with the United States to help supply the Soviet Union with food, materiel, and aircraft, the Staging Route, which ended in Fairbanks, Alaska, consisted of a line of 13 small airports, 11 of which were in Canada.

Beyond funding its own war effort, Canada faced growing demands from Britain. However, Britain, engaged in a desperate fight for survival, could no longer pay its debt to Canada, money that Canada in turn needed to pay its trade deficit with the United

States. To assist a nearly bankrupt Britain, in March 1941, the United States established the Lend-Lease program that provided military assistance to England in exchange for 99-year leases on British bases in the West Indies and Newfoundland. Ottawa worried that Lend-Lease would worsen Canada's financial plight because Britain would be able to decrease Canadian purchases. In April 1941, at a meeting at Hyde Park, New York, King told Roosevelt that by year's end the situation would compromise Canada's ability to fight the war. In the resulting Hyde Park Declaration announced on April 20, 1941, the United States agreed to increase purchases in Canada, mostly of raw materials, to balance those made by Canada in America. King was praised for the agreement, though some worried that it entwined Canada's economy, and perhaps political destiny, too closely with its southern neighbour.

CANADIANS IN UNIFORM, 1940–1942

Canada's initial overseas contingent, the 1st Division, some 18,000 strong, arrived in England in December 1939. The end of the Phoney War saw plans to involve Canadian soldiers in battle, but these came to naught. With the collapse of Denmark in spring 1940, the British and French considered an intervention in Norway, to include two Canadian battalions, but this was cancelled by the time they reached Scotland as Germany quickly conquered Norway. On June 12, 1940, some 4,000 Canadians were rushed to Brest, France, as part of the 2nd British Expeditionary Force in a desperate attempt to retain a portion of northwest Europe. However, within days, and without firing a shot, they joined a mass retreat, even, in their haste, leaving equipment behind.

Canadian soldiers settled in Britain to protect the island from a possible Nazi invasion. By 1943, their presence had grown to more than 250,000 men. Canada's Army established a Civil Affairs Branch to organize assistance, such as to help harvest crops. However, as they stayed on in England, many servicemen became bored and restless, believing themselves languishing as others were getting into action. They grew angry at British military instructors who, they said, treated them as incompetent colonials. Demoralizing as well was Britain's damp, cold climate and poor accommodations. As of late 1941, arrests of Canadian troops in Britain for drunk and disorderly conduct reached 500 monthly.

While Canadian soldiers in Britain waited for action, the story with the air force was much different. Although entering the war with only a few outdated aircraft, Canada's air force would ultimately grow to approximately 215,000 men. In December 1939, as part of Britain's Royal Air Force, Canadians assisted with attacks on German naval vessels. Early the next year, two RCAF squadrons joined the Battle of Britain, shooting down or damaging 15 German aircraft. In 1941, RCAF fighter squadrons were tasked with escorting British bombers on daytime raids into France and Belgium, though in these missions the Allies, with generally inferior aircraft, lost three planes for every one they shot down.

Figure 7.1 RCN Corvette *Shediac*, 1941 Library and Archives Canada, MIKAN 35540904.

The Royal Canadian Navy (RCN), which Mackenzie King preferred over ground troops, expanded during the war from 3,000 to 96,000 personnel. At the outset of the conflict, the RCN consisted of only three auxiliary ships, four mine-sweepers, and seven small destroyers. Canadian shipyards emphasized the construction of Corvettes, which were modest in size, less sophisticated, relatively cheap to build, and suitable for anti-submarine patrol. During the war, the RCN patrolled along Canadian and British coastlines, off India and Africa, and in the Caribbean and Mediterranean. However, its most significant contribution was to protect merchant convoys crossing the Atlantic. By 1940, a Newfoundland Escort Force, operating out of St. John's, was accompanying merchant ships some 2,000 kilometres into the North Atlantic whereupon the Royal Navy assumed control.

Expanding commitments abroad meant greater efforts to get men into uniform. To release men for active service, the federal government created three female military services: the Canadian Women's Army Corps (CWAC) on June 27, 1941, whose strength reached 21,624; the Canadian Women's Auxiliary Air Service on July 2, 1941, which in February 1942 was renamed as the Women's Division of the RCAF (RCAF–WD) and reached 17,101 personnel; and the Women's Royal Canadian Naval Service (WRCNS), established on July 31, 1942, whose numbers reached 6,781.

The expanding scope of the war also brought early rumblings to conscript men for overseas service. Defence Minister J.L. Ralston cast conscription as the fairest and most efficient system to meet military need. R.B. Hanson's caution on the issue contributed to his quick departure as interim Conservative leader and replacement in late 1941 by former prime minister and unabashed pro-conscriptionist Arthur Meighen.

Canada's ability to avoid conscription for overseas service was made possible because its army was late in becoming actively involved in combat. Its earliest engagement, at Hong Kong, was disastrous. The British assured the Canadians that the Japanese were poor soldiers and would not attack Hong Kong and risk conflict with the Empire. King did not want to send troops when the British first asked in September 1941. However, the pressure to get involved was intense, including in the

Anglophone press, which knew of Britain's request. Canada agreed to send troops in October, but all its A and B formations—those considered ready for action—were unavailable, but not those in the C category belonging to the Royal Rifles of Canada and Winnipeg Grenadiers, who required more training. Arriving in November, the 96 officers and 1,877 other ranks joined a force of 14,000 that included British and Indian troops and members of the Hong Kong Defence Corps. On December 8, 1941, the Japanese attacked. Assigned to Hong Kong Island, the Canadians did not encounter the Japanese until December 18. Brigadier J.K. Lawson, the Commander of C Force, was killed the next day. Lieutenant-Colonel W.J. Home, the highest-ranking Canadian officer, considered the fight futile, but the British garrison commander, Major-General C.M. Maltby, insisted that resistance continue, which it did until Christmas Day at the cost of 290 Canadians killed and some 500 wounded. Those who survived spent the rest of the war in Japanese slave-labour POW camps. Beatings, torture, and mock executions were common, while malnutrition left prisoners highly susceptible to diphtheria, beriberi, pellagra, parasitic worms, and dysentery.

EVACUATION AND NORTHERN DEVELOPMENT, 1942–1943

The RCMP and military intelligence had kept Japanese Canadians under surveillance since Japan's 1937 invasion of China but had uncovered no nefarious activity. Rumours circulated that in Hong Kong, and at Pearl Harbor—where Japan attacked America's Pacific fleet—local Japanese had helped the enemy. Vancouver City Council portrayed the 25,000 Japanese in the province as a "potential reservoir of voluntary aid to our enemy."[5] Eight federal MPs from British Columbia, including six Liberals, demanded that all the Japanese be moved inland. Ottawa felt compelled to act after the American government ordered its Japanese population evacuated from coastal areas on February 20, 1942. King was not overtly racist, but for him, this was purely a political calculation: he was unwilling to alienate the BC wing of the Liberal Party and the millions of Canadians convinced of Japanese-Canadian treachery.

Four days after the Americans acted, 23,000 Japanese Canadians, all located in BC, were ordered to relocate at least 160 kilometres from the coast; those who refused faced internment and forced labour. Each adult was permitted to take 70 kilograms of items, and each child 35 kilograms. Federal authorities sold off confiscated Japanese property, often at bargain-basement prices. Some Japanese with money bought properties inland, though many communities, including Calgary, Medicine Hat, and Lethbridge,

5 Patricia Roy, J.L. Granatstein, Masako Iino, and Hiroko Takamura, *Mutual Hostages: Canadians and Japanese during the Second World War* (Toronto: University of Toronto Press, 1990), 91.

Figure 7.2 Japanese Canadians being forcibly evacuated to the British Columbia interior.

refused to accept Japanese evacuees. Thousands of Japanese had no choice but to live in quickly constructed government housing complexes that averaged 400 square feet, used oil lamps and wood heat, and had no private bathroom facilities. Many ended up as labourers on sugar beet farms, a harsh job sometimes assigned to German POWs in Canada because it was difficult to find others to do it.

Fear of a Japanese attack would also transform Canada's north through the construction, mostly by America's military, of the Alaska Highway, the purpose of which was to quickly transport troops and supplies in the event of a Japanese invasion from the north. It was built in rough form between April and November 1942 and stretched over 2,500 kilometres from Dawson Creek, British Columbia, to Fairbanks, Alaska, with all but 400 kilometres located in Canada.

Besides being presented as a military necessity, the highway's construction meant thousands of well-paid civilian jobs. Several remote communities experienced an unprecedented boom, though they also struggled to cope. Dawson Creek, a community of 728 before the coming of the highway, soon totalled 9,000. Media accounts said that new economic opportunities extended to Indigenous peoples, though their involvement in better-paid jobs was minimal; typically they served as guides. The arrival of whites in remote areas also spread disease to First Peoples that often proved fatal because they had no immunity.

RISING DEMANDS AND STRAINS AT HOME, 1942–1943

By the time the Alaska Highway was completed, the federal government concluded that an attack upon Canada was very remote and it largely cancelled air raid drills by the end of 1942. Still, as the war overseas intensified, Ottawa demanded more sacrifices at home. In April 1942, the WPTB issued ration coupon books entitling drivers to only 545 litres of gasoline per year, enough for about 2,000 kilometres. In 1942 and 1943, sugar, tea, coffee, butter, and meat were rationed, because imported products became more difficult to obtain and to accommodate rising demand from troops and civilians overseas.

By 1942, more than 350,000 men had volunteered for military service, but as in World War I, the greatest challenge was in Quebec. As of October 1941, voluntary enlistment in Quebec stood at 41.6 per cent of Ontario's total, although Quebec's population was 85.5 per cent of Ontario's. King continued to face pressure to conscript for overseas service, and his opposition provided Meighen with the possibility of picking up support in English Canada.

Meighen was scheduled to run for Parliament in a February 1942 by-election in the Toronto constituency of York South. Despite large numbers of working-class voters, it had elected a Tory in every federal election since 1904. The Liberals did not run a candidate to avoid splitting the anti-Conservative vote. King undercut Meighen by announcing in the January 22 Throne Speech, which opened the parliamentary session, that his government would hold a plebiscite (a non-binding vote) in April asking Canadians if they would release Ottawa from its pledge of "no conscription for overseas service." Meighen's opponent was schoolteacher Joseph Noseworthy of the CCF. With strong trade union support, and, rather than conscription, emphasizing the need for the federal government to start planning for the post-war period so that the economic turmoil following World War I not be repeated, Noseworthy crushed Meighen by nearly 4,500 votes.

Still, for King, there remained the matter of the plebiscite, whose results were potentially catastrophic. In Quebec, 72 per cent voted "No," but in the rest of Canada nearly 80 per cent responded "Yes." King's compromise was Bill 80, which removed geographic restrictions on conscripted service. When Bill 80 was brought before Parliament, only 4 of 49 Quebec Liberals supported it, though the measure still passed. Seeking to retain national unity, King insisted he had no immediate plans to conscript for overseas service. He described his approach as "conscription if necessary, but not necessarily conscription." The best remembered quote of his political career, it "epito-mized [the] habitual caution, obliqueness and lack of commitment"[6] fundamental to his political longevity and success. For Ralston, military needs were clear-cut and he privately submitted his resignation. However, as a former militia colonel, he would not leave his post until given permission by his superior, and King, fearing a cabinet revolt, refused.

Besides turmoil over conscription, Noseworthy's victory demonstrated that Canadians were thinking beyond the conflict. Growing numbers wanted the federal government to initiate plans that included social welfare programs to offset an anticipated post-war downturn. Following Meighen's defeat, Conservatives gathered in Port Hope, Ontario, where they endorsed measures like national collective bargaining legislation, low-cost housing, and a national public health insurance scheme. At the party's convention in Winnipeg in December, John Bracken, Manitoba's premier for the past 20 years and who was first elected under the Progressive Party banner, was chosen as the new leader. As an overture to Bracken, and to underline the party's new direction, the Conservatives renamed themselves as the Progressive Conservatives.

The divisive results of the 1942 plebiscite, and the increasing demands of the war, prompted the federal government to take a more active approach toward managing information. In September, a more comprehensive Wartime Information Board replaced a rather low-key Bureau of Public Information. The Board consulted with advertising agencies and commissioned surveys from the newly created Canadian Institute of Public Opinion to gauge support for government war policies and to identify the most effective means of mobilizing people. The upbeat nature of news was evident in information con-veyed on the disastrous raid by Canadian soldiers on the French coastal community of Dieppe in August 1942. The first stories proclaimed: "It's been a wonderful day. [T]here's [not] a Canadian…whose heart didn't pound a little faster."[7]

MILITARY DEVELOPMENTS, 1942–1943

The assault on Dieppe was designed to test German defences in Europe and gather intelligence. The Americans, and especially the Soviets who were taking massive casualties, clamoured for the creation of a Western European front. General H.D.G. Crerar, then acting commander of the Canadian Corps in England, pushed for major Canadian involvement, arguing it would raise troop morale, especially since many

---

6   Cook, *Necessary War*, 290.

7   Raj Ahluwalia, *We Interrupt This Program: The News Broadcasts that Kept Us Tuned In* (Toronto: Winding Star Press, 2000).

Figure 7.3 Damaged tanks and Canadian dead at Dieppe. Library and Archives Canada, MIKAN 3195155.

were growing frustrated as they saw American soldiers, whose country declared war on Germany on December 11, 1941 (four days after doing so against Japan), playing a more active role in ground campaigns.

Many historians lay much of the blame for what happened at Dieppe on Admiral Lord Louis Mountbatten, King George VI's cousin. An ambitious naval captain who had lost three ships earlier in the war, in March 1942 he was promoted—well beyond his level of competence—as Vice-Admiral and Commander of Combined Operations Headquarters. With Dieppe, he brushed aside concerns expressed by military subordinates and in intelligence reports and ensured that the raid proceeded.

At Dieppe, the Germans had constructed a formidable defence network. The Canadians lost the element of surprise after an attacking flotilla ran into a German coastal patrol. During the raid, Allied naval and air support was inadequate, and many troops landed late and at the wrong spot. They stormed ashore in full daylight onto pebble beaches where footing was difficult and there was no cover from nearby cliffs from where the Germans opened up a deadly barrage. Of the 4,963 Canadians who participated, 907 were killed, 586 were wounded, and 1,946 were taken prisoner, making Dieppe the single most costly day for Canada in World War II.

While Canada's army was removed from action following Dieppe, its navy and air force continued to expand their roles. In February 1942, Canadian vessels became leaders in the Mid-Ocean Escort Force, which operated from Halifax and took a more southerly route than Newfoundland-based convoys. However, Canadian Corvettes remained hampered by light guns and magnetic (as opposed to more modern gyro) compasses insufficiently stable for accurate navigation. Rather than radar, the importance of which Canadian naval commanders underestimated, the asdic sets in use were regularly thrown off by underwater currents, temperature changes, rock formations, and even schools of fish.

U-boats inflicted tremendous damage on Allied merchant shipping throughout 1942. That year, the naval war

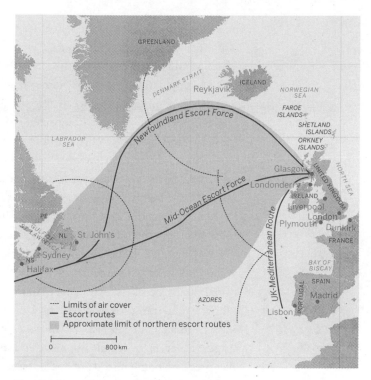

Map 7.1 Royal Canadian Navy convoy routes.

moved into the St. Lawrence where, in May, the German submarine *U-553* sank two merchant vessels. The next month, *U-132* added another three. By September, 12 more merchant ships were sent to the bottom as well as the Nova Scotia-Newfoundland civilian ferry *ss Caribou*, with the loss of 137 lives, prompting the federal government to close the St. Lawrence to ocean traffic.

By mid-1943, with the breaking of Germany's Enigma Code, heavy losses forced the U-boats to withdraw from the Atlantic trade routes, a victory to which Canada's navy made a notable contribution, especially with larger and more sophisticated vessels coming into operation. Canadians could also take pride in the April 1943 creation of the Northwest Atlantic Command, placed under Canadian Rear Admiral Leonard W. Murray, the only naval theatre of operations commanded by a Canadian officer in World War II. By war's end, RCN vessels successfully escorted 25,343 cargo vessels to their destination and wholly or partially participated in the destruction of nearly 30 German U-boats.

The role of sea and air power, both Canadian and American, was, by the early 1940s, also dramatically affecting Newfoundland. Besides convoys organized from St. John's, the Americans, ultimately 20,000 strong, began arriving in January 1941 and were stationed at St. John's, Torbay, Argentia, Gander, and Stephenville. American military leaders feared a German attempt to occupy Newfoundland, which would be disastrous for the sea-lanes between North America and Europe. Out of a population of 300,000, some 13,000 Newfoundlanders found work related to America's military presence. Approximately 6,000 Canadians also came to Newfoundland, several of whom were involved with Ferry Command that flew some 11,000 military aircraft to Britain from airfields in Gander, Newfoundland, and Goose Bay, Labrador. Ottawa worried about Newfoundland falling into America's orbit because its location made it essential to trans-Atlantic flights and Atlantic trade routes, while Bell Island provided one-third of the ore used in Cape Breton steel mills. In 1941, the Canadian government established a High Commission in St. John's and spent $16 million on improving its harbour.

Overseas, Canada's contribution to aerial combat became much more significant as part of Bomber Command, a division of Britain's Royal Air Force established in 1936. Initially, bombers focused on military targets and key infrastructure such as refineries and transportation systems. However, this expanded to civilian areas following a German bomber attack that mistakenly hit the centre of London on the night of August 24–25, 1940. Britain also moved toward "carpet bombing" as analyses showed that precision bombing did not find its targets. When Air Marshall Sir Arthur Harris took charge of Bomber Command in February 1942, the goal became to pummel Germany into submission through mass raids, sometimes with more than 1,000 planes.

Canada supplied 15 squadrons and 25 per cent of Bomber Command personnel. It suffered 9,919 killed, just over half of Canada's 17,100 air force fatalities, the highest rate among the three service branches (three-quarters of army fatalities), and certainly higher than Mackenzie King anticipated. Canada's major role in Bomber Command, and the belief among many Canadian air force personnel that they were not receiving due recognition from the British, such as for promotion, prompted growing demands for a separate Canadian-staffed and -led section of Bomber Command. The British and some Canadian air force brass resisted, claiming this was impractical and would compromise efficiency, but continued pressure resulted in No. 6 (Canadian) Group becoming operational on New Year's Day, 1943, the only non-British group in Bomber Command.

In the summer of 1943, Canada's army became heavily involved in combat. That spring, with the success of the Allies' North African campaign, preparations were made to expand into the Mediterranean, starting with Sicily. While King still feared the casualties of a ground campaign, he knew that continued resistance would cost him politically. There was also the belief that with Italian forces crumbling, involvement in the Mediterranean would bring relatively low casualties.

Some 23,000 Canadians were made part of a 140,000-strong invasion force. They had to traverse mountains via steep, narrow, and winding goat paths often blocked or booby-trapped by the enemy. They also endured Sicily's desert-like terrain, excruciating summer heat, and the threat of disease; some 1,200 Canadians in Sicily contracted malaria. They soon confronted battle-seasoned German troops with the 15th Panzer Division and the Hermann Göring Division. The month-long campaign to conquer Sicily accounted for nearly 50,000 casualties, with roughly equal numbers on both sides, that included 562 Canadians killed and nearly 1,800 wounded.

On September 3, 1943, Canadian troops joined Britain's Eighth Army in crossing the Strait of Messina into Italy. Of the 92,757 Canadians who fought in Italy, 5,764 were killed, 19,486 were wounded, and 1,004 were captured. The Italians offered virtually no opposition, as the invasion prompted a coup against Benito Mussolini and overtures to establish a separate peace with the Allies. Reacting quickly, German troops poured in, disarming more than a million Italians, jailing over 650,000, and killing about 12,000 Italian officers.

Map 7.2 Italy and Sicily.

For the Canadians, only the beginning of the campaign was relatively quiet as the Germans abandoned coastal areas, but inland they dug in for what became a war of attrition. In October, the Canadians met stiff resistance at Campobasso, located some 100 kilometres northeast of Naples. The next month, they moved northeast to cross the Sangro River, advancing in cold and sleet and through mud-soaked terrain, and on December 6, they encountered heavy German resistance at the Moro River, which became known as the "river of blood." Late December brought brutal urban warfare in Ortona, where the Canadians battled against two well-seasoned German paratroop battalions. Fighting proceeded room-by-room as the Canadians blasted their way through walls adjoining row houses, many of which were booby-trapped.

Figure 7.4 Lieutenant I. Macdonald (with binoculars) of the 48th Highlanders of Canada preparing to give the order to attack to infantrymen of his platoon, San Leonardo di Ortono, Italy, December 10, 1943.

Casualties would have been much higher had not medical services vastly improved since World War I, with blood typing and the use of antibiotics. Whereas the death rate among Canadians who reached medical services in World War I was 114 per 1,000, in World War II it was 66 per 1,000. Although stigma still surrounded battle exhaustion, the Canadians, starting in Italy, joined the Americans and British in establishing rest centres to which the psychologically afflicted were sent for a few days to rejuvenate. Canada's military made substantial efforts to provide relief and recreational services. Auxiliary services brought food, candy, tea, cigarettes, reading material, and sporting equipment to points near the front. Leave centres were established in captured cities, the first in October 1943 in Campobasso. There, the YMCA provided a canteen service as well as rooms for reading and writing, games, dances, and shows, while the Salvation Army managed lodging capable of handling up to 4,000 visitors.

POLITICAL AND SOCIAL DEVELOPMENTS, 1942–1944

Reflecting Canada's wartime contributions, the federal government lobbied for greater international recognition, especially when this coincided with national interests. Demands were made for representation on a number of Allied boards helping to conduct the war effort. In making its case, Canada advocated the Functional Principle, which proposed that in certain areas, or functions, Canada was a leading power, and thus warranted representation.

Canada first met with disappointment, as in March 1942 it was unsuccessful in securing membership on the Allied Munitions Assignment Board; Canada ranked third in Allied war production, but this still translated into only 5 per cent of the total. Canada also sought representation on the Combined Food Board. The British voiced opposition and the Americans suggested that Canada should be satisfied with membership on the less powerful Combined Production and Resources Board. Ottawa persisted, and ultimately, based on Canada's massive agricultural output, achieved success.

Within Canada, the increasing scale of the war accelerated social change, but also anxiety over the process. Between June 1939 and the beginning of 1944, some 370,000 women obtained employment in areas directly connected to the war effort, often in roles that had been the exclusive domain of men. The number of women with jobs outside the home grew from 22.7 to 33.1 per cent of the eligible female workforce aged 14 and older. Record numbers of working women were married and had children. To meet the rising demand for labour, in mid-1942 the federal government introduced income tax breaks for working couples and passed legislation to provide joint federally–provincially funded childcare facilities. Government propaganda and press commentary conveyed the message that women had taken wartime jobs out of patriotism to release men for military action and with victory overseas would return to domestic life. Yet several accounts, especially those written by female columnists, heralded the workplace contributions of women and spoke favourably of this being the basis for more permanent change. Lotta Dempsey, a future editor-in-chief with *Chatelaine*, then the most widely circulated magazine geared to Canadian women, wrote in 1943: "This was the time and the place it really started, the honest-to-goodness equality of Canadian women. It began to happen that hour when Canadian girls left desks and kitchens… stepped into overalls and took their places in the lines of workers at lathes and drills."[8]

Figure 7.5 Women munitions workers having their hair styled by fellow women munitions workers, Montreal, 1941.

At the wartime workplace, men still dominated higher-prestige and higher-paid jobs. Several factories employed female inspectors to monitor women's behaviour, such as preventing excessive fraternization with male co-workers. Still, many women spoke of being changed by their work experience, often in ways that portended ambitions extending beyond traditional female roles. They were proud of having coped with long hours and physically demanding tasks, from successfully performing "men's" jobs and from earning their own paycheque.

8 *Women at War* (Toronto: Maclean-Hunter, 1943), 10.

Figure 7.6 Recruiting for the Canadian Women's Army Corps.

Controversy also accompanied women into the CWAC, RCAF-WD, and WRCNS. The government assured Canadians that precautions were in place to prevent femininity from being compromised in the rough military world, such as uniforms designed by fashion experts to flatter the female form. Initially, women who enlisted earned two-thirds the male pay rate and were mostly confined to lower-graded jobs that reflected gender stereotypes. As of March 1945, 62 per cent of CWAC personnel were administrative clerks, and 8 per cent were cooks. Yet, to attract more female recruits, in July 1943, their basic pay was raised to 80 per cent of the male rate, and raises for achieving trade qualifications were provided on an equal basis with men.

The war also shaped the lives of Canadian children. By the end of 1944, in one of many such volunteer efforts, Ontario students raised nearly $800,000 for the Red Cross. Assignments often became patriotic lessons, such as "essays, poetry, and composition…dedicated to… the defence of democracy, the evils of fascism, and support for Canadian participation."[9] Tens of thousands of lads enrolled in cadet corps or were transported to the countryside to make up for shortages of agricultural labour.

However, with so many fathers in the military, or both parents working, it was assumed that too many children were not receiving adequate guidance. Talk swirled about girls dating servicemen, of boys joining gangs, of neglected children, and of an emerging crisis with delinquency as court appearances by juveniles rose by nearly 40 per cent between 1939 and 1942, reaching nearly 14,000. One prominent reaction was increased pressure upon working mothers to return home as soon as the war ended.

9   Cynthia Comacchio, "'To Hold on High the Torch of Liberty': Canadian Youth and the Second World War," in Geoffrey Hayes, Mike Bechthold, and Matt Symes (eds.), *Canada and the Second World War: Essays in Honour of Terry Copp* (Waterloo: Wilfrid Laurier University Press, 2012), 42.

Organized labour became another focal point. In many ways, workers were better off: unemployment evaporated, and between 1938 and 1943 the average annual pre-tax salary rose from $956 to $1,525. Countless workers were determined not to let down the country during this crisis. They clocked in record hours and produced to their absolute limit. Both the Trades and Labour Congress and the Canadian Congress of Labour officially discouraged strikes. Still, grievances mounted. Early in the war, the King government ignored union demands for compulsory collective bargaining rights. Many workers were angered by mandatory wage controls, claiming that their pay had not risen adequately since the Depression.

Organized labour's strength increased during the war as worker shortages helped the cause of unionization, since people became less fearful about losing their jobs if they supported a union. That fact, along with a burgeoning industrial work-force, resulted in an explosion of union membership from 358,967 in 1939 to 724,188 by 1944. Despite pledges from union leaders to avoid wartime strikes, organized labour began flexing its muscles. In 1943, there were 401 strikes with just over a million days lost, more than five times the total in 1939. Many Canadians demanded the internment of strike leaders, but King, with his experience in labour negotiations, chose the path of conciliation. In the spring of 1943, his government tasked the recently established National War Labour Board to undertake a comprehensive investigation of labour relations. Its report, received in August but not made public until early 1944, concluded that improvements in collective bargaining rights for labour were justified.

Although Ottawa stalled, action occurred at the provincial level. With an election slated for August 1943, the Ontario Liberals, under Premier Harry Nixon, proposed legislation guaranteeing unions collective bargaining rights if they obtained a majority of support from workers. However, under George Drew, the Ontario Progressive Conservatives supported this as well as improved pensions for the unemployed, construction of public housing, and increased funding for education. Drew's main challenge came from the CCF, which was endorsed by organized labour.

The Conservatives squeaked into office with 37 seats, three more than the CCF; the Liberals fell to third place. Drew accepted an amended version of the 1943 *Collective Bargaining Act*, which the Liberals had introduced, under which an Ontario Labour Court was established. Also in 1943, the Pattullo government in British Columbia amended the *Conciliation and Arbitration Act* to require an employer to enter into collective bargaining with a union when the provincial minister of labour was satisfied that the union held a majority of support among workers. In 1944, the Godbout government in Quebec passed the *Loi des relations ouvrières*, which facilitated successful union drives for thousands of workers.

King, like other leaders of Allied nations, concluded that the time had arrived to demonstrate a clear commitment to post-war planning, social security, and better labour relations. A September 1943 national poll showed CCF support at 29 per cent compared to 28 per cent each for the Liberals and the Progressive Conservatives. The following June, Canada elected its first CCF government when Tommy Douglas became Saskatchewan's premier.

In 1943, an Advisory Committee on Reconstruction established a subcommittee to examine social security. Its research director was Leonard Marsh of McGill University, widely considered a leading expert on social policy and a British-trained expert in social security. His *Report on Social Security* adopted many of the recommendations of a similar report by Lord Beveridge in England and advocated family allowances, better unemployment insurance and old age pensions, a public health insurance program, sickness benefits, and death benefits for dependants of the deceased. King balked at accepting such a sweeping range of proposals. He worried about the price tag and a backlash from provincial governments over excessive centralization and staked out a middle position. In the January 1944 Throne Speech, the Liberals committed to providing family allowances, a payment graduated from $5 to $8 for each child up to the age of 16. When passed by Parliament on August 1, it became Canada's first universal social program in that everyone eligible qualified (there was no means test). The next month, the federal government introduced PC 1003 (an Order in Council) guaranteeing workers union recognition if their chosen union received a majority of support.

MOVING TO VICTORY, 1944–1945

While King battled at home to keep political opponents at bay and the country united, Canadian soldiers overseas widened their fight to finish off the enemy. In Italy, in 1944, just to the north of Ortona, the Canadians confronted major German defensive lines. First there was the Gustav Line, blocking the road to Rome, which consisted of mine belts up to 100 metres deep, pillboxes, tank turrets embedded in concrete, and anti-tank ditches. Starting on May 14, I Canadian Corps battled for three days to break through its section. The Germans fell back to the even more formidable Hitler Line. The Canadians attacked on May 23, and that day Canada's 2nd Infantry Brigade took 543 casualties, a record for such a formation during the Italian campaign.

Starting in February 1945, I Corps moved from Italy to join II Corps in northwest Europe in a campaign that involved 237,000 Canadians, over 44,000 of whom became casualties, a number that included over 11,000 killed. On D-Day—June 6, 1944—some 15,000 mostly untested Canadian troops stormed ashore at Juno Beach as part of "Operation Overlord," the invasion of Normandy. Commanders of Germany's 12th SS, the main opposition, believed they could easily contain and destroy the inexperienced Canadians. D-Day brought the Canadians 914 casualties, including 340 dead, but pre-invasion estimates had predicted up to double that number, and on that first day they advanced further than any other Allied army.

The Germans quickly regrouped, and within five days Canadian losses reached 1,017 dead and 1,814 wounded, rates that corresponded to some of the worst fighting on the western front during World War I. It took 33 days for Canadian and British forces to capture Caen, a port city that Field Marshal Bernard Montgomery, Britain's highest-ranking officer, had said was possible to take by the end of D-Day. On August 21, the Canadians and other Allied forces closed the Argentan-Falaise Pocket (more frequently referred to as the Battle of the Falaise Gap) through which the Germans were retreating, thus stranding large numbers of the enemy and ending their resistance in Normandy. However, victory came at a steep price: Canada took 18,444 casualties, including 5,021 dead.

In September, Canadian forces assumed the left flank of the Allied advance and were assigned to capture the French channel ports. By October, Le Havre, Boulogne, Calais, and Dieppe were in Allied hands. However, these port facilities were badly damaged and too small and distant to handle the magnitude of supplies the Allies required. Only the Belgian port of Antwerp, located 80 kilometres inland from the North Sea along the Scheldt River, could fit the bill. Britain's Second Army had captured it, but not the surrounding area. The Canadians were tasked with clearing the Germans from the series of waterways and islands to the north of Antwerp that formed the Scheldt estuary. They had to traverse rivers, canals, water-filled ditches, flooded fields, and badly exposed roadways. Reflecting growing battlefield proficiency, they prevailed, but only after a month of bloodletting that cost 6,367 casualties, over 1,800 of which were fatal.

In February 1945, the First Canadian Army (now composed of I and II Corps) moved west to take Nijmegen in the south-central Netherlands, and south to neutralize the enemy between the Maas and Rhine rivers in Germany. In late March, the Canadians drove north to liberate the Netherlands. They were greeted with jubilation, having freed a population that had suffered severely under the Nazis. In the densely populated area around Arnhem, nearly 18,000 people starved to death during the last six months of the war. To the very end, the ground campaign cost the Canadians dearly. During the final phase of operations, extending from March 24 to May 5, the First Canadian Army suffered 6,298 casualties, 1,482 of which were fatal.

At home, King continued to resist conscription, but signals from Quebec became more worrisome. On August 8, 1944, Maurice Duplessis returned to power, as Godbout was regarded as too closely aligned with the federal Liberals. Meanwhile,

Defence Minister Ralston became more outspoken about the need to conscript after visiting troops overseas in autumn 1944 and noting that several battalions were below strength. This in turn cost lives as troops became exhausted and had less firepower with which to subdue the enemy. With Ralston no longer willing to relent, but also not offering to resign as King hoped, the prime minister turned to the defence minister's two-year old resignation offer made in response to Bill 80 and sacked him.

King replaced Ralston with General A.G.L. McNaughton, a popular figure among Canadians, although he had been sent back from England because of several botched training exercises, quarrels with Ralston, and because of his determination to resist any British plan to divide up Canadian forces as Allied reinforcements. McNaughton's new assignment was to convince a notable proportion of the 68,000 men then conscripted into the home defence force to accept overseas service. Within weeks, McNaughton admitted he could not succeed. In cabinet, support for conscription grew with likely resignations should King not act. King relented in late November 1944 but in doing so still pursued compromise. He authorized the conscription for overseas service of 16,000 men serving under the NRMA, a figure the Army's Chief of Staff identified as the bare minimum. Some 2,000 persons demonstrated in Montreal and smaller numbers in Quebec City. Still, the response in Quebec was far less violent than the reaction to conscription in World War I because King, unlike Borden, was viewed as having resisted for as long as possible and as adopting a minimalist response. In English-speaking Canada, many resented King for delaying so long on conscription, but ultimately by taking some action, he avoided a political catastrophe.

The Liberal government also held support because by 1944 not only was it introducing social welfare, but also economic plans to try to ensure a smooth transition to peacetime. C.D. Howe was transferred from Munitions and Supply to the newly created post of minister of reconstruction. At his direction, firms received more than $250 million in accelerated depreciation tax write-offs on new capital equipment between November 1944 and January 1946 to assist with reconverting to civilian production.

For many Canadians, returning to normalcy also meant getting women out of full-time employment. Mothers were made to feel guilty for not spending more time at home and, after nearly six years of war, many single women worried that time was of the essence if they wanted to avoid spinsterhood. Canada's marriage rate rose from 9 per 1,000 in 1945 to 11 per 1,000 the following year, and the fertility rate per 1,000 women from 24 in 1945 to a post-war peak of 29 in 1947, ushering in a period known as the Baby Boom. The federal government ended financial support for daycare and eliminated wartime income tax breaks for working wives. No protection was extended to women as many employers radically restructured the gender composition of their workforce. In Thunder Bay, Canadian Car and Foundry dismissed all but three of the

3,000 women it had hired to produce aircraft. Also, by the end of 1944, plans were well underway to eliminate the CWAC, the RCAF-WD, and the WRCNS.

Long-held racist attitudes also continued. As the war ended, Japanese Canadians were forced to choose between dispersal within Canada east of the Rockies or repatriation to Japan. By mid-August 1945, 10,397 Japanese Canadians, including 3,484 children, opted for repatriation. By the end of the year, 4,720 requested that their decision be reversed as they came to realize Japan was devastated. Ottawa announced that it would accept reapplications to stay in Canada if made before September 2, 1945, the official date of Japan's surrender, but would treat other requests on a case-by-case basis. In all, 3,964 returned to Japan. Unable to adjust, many applied to come back to Canada, but only 174 cases were successful.

While efforts were made to disperse or expel the Japanese, Canadians waited with much anticipation, and some trepidation, the return home of 500,000 servicemen. Mackenzie King viewed veterans as a huge voting bloc and realized military personnel did not hold him in high regard. Many denounced him for not serving in World War I—even though he was nearly 40 when it broke out—and for adamantly resisting conscription.

Determined to avoid mistakes made with veterans of World War I, the federal government started planning early for repatriation. In October 1941, it introduced the Post-Discharge Re-establishment Order. Under its provisions, those honourably discharged would receive a tax-exempt gratuity payment of $7.50 per month for time served in the Western Hemisphere, and $15 per month for time overseas. For veterans who did not claim other benefits, such as retraining, more cash was available, up to a level matching the gratuity in the form of a tax-free Re-establishment Credit intended to help them purchase, furnish, or equip a home or business. The 1942 *Reinstatement in Civil Employment Act* affirmed that healthy veterans had the right to resume their pre-military jobs, or a comparable post with their former employer, at a rate of pay equivalent to what they would have earned had they not enlisted. Grants and subsidized loans were available to those who wanted to start their own businesses, to enter commercial fishing, or, under the 1942 *Veterans Land Act,* to farm full-time or to start a small hobby farm. The 1942 *Vocational Training Co-ordination Act* provided a living allowance to any veteran who decided to retool at the government's expense, an opportunity that, after World War I, was available only to those whose injuries likely prevented the prospect of finding decent work. Qualified veterans could obtain free university education with a living allowance for a period equivalent to the time they spent in the military. Veteran benefits dwarfed all other federal social welfare costs, accounting for, between 1944 and 1948 inclusive, expenditures of $1.842 billion out of $3.621 billion.

As the next federal election approached, Mackenzie King remained concerned. His limited response to conscription left the Tories with room to gain ground. Before dissolving Parliament for an election scheduled on June 11, King's government declared its support for a *White Paper on Income and Employment* that advocated Ottawa use its new taxing, and hence spending, powers to maintain "a high and stable level of employment." The Liberals ran on the slogan "A New Social Order" for Canada. Also critical for King was good timing, as on May 8, 1945, Germany surrendered, thus deflating the contentious issue of conscription. The Liberals retained a majority, though a razor-thin one, winning 118 out of 245 seats, but they could count on support from eight independent Liberals.

CONCLUSION

As the war ended, many challenges and uncertainties lay ahead. Could Ottawa fulfill its commitment to provide effective post-war planning? Had Canada exchanged its recent colonial relationship with Britain for subservience to the United States? Would veterans effectively reintegrate into civilian life? One indication of possible future turmoil involving veterans was the VE-Day riot in Halifax. More than 1,000 naval personnel led in the looting of some 500 stores and produced $5 million in damages, three civilian deaths, and 211 arrests.

The war brought many questionable policies that historians still debate. Was there justification for outlawing groups like the Communist Party? In 1988, the Canadian government offered an official apology and $21,000 to each surviving Japanese Canadian who had been forcibly evacuated. Many accused Mackenzie King of placing the political interests of the Liberals in Quebec over the need to properly reinforce Canadian troops through conscription. King looked back to World War I, trying to avoid repeating scenarios that had split Canada along its French–English axis and that had fuelled class-based discord. His government sought to avoid Canada's involvement in the ground war to minimize casualties, though by the end of the conflict all three armed service branches had made enormous contributions.

Overseas, mistakes were made, most notably at Hong Kong and Dieppe, but Canada's military grew more skillful, becoming leaders in convoy protection, Bomber Command, and in the Mediterranean and northwest European campaigns. Canada became a major supplier of arms and commodities, factors which enabled the King government to successfully pursue greater representation internationally, though necessity also intertwined Canada more closely with the United States. Realizing Canadians' resolve that the end of the conflict not be followed by a return to pre-war economic conditions, the Liberals made substantive steps in introducing social welfare, new rights for labour, and in setting the framework for the federal government to assume a more interventionist role in post-war economic planning.

Numerous Canadians suffered tremendously during the war and would look back upon these years with sadness, bitterness, and anger. Certainly, Japanese Canadians were treated no better than Ukrainians in World War I. Their rights were ignored because most Canadians, fuelled by prejudice and panic, believed it was prudent to crush the freedoms of the Japanese in this country, even if there was no compelling evidence to justify such action. Yet, on balance, if there is such a thing as a "Good War,"[10] perhaps World War II qualifies. Its cause to crush Nazism and Fascism was unassailable. For Canada, these years saw an economic depression supplanted by an economic boom; governments assuming unprecedented responsibilities for the welfare of Canadians; and the stage set for the addition of a tenth province. Despite compromises and equivocations and, for some, betrayal, Mackenzie King brought Canada out of World War II far more united and ready to face the future than had Robert Borden a generation earlier.

---

10 This term is often applied to World War II. See, for example, Studs Terkel, *The Good War: An Oral History of World War II* (New York: Pantheon Books, 1985), and J.L. Granatstein and Peter Neary (eds.), *The Good Fight: Canadians and World War II* (Toronto: Copp Clark, 1995).

8 PROSPERITY, PREJUDICE, AND PARANOIA, 1945–1957

INTRODUCTION

The future appeared bright at the end of World War II. Democracy had triumphed over totalitarianism. Canada emerged from the conflict as a respected middle power. Still, there were doubts and unease. The celebrations following the surrender of Japan on August 16, 1945, were tempered somewhat by the dropping of atomic bombs on Hiroshima and Nagasaki on August 6 and 9. These had horrifically demonstrated the catastrophic consequences of another world war. Many feared a post-war economic slump such as that following World War I. There was worry that Canada's labour movement, whose membership had doubled during the war, would prove a threat to social order. There was also the enormous challenge of reintegrating hundreds of thousands of veterans.

The period between the end of World War II and the defeat of the Liberal government of Louis St. Laurent in 1957 were widely regarded as prosperous and socially stable. Between 1945 and 1960, Canada's population grew from 12.1 to 17.9 million. Its urban population reached 60 per cent of the nation's total, with greater Montreal climbing to nearly 2 million people and Toronto to 1.2 million. Canadians, at home and abroad, were viewed as joining a burgeoning, home-owning middle class and as enjoying happy, stable marriages and family life. There was much about which Canadians seemed satisfied. Successive large federal Liberal majority governments pointed to confidence that things were being managed effectively and that people were optimistic about the future. There appeared little tolerance for those who criticized norms, such as liberal democracy, capitalism, patriarchy, and traditional marriage and families. Many tarred the political left as being treasonous Communists. Others who did not fit in—culturally, ethnically, or socially—were ostracized. So while there seemed something of a consensus on what was normal or right, there were also the ingredients for future conflict.

FROM WAR TO PEACE

Although many of Canada's World War II veterans struggled to re-establish themselves into civilian life, overall, they were less embittered than veterans had been after World War I. Under the 1945 *Veterans Charter*, some 100,000 men retrained for over 100 trades, 75,000 qualified for government-subsidized full-size or hobby farms, and 54,000 obtained free university education.

Record numbers of Canadians rushed to the altar, eager to settle down and start a family. Canada's marriage rate rose from 9.0 per 1,000 in 1945 to 10.9 the following year, and the fertility rate per 1,000 women climbed from 24.3 in 1945 to a post-war peak of 28.9 in 1947. Canada's housing supply struggled to keep pace. In 1945, emergency regulations prohibited people from moving to Vancouver, Victoria, Winnipeg, Hamilton, Toronto, Ottawa, and Hull. Unions launched an offensive for significant salary hikes to compensate for the wartime wage freeze. In 1945, days lost to strikes topped 1 million, and in 1946 reached an all-time record of 4.5 million. Among the most prominent disputes was a 99-day strike over compulsory union membership and wages starting on September 12, 1945, at the Ford plant in Windsor, Ontario. The federal government appointed Supreme Court Justice Ivan Rand to settle the dispute. The resulting "Rand Formula" did not compel union membership but did require that everyone covered by a collective agreement pay union dues because all shared in the benefits won.

Post-war wages improved significantly; between 1945 and 1948, industrial wages in Ontario rose from 69.4¢ to 91.3¢ per hour. A peace formula took hold in which unions opted for legal legitimacy and steady workplace improvements over broader, class-based campaigns, such as to gain shop-floor control. Still, during the early 1950s, the *Ontario Labour Relations Act* was amended to delay strike action and to prevent unionization in a wide array of occupations deemed essential, including "teachers...security guards, engineers, police, fire fighters, agricultural, and horticultural workers."[1]

In a period where the Cold War and fear over the spread of Communism soon loomed large, Canada's political left faced pressure to adopt more mainstream positions. This was evident with the country's only CCF government in Saskatchewan. Despite

---

1   Charles Smith, "The Politics of the *Ontario Labour Relations Act:* Business, Labour, and Government in the Consolidation of Post-War Industrial Relations, 1949–1961," *Labour/Le Travail* 62 (2008): 120.

winning a massive landslide in 1944, with 47 of 52 seats, Premier Tommy Douglas, an ordained Baptist minister, found his government criticized by large segments of the Catholic Church, one of whose leaders portrayed the CCF as "enslaved by the mental tyranny...[of] Socialism."[2] The Church opposed the CCF commitment, delivered in 1947, to provide state hospital insurance. The CCF also passed a *Trade Union Act* under which union membership in Saskatchewan soared by 118 per cent between 1944 and 1948. In 1946, it expropriated the Prince Albert Box Company because it did not abide by the provisions of the legislation. However, the government assured that this enterprise (for which it paid fair market price) and other provincial Crown corporations turned a profit, and it held the line against raising taxes.

Canada's post-war economy inspired confidence. Fears of high unemployment dissipated as it climbed to only 3 per cent. At the end of the conflict, Canadians held $6.5 billion in accumulated savings and were eager to spend, a fact which helped to ease the economic transition from war to peace. Under the 1945 *National Emergency Transition Powers Act*, the federal government maintained control over the price of items until their supply had reached a level where removing the ceiling did not risk generating significant inflation.

The public strongly supported federal government initiatives to pursue more extensive planning and to provide social programs to ensure greater stability. Canadians remembered the Depression and feared that a hands-off approach from government risked its return. Having committed itself in the later stages of the war to more extensive welfare and Keynesian economic strategy, Ottawa was determined to carry on as the dominant power in the federation. The King government called a dominion–provincial conference for August 1945. Its intentions, spelled out in a document called the *Green Book*, spoke of institutionalizing the recent transfer of taxing powers to the federal government in exchange for transfer payments to the provinces. Ontario Premier George Drew and Quebec's Maurice Duplessis resisted the plan, as the bulk of taxes were collected in Central Canada. Finally, in 1947, with federal Finance Minister J.L. Ilsley threatening to have Ottawa proceed unilaterally, a five-year agreement was hammered out under which Ottawa retained taxing powers in exchange for transfer payments. Ontario and Quebec refused to sign, and in 1947, Ontario began its own modest income and corporate tax system.

EARLY POST-WAR FOREIGN POLICY

The post-war period would be defined by the Cold War that pitted the United States and its allies against the Soviet Union and its supporters. Many Anglo-Canadians

---

2   Peter Meehan, "'Purified Socialism' and the Church in Saskatchewan: Tommy Douglas, Philip Pocock and Hospitalization, 1944–1948," *CCHA Historical Studies* 77 (2011): 29.

still expressed primary loyalty to Britain, but the days of imperialism had passed, and England emerged from World War II battered and virtually bankrupt. The King government dismissed a suggestion made in Toronto near the end of the war by Lord Halifax, Britain's Ambassador to the United States, that Canada join a post-war Empire military alliance.

In a post-war world rapidly defined by the superpower rivalry, Canada accepted the United States as the leader in defending the "free world" against the spread of Communism. In the first two years after the war, the Soviet Union came to control governments in Poland, Romania, Yugoslavia, Albania, Bulgaria, and East Germany. Its leader, Joseph Stalin, was likened to Hitler, against whom appeasement would not work. The Communist Party of Canada, which was banned in 1941 (though allowed to reappear as the Labour Progressive Party in 1943), was not legalized until 1959.

Figure 8.1 Igor Gouzenko long hid his identity to prevent Soviet retribution. Here he appears on television in 1966.

One of the first events that touched off the four-decade Cold War occurred in Canada. On September 5, 1945, Igor Gouzenko, a cipher clerk at the Soviet embassy in Ottawa, defected after learning that he and his family were to be sent home. Gouzenko sneaked out over 100 secret documents exposing Soviet attempts to steal information about the atomic bomb, which was then solely in American hands, and to establish a network of sleeper agents across North America. This information ultimately led to the arrest of 22 local agents and 15 Soviet spies. In early 1946, Canada's federal government created the Kellock-Taschereau Royal Commission to investigate and interrogate many of those Gouzenko named. Its recommendations resulted in the establishment of a federal security panel, with military and RCMP representatives, to identify Communists in sensitive positions.

Besides being placed in the maelstrom of the emerging Cold War, Canada also sought to raise its international standing. Because of its rich uranium deposits, it was the only non-superpower to have representation on the UN Atomic Energy Commission. Lester Pearson was named the first chair of the UN Food and Agricultural Organization. Between the end of World War II and 1960, Canada established diplomatic ties with 36 countries. During this period, Canada also shed the last vestiges of its colonial past. On

January 1, 1947, the *Canadian Citizenship Act* came into effect that ended the status of Canadians as British subjects. Two years later, appeals to the Judicial Committee of the Privy Council were ended. In 1952, Vincent Massey, Canada's former ambassador to the United States, became the first Canadian-born governor general.

Many came to speak of a "golden age" of Canadian foreign policy, when, as a middle power, Canada took on a more active role in building better international relations. Yet, Prime Minister King remained wary of international commitments. He supported Article 44 of the new UN Charter permitting members to opt out of collective security. Just as after World War I, Canada gutted its military; by the end of 1946, its three services numbered fewer than 25,000 full-time personnel. Australia, not Canada, was first elected as a non-permanent member of the UN Security Council. Canada was not a major contributor of foreign aid, and much of which it provided was in the form of tied aid, meaning it had to involve the provision of Canadian goods like prairie grain.

Despite its talk of encouraging international collaboration and advancing its independent voice, Canadian foreign policy was profoundly influenced by the American–Soviet rivalry. In 1947, the King government signed a "Joint Statement for Defence Collaboration" that spoke of improving US–Canada military cooperation. The Soviets accused Canada of being a puppet of America, to which Ottawa responded by closing its embassy in Moscow.

Economics also drew Canada closer to America. A devastated Europe could not pay Canada for goods it required, money Canada needed to pay its own trade deficit with the United States. With a liquidity crisis looming, Ottawa restricted American imports and the outflow of US currency. Canada sought access to funds the United States made available to Europe under the 1947 Marshall Plan, a massive aid program to assist Europe with its post-war recovery. Several American politicians criticized Canada's discriminatory legislation, but once import controls were lifted, the United States allowed European nations to use up to $300 million annually received under the Marshall Plan to purchase Canadian goods. Support grew on both sides of the border for a comprehensive US–Canada free trade pact. A tentative five-year plan was reached in February 1948, but King balked at the last minute, recalling the disastrous political consequences of free trade for the Liberals in the 1891 and 1911 elections.

CHANGING THE GUARD, NOT THE APPROACH

In November 1948, King retired after some four decades in Parliament, more than half of them as prime minister. His replacement was Louis St. Laurent. Born in Compton in Quebec's Eastern Townships in 1882 to a French-Canadian father and an Irish mother, St. Laurent entered King's government in 1942 to replace Ernest Lapointe as justice minister. A prominent corporate lawyer before entering politics, St. Laurent ran his government like a business, treating his cabinet like a board of directors and demanding efficiency and results. Yet, he also projected a genial, grandfatherly image and became affectionately known as "Uncle Louis."

In June 1949, seven months after becoming prime minister, St. Laurent faced the electorate. His government pointed to a buoyant economy. The Liberals had established an excellent campaign team, and, with strong ties to the business community, accumulated plenty of cash for the election. The Progressive Conservatives, under the leadership of former Ontario Premier George Drew, anticipated a political revival. However, Drew came across as stiff and combative. The Liberals triumphed with 49 per cent of the popular vote and 193 of 262 seats.

The Liberals continued to benefit from a booming economy. Inflation, unemployment, and taxes remained low. C.D. Howe moved from the Department of Reconstruction—which ceased operations in 1948—to become minister of trade and commerce. He strongly encouraged foreign investment, particularly from the United States, through various incentive programs.

Figure 8.2 Cultivating the "Uncle Louis" image, the prime minister reads the comics to his grandchildren.

Canada's strong economy and its ability to afford social programs like family allowances and unemployment insurance were key in convincing Newfoundland to join Confederation. In early 1946, Britain's House of Commons announced the creation of a National Convention in Newfoundland to make recommendations for a referendum on the island's future. It convened on September 11, 1946. Initially delegates had little discussion about joining Canada. One man changed the agenda: Joseph R. Smallwood, a former union organizer, journalist, and radio commentator. He argued that union with Canada would bring Newfoundland social programs well beyond the ability of its current government. Smallwood worked out a draft agreement with Ottawa that promised Newfoundland full access to federal social programs, funds to improve its antiquated railway and to upgrade Gander airport, and for the federal government to assume Newfoundland's debt.

The Responsible Government League (RGL) opposed Smallwood, warning Newfoundlanders that their distinctiveness, self-determination, and tax dollars would all be consumed by the larger Canadian nation. There also emerged the Economic Union Party (EUP), which advocated tighter relations with America. The campaign was brutal, with Smallwood receiving death threats. On June 3, 1948, 45 per cent of Newfoundlanders voted for independent responsible government, 41 per cent for joining Canada, and 14 per cent for maintaining the current British-controlled commission government. A second referendum was slated for July 22, in which commission government was dropped as an option. Anti-confederates lacked funds, and a tenuous alliance between the EUP and RGL generated fears about Newfoundland becoming part of the United States. Confederation squeaked in with 52.3 per cent, and on March 31, 1949, Newfoundland became Canada's tenth province.

THE COLD WAR GROWS CHILLIER

In 1948, a Soviet-sponsored coup brought Communists to power in Czechoslovakia. England, France, Belgium, Holland, and Luxembourg responded with the Treaty of Brussels, which established a mutual defence pact. On April 4, 1949, Canada joined the United States, members of the Brussels pact, and other European states to form the North Atlantic Treaty Organization (NATO). Besides selling NATO to Canadians as a means of containing the Soviet Union, Canada's government argued that as a multilateral pact, no one nation, that is, the United States, would dominate NATO, thus protecting Canadian sovereignty. Canada also promoted NATO as an organization that would encourage trade, an economic aim it had inserted as Article II in NATO's Charter, though this ultimately had no impact.

At the outset of the 1950s, as part of NATO, Canada sent a brigade of 6,000 soldiers to northwest Germany. Its navy integrated into NATO deterrents against the Soviets off North America's Atlantic and Pacific coasts. In 1952, Canada's federal government established a record peacetime defence budget of $2.4 billion, nearly five times greater than two years earlier. Most of that increased expenditure related to Canada joining the American-led and UN-sanctioned "police action" to enforce collective security in Korea. Following World War II, with the Soviets occupying the northern half of Korea and other Allied troops the south, the UN temporarily partitioned the country along the 38th parallel latitude until elections were held to unite it under a single government. However,

North Korea's leader, Kim Il Sung, and his Soviet backers, wanted to unify Korea under Communist rule. On June 25, 1950, North Korean soldiers poured across the 38th parallel and overwhelmed the far weaker South Korean forces.

The United States sought UN approval to apply collective security against North Korea. At the time, the Soviet Union was boycotting the UN due to its refusal to recognize the new Communist People's Republic of China. Although UN-sanctioned, the Americans commanded and supplied over 90 per cent of the international military force. The St. Laurent government, seeking to show support but also to minimize casualties, announced that Canada would provide three outdated navy destroyers and a Royal Canadian Air Force squadron, composed of propeller-driven Vampire fighters, to assist with logistics and communications. With combat operations initially going badly for the United States, Washington called on its allies to contribute more. Britain, Australia, and New Zealand committed ground forces, prompting Canada in August 1950 to provide a brigade.

In battle, the Canadians acquitted themselves well. In April 1951, at Kapyong, they suffered 10 dead and 23 wounded but played a key role in thwarting an attack that could have struck deep into central Korea. The intervention, which lasted until mid-1953, cost 516 Canadian lives, fifth largest among the 23 UN combatants, though this paled against nearly 138,000 South Korean and over 35,000 American servicemen killed.

East–West relations began to thaw following Stalin's death on March 5, 1953. Soon after, Canada restored diplomatic relations with the Soviet Union. Trade possibilities with the Soviet Union were explored in non-strategic products like wheat. Still, at America's urging, Canada became part of the International Commission for Supervision to enforce the 1954 Geneva Accords, under which Vietnam was partitioned following the defeat of French colonial forces by Vietminh Communists. Between 1951 and 1958, Canada allowed the United States to construct three northern radar lines on Canadian soil to protect North America against a possible Soviet air attack: the Pine Tree Line at 50° latitude, the Mid-Canada Line at 54° latitude, and the Distance Early Warning Line at 70° latitude. The Cominco plant in Trail, British Columbia, provided heavy water, and Eldorado mining, operating in the Northwest Territories, provided uranium to the United States, both of which were used to produce nuclear bombs.

The Royal Canadian Mounted Police consulted extensively with American and British intelligence services to assess threats from Soviet agents. By 1954, Canadian authorities had a list of 2,700 people in the country targeted for internment in the event of war with the Soviet Union. The RCMP screened immigrants; during the first two post-war decades, some 40,000 were rejected entry into Canada for security reasons. On the other hand, in 1956, some 30,000 Hungarian refugees, fleeing from a bloody and failed revolt against a Soviet-backed Communist government, quickly gained entry into Canada as they reinforced the "ideological…interests of the country."[3]

Canadians became involved in emergency defence planning. Families stockpiled non-perishable food and other essential supplies, and many converted their basements into fallout shelters, or paid from $500 to $1,500 to build a separate bomb shelter. Municipal governments in major cities developed emergency preparation plans to deal with a nuclear attack. Over 13,000 Canadian nurses received basic training on treating casualties from an atomic bomb. High school boys trained in dousing fires and girls in first aid; elementary schoolchildren practised "duck and cover" drills.

Stable families were portrayed as a source of strength against the insidious nature of Communism. *Chatelaine*, Canada's most prominent women's magazine, wrote that primary responsibility fell to women to maintain a safe, secure home environment, including the physical health of family members, to protect against dangers of the nuclear age.

Homosexuality, a criminal offence at the time, was perceived as a threat to the family unit, as well as to Canadian security. Suspected homosexuals were fired from federal government jobs, especially if they had access to sensitive information, because it was felt that they were targets for blackmail by Soviet agents. Gay life was pursued secretly. Many homosexuals lived in sham marriages and risked arrest if caught in gay bars or other such meeting places.

CONTINENTALISM AND CONFIDENCE

Integration with America manifested itself not only in anti-Communism and the economy, but also culture. In 1951, American magazines sold 86 million copies in Canada, more than doubling homegrown counterparts. St. Laurent's handlers warned him not to appear as dismissive of Canadian culture. Days before calling the 1949 election, his government established the Royal Commission on National Development in the Arts, Letters and Sciences. Over the next year it heard from some 1,200 people; a common theme was the need for greater government support for the arts and higher education. Its 1951 report established the basis for the Canada Council. Created six years later, it supported over 1,500 annual university scholarships, pumped over $40 million annually into other university initiatives, provided money for a new National Library, and funded numerous cultural bodies such as the Winnipeg Ballet and the Stratford Shakespeare Festival.

---

3   Andrew Thompson and Stephanie Bangarth, "Transnational Christian Charity: The Canadian Council of Churches, the World Council of Churches, and the Hungarian Refugee Crisis, 1956–1957," *American Review of Canadian Studies* 38, no. 3 (2008): 310.

Despite this, Canadians remained mass consumers of American culture. Hollywood films dominated in Canadian cinemas. In 1952, the first Canadian television stations went on the air: CBFT in Montreal and CBLT in Toronto. Canadians watched homegrown products such as the Maritime musical show *Don Messer's Jubilee*. Yet, even on the CBC, the most popular programs were American, such as *I Love Lucy* and *The Jackie Gleason Show*.

American direct investment into Canada continued rising, from $3.58 billion in 1950 to $8.33 billion in 1957. The government presented Canada's economic performance as a success story. Over the 1950s, industrial output,

Figure 8.3 *Don Messer's Jubilee*. Library and Archives Canada, MIKAN 3193094.

congregated in southern Ontario and Quebec, grew by some 50 per cent. Firms were becoming more capital intensive and efficient. Between 1945 and 1957, the number of manufacturing establishments rose by 30.6 per cent but the value of production by an astonishing 161.3 per cent. In Alberta, energy production rapidly expanded with a major oil strike in Leduc in February 1947. Across Canada, farms modernized. Rural electrical customers nearly doubled to over 3.6 million during the initial post-war decade. Tractors and other major farm machinery disseminated widely. Between 1945 and 1960, the area seeded for wheat grew from 930,000 to 1 million hectares, but the number of bushels produced from that land skyrocketed more than 60 per cent to over 500 million. Unemployment remained low, hovering between 2.8 and 5.9 per cent between 1945 and 1957. Canadians were earning more: between 1945 and 1960, the average annual salary nearly doubled from $1,649 to $3,176.

Canada's housing market remained red hot, fed by rising incomes, low down payment requirements and mortgage interest rates, and affordable prices. The 1944 *National Housing Act* halved the down payment requirement to 10 per cent and the Central Mortgage and Housing Corporation, a government agency established in 1945, helped keep mortgages fixed for as long as 25 years, up to five times the pre-war standard, and at rates as low as 4 per cent. Nearly 368,000 homes were constructed between 1945 and 1949, and in practically every year throughout the 1950s, over 100,000 new residential homes were built.

One million Canadians settled in suburban communities between 1945 and 1960, a trend made possible by expanding car ownership and road construction. Large builders used standardized designs and pre-assembled parts, mostly to construct single-storey bungalows or larger ranch-style homes. Some criticized new suburban developments for their uniformity, blandness, and for subliminally encouraging conformity. Yet, countless Canadians were thrilled to leave overcrowded city centres for new, affordable homes and family-friendly neighbourhoods. The suburbs provided young couples with entry into home ownership, and in the context of the Cold War "demonstrat[ed] the superiority of Western capitalism."[4] Home ownership grew at an unprecedented rate, rising from 57 to 65 per cent between 1941 and 1951.

New massive, planned communities emerged, such as Don Mills, north of Toronto, on some 800 hectares of farmland. Toronto business tycoon E.P. Taylor had initially slotted this space for a new commercial brewery but reconsidered in 1951 in light of increased demand for suburban housing. By the end of the decade, Don Mills was a community of 25,000 residents. Former hamlets—such as Scarborough and North York outside Toronto, and Burnaby and Coquitlam outside Vancouver— exploded in population. In the first three decades following World War II, the share of greater Vancouver's population living in suburban areas nearly tripled to just over 60 per cent. In 1953, Toronto annexed several surrounding townships, villages, and boroughs to create a metropolitan government to better plan for future growth.

With rising incomes, retail sales in Canada increased from $4.57 billion in 1945 to $13.47 billion in 1955. The television became a household staple, with sales rising from just 325 sets in 1948 to over 100,000 by 1953, as mass production and huge demand brought falling prices from economies of scale. Car registration skyrocketed from 1.16 million in 1945 to 4.1 million in 1960. Air travel, though still relatively expensive, also expanded—from 81,600 passengers in 1946 to 429,000 in 1955—as technology and safety advanced notably during World War II, as well as with more air routes, airports, and airlines as the government-owned Trans-Canada Airlines was joined by the privately owned Canadian Pacific Airlines in 1942.

Government spending helped fuel the post-war boom. Ottawa led the way with several massive infrastructure projects. In 1948, it provided $150 million to complete the Trans-Canada Highway. It forged ahead with the St. Lawrence Seaway, prodding the United States to share the costs—which for Canada reached nearly $1 billion between 1955 and 1959—by threatening to proceed unilaterally and thus manage the waterway.

---

4   James Onusko, "Childhood in Calgary's Postwar Suburbs: Kids, Bullets, and Boom, 1950–1965," *Urban History Review* 43, no. 2 (2015): 27.

Figure 8.4 Aerial shot in 1955 of the planned Toronto community of Don Mills.

The federal government made moderate improvements to social programs while maintaining low taxes. In 1952, the income-based means test for Old Age Pensions was removed for those 70 and older, though it was applied to those 65 to 69 as they became eligible for this benefit. In 1957, the federal Liberal government introduced the *Hospital Insurance and Diagnostic Services Act*, under which it pursued shared-cost agreements with the provinces—which were completed by 1961—to provide Canadians with free hospital care and laboratory and radiological diagnostic services for a range of medical needs.

With the public generally supportive of Ottawa's stronger role, federal–provincial disputes remained low-key, at least in English Canada. In 1948, Leslie Frost succeeded George Drew as Ontario's premier; Frost's greater amiability, self-proclaimed small-town values, and longevity in office, lasting until 1961, earned him the affectionate nickname of "Old Man Ontario." In 1952, Frost's government agreed to a five-year tax rental agreement with Ottawa in which Ontario largely ceded control over income and corporate taxes in exchange for a larger subsidy. Alberta's Social Credit government moderated its doctrines under Ernest Manning, who took over after William Aberhart's death in 1943. The Manning government courted investment, provided price supports to farmers, and followed a fiscally conservative approach.

NOT LIKE THE OTHERS

In Quebec, Maurice Duplessis's *Union Nationale* government, despite aggressively courting Anglo-Canadian and American investment, used French-Canadian nationalism to combat federal power. In 1948, Duplessis symbolically adopted the *fleur-de-lys* as Quebec's flag. Three years later, his government rejected federal funding for universities—casting it as interference in education—and in 1954 created its own income tax to force the federal government to retreat from this area. In 1953, the *Union Nationale* established the Quebec Royal Commission of Inquiry into Constitutional Problems. The five-volume report, released in 1956, presented Confederation as a pact between the English and French that inherently gave Quebec special status to protect and promote the French language and culture.

Duplessis projected a folksy charisma that endeared him to Francophones, especially those living in rural areas, to whom he cast himself as a protector of their way of life. Many revered *le chef*, or the chief, as he was called, as the only one capable of running the province. To others, he was a corrupt demagogue. With reason, many believed that only areas that voted *Union Nationale* received decent government services, something that helped keep rural Quebec, which required electrification, strongly behind the *Union Nationale*. For Quebec dairy farmers, Duplessis refused to authorize the sale of margarine, the 1886 ban of which in Canada was overturned by the courts in 1950, but did not appear in Quebec until 1961. Support from rural areas paid off handsomely because with the government resisting electoral readjustment, rural Quebec held over half the seats in the provincial legislature, despite having only one-third of the province's population.

Duplessis portrayed Quebec as morally superior based upon its agricultural and Catholic nature. Quebec's powerful Roman Catholic Church strongly backed Duplessis, especially since his government permitted it to retain control over schools and most social services for Francophones, a practice that also saved the provincial government a great deal of money. The church also firmly endorsed Duplessis's efforts to repress the political left, which it cast as spreading social disorder and atheism, and Jehovah's Witnesses for denouncing Catholicism and the Pope.

Anglo-Canadian and American business interests supported the *Union Nationale* because they enjoyed low taxation and faced little or no pressure to process resources in Quebec. Between 1953 and 1959, US investment in Quebec doubled to $4 billion, and Americans dominated in areas that included industry and resource development. The provincial government maintained it was collecting substantial royalties and that investment created good jobs. However, with most large firms operating in English,

Francophones were confined to the lower rungs, earning, on average, two-thirds of their English-speaking counterparts.

Duplessis was strongly anti-union, claiming he was protecting the province from outsiders and Communists. His government barely tolerated the *Confédération des travailleurs catholiques du Canada* (CTCC), despite its heavy church involvement and advocacy of joint committees of labour and management, rather than strikes, to settle disputes. André Laurendeau, the editor-in-chief of *Le Devoir*, one of Quebec's most influential newspapers, condemned Duplessis as a *roi nègre*, a token local ruler acting on behalf of imperial American interests.[5]

Forces for change were brewing in Quebec, but it would take Duplessis's death in 1959 to unleash the process. While Duplessis's power base was rural Quebec, the province's urban majority continued to grow. Federal government programs like unemployment insurance and family allowances started cutting into Church power and influence. More Quebeckers expressed frustration with the power yielded by Anglo-Canadians and Americans. Reformist elements in the Catholic Church cast Duplessis's government as corrupt because of its vast use of patronage and reliance on corporate contributions.

Organized labour grew more hostile. This became evident during the five-month-long strike, starting on Valentine's Day 1949, by some of Canada's poorest paid and overwhelmingly Francophone miners against the American-owned Johns Manville Corporation at Asbestos in Quebec's Eastern Townships. Chaplains in the area backed the strikers and dismissed the government's claim that Communists were fomenting class conflict. The strike spread to neighbouring, smaller mines. Because workers did not wait for the establishment of an arbitration board before striking, they were deemed in violation of Quebec's *Loi des relations ouvrières*, and their strike, which had grown to include some 5,000, was declared illegal. The government dispatched police to protect replacement workers. The dispute finally ended after strikers trying to close the mines clashed with police who, after reading the *Riot Act*, threatened to open fire.

Many Quebec intellectuals stressed the need for political change. These included Pierre Trudeau, then a young, left-wing lawyer and academic who witnessed events at Asbestos. Trudeau cast the strike as an awakening among Francophones to a repressive government. It was a message that he and a number of social scientists, primarily at Laval University, also disseminated by establishing in 1950 a small-circulation, but soon influential, publication called *Cité libre*.

---

5   David Meren, "An Atmosphere of *Liberation*: The Role of Decolonization in the France–Quebec Rapprochement of the 1960s," *Canadian Historical Review* 92, no. 2 (June 2011): 263–94.

NEWCOMERS AND FIRST PEOPLE

Beyond the recurrent French–English dynamic, Canada was becoming more diverse. Immigration became a major source of population growth. Between 1946 and 1952, Canada provided refuge to 164,000 displaced persons from war-torn Europe. Immigrants were selected for occupational skills needed in Canada, but also on the basis of those who would not significantly alter Canada's white and Christian character. Of the 250,000 Jewish survivors of the Holocaust, Canada accepted only 8,000.

In 1947, in an official *Statement on Immigration*, Prime Minister King spoke of Canada's "absorptive capacity," meaning not only its need to keep the number of newcomers to a level that would not increase unemployment and strain social services, but also to prevent altering Canada's racial character. Of the Chinese, King remarked in Parliament: "Any considerable Oriental immigration would…give rise to social and economic problems…that might lead to serious difficulties."[6]

Canada favoured immigrants from Britain; 800,000 arrived between 1946 and 1967, pushed by economic difficulties at home and pulled by family ties in Canada and the perceived ease of cultural adaptation. The aggregate population of other Europeans grew significantly, particularly Germans, many of whom were skilled workers, and Italians, a large percentage of whom went into the building trades. However, Canada remained overwhelmingly white. The percentage of Canadians of non-European origin grew from 0.1 per cent in 1941 to 0.5 per cent in 1961.

It took time and typically more than one generation for newcomers to start climbing the social ladder. By the end of the 1950s, Italians comprised 33 per cent of Toronto's general labourers, but only 2 per cent of its professionals. Nevertheless, most Italian families had saved enough money to purchase a home, and many sponsored family members to settle in Canada. In 1944, Ontario's government outlawed workplace discrimination based on race, and in 1951 did the same with housing covenants designed to keep certain groups out of neighbourhoods. Still, a high burden fell upon the complainant to prove racism. Canada contained social clubs and neighbourhoods that quietly restricted themselves to white gentiles. In November 1946, Viola Desmond was fined $20 and sentenced to 30 days in jail for sitting in the "White Only" section of a movie theatre in New Glasgow, Nova Scotia, and the law under which she was charged was not repealed until 1954. Not until 1962 did Canada's *Immigration Act* eliminate racial considerations for applicants, such as the likelihood of them adapting to a cold climate, something used to disqualify blacks from warmer areas.

---

6   Alan G. Green, *Immigration and the Post-War Canadian Economy* (Toronto: Macmillan of Canada, 1976), 17, 21.

While many immigrants started ascending the social ladder, things remained dismal for Canada's First Peoples. The post-war economic boom passed Indigenous peoples by. Such was the conclusion of two federally commissioned surveys led by Harry Hawthorne, the founder of the University of British Columbia's anthropology program, and his wife and academic colleague, Audrey. Their first report, released in 1955 (whose conclusions were echoed in the second in 1966), emphasized the pitiable economic status of Indigenous peoples. Their employment was largely confined to low-paid jobs in primary industries and as farm labourers. They also remained on reserves often without electricity and running water, and dependent upon scarce government assistance controlled by Indian Agents.

Indigenous peoples who fought for Canada in World War II were excluded from government veterans programs, such as loans to start a business or a farm, because they were judged as lacking competence or responsibility to cope with debt. Indigenous children, as wards of the state, were forced into residential schools where pressures to assimilate were accompanied by psychological, physical, and sexual abuse and where decrepit conditions produced shockingly high mortality rates. Pressure from the National Indian Brotherhood resulted in a 1946 Special Joint Senate-House of Commons Committee to consider changes to the 1876 *Indian Act*. However, the only meaningful action was a 1951 amendment legalizing the *potlatch*, the ceremonial distribution of gifts.

SAFEGUARDING SOCIAL STABILITY

Despite rapid change, in many ways post-war Canadian society appeared increasingly traditional. In part, this was a reaction to the perception of moral laxity and challenges to conventional gender roles during the war. Certainly, things were not clear-cut. More Canadians identified themselves as churchgoers in the 1950s, but religious leaders complained about irregular attendance and a lack of devoutness. Montreal teemed with nightclubs and brothels, enough to draw visitors from across North America. When police finally cracked down, many Montreal prostitutes left for Windsor, which enjoyed the reputation as a destination for sex tourists, especially for well-paid Detroit automobile workers.

Still, the popular image remains one of a socially conservative post-war Canada. A principal basis for this relates to women's experiences. In the world of fashion, reacting against wartime austerity that simplified clothing and saw women don jeans and overalls for factory work, in 1947 the internationally known and trend-setting French designer Christian Dior came out with his *New Look*, which was characterized by full skirts, cinched waists, and exaggerated bust lines. Swimwear became more provocative, with the bikini debuting in 1947. In Hollywood movies, strong and resourceful wartime heroines were replaced by wholesome and pretty women like Doris Day and Audrey Hepburn, or by sex kittens such as Jayne Mansfield and Marilyn Monroe.

The overwhelming message to post-war women was to devote themselves to marriage and motherhood. In the years following World War II, Canadians married younger, a trend bolstered by the strong economy and the belief they could support a family. Between 1945 and 1958, the average age of brides dropped from 25.3 to 24.8 and of grooms from 29 to 27.7. The affordability of suburbia made it possible for more women to stay at home where they could focus on raising children.

Giving birth was portrayed as the fulfillment of a woman's life. Abortion remained illegal until 1969; nurses or doctors who participated in this procedure risked imprisonment, thus leading many desperate women to ill-regulated or self-induced, botched abortions that produced thousands of deaths. The post-war period ushered in the so-called Baby Boom, a trend that extended until the early 1960s. Between 1946 and 1957, the number of babies born per year went from 300,547 to 469,903. A new army of child psychologists, public health nurses, and other experts dispensed advice to women on child rearing. The most widely sold work, only exceeded in sales by the Bible, was the *Common Sense Book of Baby and Child Care* by American Dr. Benjamin Spock. Released in 1946, it emphasized the need for a "steady, loving person" (i.e., the mother) as a "promise of security"[7] for the baby and child. Canadians joined this emerging group of celebrity childcare experts, the most prominent being William Blatz of the University of Toronto's Institute of Child Study and Samuel Laycock, professor of child psychology at the University of Saskatchewan. Both stressed that mothers "devote themselves to ensuring their children's social, emotional, and psychological well-being."[8] Canada's federal government printed pamphlets such as *The Canadian Mother and Child* that echoed such messages.

Some women chaffed against this type of life. A 1956 study by three sociologists entitled *Crestwood Heights*, which focused on an upper-middle-class section of Toronto, shed some much-needed light on the reality of women's lives at the time. While many of the housewives interviewed expressed satisfaction, several used words like "humdrum" and "monotony" to describe their daily routine.[9]

---

7 Doug Owram, *Born at the Right Time: A History of the Baby Boom Generation* (Toronto: University of Toronto Press, 1996), 33.

8 Mona Gleason, "Psychology and the Construction of the 'Normal' in Post-War Canada, 1945–1960," *Canadian Historical Review* 78, no. 3 (1997): 445.

9 Veronica Strong-Boag, "Home Dreams: Women and the Suburban Experiment in Canada, 1945–1960," *Canadian Historical Review* 77, no. 4 (1991): 503.

It took a generation after the end of World War II for Canada's female job participation rate to reach its 1944 peak. Employment of single women was still widely perceived as temporary until marriage, and earnings from wives and mothers as supplementing the male "breadwinner." Women remained trapped in poorly paid job ghettos. In 1951, 96.4 per cent of stenographers and typists, and 88.9 per cent of sewing machine operators, were women. Men earned more for doing the same job. At a time when a male sewing machine operator made $1.20 an hour, women received 80¢.

Still, some progress was evident. The National Council of Women of Canada and the Canadian Federation of Business and Professional Women, largely run by elites, allied with women trade unionists to campaign for equal pay for equal work. On April 5, 1951, Ontario's government passed the *Female Employees Fair Remuneration Act*. By the end of the decade, eight other provinces followed suit, as did the federal government in 1956. However, the legislation had major gaps, particularly in specifying what constituted equal work, thus allowing assumptions about greater male strength and competence to nullify equal pay.

The early post-war period also focused socially conservative pressures on youth. As the Baby Boom generation matured, and stayed in school longer than their parents' generation, a separate youth culture became more evident with its own terms and tastes, some of which worried older Canadians. In magazines, school lessons, films, and on television, the dominant message was for youth to seek acceptance over individuality and to respect authority. School boards intensified education in citizenship that emphasized themes like nationalism, rights and responsibilities in a democracy, and the value of freedom. Boys were expected to work hard in school as a means of getting ahead and to prepare for their roles as the family breadwinners. Girls, though presented with more career possibilities than their mothers, were to remain ladylike and not show too much intelligence lest they scare off potential suitors.

Such trends were fed by the fear of more young people going awry. Court appearances by juveniles rose from 7,304 in 1950 to 16,009 by 1960. In large part, this was due to demographics as the maturation of Baby Boomers created a massive teenage population. Still, to many, a crisis was brewing. Increased fear over delinquency was evident not only in large cities, but reached into smaller, even remote communities. If the *Prince George Citizen* in the 1950s was to be believed, the "capital of British Columbia's northern interior was besieged by juvenile delinquents threatening the well-being of school children and adults alike." Such accounts reflected reports from across North America, the community's "reputation as a hard-drinking lumber town"[10]

10 Jonathan Swainger, "Teen Trouble and Community Identity in Post-Second World War Northern British Columbia," *Journal of Canadian Studies* 47, no. 2 (2013): 151, 153.

and the desire of its leaders and emerging middle class to create a greater aura of respectability.

During the late 1940s "zoot suiters"—who wore outlandish outfits that included a long and loose-fitting jacket and high-waisted baggy trousers—garnered widespread media. The zoot suit was emblematic of freedom and rebelliousness, characteristics attributable to youth. In 1949, Toronto City Council passed a resolution demanding that zoot suits be outlawed. The next decade, the leather-jacketed hoodlum became prominent in public consciousness. Among official inquiries into rising delinquency were a 1950 Mayor's Committee in Toronto, and one led in 1958 by Ontario's attorney general. Threats to family stability—working mothers, single parenthood, alcoholism, and poor housing—were named as culprits.

Popular entertainment aimed at youth came under attack. Crime and horror comic books were one such source. Critics denounced them for perverting young minds. Davie Fulton, the federal Conservative member representing Kamloops, British Columbia, championed the campaign against this source. He pointed to studies by New York psychiatrist Dr. Fredric Wertham on "The Psychopathology of Comic Books" that garnered extensive media coverage across North America. For Fulton, proof of the dangerous influence was evident in a Dawson Creek, BC, robbery and murder committed by a 13- and an 11-year-old boy, both of whom "admitted to reading loads of comic books."[11]

In December 1949, Fulton introduced a Private Member's Bill that quickly passed through Parliament and the Senate to ban the importation into Canada of "any magazine or book…devoted to the pictorial presentation of crime" and "any publication a dominant characteristic of which is the undue exploitation of sex."[12] Several booksellers received fines, up to $1,000, and some communities organized public burnings of comic books.

Over the 1950s, movies eclipsed comic books as a source of concern regarding youth. To counteract declining movie attendance that came with the spread of television, movie producers and theatre owners undertook several initiatives: widescreen epics, 3-D films, drive-ins (which many saw as encouraging immorality), and movies aimed at an expanding adolescent market. Many films were innocent or purposefully inane like *I Was a Teenage Frankenstein*. Others were criticized for providing sympathetic or glamorized treatment of alienated, defiant, and delinquent youth. Among those that stood out was *Rebel Without a Cause*. Released in 1954 and starring teen idol James Dean, it revolved around misunderstood teenagers from middle-class

---

11 Sgt. John Burchill, "Dick Tracy Gets Smacked Down: Crime Comics in Manitoba," *Manitoba History* 77 (2015): 30.

12 Augustine Brannigan, "Mystification of the Innocents: Crime Comics and Delinquency in Canada 1931–1949," *Criminal Justice History* 7 (1986): 111.

suburban homes. It garnered tremendous attention because of Dean's own reputation as a rebel and his death later that year in a high-speed automobile accident; among the film's scenes was the death of a teenager in a drag race with stolen cars.

Rock and roll music was also condemned for corrupting youth. With roots in black American rhythm and blues, many cast rock music as a racial threat. Its loud and aggressive nature and the audacious style of many performers was thought to encourage sexual revolt, none more so than in the case of its first white superstar, Elvis Presley, whose on-stage pelvic gyrations threw female spectators into fits of sexually charged frenzy. In 1957, an Ottawa Catholic school suspended several teenage girls for attending a Presley concert.

Figure 8.5 In 1957, the National Film Board released *Being Different*. It follows a 13-year-old boy who faces ridicule from his friends for collecting butterflies. The lad struggles as to whether he should continue or give up his hobby to conform.

CHANGING THE GUARD, 1956–1957

Despite signs of dissent, few Canadians in the mid-1950s would have predicted defeat for the federal Liberals. The economy remained strong, the government appeared as effective managers, the Liberal Party was well organized and financed, and St. Laurent remained far more popular than opposition leader George Drew. In 1953, the Liberals were re-elected with a huge majority of 172 seats, compared to 51 Conservatives, 23 CCF, and 15 Social Credit. By the mid-1950s, however, there was a growing sense that the Liberals had become aloof and arrogant. Although Canada continued to court American investment, there was also mounting unease that the country was risking its sovereignty.

Controversy came from the decision to build an oil pipeline from Alberta to Ontario. In early 1956, C.D. Howe arranged for two rival groups—one American and one Canadian—to partner on constructing the project under the name of Trans-Canada Pipelines. In May, the new company said it required $80 million in emergency government financing to keep things on schedule. Parliament needed to authorize this. However, the CCF wanted a Canadian Crown corporation to build the pipeline while the Conservatives demanded that Canadians be the senior partners in the project. The opposition began a filibuster—a series of lengthy speeches designed to paralyze Parliament—to which the Liberals responded with closure that put a deadline on debate. The opposition effectively portrayed the Liberals as subverting Parliament's authority and the democratic process to serve American corporate interests.

Concern over growing American influence was also expressed in a Royal Commission on Canada's Economic Prospects. Placed under economist and future federal Finance Minister, Walter Gordon, the commission issued a critical report shortly before the 1957 election. With the United States controlling, for example, 70 per cent of Canadian petroleum production and 43 per cent of Canadian manufacturing, the report concluded that this led to an excessive outpouring of profits to the United States rather than their reinvestment to keep Canadian-based enterprises modern and competitive.

Canadians showed growing distaste for American show-trials and public shaming of suspected Communists, something which had spilled over into Canada. On April 4, 1957, Herbert Norman, Canada's ambassador to Egypt, leapt to his death from a Cairo apartment building. As a student at Cambridge in the 1930s, Norman had flirted with Marxism. Completing a PhD at Harvard, he became a leading expert on modern Japan. Brilliant and driven, in August 1946, he became head of Canada's legation in Tokyo. However, as the Cold War intensified, concerns grew in the US Congress over Norman having access to sensitive documents, concerns that were made public in autumn 1950 and produced an RCMP investigation. Norman was cleared, but reassigned to become Canada's High Commissioner to New Zealand, a post that one former colleague described as "exile…for someone of [his] calibre." Six years later, he returned to the diplomatic limelight as Canada's ambassador to Egypt. The US Congressional Subcommittee on Internal Security fretted over Norman being ambassador to a country perceived as a Soviet proxy and made public innuendos about his Communist sympathies. Norman slipped into depression, spoke of people out to "destroy him," and dreaded the prospect of again facing "question after question."[13] His suicide, only months before the federal election, hurt the Liberals who, despite condemning America's role in this tragedy, many Canadians saw as too closely aligned to the United States. More Canadians wanted the country to work toward easing the American-Soviet arms race. Concern mounted with scientific studies showing increased radioactive fallout from superpower testing of nuclear weapons and that no one, even those with bomb shelters, would survive a nuclear war.

---

13 Roger W. Bowen (ed.), *E.H. Norman: His Life and Scholarship* (Toronto: University of Toronto Press, 1984), 60–68.

The perception of the Liberals as too pro-American was also fuelled by the autumn 1956 Suez Crisis. The roots of the crisis lay in the rise of post-war Arab nationalism and the fact that Britain and the United States rejected assistance to Egypt to build the Aswan Dam because of Egypt's strong ties to the Soviet Union. Egyptian President Gamal Nasser responded by nationalizing the Suez Canal, a 162-kilometre waterway connecting the Nile River to the Mediterranean Sea that had been financed by private British and French interests and remained under lease to these nations. Britain and France rejected Egypt's offer of monetary compensation. There was rising concern that Nasser, to get his way, would close the canal, which was a key international trade and transportation route. Worsening the emerging crisis, Egypt, in a move against its archenemy Israel, blocked the Straits of Tiran, Israel's only outlet to the Red Sea, and permitted Palestinian fighters to attack Israel from Egyptian territory.

On October 29, 1956, Israeli forces, as prearranged with Britain and France, crossed into the Sinai Peninsula on Israel's southern border. The Israelis quickly defeated Egypt's inferior military and moved toward the canal. The next day, the British and French governments, using a UN resolution calling for an immediate ceasefire, moved to occupy a zone around the canal to establish a buffer between the Israelis and Egyptians. As expected, Nasser rejected the ceasefire. On October 31, the British and French responded by attacking Egyptian forces by air. The Soviet Union then threatened to intervene to protect Egypt. Fearing that things were spiralling out of control, the United States demanded that the invading forces withdraw. American President Dwight Eisenhower was incensed that the Europeans had planned the intervention in secret. St. Laurent was also annoyed with British Prime Minister Anthony Eden for publicly stating his hope for Canadian support. St. Laurent made clear this was not forthcoming; but he added what many Anglo-Canadians considered as an insult when he publicly stated that Britain's days of acting like the "superman" of Europe had passed.

Canada would make a major contribution to diffusing the Suez crisis. It enjoyed excellent diplomatic links to both the United States and Britain. External Affairs Minister Lester Pearson could deal effectively with Nasser, having had constructive discussions with him the previous year on regional issues. Pearson proposed and helped shepherd through the UN the establishment of a multinational "emergency force" under an integrated UN command to monitor a ceasefire and the withdrawal of foreign forces from Egypt. For his role, Pearson won the 1957 Nobel Peace Prize. Although garnering praise, many Anglo-Canadians charged that Canada had deserted the mother country to do America's bidding by helping to push Britain out of Egypt. One poll showed that 43 per cent of Canadians supported Britain's actions in Suez compared to 40 per cent who expressed opposition.

By the end of 1956, the Liberals faced tougher political opposition. On December 14, 1956, the Progressive Conservatives turned from an ailing George Drew to select John George Diefenbaker as their new leader. Diefenbaker was raised in modest circumstances on a 65-hectare homestead near Prince Albert, Saskatchewan. He initially made his mark as a trial lawyer, often accepting unpopular cases to support people with few resources. A strong civil libertarian, he had been one of the few MPs to oppose the forced evacuation of Japanese Canadians during World War II. Elected to the House of Commons in 1940, Diefenbaker ran unsuccessfully for the party's national leadership in 1942 and 1948 before attaining success at the Progressive Conservatives' 1956 convention. A strong orator, he projected the image of a crusading populist who approached issues with a sense of righteousness. His hero was John A. Macdonald, a nation-builder who, he said, protected Canada from American domination and remained loyal to Britain.

The Liberals were initially pleased with Diefenbaker's selection because he was not the choice of the Tory establishment, who saw him as unpredictable and as less friendly to business interests. A January 1957 public opinion poll placed the Liberals comfortably ahead at 48 per cent compared to 31 per cent for the Progressive Conservatives. However, leading up to the federal election on June 10, Diefenbaker proved to be an outstanding and tireless campaigner. He criss-crossed the country by train and fed off the energy of ever-larger crowds, who enthusiastically responded to his self-proclaimed outsider status and portrayal of the Liberals as kow-towing to American and big business interests. St. Laurent remained popular, but at 75 years old he appeared tired and sometimes cranky. The Liberals won the popular vote with 40.9 per cent compared to 38.9 per cent for the Tories, but when it came to parliamentary seats, the Progressive Conservatives achieved a razor-thin minority government with 112 seats compared to 105 Liberals and 48 for the other parties.

CONCLUSION

Canada during the late 1940s and most of the 1950s was increasingly prosperous. More Canadians were coming to share in the good life, becoming part of a growing middle class. Optimistic about the future, they married younger and produced more children. Canada discarded the last vestiges of its colonial past—developing its own citizenship, ending references to the JCPC, and appointing a Canadian-born governor general— and its federal government invested to support Canadian culture. As a middle power, it expanded its presence abroad and made notable contributions at the UN. There was widespread agreement among Canadians that the Soviet Union and its Communist allies were bona fide threats to freedom and that some curtailment of civil liberties was justified to ferret out those intent on harming Canada. Unions appeared less militant and the political left more moderate. Louis St. Laurent, who ran his government like a business and exuded a quiet confidence and comforting grandfatherly image, seemed to personify the era.

However, there were cracks in the apparent consensus. Many Canadians were left untouched by the country's growing prosperity, several provincial governments opposed Ottawa's power, many criticized Canada's close ties with America, and notable numbers condemned, or themselves suffered from, Cold War campaigns to root out Communists. Pressure, and sometimes coercion, played a role in keeping women in the domestic sphere and compelling youth to behave with restraint.

Diefenbaker would be less pro-corporate and less pro-American. However, growing turmoil would also mark his years in office, as the 1960s witnessed more intense political, social, and cultural change. Much of what followed in the 1960s represented a reaction to, and often a rejection of, values, conventions, and approaches typifying the initial post-war period. Some cleavages and conflicts that had marked Canada in earlier years had been addressed, though by no means in ways that satisfied all. Now the country was about to embark on new paths that brought different, and often long-ignored, controversies to the forefront.

9 THE SEARCH FOR JUSTICE AND EQUALITY, 1957–1967

INTRODUCTION

The decade leading to Canada's centennial in 1967 was supposedly marked by dramatic change where the new dynamisms were dissent, rebellion, and protest. It was, we are often told, a period when the young, especially those on university and college campuses, confronted the established and the entrenched, whether in business, government, or religious and educational institutions, and where old mores and cultural practices were challenged and toppled. In the new society that began to emerge in the period, there were changes in social practices and a new awareness of the injustices that had marked Canada for generations. "British" Canada was challenged when a new search for identity began. Long neglected regions chafed under an economic system that left them socially and economically marginalized, Indigenous and Métis peoples demanded greater autonomy and a greater share of the nation's wealth, women and various ethnic groups demanded equality and inclusion in the mainstream of Canadian society, and provinces, particularly Quebec, sought greater control of its own affairs within the Canadian state. While many existing institutions changed and new ones were established, and new social practices and new public and private morality took root, no one had any certainty over how the choices made in the period would turn out. Canadians were responding to a changing world and attempting to solve problems that confronted them. Their goal was to find justice for communities within while building a strong national community.

A new, liberal consensus had emerged in the immediate post-war period that governments should provide citizens with certain social rights. This was reflected best in the emergence of a welfare state that provided a variety of income transfers to individuals and transfers of cash from Ottawa to the provinces for a variety of programs. The state had an obligation to provide for the well-being of its citizens, yet, despite the riches of general prosperity, Canada was poor in too many ways and many Canadians were unhappy and dissatisfied with their lot. On the surface they appeared to rebel, the defining markers of which included new social mores and a growing aura of protest across a wide cross-section of society: women, First Nations and Métis peoples, and workers and immigrants who considered Canada unjust; Quebec's fractious Quiet Revolution; rising anti-Americanism; new notions of Canadian nationalism; and rampant regional discontent. Social and economic unrest became hallmarks of Canada as disadvantaged citizens and regions demanded greater fairness and social and economic justice.

Yet, at decade's ends, it is hard to find evidence that the discord among Canadians had fundamentally changed the country. In many ways, the "turbulent" decade was a reflection of uncertainty and a continuation of the problems and issues that, in many ways, had defined Canada since Confederation. Canada's political system and its traditional power brokers remained ensconced in their places of privilege at the end of the decade, and life for many of Canada's marginalized peoples had not changed significantly even if the seeds of a new Canada had been planted. Quebec, Indigenous peoples, women, new immigrants, and regions, among others, continued to demand redress of their grievances at decade's end. When Canada celebrated its centennial, the nation was remarkably like it had been when the decade began.

SIGNS OF CONFLICT: A NEW GOVERNMENT AND A NEW BEGINNING?

News that all was not well in Canada in the 1950s came from an unlikely source: the Royal Commission on Canada's Economic Prospects. In 1956, long-time Liberal backer and commission chair Walter Gordon reported a high level of discontent after travelling extensively across Canada. Deficiencies in infrastructure and the lack of amenities was one problem, and it threatened the social, cultural, and economic well-being of citizens. Large numbers of Canadians had incomes insufficient for their needs: families were unable to care decently for their children and too many of the elderly lived in abject poverty. Gordon warned of festering tensions, notably between the two historic communities of French- and English-speaking Canadians, but also of various ethnic groups that believed they were marginalized and discounted. There was considerable disenchantment in the regions, notably in the Atlantic and throughout the Prairies, where many believed the post-war economic boom had missed them. Many workers similarly were disenchanted. Gordon noted metaphorically that Canada "could do with fewer level-crossings and more museums"[1] and warned of troubles ahead unless the cleavages in the country where immediately addressed.

The extent of the discontent became evident on June 10, 1957, when Canadians repudiated the long-serving Liberal government in favour of John G. Diefenbaker and his Progressive Conservatives. Diefenbaker came to office an outsider. Even Conservatives questioned his bona fides, and his agrarian populist roots worried many in the party. Growing up in Saskatchewan, he witnessed first-hand the discrimination toward French Canadians, First Nations' peoples, Métis, and European immigrants. As a young lawyer, he had earned a reputation for defending the disadvantaged and marginalized. He promised not merely the reconciliation of English- and French-speaking Canadians, but the inclusion of all ethnic groups within the Canadian nationality. Canada could do better. For those whom prosperity had missed, such as farmers in Western Canada, his message resonated. They saw themselves as victims of the business and financial interests of Central Canada. Many others, especially in rural areas, believed their predicament resulted from an uncaring state. Many of those who had shared most in the post-war economic boom were disillusioned that their nation did not seem to have any great purpose.

Diefenbaker promised a new Canada and found a receptive electorate. A few days after the Conservative victory, he and his wife, Olive, made their own way from Saskatoon to Ottawa. They carried their own luggage and boarded a Trans-Canada Air Lines flight from Saskatoon, as the prime ministerial plane was busy flying defeated Liberal cabinet ministers back to Ottawa to clean out their offices. Diefenbaker became Canada's thirteenth prime minister on June 21, 1957, and held the position until 1963. During that time, he never lived up to his promise or the optimism he had inspired in Canadians.

Diefenbaker launched his term as prime minister with a fury of activity. Even before Parliament met, the cabinet, which included Ellen Fairclough as the first women federal cabinet minister, was busy. The new government gave federal employees a pay raise, provided assistance to coalmines in Nova Scotia, dispatched officials to Europe to find markets for Canadian grain, and provided price support for Canadian turkeys. It also created a Royal Commission to investigate the energy sector, increased Old Age Pensions, introduced a series of tax cuts to help lower-income Canadians, amended the

---

1 Canada, Royal Commission on Canada's Economic Prospects, *Final Report* (Ottawa: Queen's Printer, 1957), 14.

Criminal Code to ensure the humane slaughter of animals, and passed a host of measures to deal with pressing social and economic problems. The torrid pace continued after Queen Elizabeth II opened Parliament on October 14, 1957, the first monarch to do so.

Canadians were not accustomed to such an active Parliament. Neither was Louis St. Laurent, Liberal leader and prime minister since 1948. He resigned and the party selected Lester B. Pearson, the serious-minded, steady, but stuffy former secretary of state for External Affairs and Nobel Laureate, as his replacement. Pearson embodied the arrogance of a party accustomed to power. He immediately presented a motion in the House of Commons calling upon Diefenbaker to turn the government back to the more-experienced Liberals. It was not an auspicious beginning. Diefenbaker took full rhetorical flight, fuming at Liberal

Figure 9.1 H.M. Queen Elizabeth II, being greeted by Prime Minister the Rt. Hon. John G. Diefenbaker and Mrs. Diefenbaker at a Government Reception at the Chateau Laurier, October 15, 1957.

arrogance. He dissolved Parliament, called new elections, and logged more than 20,000 miles expounding on Liberal arrogance in 103 speeches in 180 constituencies.

The campaign was all Diefenbaker, Canada's first charismatic twentieth-century leader. Canadians had found a new nationalist who invoked a vision not seen since the days of John A. Macdonald. Canada was a northern nation with boundless opportunity. It had the capacity to create equality of opportunity for all. Diefenbaker invited Canadians to join his vision of "One Canada." Thousands braved the bitter February winter in 1958 to attend Conservative rallies and congregated along the railways lines to get a glimpse of the new prime minister. Even Maurice Duplessis, the premier and demagogic kingpin of Quebec, turned his *Union Nationale* political machine to Diefenbaker's cause. The Conservatives secured the largest victory in history to that point, winning 208 seats, including 50 from Quebec, and 53.7 per cent of the popular vote, the highest ever recorded in any peacetime federal election. Diefenbaker was at the height of his political power, but it would be fleeting.

A NEW NATIONAL POLICY IN A RECESSION

Although Diefenbaker promised a new vision for Canada, he had to deal with something more mundane: a stubborn recession. The first signs of a souring economy were evident earlier, but it became the new Conservative government's responsibility. Exports declined in 1957 and 1958 and did not recover until 1961. Consumer demand stagnated and only increased after 1961. New investment dropped by 18 per cent in 1956 and continued to decline until 1962. The unemployment rate jumped to 8 per cent in 1958 and remained high until 1962. In Ontario, for instance, the government provided public assistance to unemployed "employables"—a phenomenon not seen since the Great Depression.

Diefenbaker attempted to stimulate the economy through various Keynesian policies by providing further income support to individuals and infrastructure investment. The government gave the provinces $87 million to spur economic recovery and increased transfers for health insurance plans. New highways were constructed through the Yukon and the Northwest Territories to open the North, and the South Saskatchewan River Dam was constructed, but such initiatives could not bring the country out of recession. The government came to believe that workers no longer had the proper skills or qualifications needed for the new Canadian economy and introduced the *Technical and Vocational Assistance Act* (*TVTA*) in 1960 to fund investment in technical and vocational education in the provinces. The stimulus package increased public expenditure by 32 per cent.

Although the government attempted to align its fiscal policy—its decisions on taxation, borrowing, and spending—to deal with the recession, it also believed that Canada's restrictive monetary policy exacerbated the economic difficulties the country faced. Monetary policy is the basis upon which a government makes decisions to control the amount of money in circulation, usually to control the level of inflation. In Canada, monetary policy is controlled by the Bank of Canada, a Crown corporation accountable to Parliament, but which operates independently of the government.

James Coyne, the Bank's governor, had been appointed by the Liberals, and Diefenbaker did not trust him. So long out of power, Conservatives arrived in Ottawa reluctant to trust any civil servant. Perhaps Diefenbaker's suspicions were justified as he faced daily in the House of Commons a number of former civil servants—Lester Pearson, Mitchell Sharp, Jack Pickersgill, and others—who had left the civil service for the Liberal Party.

Coyne pursued a policy of tight money, keeping interest rates high to limit borrowing and control inflation. Such a tactic led to an over-valued Canadian dollar and forced Canadians to borrow capital in the cheaper American markets, forcing up the Canadian exchange rate, which in turn made exports more expensive—all of which further limited economic recovery. Economists and the public alike called for Coyne's dismissal, but when the government asked him to step aside, he refused. Diefenbaker then foolishly released details of the governor's lucrative pension, sparking a feud that created additional uncertainty in financial markets. The fiasco with the governor, together with the government's decision to fix the exchange rate for the Canadian dollar at 92.5¢ American, raised serious questions about Diefenbaker's ability to manage the nation's financial and economic affairs.

CONFRONTING REGIONAL ECONOMIC DISPARITY

Fulfilling an election promise, the Conservatives also attempted to address regional economic disparity across Canada. Whether measured in levels of income, gross provincial product per capita, or rates of unemployment, there were considerable differences between the various provinces and regions. Even in periods of economic prosperity, those disparities remained. By the late 1950s, it was clear the Atlantic region had fallen far behind the rest of the country. Per capita income in the Atlantic provinces was well below the national average. Nova Scotia, the economic leader of the region, had a per capita income 75 per cent of the national average; Newfoundland's stood at 54 per cent, whereas Ontario's per capita income was 120 per cent of the national average. In the early 1960s, 38.5 per cent of new homes built in the Atlantic provinces were without flush toilets; just 8.7 per cent of those in Ontario had no indoor plumbing.

One of the most obvious signs of regional disparity was rural poverty. Diefenbaker, who was the first prime minister to make regional inequalities a priority, launched a series of initiatives to correct the problem. He believed, though, that the solution to low incomes was not through the provision of income support to individuals, but by creating the necessary infrastructure to foster new economic development. He introduced the "Atlantic Provinces Adjustment Grants," allowing the provinces to undertake large-scale capital projects, such as in hydroelectric development, to attract industry. This initiative was followed by the Atlantic Provinces Development Board in 1962. Staffed by federal officials from various government departments, it was the first attempt to develop a comprehensive regional development strategy aimed at improving the basic infrastructure of a region. Its $186 million budget was aimed primarily at highway construction, water and sewage projects, the creation of industrial parks, and the generation and transmission of electrical power, all with an eye to attracting manufacturing enterprises to the region. The *Agriculture Rehabilitation and Development Act* (ARDA), another federal–provincial initiative, was designed to improve the viability of rural communities through better resource use and retraining of workers to facilitate the transition of marginal farmers to better employment opportunities.

When the Liberals returned to power, these initiatives were broadened, not cancelled. ARDA turned its focus to development in non-agricultural and resource sectors to absorb the surplus labour from farming and fishing. In 1966, the Fund for Rural Economic Development (FRED) diverted funds to the most economically depressed areas of Canada—the Gaspé Peninsula in Quebec, two regions in New Brunswick, all of Prince Edward Island, and parts of northern Manitoba—with particularly low incomes and little hope of private-sector economic development in order to augment both infrastructure and economic investment opportunities.

The provinces, too, attempted to promote development in economically depressed areas. When Robert Stanfield became premier of Nova Scotia in 1956, he recognized that many of the small rural communities that depended on agriculture, fishing, and coal faced terrible poverty. With low productivity and antiquated equipment, many were struggling to survive, and Stanfield believed the best solution lay in creating manufacturing and factory jobs. He created the Industrial Estates Limited with Frank Sobey—best known for the chain of grocery stores across Canada—as president to encourage financial support for small-scale textile, fish-processing, and hardboard plants to establish in the province.

Many of the economically challenged provinces followed Nova Scotia's lead and used state capital to facilitate development. In New Brunswick, the first Acadian elected premier, Louis Robichaud, led his Liberal Party to victory on the promise of change. His Equal Opportunity Program attempted to better the lives of rural citizens through improvements in education, health, and social services as well as economic development. Joseph R. Smallwood, one of Canada's most colourful premiers, attempted to create an industrial revolution in Newfoundland and Labrador through the Newfoundland and Labrador Corporation, and by convincing Ottawa to participate in funding the resettlement of thousands of isolated fishing communities, such as Pushthrough on the southwest coast of Newfoundland, to larger towns that were designated as growth centres. The promised jobs never came, but most of the resettled families found themselves with much better social services and amenities, including schools, medical facilities, running water, and electricity.

There were other relocation schemes across Canada as well. In Nova Scotia, there was also relocation of people, most notably from the Halifax suburb of Africville. It was one of city's oldest and largest black neighbourhoods, but through years of neglect and racism it became one of the worst slums in the country. In the rush of urban renewal sweeping North America, the city council relocated the citizens of Africville to another part of the city. At the time, urban planners across North America praised the relocation, but the citizens of Africville saw it as the destruction of their vibrant community and as an overt act of racism. In February 2010, Peter Kelly, the mayor of

Halifax, apologized to the people of Africville and their descendants for the decision and provided $3 million in compensation to build a church and interpretive centre at the site of the former community. Many Indigenous communities in northern Canada were relocated to make way for hydroelectric development, with little thought given to the impact on those forced to move.

Did such state-sponsored policies work? Some were spectacular failures (such as Nova Scotia's expenditure of millions of dollars to lure Clairtone, an innovative hi-fi and colour television firm founded by Peter Munk and David Gilmore, to Stellarton, Nova Scotia), but there were also some successes, such as the establishment of the Michelin tire plant in Bridgewater. Some have argued governments wasted millions of dollars with limited success, while others maintain that people have a right to live in the parts of the country they have always called home and that, moreover, it is the state's responsibility to help them do so. If nothing else, government expenditure in the depressed regions allowed citizens to earn a higher level of income than would have been possible without state intervention. What did become clear by the late 1950s was that governments could no longer ignore the fact that not all regions and not all Canadians shared equally in the nation's wealth. They had to be proactive in finding a solution. However, the federal programs were designed and implemented to deal with specific problems and lacked an overall strategic approach. Even within federal and provincial government departments there was little evidence that they worked together to create an integrated plan for depressed regions. The lack of coordination between the federal and provincial governments remained a major problem, and each new initiative seemed to be planned and implemented without much consideration of what was happening elsewhere. By the end of the 1960s, there emerged a consensus that regional disparity could not be adequately addressed without a centralized federal agency with the necessary authority to coordinate all federal regional development efforts and a mandate to work cooperatively with the provinces.

NATIONAL STANDARDS AND MEDICARE

Because of the uneven distribution of wealth across the country, some provinces had a larger tax base than others. This meant that a poorer province such as New Brunswick would have much less revenue than would a wealthier province such as British Columbia or Ontario. The level of public services provided in a wealthier province would consequently be much greater than those in economically disadvantaged ones.

The solution to the fiscal imbalance and the obvious unfairness created by it was first broached in the formal equalization program in 1957. Designed to provide a reasonable measure of equality of services across the country that, otherwise, poorer provinces would not have been able to afford, the program guaranteed that the revenue for each province would be raised to the per capita level of that of the wealthiest two provinces. Equalization grants were paid out of the general revenue that Ottawa collected. Wealthier provinces did not contribute directly to the equalization program.

Equalization was only one way of sharing the national wealth. Another was shared-cost agreements between the federal and provincial governments. These were programs that the federal government offered to the provinces but were conditional on the province contributing (usually) 50 per cent of the cost. Equalization transfers could be spent however the province wished, but conditional grants were different. They allowed the federal government to set national priorities and to meet the social needs of all Canadians, regardless of where they lived. In 1953–54, Ottawa's expenditure on such programs was $75 million; by 1963, it was more than $935 million. Diefenbaker had established 15 new shared-cost programs, and several were especially expensive. The hospital insurance plan, introduced in April 1957, cost nearly $400 million annually. Still, Canadians demanded that the state deal with existing injustices and inequalities, and Ottawa's response often came in shared-cost agreements.

Most Canadians wanted a national health plan, and although there was little agreement on what form it should take, it, too, was provided through a shared-cost conditional arrangement. The drive for a national system of publicly administered and state-funded medicare in Canada began in Saskatchewan, where a comprehensive prepaid and compulsory medical insurance program was introduced in 1961, nearly two decades after Tommy Douglas had led his Co-operative Commonwealth Federation (CCF) party to victory. By the time the *Medical Care Insurance Act* passed the provincial legislature and was to become law on July 1, 1962, Douglas had been recruited to lead the New Democratic Party, which had emerged from a union of the old CCF and the Canadian Labour Congress. Woodrow Lloyd became the new Saskatchewan premier and had to deal with an assault from the province's doctors who opposed the plan for state-run medicine. Medicare would become one of the major victories for social justice and equality of the period.[2]

Spurred by the public interest and widespread support for the innovative legislation in Saskatchewan, the federal government considered creating a plan to cover all Canadians. As a first step, the Diefenbaker government appointed Supreme Court Justice Emmett Hall to head a Royal Commission on Health Services. When the report was issued in 1964, Diefenbaker was no longer prime minister, but Hall

2   Alvin Finkel, *Social Policy and Practice in Canada. A History* (Waterloo: Wilfrid Laurier University Press, 2006), Chapter 8, "The Medicare Debate, 1945–1980."

recommended publicly funded, comprehensive universal insurance not only for doctors' services but for prescription drugs and home care, as well as dental and optical services for some groups.

SEARCH FOR BALANCE: CANADIAN–AMERICAN RELATIONS

During Diefenbaker's years as prime minister, Canada's relationship with the international community was marked by great uncertainty and a greater desire for Canadian independence. Many Canadians were particularly concerned about the growing interdependence of Canada and the United States, but there was no easy way to set Canadian priorities apart from those of the Americans. This was a period of great homogenization in North America and Europe, and no matter how hard some Canadians tried to keep their country separate, the United States exerted—usually without much effort—a profound influence on Canada.

Diefenbaker never had an easy relationship with the Americans. He, more than any recent prime minister, worried immensely about the coziness of Canada's leadership with the Americans. It is important to remember that while he was prime minister, the Cold War was the most important factor in Canadian foreign policy and any confrontation between the United States and the Soviet Union was certain to affect Canada. The Arctic was no shield against nuclear warheads.

Shortly after Diefenbaker became prime minister, he signed the North American Air Defense Command (NORAD) Agreement to provide continental air defence, although the agreement left Canada in a subordinate role in a defence alliance based on nuclear deterrence. He approved NORAD without consulting either his cabinet or the Department of External Affairs, and without parliamentary debate, claiming later that the Canadian military and the previous government had already approved of the plan. During the furor that NORAD aroused in Parliament in 1958, the decision to create the alliance was never criticized, only the process that Diefenbaker had followed. The threat from Soviet bombers was real in 1958, and NORAD was a logical military development for a "Cold Warrior" like Diefenbaker.

By the time NORAD was fully functioning, surface-to-air missiles, such as the Bomarc-B, had become the major defence against incoming bombers, not interceptor jets. Yet, Canada had invested heavily in A.V. Roe Canada, a division of the British aerospace company Hawker Siddeley, to produce an all-Canadian interceptor, the AVRO CF-105, or AVRO Arrow, as a measure of protection against the Soviets. The Arrow also promised to stimulate the Canadian aviation and high-tech industry, but it had become obsolete even before it went into production. Over budget and without a market outside Canada, the previous Liberal government had planned to cancel it, but when Diefenbaker did so, he paid a high political price. Canadians remain attached to the Canadian-designed and built delta-wing supersonic interceptor.

By 1962, Diefenbaker was wavering on his commitment to continental defence because the anti-aircraft Bomarc missiles, already installed in Canada, had to be armed with nuclear warheads. Ever the populist, Diefenbaker was surprised when thousands took to the streets and wrote to him personally to protest Canada joining the nuclear club. Even though public opinion polls showed support for nuclear arms, Diefenbaker was swayed by the views of those ordinary Canadians who took the time to write. His cabinet was split on the nuclear issue, and when Diefenbaker eventually decided not to accept nuclear warheads, his minister of defence resigned. The Liberals initially opposed nuclear weapons, only to change their minds later. The Americans were furious, claiming Canada's wavering on arming the Bomarcs left the United States vulnerable to Soviet attack.[3]

Relations between Canada and the US deteriorated even further during the Cuban Missile Crisis in October 1962. Although Diefenbaker harboured deep suspicions of the Soviet totalitarian system, he was also worried about US President John F. Kennedy's hawkishness toward the Communists, even after the Americans discovered Soviet missiles were being deployed in Cuba. Kennedy imposed a naval blockade, demanding withdrawal of Soviet weapons. Before he told Americans in a television broadcast on October 22 of his decision to confront the Soviets, Kennedy sent a special envoy to brief Diefenbaker and request that the Canadian forces within NORAD be put on alert in case of a Soviet military reprisal against US action. Diefenbaker had expected to be consulted on North American defence, not merely told what the Americans had already decided. For three days, he refused to bow to American pressure and the photographic evidence they had given him of the Soviet presence in Cuba. Diefenbaker called for a UN inquiry into the Cuban situation as a way of resolving the crisis, but in the face of unrelenting pressure, he authorized the use of the Canadian military if it became necessary. By then Kennedy and his advisors concluded that Diefenbaker could not be trusted to protect American interests and had to go.

Some have seen the dispute as evidence of Diefenbaker's nationalism; others have seen it as a failure of Canadian leadership. Diefenbaker maintained that he had to protect Canada from American military control. After the Soviets backed down, Kennedy was hailed as a hero even within Canada, and Diefenbaker was made to look foolish and indecisive in the face of imminent danger. There is some evidence that the

---

3 Jamie Glazov, *Canadian Policy Towards Khruschev's Soviet Union* (Montreal and Kingston: McGill-Queen's University Press, 2002), 112–22.

Figure 9.2 Prime Minister John Diefenbaker with President John F. Kennedy and Governor General Georges Vanier during Kennedy's visit to Ottawa, May 1961. Jacqueline Kennedy and Mrs. Diefenbaker follow.

Kennedy administration worked thereafter to get rid of Diefenbaker, one of the last Canadian nationalists to confront American hegemonic leadership.

INDIGENOUS CANADIANS: LAYING THE FOUNDATION OF CHANGE

Despite more than three generations of official state policy to assimilate Canada's Indigenous peoples, they showed remarkable resilience despite obstacles of poverty, unemployment, and discrimination. By the late 1950s, their numbers increased markedly and change in Indigenous societies rivalled that of any other group or province during the 1960s. The civil rights movement in the United States and the resistance of colonized peoples throughout the world spurred much of the reconsideration of Indigenous peoples in Canada. The prolonged post-war economic prosperity had had little impact on them, however, and many Canadians were shocked by the deplorable conditions in which Indigenous peoples lived.

Residential schools continued to operate, and assimilation remained the goal of the state. Yet, Diefenbaker took an important step toward greater equality when Indigenous people were awarded the right to vote without surrendering their status and their treaty rights, which had been a precondition of their attaining the franchise since Confederation. This was largely a symbolic move, as many Indigenous people chose not to cast their ballot, but the first to do so voted federally on the Rice Lake Band near Peterborough, Ontario, in a by-election on October 31, 1960. James Gladstone, a member of the Blood Tribe of the Blackfoot Nation, became the first status Indian appointed to the Senate two years earlier.

Steps toward significant change came largely from Indigenous peoples themselves, not from the state or other Canadians. They created political organizations to make their voices heard, but with so many different groups spread across Canada, there was no single Indigenous voice. In 1961, the National Indian Council was created to represent three of the four major groups: Treaty and Status Indians (those recognized by the federal government as registered under the *Indian Act* and entitled to a wide range of programs and services offered by federal agencies, provincial governments, and the private sector); non-status peoples (persons who considered themselves "Indians" but were not recognized as such by the *Indian Act*, usually because they could not prove their status or had lost their status); and the Métis people. The Inuit were not included. While the National Indian Council hoped to create unity among all Indigenous peoples, this proved impossible; in 1968 it broke into two groups—the National Indian Brotherhood, which represented Status and Treaty groups, and the Native Council of Canada, which represented the Métis. They began a discourse of equality, treaty rights, and land ownership.

In 1964, the Hawthorn Commission, which had undertaken a comprehensive investigation into conditions of Indigenous peoples at the request of the minister of the Department of Citizenship and Immigration, reported that Indigenous peoples had not been assimilated and recommended that the federal government abandon the racist policies it had pursued since 1867. The report did not recommend Indigenous self-government but preferred what it called "citizens plus." There is no single definition of the concept of self-government, but it was generally assumed to mean that Indigenous peoples would regain control over the management of affairs that directly affected them and would allow them to preserve their communities and cultural identities. According to the Hawthorn Report, First Peoples would enjoy all the rights and benefits of Canadian citizenship, but they would remain "Indians" and could expect the federal government to protect their lands and acknowledge their special rights as "charter members of the Canadian community." The Hawthorn Report also noted that reserves lacked a sufficient resource base to support the growing Indigenous population. The Pearson government realized that Indigenous policy in Canada had to be redefined, but Pearson resigned before he might have reached any accommodation with Indigenous leaders, as he had attempted with Quebec. His replacement, Pierre Trudeau, would counsel no such status for First Peoples, even though self-determination, equality, and treaty rights had clearly emerged as part of the Indigenous discourse.

CHALLENGING INEQUALITIES AND REVAMPING IMMIGRATION

Diefenbaker was committed to the extension of basic rights and ending discrimination. In 1960, he introduced a Bill of Rights, which included fundamental freedoms for all Canadians. It applied only to matters under federal jurisdiction, but it was the first attempt by the state to establish basic rights in Canadian society, and it laid the foundation for the 1982 Charter of Rights and Freedoms. Diefenbaker also waged a human rights crusade in the Commonwealth, particularly against the apartheid regime in South Africa. The Canadian government had traditionally refrained from interfering in the internal affairs of member nations in either the Commonwealth or the United Nations, but Diefenbaker insisted that South Africa should not be a member of the Commonwealth unless it provided equal opportunity for all people, regardless of race, colour, or creed. Rather than change its system of apartheid, on May 31, 1961, South Africa became a republic and ended the Queen's status as head of state. Another Canadian prime minister would play a pivotal role in having the Commonwealth impose sanctions against the racist regime in South Africa in the 1980s. These helped bring an end to apartheid, and South Africa was readmitted to the Commonwealth in 1994.

Canada remained a desirable destination for many people seeking a better life throughout this period, but in the 1960s, Canada did not want just any immigrants, even if one of Diefenbaker's first acts was to grant an amnesty to all illegal alien residents in the country. His attempt to restrict admission of non-dependant relatives of immigrants already in Canada in favour of educated and skilled immigrants who would better meet long-term labour needs angered many Italian, Greek, and Portuguese citizens who had come to Canada after World War II. In the face of their opposition, the government relented and maintained the family sponsorship program, but the traditional source of immigrants in continental Europe and the United Kingdom was declining. As it looked elsewhere for its immigrants, Canada would cease to be a "British" country and a new Canada would emerge. Canada's refugee policy was restructured to ensure that political refugees were legitimate and not trying to jump the queue. In 1962, Fairclough introduced major reforms to Canada's immigration policy to reflect the country's new priorities. She also eliminated the overtly racist features of Canada's immigration laws by eliminating national preferences, and hence racial discrimination, although European immigrants retained the right to sponsor a wider range of relatives than others. In 1967, the Department of Immigration was created, and a formal points system was introduced.

DIEFENBAKER GOVERNMENT IN TROUBLE

The bloom quickly faded from the Diefenbaker rose, but no other leader seemed to excite a majority of voters. The uncertainty of the decade was perhaps best reflected in its politics. Within four years, Diefenbaker squandered his huge majority and on June 18, 1962, was reduced to a minority; his hold on the West and much of Atlantic Canada seemed secure, perhaps because he had attempted to address their grievances. The industrial heartland of Ontario and Quebec deserted him, but the emergence of Social Credit in Quebec, where Réal Caouette's brand of conservative rhetoric appealed to rural Quebeckers, prevented the Liberal Party from gaining a majority. The NDP never lived up to expectations. It won 19 seats in 1962 but never became a factor in national politics throughout the decade.

Diefenbaker struggled in the minority parliament and his party's support dropped even further during the Cuban Missile Crisis. Many members of his own party turned against him and attempted to have him replaced as leader. Despite all of the Conservative woes, however, voters did not trust the Liberals under Pearson enough to give them clear control of the government. This despite the fact that the Liberals re-packaged their party and their leader—Pearson dropped his trademark bow-tie, for instance, and the party recruited a number of younger candidates who favoured progressive social legislation. Pearson won a minority in 1963, a feat repeated in 1965, even though by then Diefenbaker was so badly mauled by his own party that Pearson's failure to win decisively speaks volumes not only about how Pearson failed to captivate the imagination of the country, but also about the uncertainty of the period. Only two years apart in age, neither Pearson nor Diefenbaker seemed right for the nation.

EXPANSION OF THE WELFARE STATE AND SOCIAL CITIZENSHIP

Pearson demonstrated that a minority government, operating from a centrist position and depending on the left for support, can produce successful and progressive legislation. He created a new social Canada. Over the span of five years, he implemented a wide range of new social legislation. The new policies included a universal system of medical insurance (despite the opposition of some of the provinces and the insurance companies), a national contributory pension plan, the extension of family allowance benefits to 16- and 17-year-olds to keep them in school, interest-free loans to make post-secondary education more accessible for lower-income Canadians, and substantially funding operating costs of colleges and universities. Pearson also understood the growing tensions in Quebec and appointed a Royal Commission to study bilingualism and biculturalism. More reluctantly, he appointed a commission to study the conditions facing women in Canada, but he enthusiastically promoted new Canadian symbols.

Pearson never envisioned the social programs Canada ended up with in the 1960s. During the 1963 election campaign, he had promised free medical services only to children under 16 and to persons over 65. All others would have to pay the first $25 of any medical visits. When the Diefenbaker-appointed Hall Commission recommended that the federal government pay 50 per cent of any provincial medicare program that provided universal coverage, Pearson was forced to rethink his plans. The New Democrats—whose support he needed to govern—immediately endorsed Hall's recommendation. So, too, did many Canadians, but Pearson and his government moved cautiously.

The provinces were divided on what form medicare should take and how it should be administered, even though they all supported the concept. Quebec refused any shared-cost or conditional programs that were designed and controlled by the federal government. Alberta wanted a program that allowed user fees and provided a role for private insurance companies. British Columbia, Manitoba, and Ontario all insisted that provincial governments knew the health needs of their citizens better than Ottawa did and wanted the federal government simply to provide the financial resources so provinces could implement their own systems. The remaining, poorer provinces were just happy to have Ottawa contribute to programs they could not themselves afford. During the 1965 federal election campaign, Pearson finally committed his party to a Hall-style medicare system, but it would not be until July 1, 1968, when Ottawa made funds available to the provinces, that Canada finally had a national health insurance program, often referred to as medicare. Medicare was not a single national program, but 12 health insurance plans run by provincial and territorial governments that agreed, in exchange for federal funding, to adhere to a set of national principles. These included universality of coverage; portability of coverage when people lived outside their home province; comprehensive coverage of physician's services; public administration of the provincial plans; and accessibility without user fees. If the provinces adhered to these national standards, they were eligible to claim 50 per cent of the cost of their medicare programs.

Health care soon became one of the largest expenditures for governments and one of the defining characteristics of social citizenship in Canada. It was not the only program, however. The 1960s also saw Canada establish a national contributory pension plan to build on Old Age Pensions first introduced in 1927. Diefenbaker had introduced an initiative in 1962 that allowed Canadians employed outside the home to save for a pension, and even appointed a commission to investigate a contributory pension plan for Canadians. After long and protracted negotiations with the provinces, the Canada and Quebec Pension Plans were introduced in 1966. These were self-supporting plans financed with contributions from employees and employers.

Another development was the Canada Assistance Plan (CAP) in 1966. One of the best examples of cooperative federalism—the term given to Pearson's negotiations with the provinces to avoid a constitutional crisis over jurisdiction of social policy—CAP was an attempt to regularize federal involvement in provincial social programs by establishing a comprehensive financial arrangement between the federal and provincial governments. The federal government agreed to share equally with the provinces the cost of such programs as old age assistance, assistance for the disabled, pensions for the blind, and unemployment assistance. The initiative allowed the provincial governments to manage an array of social programs, but it also allowed the federal government to set national standards. Because CAP had not set any limit on provincial spending on their social programs, Ottawa soon realized that public spending could quickly get out of control when it was left picking up the tab for provincial spending.

Even so, developments in this period responded to some of the social tensions within the country. Canada had embraced a common set of social rights, shared and available to all citizens, in the hopes that it would not only ameliorate conditions for the marginalized and poor but that it would enhance a sense of community and strengthen social cohesion. Because of the redistributive nature inherent in some of these social programs, they heightened the level of attachment to the nation and encouraged citizens to see themselves as members of a single community, enjoying a common set of rights and sharing a common set of obligations. In Canada, as in other Western nations, the development and expansion of social programs in the 1960s encouraged a new sense of citizenship. Medical care and state support during periods of personal turmoil became, like public education, a right of Canadian citizenship.

QUEBEC AND THE QUIET REVOLUTION

The country had to deal not only with rising expectations among its citizens, but also with demands from the provinces for greater autonomy. Provincial governments emerged as the articulators of regional and provincial interests in the 1960s, and Quebec was the most insistent on changes to intergovernmental relations. In fact, a generation of Canadians grew up trying to understand Quebec's place in Canada and how its aspirations could be accommodated within the national community.

"The Quiet Revolution" is the phrase used to describe the rapid social, economic, and cultural changes in Quebec that began in the 1950s and blossomed in the early 1960s. French-speaking Quebeckers also took greater control of their economy and developed the self-confidence to change their society to become more like the rest of North America. They also saw themselves as a nation ready to assume greater control over its own affairs.

Evidence of the socio-economic transformation of Quebec accelerated after the end of World War II and became increasingly apparent after the death of Premier Maurice Duplessis in 1959 and the election of the Liberal Party in 1960. While Duplessis had worked with the Roman Catholic Church and other elites to perpetuate the myth of a rural agrarian society, Liberal Jean Lesage embraced modernity and severed many of the links between church and state. He also embraced an interventionist state to create a secular and modern society in Quebec. Many on the left, though, re-imagined Quebec as having been in a state of colonization since 1867 and embraced the decolonization rhetoric of subjugated peoples akin to those in the Third World. The most famous statement of Quebec's colonized status came from Pierre Vallières's 1968 treatise *Nègres blancs d'Amérique*.[4]

The changes were championed by the middle class that had emerged in the 1950s and had found employment after World War II in the vast bureaucracy of the Catholic Church. However, they chafed under the traditional nationalism that the Church and state promoted and welcomed modernity, even if they were merely instituting one form of nationalism for another. The Catholic Church—like other established churches across Canada—started to lose its control over society, reflected most obviously in a rapid decline in attendance. Women and men deserted the religious orders, and new recruits dwindled. A 50 per cent decline in the birth rate from 1959 to 1969 was further indication of the rejection of Catholicism in Quebec.

The Quiet Revolution saw the interventionist state as a positive development. Duplessis had long worked with foreign capital to exploit the province's resource sector and to supply pliant workers for manufacturing enterprises, but under Lesage the province turned to state capital as a source of economic development—the same strategy that had been employed in many other provinces. For many Quebeckers, state capitalism was a means of not only limiting the control of foreign capital, but also of ensuring that all new jobs created by the state would be filled by French-speaking Quebeckers. French would be the workplace language.

---

4 David Meren, "An Atmosphere of *Liberation*: The Role of Decolonization in the France–Quebec Rapprochement of the 1960s," *Canadian Historical Review* 92, no. 2 (June 2011): 277–78.

One of the best-known and most symbolic events of the Quiet Revolution was the nationalization of hydroelectricity.[5] Hydro-Québec was created in 1944, with the expropriation of the electricity and gas assets of the Montreal Light, Heat and Power Company, a powerful monopoly in Montreal, to create a provincial Crown corporation to run the utility. Lesage gave Hydro-Québec control over all sites that had potential for hydro power not held by private interests and began the process of changing the language of work at the corporation's head office and at all of the work sites. In February 1962, René Lévesque, the provincial minister of natural resources who was previously a popular television journalist, announced a plan to complete the process begun a generation earlier of nationalizing all power companies in the province. With the province divided on the issue, Lesage called an election to let the people decide. The Liberals presented the nationalization of the power companies as a means of ending economic colonialism by kicking the foreign, usually English-speaking companies, out of the province. He chose *maîtres chez nous* as his campaign slogan and easily won re-election. The government bought 80 companies involved in the private generation of electricity for $604 million, making Hydro-Québec the world's largest hydroelectric generating company.

Hydro-Québec was not the only instance of state capitalism in the province. In 1961, Lesage created an economic planning council that examined the province's economic potential and the role the government should play in developing it. He followed in 1964 with the *Société générale de financement*, a provincially administered corporation to fund Quebec companies with plans to invest in the province. The government also dispatched bureaucrats throughout the province to assist with regional economic development plans. All these initiatives, together with new expenditures in health, education, and social services, were costly, and the provincial debt soared dramatically. After the Quebec Pension Plan was created, the government established the *Caisse de dépôt et placement du Québec* to oversee the pension plan and invest the funds in economic initiatives in the province.

The Quiet Revolution also signalled a change for Quebec's role in Confederation, though Quebec had rarely seen itself as just another of the provinces. In the new spirit of nationalism, many Quebeckers saw their province as their primary state. Lesage established a ministry of federal–provincial relations to deal with Ottawa, and those that followed him in the premier's office clearly saw themselves as the equal of the prime minister of Canada. Quebec was rapidly beginning to act as a nation; it wanted greater power, greater financial resources, greater autonomy, and less federal involvement in the province, except for the unconditional transfer of funds from Ottawa. For

---

5   See Susan Mann Trofimenkoff, *The Dream of Nation: A Social and Intellectual History of Quebec* (Toronto: Gage Publishing, 1983).

many, this assertiveness marked the end of the colonialism they had endured since the Conquest in 1763.

To control its destiny, many Quebeckers believed that the provincial government had to have control of many of the social programs that were managed and paid for in Ottawa. When Lévesque became Family and Social Welfare minister in 1965, he announced that he wanted control of all federal social security programs and that federal involvement would be limited to providing funding for them. Lévesque maintained that Quebec City knew better than Ottawa the particular needs of his province—a claim initially made in the 1963 *Rapport du comité d'étude sur l'assistance publique, Québec* (the Boucher Report). Only with total control of its social security program, Lévesque claimed, could Quebec deal effectively with the poverty within its provincial boundaries.

In 1966, Lévesque demanded that Ottawa either radically reform the family allowance program to meet the priorities of Quebec or, barring that, transfer funds for the program to the provinces. He insisted on using the word "repatriation," suggesting that the province was taking back responsibility for a program that was constitutionally within its jurisdiction. Of course, the reforms that Lévesque enunciated followed closely the *maîtres chez nous* rhetoric of a more autonomous Quebec. While the province had opted out of several federal–provincial programs throughout the 1960s, most notably the Canada Pension Plan and Youth Allowances, giving the provinces control over family allowances was particularly troubling for the federal government. Ottawa had established the program as a purely federal initiative as part of the welfare state it attempted to create following the end of World War II. If Quebec was given exclusive control over the family allowance program—which was seen, in part, by federal political leaders as an important aspect of Canadian citizenship—it would represent an erosion of the power of the national government and the strengthening of provincialism. In the case of family allowances the federal government refused, but in other areas of social policy, such as the Canada/Quebec Pension Plan, Quebec had more success.

Although the Liberal government in Quebec remained popular and earned 47 per cent of the popular vote in the 1966 provincial election, it nonetheless lost to the *Union Nationale*, which captured just 40 per cent of the vote but a majority of the seats, many of which were in rural areas. The election of Daniel Johnson (who died in 1968) did not reverse demands from Quebec for special status in Confederation. Johnson had campaigned on *Égalité ou Indépendance*, raising the possibility of independence if Ottawa did not recognize Quebec as equal to Canada. Once in office, he pushed hard for constitutional change that would recognize Canada as the union of two nations rather than of 10 provinces. He changed the name of the Legislative Assembly of Quebec to the National Assembly as part of rebranding Quebec's collective identity. The new nationalist movement dismissed the old identifier of French-speaking Quebeckers and adopted *Québécois* to describe the people of Quebec.

Even Johnson's fervent nationalism and his desire for a new federal arrangement failed to satisfy many Quebeckers. At first, those who sought independence from Canada looked to Pierre Bourgault's *Rassemblement pour l'indépendance nationale* (RIN) and the *Ralliement national* (RN), which, together, captured only 9 per cent of the popular vote in the 1966 provincial election. The RIN had come to prominence for its violent protests during the visit of Queen Elizabeth in 1964. The independence movement became a more potent political force when René Lévesque left the Liberal Party, convinced that it would never demand sovereignty for Quebec, and created the *Mouvement Souveraineté-Association* (MSA) in 1968. A year later he created the *Parti Québécois* (PQ), to work for a sovereign Quebec state. Even the federalist parties—the label attached to those committed to Quebec remaining in Canada—wanted special status for Quebec within the Canadian federation.

PEARSON: CONFRONTING THE NEW REALITIES

When the federal Liberals returned to power in 1963, Pearson recognized that something profound was happening in Quebec. He realized, too, that Ottawa had to deal with the new reality, though, like most people in English-speaking Canada, he looked at Quebec with bewilderment, wondering what it really wanted. Pearson, the former diplomat, chose a path of pragmatic accommodation, often with the support of Ontario Premier John Robarts.

Pearson's first task was to try to understand events in Quebec. To do that, he appointed the Royal Commission on Bilingualism and Biculturalism with two co-chairs: André Laurendeau, a leading Quebec journalist who convinced Pearson to take separation seriously, and Davidson Dunton, the president of Carleton University. The commission travelled the country to raise the consciousness of ordinary citizens to the fact that Canada was a bilingual and bicultural nation. It recommended that French and English be the two languages of the federal government. A large number of citizens of neither French nor English ancestry, however, argued that they were left out of the duality narrative. By then, it was clear that Canada was no longer a bicultural and bilingual nation, but a multicultural one: one in four Canadians could not trace their ancestry to either French or British origins. Of course, the French–English dichotomy had always ignored Canada's First Nations and Métis peoples.

Pearson also reached out to intellectuals and union leaders in Quebec who feared the new nationalism was as destructive as the old one. They were worried about what was happening in their province and harboured contempt for those who wanted to distance

Quebec from the rest of Canada. Pearson convinced three middle-aged men to join the Liberal Party: Pierre Trudeau had long fought Duplessis, but he refused to enter the political arena and spent his time carping from the sidelines; two others, journalist Gérard Pelletier and labour leader Jean Marchand, shared Trudeau's fear that the policies being pursued by the provincial government in Quebec would lead to its isloation from the rest of North America. They believed that Quebec's interests could be best served if they joined the federal government in Ottawa, but they did not agree with Pearson's policy of accommodation. They refused to accept the premise of the Quebec provincial government that Quebec was the "homeland" of French-speaking Canadians; they believed that the development and protection of French was a responsibility of the federal government and that French-speaking Canadians should be at home in any part of Canada.

Many had hoped that the Quiet Revolution would make Quebec like all of the other provinces (though they were never sure what that would be), but clearly this was not happening. What Canadians witnessed in Quebec was troubling, especially the violence that seemed to be engulfing the province. On May 31, 1963, *Time* magazine ran a headline "Bombs in the Quiet Land" that spoke of a reign of terror in Quebec. Over an 11-week period, a series of explosions had killed a security guard and injured several people, including a bomb specialist with the Canadian Army. The targets were Government of Canada buildings in both Montreal and Quebec City. Much of the violence was attributed to the *Front de libération du Québec* (FLQ), which *Time* described as "a lunatic fringe of violent nationalists whose aim is the secession of French-speaking Quebec from the rest of English-speaking Canada."[6] Perhaps the most troubling event occurred during France's President Charles de Gaulle's visit to Quebec during the 1967 Centennial celebrations. Quebec had opened Maison du Québéc in Paris in 1961, and de Gaulle wanted Quebec to be a separate state. Pearson and his officials were worried, but did not really think de Gaulle would encourage Quebec independence during his visit; however, he did precisely that. Speaking to a large, enthusiastic crowd in Montreal, de Gaulle shouted, "*Vive Montréal! Vive le Québec! Vive le Québec libre! Vive, vive, vive le Canada français! Et vive la France!*" bringing a thunderous response from those assembled below the balcony of the Montreal City Hall. Pearson was outraged and cancelled his meeting with de Gaulle, who hastily departed Canada.

CANADIAN–AMERICAN RELATIONS

When he discovered that Canadians were worried about the level of foreign ownership in the late 1950s, Diefenbaker promised to divert a portion of Canada's trade away

---

6   "Bombs in the Quiet Land," *Time*, May 31, 1963.

from American to British markets. It was a futile gesture, as Britain was increasingly looking toward Europe and membership in the European Economic Community. While Diefenbaker often confronted the Americans, Pearson attempted to find some accommodation with them during a period of rising nationalism and growing anti-Americanism in Canada. American capital had come to control important sectors of the economy, including 75 per cent of oil and gas, 60 per cent of mining, and 60 per cent of manufacturing. Pearson introduced legislation to protect Canada's fledgling magazines, but undermined his own legislation by exempting *Time* and *Reader's Digest*, the two American giants that dominated the Canadian media marketplace. The Liberals' first budget in June 1963 proposed a 30 per cent tax on foreign takeovers of Canadian businesses and a series of measures designed to limit foreign control of the Canadian economy. Because of pressure from the United States as well as the Canadian business community, the measure was withdrawn and the Finance Minister, Walter Gordon, eventually resigned. Nor was Canada particularly supportive of the attempts to liberalize international trade that might have reoriented exports away from the United States. In the 1964 negotiations over the General Agreement on Trade and Tariffs, initially introduced in 1947 to liberalize international trade, Canada refused to participate in the general lowering of tariffs. Rather, it favoured a product-by-product scheme, arguing that any general lowering of the tariff unfairly hurt resource-export nations and those dependent on manufactured imports like Canada.

Despite the rhetoric of liberal internationalists like Pearson, Canada preferred bilateral treaties when it came to trade. The best example of this is the Auto Pact, signed between Canada and the United States in January 1965. The auto sector is really a microcosm of Canada's economic relationship with the United States. Canada had lost its indigenous auto manufacturers in the 1920s when all of the Big Three US companies—Ford, General Motors, and Chrysler—formed strategic alliances with Canada's struggling auto sector that saw American cars assembled in Canada to gain access to Canadian and Commonwealth markets. Like the Americans, Canadians loved their cars, and Pearson convinced the US to integrate the North American car and auto parts industries into a single market. The result was the Auto Pact that protected a share of the continental market for Canadian producers and kept some of the high-paying jobs in automobile production in Canada. The Auto Pact guaranteed minimum production levels in Canada. It is ironic that Pearson, who began his tenure as prime minister as an economic nationalist, created a single North American auto zone, which was an important step in the economic integration of Canada and the United States.

Yet, at Temple University in Philadelphia, Pearson suggested that the United States halt its bombing of North Vietnam. President Lyndon Johnson, who assumed the presidency after Kennedy's assassination, was so angry with Pearson's comment on the Vietnam War that he grabbed the prime minister by the shirt collar, lifted him off the floor, shouted "You pissed on my rug!," and told him to keep his nose out of American affairs. Pearson's speech played well in Canada, however.

INVENTING CANADIAN SYMBOLS

Given the divisions that had become apparent in Canada by the 1960s, Pearson hoped that a reconstructed national identity would restore unity. One of his most important acts was to create a new flag. More than 80 per cent of Canadians surveyed in 1958 said they wanted a national flag that was not already flown by another country. In 1963, Pearson promised to deliver a new flag if elected prime minister. In 1964, when he announced his plans to do so, however, large numbers of Canadians were either indifferent or downright hostile. Diefenbaker opposed the idea, as did the Royal Canadian Legion. Legionnaires in Winnipeg booed Pearson when he told them that the Red Ensign, a flag of the British merchant marine but used for generations as a Canadian flag, was no longer acceptable for Canadians in the 1960s. He wanted the maple leaf, which had long been seen by many as one of Canada's enduring symbols.

Many in French Canada were ambivalent to the debate that ensued, pitting those who favoured a new flag against those that wanted to retain the symbols of Canada's past. A parliamentary committee was tasked with considering various designs for a new flag. It unanimously selected the current maple leaf flag suggested by Liberal MP John Matheson. After passing a closure motion, Parliament voted 163 to 78 to adopt a new flag at 2 AM on December 15, 1964. On February 15, 1965, Canadians raised for the first time an official national flag that did not include the Union Jack. The Maple Leaf quickly became an important Canadian symbol.

Like so many of Canada's twentieth-century prime ministers, including Diefenbaker, Pearson had no success amending the constitution. Each time since 1867 that Parliament wanted to change Canada's constitution, it had to make a request to the British House of Commons in London. Like Diefenbaker, Pearson saw this as a slight to Canadian nationhood, and he attempted to change the procedure by building on the work of E. Davie Fulton, the minister of justice in Diefenbaker's cabinet. A dominion–provincial conference in 1960 had agreed that Ottawa should have the consent of all provinces before changes were made by the federal Parliament to a variety of items. These included the use of the French and English languages, education rights, the assets of a province, the legislative powers of a province, provincial representation in the House of Commons, and the amending formula itself. There was even a desire at the time among some of the provinces for a flexible constitution that would allow any province to transfer or delegate a matter of exclusive provincial jurisdiction to the federal government and, at the same time, allow the provinces to assume responsibility for areas within the federal purview. First ministers had also agreed by early December 1961 on an amending formula that allowed the federal Parliament to amend the constitution if supported by two-thirds of the provinces that together had more than 50 per cent of the population of Canada. The Fulton formula, as this constitutional package was called, was rejected by Quebec when it failed to get control over unemployment insurance, which the provinces had surrendered to Ottawa in the early 1940s.

Pearson's government attempted to bring closure to the Fulton proposal in 1964, when Guy Favreau, then minister of justice, presented a new proposal that retained the main features of the Fulton formula but added provisions granting Parliament exclusive power to make amendments to the Constitution of Canada concerning the executive government of Canada, the Senate, and the House of Commons. At the 1964 conference, all the premiers agreed with the proposed procedure, but Jean Lesage, premier of Quebec, later changed his mind amid stiff opposition in Quebec.

NEW DEMANDS FROM WOMEN'S GROUPS

The decade was not an easy one for women. In the immediate post-war period, it was clear that domestic duty was the centre of life for most women. Throughout the 1950s, the media and prominent women, such as Dr. Hilda Neatby, one of the pre-eminent historians of her generation, continued to emphasize the centrality of family and women's role in that Canadian institution. Interestingly, though, the role of women outside the home became a frequent topic in women's magazines in both English- and French-speaking Canada. Under the editorship of Doris Anderson after 1957, *Chatelaine/Châtelaine* carried groundbreaking articles on the problems of working mothers, pay equity, abortion, divorce, and family violence. She advocated social change and emerged as one of the leaders of the feminist movement in Canada, committed to bringing about fundamental change for women.

The period saw growth in women's activism, now referred to as the "second wave" of feminism to distinguish it from the earlier women's movement at the beginning of the twentieth century. There was little unity in the women's movement, but most efforts were directed toward the systematic obstacles that helped define women's place in society. Although only a small number of Canadian women were actually involved with the women's liberation movement, limited as it was primarily to university campuses and assuming the rhetoric of the liberation movements of colonized people around the world, it has come to define women's protest during this period. While some women involved in the movement protested against such events as bikini contests in Toronto, other women were working hard to change gender stereotypes about what a woman could and could not accomplish. During the winter of 1968, Nancy Greene earned a place for women in Canadian sport with her gold-medal performance in the giant slalom at the Grenoble Olympics; she worked as a secretary to cover her training costs.

The women's movement responded to some of the major issues of the period, and it included many women who were moved by a particular concern or worry. One issue was the danger posed by the possibility of nuclear war. This prompted Peggy Hope-Simpson, a young mother living in Halifax, to launch the Voice of Women (VOW) in Nova Scotia; VOW had begun in 1960, when *Toronto Star* columnist Lotta Dempsey urged women to join together to oppose nuclear war. The Nova Scotia branch organized an international

Figure 9.3 Women remained responsible for most household duties during the 1960s. Here a woman is selecting meat from a butcher in a grocery store.

women's conference in 1962 that included women from the Soviet Union and other Communist countries; they called on the United Nations to designate an International Year of Peace. Howard Green, Canada's minister of external affairs, later claimed that the VOW contributed to the government's decision in 1962 to delay putting Canadian forces on alert during the Cuban Missile Crisis. A new era had arrived in public participation in the democratic process and it would not belong simply to the nation's youth.

Laura Sabia met the same kind of enthusiasm for her cause. She had a privileged upbringing, attending a private boarding school in Quebec where she resented the fact that the nuns had to bow to the priests, and she never accepted the role that women had in Canadian society. She went to McGill University with hopes of becoming a lawyer but followed the pattern of many female students and soon found herself married and raising four children. In St. Catharines, Ontario, she became active in local politics and the host of a radio phone-in show and embraced some of the emerging social issues of the day. When she challenged the Catholic Church on abortion, she asked, "What do 100 celibates in Rome know about women's bodies?" When the Royal Bank ran an advertisement of "Mary the Happy Teller," she found it insulting to women and led a campaign

Figure 9.4 Women march in 1961 proclaiming "No Nuclear Arms for Canada—Pas d'armes nucléaires pour le Canada."

to have it withdrawn. Not only was the ad dropped, but her campaign led to two women being added to the bank's all-male board.[7] She became one of the revolutionaries of her time.

Sabia is best known for pushing the Canadian government to appoint a Royal Commission to investigate the status of women in Canadian society. She assembled a coalition of 32 women's organizations, including the *Fédération des femmes du Québec*, to lobby for the creation of the Royal Commission on the Status of Women. When Pearson refused, Sabia was outraged and told the *Toronto Globe and Mail* that Pearson would regret his decision when she led 3 million women to Ottawa. When the newspaper ran Sabia's comments as its lead story, Pearson changed his mind and Sabia got her Royal Commission to "inquire into and report upon the status of women in Canada, and to recommend what steps might be taken by the Federal Government to ensure for women equal opportunities with men in all aspects of Canadian society." Florence Bird, a CBC journalist, was appointed chair, and the commission reported in 1970. The commission was important because,

7 http://www.coolwomen.ca/coolwomen/cwsite.nsf/vwWeek/14125A1469DB08CC85256D12005CBEB5?OpenDocument.

for the first time, it legitimized the concerns women had regarding their status. It also raised women's issues and status to matters of national consciousness.

One of the most important developments for women was the introduction of the first oral contraceptive, Enovid, known simply as "the Pill" in 1960. Even though doctors agreed that there were adverse side effects to the Pill, it was enormously popular among Canadian women; in its first year on the market, doctors issued more than 10,000 prescriptions for the drug and within five years, the number had increased to 750,000. The Pill gave women more control over childbearing, and it allowed them greater freedom to choose a career over what had been the only other real option available to many women—motherhood. Nonetheless, Canada still had oppressive laws regarding the display and selling of contraceptive devices. In 1960, Toronto pharmacist Harold Fine was jailed for selling condoms, and it was not until 1968 that the Criminal Code of Canada was amended to deal with contraception and abortion.

Regardless of the improvements in the lives of Canadian women, for many women the major focus was still on the home. Women were largely responsible for the home and it was their role as wives and mothers that concerned many in Canadian society. Although it was far from the reality, the idealized Canadian woman lived in the suburban communities that sprang up around Canada's larger cities. There has been much criticism of the lack of community in the early suburbs and the isolation many women felt there. At the beginning of the 1960s, only one married woman in five was in the paid labour force, though by 1970 there had been dramatic gains, as one in three married women worked outside the home. Most women in the paid workforce were still in clerical and retail positions and traditional jobs such as teaching and nursing.

EMERGING NEW VALUES

The federal government had to respond to other changing social mores, and it fell to Pierre Elliott Trudeau, the justice minister in Pearson's government, to change Canadian law to reflect the demands of an increasingly modern and secular society. Although he was a devout Catholic, Trudeau introduced his controversial Omnibus Bill (72 pages in length and containing 109 clauses) in the House of Commons on December 21, 1967, proposing massive changes to the Criminal Code of Canada. During the debate that followed, Trudeau uttered his most famous words: "There's no place for the state in the bedrooms of the nation." The legislation decriminalized homosexual acts performed in private and between adults and amended the abortion laws to make it legal for women to get an abortion under certain conditions (although all references to abortion would not be removed from the Criminal Code until 1988). The bill also legalized lotteries, introduced some restrictions on gun ownership, and

Figure 9.5 Photograph depicting a group of young people sitting on the sidewalk in Yorkville in Toronto, one with a sign that reads "Freedom for the Oppressed."

permitted police to perform Breathalyzer tests on suspected drunk drivers if they had reasonable and probable cause. It changed divorce laws and decriminalized the sale of contraceptives. The bill was passed into law in 1969, only after it had generated intense and acrimonious debate both inside and outside the House of Commons.

Young Canadians, particularly university students, demanded change, and one of their concerns was American influence in Canada, even though Canada's culture became increasingly American and international at the same time. They belonged to the Baby Boom generation—children born in the post-war period who became teenagers in the 1960s. They wanted a different life from their parents and grandparents, and they would change the music, fashion, and many of the values of an earlier generation. Like youth throughout the Western world, boys and young men let their hair grow, and young men and women alike chose blue jeans as their attire of choice. They embraced American and British rock groups, and when they found their own stars—such as Gordon Lightfoot, Joni Mitchell, or Neil Young—they were hardly distinguishable from their American and British counterparts. The American civil rights movement and American protests against the Vietnam War drove much of the Canadian protest movement, but the Baby Boom generation here, as elsewhere, helped shape the new morality of the period. They raised questions about the capacity of governments to control their lives and protect society from the excesses of corporate greed. The public debate that the generation engendered recast old mores and created new social issues. This was particularly true with the degradation of the environment.

Of course, conservation was not new in Canada in the 1960s. John A. Macdonald had created the first national park in the 1880s at Sulphur Springs in what is now Banff National Park, but that first environmental movement was aimed at protecting tourist areas for the wealthy or the efficient management of natural resources. In the 1930s, Ducks Unlimited Canada was established to protect Canada's wetlands for hunting enthusiasts, and federal and provincial governments attempted to protect forests and manage agricultural land uses. In the late 1950s, Canadians became more concerned about the ecological system and pollution. Some of this was predicated on the fear of nuclear destruction, but pollutants became a huge concern when Rachel Carson popularized the concept of ecology in her influential book *Silent Spring* (1962), which warned of the long-term effects of misusing pesticides. Those who dismissed the early environmentalists as alarmists would soon realize what was happening to the ecosystem. In June 1969 Lake Erie—declared "dead" earlier in the decade—caught fire where the Cuyahoga River empties into the lake at Cleveland, Ohio. The Canadian side of the lake was no better, and the Great Lakes became the focus for the fledgling environmental movement in the 1960s.

One issue was detergents that were being dumped into Lake Ontario throughout the Golden Horseshoe of southern Ontario, the region that accounted for much of Canada's manufacturing capacity and its post-war growth. A wide range of effluents were discarded into the lake from homes and industries alike. The synthetic detergents that had displaced soaps made from biodegradable animal or vegetable fats were not easily broken down, and they accumulated in the waters in the Great Lakes water system. Governments and industry—often reluctantly—worked to solve the problem of the proliferation of foam through the use of more biodegradable materials, but such measures did little to control the massive growth of algae, or *cladophora*, which fouled local beaches around Toronto. The public outcry against the pollution spawned such organizations as Pollution Probe and helped to create the modern environmental movement in Canada. Pollution Probe began a concerted campaign to force the federal government to amend the *Canada Water Act* to regulate the phosphorous content in detergents.

Pollution was not just a problem in the major industrial centres. Long Harbour, Newfoundland, a community with a long history in the fishery, experienced environmental and health-related problems after the Electric Reduction Company of Canada Industries Limited (ERCO) was lured to the province with generous subsidies from the provincial government to produce phosphorus. Within months of the plant going into production, fishers began finding dead fish in Placentia Bay, and the minister of fisheries ordered the fishery in the area closed; the plant also closed voluntarily for a brief period on May 2, 1969. Emissions from the plant killed local vegetation, deformed moose and rabbits were found near the plant, and citizens there experienced air pollution for the first time. The plant remained open until 1989.

Expo 67, to celebrate the nation's centenary, seemed to mask many of Canada's problems, including what humankind was doing to the planet. Montreal built an island for the world's fair, in the middle of the St. Lawrence River, from the soil that had been excavated to build a new subway. The theme for the extravaganza was Man and His World/Terre des Hommes. The 113 pavilions built by participating nations all had a futuristic design, including that of Germany, which erected a 15-storey-high multi-peak plastic tent. For the millions who visited the site, La Ronde (the amusement park section) and the *Bluenose II* (a replica of the famed and historic Nova Scotia sailing vessel) were two of the most popular attractions. The fair was proclaimed the greatest ever. Canadians celebrated the achievement and were proud that their nation had reached its one hundredth anniversary. The celebration was not just in Montreal, though. In communities across the country, Canadians celebrated not just with picnics, but with the construction of hockey rinks, playgrounds, and arts and cultural centres.

However, more difficult times lay ahead. Quebec had made it clear that the current situation was unsatisfactory, the regions harboured much discontent toward the centre, women demanded major systemic change, Indigenous peoples agitated for fuller recognition of treaty rights, multicultural groups wanted equal recognition with citizens of French and English ancestry, and too many Canadians lived in poverty. The nation would be shaken to its very core in the years ahead.

10 CONFRONTING INJUSTICES, SEARCHING FOR INCLUSION, 1968–1984

INTRODUCTION

O n Saint-Jean-Baptiste Day, June 24, one day before the 1968 federal election, a group of protesters showered Pierre Trudeau, Canada's new prime minister, and a group of dignitaries with rocks and bottles, some containing paint and acid, shouting "*Trudeau au poteau*" (Trudeau to the gallows). Trudeau, who had already so captivated Canadians that a journalist had dubbed the adulation Trudeaumania, refused to flee even as others scurried away while a riot erupted on the streets of Montreal. As images of the riot flashed across the country, Canadians believed they had finally found a resolute leader to stand against the separatists in Quebec who were threatening to destroy Canada. The following day, Trudeau captured 45 per cent of the popular vote and 155 seats in the House of Commons, the first majority for any political party since 1958.

Trudeau, the flamboyant "non-politician," led Canada in the liberalizing spirit of the age, charting for it an independent international role, quelling Quebec separatism, building national unity, and forging a pluralistic "just society" that promised equality rights and equal opportunity for all. These goals and aspirations were embodied in such initiatives as the Third Option, in the National Energy Program, in the *Official Languages*

Act, in multiculturalism, and in a new Charter of Rights and Freedoms, as well as in new initiatives in social welfare, redressing Indigenous and regional grievances, and efforts to improve the status of women and minorities. His determination and single-mindedness were resolute. Compromise, long considered a necessity for any successful prime minister, was not Trudeau's forte. Yet, he transformed Canada, but in doing so, he alienated large segments of the population, nearly destroyed the Liberal Party, and, many have argued, left the country less unified than he had found it.

Figure 10.1 Prime Minister Pierre Elliott Trudeau.

THE LIBERALIZING SPIRIT

Trudeau excited Canadians with his charisma and promise of a just society. He modernized Canada when he tackled outdated laws on abortion, divorce, and homosexuality and symbolized the hopes of many for a new and different Canada. This clearly set him apart from his peers. The language Trudeau used to justify legislation on issues such as sexual relations now seems oddly antiquated, but at the time it was progressive. Trudeau and his Minister of Justice, John Turner, considered abortion and homosexuality immoral and sinful, but they insisted that what consenting adults did in private should not concern others. Trudeau had no intention of "sending policemen into the nation's bedrooms." His government would neither make abortion any easier nor condone homosexuality, but it realized neither was a crime. To ensure passage of his legislation in Parliament, covering a range of social issues—legalizing abortions under strict conditions, permitting lotteries, placing restrictions on gun ownership, and changing laws on drunk driving—he opted for an Omnibus Bill, so as not to allow those opposed to defeat any single measure they found objectionable. The legislation became law in May 1969 after an acrimonious debate. Trudeau was a progressive intent on remaking Canada.

For many women's groups who wanted abortion to be more accessible, the legislation offered a mere veneer of progress. Section 251 of the Omnibus Bill allowed a woman to obtain an abortion but only in a hospital, and only when authorized by the medical profession. Women dismissed the legislation, claiming it perpetuated the state's regulation of their bodies and reproductive rights. The Abortion Caravan, a group organized by the Vancouver Women's Caucus, led the opposition to the new abortion laws. They took the matter directly to the prime minister, placing a coffin on the lawn of 24 Sussex Drive, his official residence, to represent women who had died seeking illegal and unsafe abortions. They maintained that abortion was not a medical or criminal matter but a woman's choice. Only when the state recognized this would women be assured a fair measure of equality.

Trudeau dismissed their cause, prompting 30 members of the group to chain themselves to chairs in the Parliamentary Gallery, closing the House of Commons for the first time because of a protest in the public galleries. Later, they ambushed Trudeau at a press conference, demanding again that he broaden his reforms to immediately legalize all abortions in Canada. Again, he was dismissive and challenged the women to get involved in politics (as he had) and make the changes themselves if they did not like the way he was running the country.[1]

Trudeau's attitude strengthened the burgeoning women's movement. It also ushered in a new activism among women that became known as "second-wave feminism." It developed as part of the general

Figure 10.2 "...I trust the membership committee is keeping a wary eye on this tomfoolery." Women's issues faced considerable opposition, as this cartoon depicting members of the "Anathema Club" worrying about the Royal Commission on the Status of Women shows.

radicalization of the period and was committed to the idea of substantial equality of women with men. It focused on reproductive rights and reproductive freedom, sexual harassment and sexual freedom, and equality of work. It also embraced the idea that females in political office and other places of leadership would bring female interests to politics, government, and throughout society. The presence of women generally would also change how Canada functioned. The protest against the abortion laws brought such groups as the National Council of Women, the Canadian Committee on the Status of Women, and a large number of provincial and local women's organizations together in the fight for equality.

One of the landmarks for the women's movement was the report of the Royal Commission on the Status of Women in Canada, appointed in 1967. The report confirmed what many women knew already: women occupied an unequal place in Canadian society

---

1   Christabelle Sethna and Steve Hewitt, "Clandestine Operations: The Vancouver Women's Caucus, the Abortion Caravan, and the RCMP," *Canadian Historical Review* 90 (September 2009): 463–95; and CBC, "The Omnibus Bill Doesn't Go Far Enough," CBC Digital Archives Website, http://www.cbc.ca/archives/entry/the-omnibus-bill-doesnt-go-far-enough.

and suffered inequality and discriminatory policies in almost all aspects of life. They were under-represented in political institutions, were denied equal access to educational opportunities and jobs, earned a portion of men's wages, and were treated unfairly under the law, particularly when it came to property. The report offered 167 recommendations covering all aspects of women's lives, but the irrefutable evidence of the discrimination women faced was the report's greatest contribution. It created in the public consciousness an awareness that the treatment of women had to change, and leading that demand for change was the National Action Committee on the Status of Women (NAC), an independent lobby group created to fight not only for change but to keep women's issues on the public agenda. The federal government provided NAC with much of its funding. It also created within the bureaucracy several administrative units to deal with women's issues.

EQUALITY

Trudeau also tackled Canada's language laws to create greater equality for French- and English-speaking citizens. When he worked briefly in the federal civil service in the 1950s, he had been shocked that Ottawa functioned solely in English. An Official Languages Bill was introduced on October 17, 1968, to guarantee Canadians fundamental language rights. Building on the program of language training that began in the federal public service in 1964, it established English and French as the official languages in the federal civil service, all Crown corporations, and all federal courts where either minority group constituted at least 10 per cent of the population (called bilingual districts). In introducing the bill, Trudeau insisted that "We want to live in a country in which French-Canadians can choose to live among English-Canadians and English-Canadians can choose to live among French-Canadians without abandoning their cultural heritage."[2] A language commissioner was appointed to investigate infractions of the Act.

There was much criticism to the new legislation, particularly in Western Canada. Former Prime Minister John Diefenbaker saw the legislation as pandering to French Canadians, although Diefenbaker himself had earlier introduced simultaneous language translation in the House of Commons. When the bill came to Parliament, 17 Conservatives—all but one from Western Canada—vowed to vote against it, but Robert Stanfield, the Conservative leader, was able to keep most of his party in line. The legislation passed into law in July 1969 without a recorded vote so as not to emphasize the anti-Quebec sentiment in Parliament. The new language laws were a further indication that the government wanted a new Canada, one in which French- and English-speaking Canadians could feel at home. It was not compulsory

---

2 House of Commons, *Debates*, October 17, 1968.

bilingualism, but Trudeau believed that Quebec could be kept in Canada by ensuring that Francophones could participate significantly in the federal state.

UNITY AND REGIONAL ECONOMIC DISPARITY

Trudeau understood, too, that social and economic disparity were as great a threat to national unity as was language. By the late 1960s, economic disparity in levels of incomes and employment persisted across Canada. Ottawa had demonstrated earlier that it was prepared to intervene directly to promote economic growth in the depressed regions of Canada. However, despite a variety of federal initiatives to reduce rural poverty through transfer payments to provinces and individuals, and a spat of initiatives to spur development in the depressed regions, the gap between the poorest and the wealthiest provinces narrowed only marginally. Only Ontario, Alberta, and British Columbia had per capita incomes that exceeded the national average.

Trudeau decided shortly after the 1968 election that regional development priorities would be directed to areas east of Quebec City, the most economically depressed regions of Canada. He declared that "if the underdevelopment of the Atlantic provinces is not corrected, not by charity or subsidy, but by helping them become areas of economic growth, then the unity of the country is almost as surely destroyed as it would be by the French-English confrontation."[3] As he had done with the language file when he put his trusted friend Gérard Pelletier in charge, Trudeau turned to another trusted friend— Jean Marchand, who had come to Ottawa with him and Pelletier as the "Three Wise Men" in 1965—to be the minister of the Department of Regional Economic Expansion (DREE). The new regional development strategy was to promote economic growth in the most economically depressed regions. To do so, Ottawa adopted a model of economic development known as the "growth pole" concept. This held that economic growth does not occur everywhere at once, but begins in particular centres and then spreads through-out a larger economic zone. By first improving the regional infrastructure through improved transportation networks, water and sewer systems, and educational facilities, and then offering generous cash incentives and tax breaks, the government believed it could attract new manufacturing industries to economically challenged regions.

Trudeau and Marchand soon discovered, however, that all politics in Canada is essentially regional and all government expenditure political. In the first years (1969–72) of the government's initiative, nearly 80 per cent of the regional development budget was expended in the Atlantic provinces and eastern Quebec. Beginning in 1973,

---

3   Quoted in Donald J. Savoie, *Regional Economic Development. Canada's Search for Solutions* (Toronto, University of Toronto Press, 1986), 28.

however, DREE funds were spread more equitably across Canada, and to both rural and urban areas, as regional development decisions became increasingly influenced by political dynamics. The wealthier provinces insisted that they, too, had depressed economic regions that would benefit from federal assistance. Ontario, Alberta, and British Columbia—all traditional net contributors to the federal coffers—were subsequently included in regional economic development programs to ensure that they, too, received a share of the federal monies. Canada's major cities also demanded a share of federal infrastructure spending. Following the 1972 election, when Trudeau's majority disappeared and he barely won a minority victory, the Liberal government provided considerable amounts for regional development to Western Canada where it won only 6 of 68 seats. Montreal, too, was a clear beneficiary of regional development funding when it returned a large number of Liberal MPs to Ottawa who argued that Quebec's economic strength was dependent on the economic well-being of that city. Once Montreal was included, Ontario MPs insisted that parts of Ontario should be able to avail of funds for regional development: three counties in eastern Ontario were subsequently added to the federal funding program. After the election of the *Parti Québécois* in 1976, DREE allocated additional funds to Quebec to strengthen the federal presence there and stem the tide of separatist sentiment. With such compromises and negotiations to include all Canada, Atlantic Canada saw its share of regional development funds drop to 39 per cent by 1978, even though it remained the most economically depressed region in the country.

Canada's attempt to end regional economic disparity failed. Although Trudeau had initiated his regional development strategy as a way to strengthen national unity, most of the provinces became embroiled in quarrels with Ottawa over how few of the federal dollars actually came to their particular province and how Ottawa ignored their real economic needs. Many provincial politicians and governments were annoyed that federal MPs used DREE funds to announce new infrastructure projects and job creation programs without any provincial consultation but as ways to deliver goodies to their local constituencies. In 1982, Trudeau disbanded DREE and transferred its policy role and programs to a new Department of Regional Industrial Expansion (DRIE). With the reorganization, the government turned its focus away from eliminating regional economic disparity to preserving the industrial heartland of Canada, particularly in Ontario where the manufacturing sector encountered difficult times.

During Trudeau's term in Ottawa, more than $7 billion was spent to address regional economic development. Billions more were spent in federal equalization programs. While economic disparity was not eliminated, incomes per capita narrowed across Canada, even if the ranking of those provinces in the have-not category did not change. Still, earned income per capita—that is, incomes that do not include government transfer payments such as unemployment insurance—hardly changed over the period. Regional economic disparity remained as much a factor in Canada at the end of the Trudeau period as it was at the beginning.

EQUALITY AND SOCIAL POLICY

The Trudeau government also promised to create a more equitable social security system for Canadians. Despite the progress made in health care, contributory pensions, and social assistance in the 1960s, many Canadians were shocked when the Economic Council of Canada reported in its *Fifth Annual Review: The Challenge of Growth and Change* in 1969 that one in five Canadians lived in poverty. Canada was a prosperous nation, spending more than $4.4 billion on social welfare: How could so many of its citizens, including many who worked full time, be poor?

Canada was not alone among the world's nations to rediscover its poor in the midst of the national prosperity; the United States and many European nations did as well. As US President Lyndon Johnson had declared war on poverty in the mid-1960s, Trudeau promised a just society. Many of the changes in federal social policy were initially motivated by that pledge, but as with the promise of eliminating regional disparity, it went unfulfilled. The first reforms came to the unemployment insurance (UI) program, which had first come into effect in 1941 to assist workers temporarily unemployed. In 1971, the program was broadened to cover virtually all workers in Canada; it added maternity, sickness, and retirement benefits for workers. It also increased benefits from 43 per cent of earnings to 66.6 per cent, to a maximum of $100 per week. In economically depressed regions where seasonal employment was common, the unemployed could collect benefits for 51 weeks after eight weeks of work. However, the notion that Canada, a prosperous nation with a rising standard of living, could afford a social security system that provided a generous array of supports—such as those covered in the revisions to the unemployment insurance program—did not last long. When unemployment rose dramatically in 1972 and 1973, and the government had to inject more than a billion dollars into the UI account, it moved quickly to increase the qualifying period, reduce benefits, and, by 1978, use the income tax system to claw back UI benefits from higher-income earners.

By the end of the 1970s, the government was motivated more by fiscal constraint than any notions of a just society. This is evident with family allowances. Canada's best-known universal social program, introduced in 1945, family allowances paid a dividend for children under the age of 16 to aid mothers in their upbringing. By the late 1960s, the program cost $560 million or, on average, slightly more than $7.20 monthly for each child in Canada. During the 1968 leadership race, Trudeau had insisted that Canada end universality, or the paying of benefits to all recipients regardless of income level. He favoured selectivity in social transfers to get more money into the hands of low-income families. Those reforms would help achieve Trudeau's just society, but federal–provincial conflicts, political considerations, and fiscal pressures soon became the main drivers of social policy reform, not social justice. Trudeau's proposal, in 1970, to eliminate universality in family allowances and transfer the dollars previously going to well-to-do families to those in greatest need would have substantially increased the monthly benefits for low-income families. Public opinion polls showed that the majority of Canadians supported such targeting. The proposed Family Income Support Program was to completely reform the family allowance program, change it from a universal to a targeted one, and increase average benefits for each child from about $7 to $20 per month.

Although anti-poverty groups welcomed the proposed reforms, the government retreated from its plan for three reasons. First, many women's organizations were opposed because it would have terminated benefits for 1.2 million families (39 per cent of recipients), and mothers who received monthly cheques would lose this income if benefits ceased. Second, the Liberal government was reduced to a minority in the 1972 election and the New Democratic Party, which held the balance of power in Parliament, threatened to withdraw its support if the universality provisions were removed from social security programs. Third, the family allowance program became embroiled in a constitutional quarrel, particularly between Ottawa and Quebec City. Although Trudeau and the premiers had come close to reforming Canada's constitution at the Victoria Constitutional Conference in 1971, the deal fell apart when Ottawa refused to concede control over social policy to Quebec. Trudeau subsequently named Marc Lalonde, his principal secretary and another trusted advisor, the new minister of national health and welfare to find a solution that would appeal to Quebec. The government subsequently increased family allowance benefits to $20 per month and allowed the provinces to determine how the benefits were to be distributed, but the federal government continued to issue the monthly cheques to mothers. This allowed Quebec a measure of control over the program, but it meant that targeted social spending to the poorest families, which had initially been the primary goal of family allowance reform, would wait. The cost of the program reached $1.9 billion by 1976.

In 1978, the federal government finally introduced major changes to children's benefits when it created a Refundable Child Tax Credit Program, which was designed to funnel more money to lower-income families through income-tested supplements to universal family allowances. Average family allowance benefits were reduced to $20 from $25.68. The money saved was transferred by means of a tax credit to low- and moderate-income families. Families with annual incomes less than $18,000 received a tax credit of $200 per child for those under the age of 18; the amount of the tax credit was reduced as family incomes rose to $26,000, at which point it disappeared completely. What governments had discovered was that they could use the tax system to deliver social benefits. Ending universal coverage—as the Trudeau government had attempted—was politically dangerous, but reforming social programs through the income tax system came with much less risk. This was a revolutionary change, and it would be used increasingly to radically transform Canada's social security system.

EQUALITY AND INDIGENOUS PEOPLES

If there was one group that stood to benefit from Trudeau's promise of a just society it was Indigenous peoples, who continued to struggle in Canada. The Pearson government had commissioned a study by Dr. Harry Hawthorn to investigate the situation of Indigenous peoples, with the hope of then preparing a plan to deal with the difficulties they faced. The Hawthorn Report presented a depressing portrait of Indigenous communities: earnings per capita, health and education outcomes, mortality rates, and a host of socio-economic measurements were far below the Canadian average. Yet, Hawthorn recognized that First Peoples had survived Canada's assimilationist and neo-colonial policies and that Canada must recognize them as a distinct community. He recommended that the federal government treat Indigenous peoples as "citizens plus" because of their inherent title and treaty rights.

The Trudeau government followed with a series of consultations with Indigenous organizations across Canada as part of its promise of a new Indigenous policy. The National Indian Council (NIC) made it clear that Indigenous peoples held dearly to their identity. It also asked for an Indian claims commission to settle the increasing number of land claims that were being launched by groups across Canada, following a similar process that had already begun in the United States. (A land claim is a formal request from an Indigenous community stating that it is legally entitled to land—or financial compensation—as part of the unfinished treaty-making process, or that the federal government did not fulfill its fiduciary responsibility to Indigenous peoples who had signed treaties with the Crown.) However, when the Indian Affairs minister, Jean Chrétien, announced the government's preliminary policy—*Statement of the Government of Canada on Indian Policy*, better known as the White Paper—in 1969, it was clear that the government had ignored much of what Indigenous communities had told it.

The White Paper proposed that the special relationship between First Peoples and the Government of Canada be severed, and all Indigenous peoples be fully integrated into Canadian life. The legal difference between Indigenous and non-Indigenous peoples would be replaced by what the government considered equality. This would mean the abolition of Indian status (which entitled Indigenous peoples to a wide range of programs and services offered by the federal government), the transfer of control of reserve lands to First Nations peoples, and the integration of services for Indigenous and Métis people into the various federal and provincial departments of government. Indigenous peoples would then interact with their governments as individuals and not as members of a separate group with legal and constitutional rights.

Following on the civil rights movement in the United States and Australia, Trudeau's Indigenous policy called for the integration of minority and racial groups into mainstream society. Many white middle-class families felt similarly, demonstrated perhaps by the large numbers that had adopted First Nations' children in what is now known as the Sixties Scoop, a process that has been likened to the devastating impact of residential schools. The conditions on reserves had attracted little attention from the Canadian civil rights movement. Chrétien provoked Indigenous communities even more when he said that their disadvantaged position was attributable not to government policy or racial prejudice but to the fact that they had special status. Their legal and constitutional status as "Indians," and the policies that resulted from it, he contended, had kept them separate and behind other citizens. Although Trudeau called for fairer treatment of disadvantaged groups and regions and had consulted Indigenous groups, his strong commitment to liberal values and individualism made him unsympathetic to any special treatment that Hawthorn had recommended or that had existed in the treaties negotiated between the Crown and Indigenous peoples after Confederation. He found the notion of treaty rights between two groups within the same society at odds with his notion of common and equal citizenship. No group in Canada, he insisted, required special status. Moreover, he dismissed all attempts to redress past injustices. His goal was justice for all citizens in our own time, but that did little to satisfy First Nation demands. Historian J.R. Miller has argued that the government's Indigenous policy "was a response to values within the policymaking arena, not to the basic problems facing Indians."[4] The central agencies in the federal government, such as the Prime Minister's Office, controlled by the prime minister and his political staff were most concerned with pursuing policies that conformed to Trudeau's philosophy of individualism and equality and the belief that no ethnic and racial group had any special claim in Canada.

That Trudeau's proposals for Indigenous peoples came in a White Paper (a term given to the government's preliminary position on a particular policy) was an irony not lost on First Nations communities. Although there was support among some Indigenous groups for the government's proposals, most dismissed them as the ultimate triumph of the government's assimilationist and colonialist policies designed to eliminate Canada's

---

4 J.R. Miller, *Skyscrapers Hide the Heavens. A History of Indian-White Relations in Canada*, 3rd ed. (Toronto, University of Toronto Press, 2000), 334.

Indigenous peoples. The Chiefs of the Indian Association of Alberta responded with *Citizens Plus: The Red Paper*, which emphasized the importance of the historical treaties in the relationship between First Nations people and the federal government, presented a case for Indigenous self-sufficiency and self-governance, and rejected any notions of assimilation. It was an act of resistance by Indigenous people and marked the further politicization of their organizations, which felt they had to defend themselves, their collective identities, and their existence as distinct peoples from the state. Indigenous peoples made it clear that they would no longer be content to occupy the margins of Canadian society. The Red Paper was adopted by the National Indian Brotherhood (NIB) as its official response to the White Paper. Almost immediately, First Nations, Inuit, and Métis people became part of an international network to protect the human rights of Indigenous peoples, and they turned to the courts to build a legal case for their continuity as distinct peoples and separate nations within Canada. The federal government subsequently assisted the Indigenous organizations by dramatically increasing funding to the NIB and more than 20 other similar organizations across Canada.

Although the socio-economic condition of Indigenous peoples improved only slightly during the Trudeau period, they made huge strides in asserting their historical claims, especially through the courts. In 1973, the Supreme Court of Canada ruled against the land claim of the Nisga'a of British Columbia. However, for the first time the Court recognized in the *Calder* case that Indigenous title existed in Canadian law, prompting Trudeau to quip to a group of First Nations leaders, "Perhaps you had more legal rights than we thought you had when we did the White Paper."[5] Ottawa then agreed to deal, through the Office of Native Claims, with Indigenous claims against lands not under treaty.

When Quebec began a vast hydroelectric development of the James Bay watershed without addressing the territorial claims of the Cree and Innu who lived there, those groups secured a court injunction to stop the development. In 1975, a deal was worked out that gave James Bay Cree $150 million in grants and royalties over 10 years and control over lands that were not flooded in exchange for surrendering 1 million square kilometres to allow the hydroelectric project to proceed. These were important milestones and, as we will see when we turn to the constitutional renewal, Indigenous organizations demanded that they, too, participate in that process.

FOREIGN POLICY: SEEKING NEW DIRECTIONS

Trudeau wrote in his *Memoirs* that he was "neither fascinated by the study of foreign policy nor especially attracted by the practice of it," but he knew he did not like how

5 Miller, *Skyscrapers Hide the Heavens*, 343.

Canada had practised foreign policy in the past. He was critical of both its style and content, and in his first foreign policy speech in May 1968, he promised diplomatic recognition of the People's Republic of China, a review of Canada's commitment to NATO, and a reassessment of Canada's assistance to Third World countries. The government eventually outlined its major objectives in the much-anticipated *Foreign Policy for Canadians*. It identified six priorities: sovereignty and independence, peace and security, economic growth, social justice, quality of life, and a harmonious natural environment. Trudeau also promised to promote Canada's Francophone traditions in foreign policy and create better relations with other Francophone states around the world. The review also made it clear that Trudeau and his closest advisors, not the professional bureaucrats who played a strong role in foreign policy since World War II, would decide Canada's foreign policy. Trudeau appointed Ivan Head, his former constitutional advisor, as his principal foreign policy advisor. As he did with much of Canadian public policy during the period, Trudeau personalized Canadian foreign policy and insisted that economic growth and national unity would replace international security as Canada's major foreign policy priority. Foreign policy became an extension of domestic policy.

Trudeau wanted to exert Canada's independence and reorient its diplomacy away from what he considered Canada's preoccupation with the United States and Europe. The best way to do so, he believed, was through *rapprochement* with the Soviet Union and other Communist countries. He befriended Communist Cuba and insisted the West learn to understand Communist governments around the world. He delivered on his promise when he recognized the People's Republic of China in 1970, an act that many, including Trudeau, thought would anger the US, although in reality the Americans had also been secretly courting better relations with China.[6] Trudeau also saw the establishment of official diplomatic relations with China, with a population of nearly a billion people, as an important market for Canadian exports. Relations with China led to a new era of Sino-Canadian trade. In 1973, the Canadian-Chinese Trade Agreement gave each country the tariff rate it applied to its most favourable trading partners. That same year, a Canadian trade fair in Beijing attracted about 600 Canadian officials and business leaders; Chinese Premier Zhou Enlai even attended. The two countries also established a Joint Economic and Trade Committee that sought ways to solve any economic and trade-related concerns between the two nations. By 1973, Canadian exports to China had doubled, and it became an important market for sulphur, wood pulp, newsprint, wheat, and metals such as aluminum and copper.

---

6   See, for example, S. Beecroft, "Canadian Policy Towards China, 1949–1957: The Recognition Problem," in P. Evans and M. Frolic (eds.), *Reluctant Adversaries: Canada and the People's Republic of China, 1949–1970* (Toronto: University of Toronto Press, 1991); and N. St. Amour, "Sino-Canadian Relations, 1963–1968: The American Factor," in the same publication.

Canadian attitudes toward NATO also changed. There were concerns that the alliance was increasingly dominated by the United States and that European nations seemed unwilling to provide for their own defence. Moreover, by 1968, the Communist threat in Europe had diminished and many Canadians were growing wary of the US war in Vietnam. Following nearly a decade of détente, or relaxed tensions with Moscow and other Warsaw Pact countries, and notwithstanding the Soviet-led invasion of Czechoslovakia in 1968 (after it flirted with Western-style democratic reform), Canada halved its commitments to defending Europe under NATO without any consultation with its allies. Trudeau considered pulling Canada out of NATO entirely, but his cabinet refused. Canada's allies in NATO complained regularly throughout the 1970s of its cuts to its military expenditure and that the country was not pulling its weight in the alliance as Canada reoriented its defence priorities toward protecting Canadian sovereignty.[7]

The Soviet Union was particularly impressed with both Trudeau's rhetoric and his actions. It saw him as asserting Canadian independence from the United States and invited him to Moscow for a state visit in 1971, the first of any Canadian prime minister. While there, Trudeau emphasized the shared northern experiences of both countries and mused about the dangers of American influence in the cultural, economic, and military life of Canada. Trudeau's state visit went well and Trudeau invited Soviet Premier Alexei Kosygin to Canada.

During these meetings, Canada and the Soviet Union discussed the possibility of a hockey competition between the best players in both countries. Sport has frequently been used to ease tensions and strengthen bilateral relations between countries, as when the American National Table Tennis Team travelled to China in 1971 for a series of matches that became known as "Ping Pong Diplomacy." In Canada, where hockey had long been the national winter pastime, Canadians had become embarrassed with their poor play in international competition. The Soviets were the dominant hockey nation in the early 1950s, but for Trudeau, hockey, foreign policy, and domestic politics became intertwined. While a hockey tournament might strengthen Canada's relationship with the Soviet Union, it offered the potential for something greater to Trudeau: strengthening national unity.

On April 18, 1972, the Canadian government and the National Hockey League agreed to an eight-game series with the USSR that would allow Canada's professional hockey players with signed contracts with the National Hockey League play for the first time in an international competition with the Soviets. Of course, the

---

7   Dean F. Oliver, "Canada and NATO." Dispatches: Backgrounders in Canadian Military History. Canadian War Museum, 2009. http://www.warmuseum.ca/cwm/explore/military-history/dispatches.

Canada–Russia hockey series was no mere cultural event. Both Leonid Brezhnev, the political leader of the Soviet Union, and Trudeau believed that sport played an important role in the development of their nations. For Brezhnev, the series was an opportunity to prove that Russian athletes were the best in the world and to show the West that the Communist way of life was working well. For Trudeau, who often attended major sporting events and was himself athletic, the series would build unity and cohesion at home. Many Canadians saw the game as a contest between an evil Communist empire and a virtuous liberal democracy.

The Canada–Soviet series, held in September 1972, became among the most memorable moments in Canadian history. The Soviets surprised the Canadians with their superb skills and their excellent conditioning and won two and tied one of the four games in Canada, prompting fans in Vancouver—the games were played in four different Canadian cities, itself an act of nation building—to boo their team for its poor performance. The series moved to Moscow for the final four games and the Canadians won in dramatic fashion when Paul Henderson scored at 19:26 of the third period of the final game. Trudeau got his wish as Canadians came together in a moment—albeit fleeting—of national unity rarely seen in Canada.

Even though Trudeau turned his attention to China and Russia, he could not escape the fact that the United States remained the most important foreign power for Canada—even if many Canadians disliked the American empire. Increasingly, American wariness toward Trudeau turned to suspicion and hostility. President Richard Nixon was furious when Trudeau's government condemned American bombing in North Vietnam in a motion in the House of Commons. When Nixon launched his New Economic Program in 1971 to revive the American economy, it considered Canada as just another trading partner, no different from the Western Europeans and the Japanese, ignoring the "special relationship" that had developed over decades between the two North American neighbours.

Canada announced that it would pursue what it termed the "Third Option," an attempt to reorient Canadian trade to Europe and Asia and away from a reliance on the United States. Canada subsequently developed closer ties with both Japan and the European Community, but neither trade relationship was able to significantly alter the longstanding trading relations with the United States. Neither was Trudeau's attempt at economic nationalism to reduce American control of the Canadian economy. In 1971, the government created the Canada Development Agency to foster greater Canadian ownership of businesses by investing heavily in companies operating in Canada. The Foreign Investment Review Agency (FIRA), created in 1974, to control foreign investment by reviewing all acquisitions of Canadian firms to determine that such transactions were in the national interest, only resulted in long delays for business transactions and angered both American entrepreneurs and the Canadian business class. FIRA turned down very few foreign acquisitions of Canadian firms.

Canada attempted to assert its independence in the energy sector following the Arab–Israeli War in 1973, after the Organization of Petroleum Exporting Countries (OPEC) imposed an embargo on the shipment of oil to Israel's allies. Because the United States was dependent on foreign supplies of oil and Israel's strongest ally, it was particularly hard hit and saw Canada as a relatively secure alternative. However, when Canada adopted an increasingly nationalistic energy policy as it struggled to deal with a rapid increase in world oil prices and its own self-sufficiency, it further angered the Americans. Canada even considered an embargo on oil exports, but settled for a tax increase on exports despite the objections of Americans—and Albertans. Canada created Petro-Canada as a Crown corporation in 1975 to garner a greater share of the oil and gas sector that was largely in American and foreign hands.

A similar trend was evident in cultural policy, though Canada and the US disagreed on what constituted culture. To Canada, culture included television, movies, books, and magazines, but the United States considered these as consumer goods that should not be treated any differently than the movement of potash, for example, when it crossed the Canada–US border. American cultural exports dominated popular culture in Canada, and the government—and Canadians, too—wanted to reverse that trend. Through the Canadian Radio-television and Telecommunications Commission (CRTC), established in 1968, radio stations had to include at least 30 per cent Canadian content on commercial radio and increase the level of Canadian programming on television to 60 per cent. To allow Canadian films and books to compete with American ones, the government increased funding to the Canadian Film Development Corporation and provided subsidies to book publishers. In 1975, the federal government introduced measures to disallow Canadian businesses from claiming advertising costs as a business expense for tax purposes in so-called split-run publications—and on US border television stations—unless those magazines had 75 per cent Canadian content. Split-run editions were American magazines reprinted in Canada for the Canadian market with little or no Canadian content. The new measures were aimed primarily at the Canadian editions of *Time* and *Reader's Digest*. *Reader's Digest* chose to Canadianize, but *Time* did not.

Although Trudeau expressed a deep-seated animosity for any form of nationalism, his policies of economic and cultural nationalism not only appealed to a national-ist sentiment in Canada, but to the sense of anti-Americanism that runs deep in Canadian society. Despite the array of policies aimed at protecting Canada's cultural and economic sovereignty, Canada could not ignore that it was a North American state and cooperation with the United States was not only inevitable, but necessary. In spite of his bravado and rhetoric during his early years as prime minister, Trudeau came to understand this, especially after the Cold War heated up with the Soviet invasion of Afghanistan and the American military build-up under President Ronald Reagan. In 1983, Trudeau allowed the testing in Canada of US cruise missiles that flew close to the ground to avoid detection by radar. The testing demonstrated Canada's commitment to the modernization of NATO as a nuclear deterrent. Testing the missiles in Canada, where the terrain was similar to that of the Soviet Union, allowed the North American Aerospace Defense Command (NORAD) to develop the technology to destroy Soviet cruise missiles heading to North America. Finally, and perhaps as a complete reversal of Trudeau's early foreign policy, the Canadian government began talks with the Americans in 1983 on the subject of free trade.

Historians J.L. Granatstein and Robert Bothwell titled their book on Trudeau's foreign policy *Pirouette*. They argue that Canadian foreign policy came full circle between 1968 and 1984—hence, a foreign policy pirouette. When Trudeau assumed office, he had rejected the Pearsonian mantra that Canada could be a helpful fixer or an "international boy scout"—as Canada was sometimes derisively known—on the world's stage. Yet, in one of his final acts as prime minister, he embraced Pearson's approach and attempted the role of global "fixer" when he undertook a tour of foreign capitals to promote world peace and lessen the growing tensions, especially between the United States and the Soviet Union. As an elder statesman, Trudeau received praise for his peace initiative, but none of the major leaders took him seriously, an indication, perhaps, of how little influence Canada and Trudeau had in international affairs.

FISCAL FEDERALISM, PUBLIC FINANCES, AND LABOUR

The Canadian federation, with its divided jurisdiction between the national and provincial governments, has tensions built into the system, much of them over the federal spending power. Since the end of World War II, the federal government had the financial capacity to fund national priorities and introduce new programs in a variety of policy fields, even though the provinces insisted that Ottawa was invading areas of their jurisdiction. The whole system of transfer payments from the federal to the provincial and territorial governments is called fiscal federalism, and these intergovernmental transfers either take the form of conditional grants or block grants. Block grants were usually simple transfers, such as equalization grants, that came without any conditions; the funds could be spent however the provinces decided. Conditional grants were different: they placed significant conditions on how the funds transferred by Ottawa could be spent.

Ottawa used its financial resources to encourage—and sometimes to coerce—the provinces to embrace federal policy initiatives. This has been true of the federal health grants and universities grants. Although provinces depended on transfers from

Ottawa, they resisted Ottawa's setting of priorities within their areas of jurisdiction. As a way to improve federal–provincial relations and to return to some semblance of fidelity to the original BNA *Act*, the federal government under Trudeau promised to introduce new national programs only if they enjoyed the support of provincial legislatures in at least three of the four regions of Canada. Ottawa would provide financial compensation on a per capita basis to those provinces that chose not to participate in any of the federal programs if they introduced similar programs.

For much of the post-war period, governments were expected to provide economic leadership. Through their Keynesian approach, they attempted to even out the economic ups-and-downs of the business cycle, and also to improve health, education, income support, and other social benefits for all citizens. By the early 1970s, however, the growth and prosperity that Canada had enjoyed for much of the period since 1945 slowed, and governments had less money to spend. Moreover, inflation and unemployment rates rose sharply, and the federal deficit ballooned from $667 million in 1968 to $10.9 billion in 1979 and $32.5 billion in 1983. During that same period, Canada's federal debt increased from $19 billion to $157 billion. Such increases forced a major rethinking, not only about economic management and the role of government, but also of the relationship between the provinces and the federal government.

The economic crisis in the early 1970s was triggered largely by the huge increase in commodity prices around the world, particularly in crude oil. The oil-producing countries in the Middle East placed an embargo on oil shipments when the Arab–Israeli War (also known as the Yom Kippur War) broke out in 1973, sending the price up dramatically. The increase in oil prices helped drive inflation to over 10 per cent in 1974 and 1975, and it remained high for much of the decade. Unemployment jumped from less than 5 per cent in 1973 to 11 per cent in 1982, and Canada's domestic banks increased the prime rate for their best customers from 7 per cent in 1968 to nearly 23 per cent in 1981.

To deal with the economic crisis and rampant inflation, the government introduced a comprehensive system of wage and price controls overseen by the Anti-Inflation Board (AIB) in late 1975 to manage the situation. The AIB was given authority to review wage settlements in large companies and reverse increases if excessive. Similarly, it monitored price increases and profit margins of large companies and had the authority to reverse any increases. These tactics were not particularly effective in addressing the economic situation, and they caused a rift not only between the federal and provincial governments, but also mobilized the labour movement, which saw the anti-inflation program as an attempt by both the state and big business to limit wage increases for workers and interfere with the fundamental right of collective bargaining. On October 15, 1976, the Canadian Labour Congress (CLC) led a day of protest against wage and price controls and the Trudeau government. Unions became increasingly militant as they struggled to protect the wage gains they had made in the 1960s and early 1970s, as both federal and provincial governments sought to stem those increases. In 1982, the federal government imposed wage limit increases of 6 and 5 per cent for two years—a policy later adopted by most provincial governments. Although such policies further angered workers, the situation would get much worse for labour as the economy contracted further in the coming years.

As the economic woes continued and government expenditure began to outstrip revenues, the federal government reduced its transfers to the provinces as one way to control expenditures. Ottawa was particularly concerned about cost-sharing programs that had been instituted in health care, social assistance, and post-secondary education, for instance, where it had promised to reimburse the provinces for 50 per cent of their spending. Such an arrangement with the provinces left Ottawa vulnerable, as it reimbursed the provinces for half the costs of many provincial programs over which it had no control. It demanded greater certainty with the amount of cash it transferred annually to the provinces, and in 1977, it introduced the *Established Programs Financing Act* (*EPF*), which replaced cost-sharing programs for health and post-secondary education and set clear limits on Ottawa's financial liabilities. In exchange for setting limits to federal transfers, Ottawa allowed the provinces to set their own spending priorities. The advantage for Ottawa during a period of rising deficits was that federal spending became predictable in certain areas, as the transfer was limited by the growth in per capita gross national product (GNP). The change in financial dynamics meant that national programs started to disappear and the Canadian federation became more decentralized, as each province could set its own priorities without regard to national ones. It is noteworthy that no new social programs were introduced in this period, as all governments became concerned about how to pay for those that already existed.

OTTAWA AND THE PROVINCES: HOW TO BUILD A STRONGER NATION?

The movement toward greater decentralization was disturbing to Trudeau, and his administration attempted to reverse the trend with a more centralist and stronger federal government. Not surprisingly, this new orientation heightened tensions between the federal government and the provinces, which were in no mood to relinquish any of their constitutional powers to Ottawa. This period of "conflictual federalism" was played out across Canada, particularly in Alberta, which had gained extraordinary economic wealth with its huge oil reserves; in Newfoundland, which fought Ottawa over control of offshore oil and gas; and in Quebec, where the separatist *Parti Québécois* was elected in 1976 with its goal of sovereignty-association with Canada.

Western Canada's discontent with Confederation has a long history. It began shortly after John A. Macdonald introduced the National Policy in 1879, with a tariff that favoured the manufacturing industries in Quebec and Ontario. The West believed that its resources were feeding the wealth of Central Canada, and its interests were not reflected in the country's political institutions such as the House of Commons and the Senate. This discontent, often called "Western Alienation," has had various manifestations, notably in the rise of the Progressive Party in 1919, but it reached its zenith during the 1970s, when Ottawa revived the historical sense of grievance in dealing with an energy crisis. When oil prices increased in 1973–74 from $3 per barrel to more than $12, many Canadians wondered why they had to pay the international price when Canada had plenty of oil. In other words, they asked why there was not a made-in-Canada price for Canadians. Ottawa agreed, and to keep the domestic price below the world price it imposed an export tax on Alberta and Saskatchewan oil shipped to the United States. It then used the revenues gained on these exports to lower the price Canadians in Eastern Canada had to pay for imported oil. Such a policy pitted Western oil-producing provinces against the consuming ones in Eastern Canada. The Western provinces were angry because Ottawa's policies reduced the revenues coming to the provincial treasuries. They responded by increasing the royalty rates charged on Crown lands, but Ottawa refused to allow oil companies to deduct these costs from their federal corporate taxes. In the general election following the dispute between the Western provinces and Ottawa, Alberta and Saskatchewan did not elect a single member of the federal Liberal Party and British Columbia sent only one Liberal MP to Ottawa. The region's anger against Trudeau helped elect a minority Progressive Conservative government led by Albertan Joe Clark in 1979. By the time Trudeau returned to office in 1980, the outbreak of the Iran–Iraq War sent Canada into another energy crisis that again saw dramatic increases in the price of oil. Before the new oil crisis renewed the anger in Alberta, however, Canada had to deal with the threat of Quebec separation.

CHALLENGING CANADA

Trudeau believed that there should be no special status for any person or any province in Canada. That was evident in the White Paper on Indian policy, but it would also prove true in his dealings with the provinces, especially Quebec. Trudeau feared the withering of the national community and resisted all attempts that he believed weakened the federal government. Quebec, on the other hand, had long held that it was never a province like the others and that it deserved a special place in the Canadian federation. Many Canadians feared that the worldwide liberation movement—marked by race riots and the Black Panther resistance in the United States, the students' confrontation with police in Paris in 1968, and violence in Northern Ireland—would blossom in Quebec. However, when Robert Bourassa led the Quebec Liberal Party to a decisive victory in April 1970, it seemed that the radical element remained on the margins of Quebec society. That soon proved to be an illusion. On October 5, 1970, the *Front de libération du Québec* (FLQ), a terrorist group founded in 1963 and responsible for more than 200 bombings by 1970, kidnapped British diplomat James Cross. It demanded that the FLQ manifesto be read over the radio and that all convicted or detained FLQ members, whom it called political prisoners, be released. The Quebec government agreed to the former, refused the latter, and offered the kidnappers safe passage out of Canada in exchange for Cross's release; that same day, a second FLQ cell kidnapped Pierre Laporte, the Quebec minister of labour. Quebec asked Ottawa for assistance.

The federal government proclaimed the existence of a state of "apprehended insurrection" in Quebec and on October 16 invoked the *War Measures Act*, legislation that had been first used during World War I. The army was dispatched to Quebec, the civil rights of all Canadians were suspended, the FLQ was banned and more than 465 people were arrested, most of whom were never charged with any crime. Two days later, the FLQ strangled Laporte and stuffed his body into the trunk of a car. Cross was released in exchange for safe passage of the kidnappers to Cuba. Paul Rose and Francis Simard, two of the terrorists who had kidnapped and murdered Laporte, were arrested, convicted for kidnapping and murder, and given life sentences. They were both released in 1982.

The invocation of the *War Measures Act* has remained controversial. At the time, the FLQ claimed it had a membership of 100,000 revolutionaries, armed, organized, and ready to fight for Quebec independence. Rallies in support of the FLQ were held at the Université de Montréal and the Paul Sauvé Arena; many intellectuals, union leaders, and media personalities appeared sympathetic, and few rushed initially to condemn the FLQ and its tactics. However, more than 88 per cent of Canadians (and 85 per cent of Quebeckers) supported Trudeau's invoking of the *War Measures Act*, although over time many have come to wonder if Trudeau and the federal and provincial governments overreacted to the crisis.[8]

Most in Quebec did not support revolutionary liberation movements, and they gave Bourassa a second overwhelming victory in 1973, even though the *Parti Québécois*, a nationalist social democratic party with strong support from the labour movement, captured 30 per cent of the popular vote. Following the election, leader

---

8   Manon Leroux, *Les silences d'octobre: le discours des acteurs de la crise de 1970* (Montréal: VLB Éditeur, 2002); and William Tetley, *The October Crisis: An Insider's View* (Montreal and Kingston: McGill-Queen's University Press, 2006).

Figure 10.3 Hon. Pierre Laporte's coffin leaving the Court House, Montreal, Quebec, October 20, 1970. He was murdered by members of the FLQ.

René Lévesque convinced party members and supporters—usually called *péquistes*—to accept sovereignty-association with Canada rather than outright independence. Sovereignty-association meant that Quebec, though politically independent from Canada, would continue an economic partnership with it. The PQ also promised that it would not unilaterally declare independence from Canada but would hold a referendum on sovereignty-association during its first term in office. The party changed the rhetoric of independence and became more acceptable to voters. Lévesque insisted that Confederation was a financial drain on Quebec and it could only reach its true aspirations—economic as well as social and cultural—if it were free of the burdens of the federal government. Trudeau's promise of a bilingual and bicultural society had done little to satisfy a Quebec that desired greater autonomy and cared little about any attempt to accommodate French-speaking minorities outside of Quebec or Trudeau's promotion of the French language within the federal civil service. The PQ cruised to an easy victory in 1976. It immediately strengthened the French language through Bill 101, prohibiting the use of English in many instances.

QUEBEC REFERENDUM ON SOVEREIGNTY-ASSOCIATION

The Quebec government held its referendum on sovereignty-association in 1980. The question put to voters was cumbersome, but its intent was clear: "[D]o you agree to give the Government of Québec the mandate to negotiate the proposed agreement between Québec and Canada?" A *oui/yes* vote meant that Quebec would negotiate a new arrangement with Canada that, it was believed, would recognize Quebec as politically independent but continue its economic ties through a mutual free trade zone that would also share Canada's monetary system. The PQ maintained that goods and people would pass freely across Quebec's borders into Canada. A yes vote would be business as usual with the rest of Canada.

The stakes were high and the campaign rhetoric bitter. Lévesque was clearly the leader of the *oui* side, and his campaign was an impassioned plea for nationhood. It was particularly well-organized and fairly effective, but two developments in the final days of the campaign turned the tide against the sovereigntists. First, Lise Payette, the highly respected Québécoise feminist and minister of consumer affairs, cooperatives and financial institutions, offhandedly referred to women supporting the *non* side as "Yvettes," after a submissive young girl familiar to most women from elementary school. Then, she called Madeleine Ryan, the wife of provincial Liberal leader Claude Ryan, an Yvette, inadvertently mobilizing an army of opposition from women and sympathetic media that bolstered the federalist cause. More than 14,000 women staged a massive "Yvette" rally in the Montreal Forum to support the *non* side. Many commentators have suggested that Payette's mistake helped turn the momentum away from the sovereigntists.

Second, Trudeau intervened. When the PQ announced the referendum, he had retired from politics, after losing the June 1979 federal election to the Progressive Conservatives and Joe Clark. The PQ were delighted that Trudeau—their long-time nemesis—was gone; they saw Clark, an English-speaking Albertan who, at 39, was the youngest prime minister in Canada's history, as no match for Lévesque. They had not counted on Clark's government surviving only seven months and Trudeau returning as prime minister in early 1980. In perhaps his most eloquent and momentous speech, at Paul Sauvé Arena in Montreal on May 14, Trudeau, referring to the PQ as hucksters, said: "We won't let this country die, this Canada, our home and native land…We are going to say to those who want us to stop being Canadians, we are going to say a resounding, an overwhelming No!"[9] Yet, he made it clear that a *non* vote would not be interpreted as an indication that everything was fine with the way Canada operated. In the February 1980, election Trudeau clearly had Quebec in his back pocket, winning 74 of 75 of the province's seats, and 59.5 per cent followed him into voting for Canada in the referendum.

Trudeau's promise of constitutional reform helped turn the tide of the campaign, as the Québécois saw a *non* victory as leading to fundamental change to their place in the Canadian Confederation. However, Trudeau never spelled out what his promise meant and it is unlikely—given his views about special status—that he ever contemplated

---

9   Pierre Elliott Trudeau, *Transcript of a speech given by the Right Honourable Pierre Elliott Trudeau at the Paul Sauvé Arena in Montreal on May 14, 1980.* (Ottawa: Office of the Prime Minister, 1980), 15.

greater powers for Quebec. He did not mention at any time during the campaign his hope for a new Charter of Rights and Freedoms, which would be the basis of a new Canadian citizenship and would transcend any sense of ethnicity and particularism. Just what Trudeau meant by his promise of change and what French-speaking Canadians in Quebec thought he meant has been the subject of considerable debate since that time.

CONSTITUTIONAL ODYSSEY

Twenty-three days after the Quebec referendum, Trudeau met the premiers at 24 Sussex Drive, hoping finally to change the constitution. Trudeau's first attempt had ended in failure when Quebec refused to ratify the proposals agreed to in Victoria in 1971. In 1975, when the premiers met for their annual meetings in St. John's, Trudeau again invited them to consider a constitutional conference to discuss patriation of the Constitution and an amending formula. However, Frank Moores, the Newfoundland premier and chair of that year's premiers' conference, replied that the premiers wanted to consider the distribution of powers, control of natural resources, and other important matters.[10] There was no progress, perhaps because this was a period of poisoned relations between Trudeau and the premiers: between 1975 and 1980, the Supreme Court heard 80 constitutional cases dealing with the division of federal–provincial powers—two more than it had heard in the previous quarter century.

The federalist victory in Quebec and Trudeau's promise of a new constitutional deal after the referendum gave an added impetus to the long, protracted history of constitutional reform in Canada. However, there was no indication that success would be either imminent or easy. When Trudeau and the first ministers sat down to discuss the Constitution over dinner in September 1980, he dismissed the premiers' list of priorities as a provincial "shopping list"[11] and left the formal dinner he was hosting before the dessert arrived. Federal and provincial officials had spent the previous summer negotiating various proposals from the two levels of government, but Trudeau remained convinced that the premiers had only their pet constitutional projects and no sense of what Canada should be. A rejuvenated Trudeau, with a new lease on political life—from the Canadian people in the 1980 general election and from the Québécois in the referendum—had his own list, and constitutional renewal would be on his terms. He had broadened his constitutional list to include a Charter of Rights, reform of the Senate and Supreme Court, a commitment to the principles of equalization, and the reduction of regional

---

10 Peter H. Russell, *Constitutional Odyssey: Can Canadians Become a Sovereign People?* 3rd ed. (Toronto, University of Toronto Press, 2004), 98.

11 Quoted in Russell, *Constitutional Odyssey*, 110.

disparities. All of these measures were designed to strengthen the Canadian economic union and Ottawa's ability to manage national interests; Trudeau was determined not to allow the provinces to sunder the Canadian political community.

CREATING A NATIONAL ECONOMY

With the PQ firmly in power in Quebec, constitutional negotiations were bound to be difficult, but when Trudeau attempted to establish federal authority over the oil and gas industry in a new energy crisis in 1980, he incurred the wrath of the West and energy-rich provinces in Atlantic Canada. After the first oil crisis in 1973 and 1974, the federal government had negotiated a series of bilateral agreements with the oil-producing provinces, but these agreements expired in mid-1980 during another precipitous rise in oil prices spawned by the Iran–Iraq War. After the federal government failed to negotiate new agreements that satisfied the goals and objectives of the provinces, Trudeau unilaterally introduced the National Energy Policy (NEP) on October 28, 1980. The NEP had three objectives: first, to increase Canadian participation in the oil and gas sector, or "Canadianize" it, in the view of the media; second, to establish Canadian self-sufficiency to ensure security of supply for the domestic market; and third, to achieve fairness in the domestic price. The federal government hoped to control the domestic price by garnering a greater share of the revenue from the oil produced in the West and subsidize expensive oil imports in Eastern Canada. Ottawa believed that such a "national" approach would insulate the economy from sharp spikes in the cost of oil imports and lessen the impact on consumers and the manufacturing sector in Ontario and Quebec. The NEP increased Ottawa's share of revenues from 10 to 24 per cent, with the remainder to be shared between the provinces and the oil companies. The government also introduced a special tax on the oil and gas sector to finance the expansion of state-owned Petro-Canada, created in 1975 and mandated to assume a large role in developing Canada's energy resources. In 1983, with the purchase of a number of oil refineries and service stations from BP Canada, Petro-Canada played a major role in the development of Canada's oil sands and East Coast oil fields and became a symbol of Canadian economic nationalism.

Alberta and Saskatchewan were outraged. They claimed that because the export levy was placed only on oil—and excluded other commodities such as lumber or electricity—it amounted to discrimination against them, the oil-producing provinces. Alberta Premier Peter Lougheed told Albertans in a televised address that what Trudeau had done was akin to "having strangers take over the living room." He immediately reduced oil production by 15 per cent, delayed two oil sands projects, and took Ottawa to court. He succeeded in forcing Ottawa to negotiate a new pricing and taxation arrangement for the oil sector, but the damage was done: the West never forgave Trudeau for his centralist policies and the NEP still rankles many in Western Canada. With cuts in oil production in Alberta, exploration was significantly curtailed, bankruptcies soared, and real estate prices crashed by about 40 per cent; it has been suggested that the NEP cost Alberta between $50 and $100 billion in revenue. Moreover, the Western provinces railed against the powers of the federal government and the imbalances in Confederation that allowed Ottawa to intervene in the taxing of oil and gas to give consumers in Ontario and Quebec cheaper gas prices. The energy issue developed into a federal–provincial constitutional power struggle, and the West demanded constitutional reform to give it a stronger voice in the national policymaking process.

A NEW CONSTITUTION AND ONE DISSENTING PROVINCE

The constitutional process was not an easy one, but Trudeau believed that it was critical to reverse the anger in the West as well as in Quebec. He saw Canada slipping either toward "a community of communities or ten quasi autonomous states"[12]—either way, it was a threat to the country's survival. He wanted to reform the Constitution to create a strong and coherent national state by strengthening the powers of the federal government. He also hoped to forge a durable and stable national state as a way to create a renewed political identity through a charter of common and shared rights and freedoms. Trudeau wished to see Canada embrace a civic nationalism—that would replace all forms of ethnic nationalism—based primarily on a shared language, culture, and heritage, or what Michael Ignatieff has called "blood" in his influential book *Blood and Belonging: Journeys in the New Nationalism.*

Civic nationalism was an attempt to replace ethnicity as the defining national characteristic, with a new political bond based on a philosophical vision around liberal individualism. It would be the organizing principle for the nation-state. These ideals promoted diversity and the respect for cultural diversity, or multiculturalism, which was a reversal of early government policy to assimilate immigrants. Canada had introduced an official policy of multiculturalism in 1971, which ensured that all citizens in Canada could keep their identities and take pride in their heritage. This meant that the state would not privilege one culture over another, as it had attempted to do with promoting the "Britishness" of Canada for generations; rather, culture was an individual matter, and all individuals had the right to maintain and celebrate their individual culture. Multiculturalism asked Canadians to accept all cultures and

12 Quoted in David Milne, *Tug of War: Ottawa and the Provinces Under Trudeau and Mulroney* (Toronto: James Lorimer & Company, 1986), 15.

to realize that pluralism and ethnic diversity would strengthen—not threaten—the Canadian identity. In all of this, Trudeau believed his vision and his constitutional reforms would satisfy Quebec as well as build a stronger bond between the national government and all Canadian citizens.

Trudeau's vision was to reinvent Canada, and it encountered stiff opposition, as many feared the government's policy of multiculturalism would undermine the British and French heritage; in Quebec, many feared that multiculturalism would weaken Quebec nationalism. Indigenous peoples refused to see themselves as members of a multicultural Canada. Many in the immigrant and multicultural communities, though, appreciated the official recognition of their heritage and culture, but they hoped that official acceptance of multiculturalism would eliminate the racial prejudice and discrimination they faced in Canadian society and provide equal access to employment and educational opportunities. Civic nationalism was intended to achieve Trudeau's vision of a Just Society and construct a fair and equitable Canada. There can be no doubt that Trudeau's policies and constitutional reforms embodied a particular ideal for Canada.[13]

Patriating the constitution from the British Parliament was the final act of nationhood that began with Confederation itself. A *Canadian Citizenship Act* had come in 1947, and a new flag in 1965. Trudeau himself had attempted to strengthen the Canadian identity when he eliminated the use of the term "Dominion" from Canada to create a "Government of Canada" and began a process to rebrand the nation with bilingual designations such as Canada Post and Statistics Canada. The ability to amend its own constitution in its own Parliament, rather than having to ask the British government to do so, would end years of embarrassment for many Canadians.

Less than a month after the September 1980 constitutional conference ended in failure, Trudeau took to the national airwaves and told Canadians that given provincial intransigence he would proceed unilaterally with constitutional reform. He promised an amending formula, a commitment to the principle of equalization and the reduction of regional disparity, a Charter of Rights and Freedoms, and the use of a referendum to approve future constitutional amendments. He termed these proposals the "people's package," clearly an attempt at appealing to the national community of individual citizens as opposed to working through the provincial premiers, who he presented as self-interested and greedy. Trudeau had donned a populist mantle and invited Canadians to participate in a series of televised hearings on the constitution that eventually resulted in a series of amendments to his proposals, giving constitutional recognition of rights for women, Indigenous peoples, and disabled individuals,

---

13 These ideas are developed in Andrew Nurse, "Narrating the Nation: An Introduction," in Raymond B. Blake and Andrew Nurse (eds.), *Beyond National Dreams* (Toronto: Fitzhenry & Whiteside, 2008), 1–8.

as well as recognizing the multicultural nature of Canada. Although New Brunswick and Ontario supported him, Trudeau had ushered in a new constitution-making process that privileged public and popular participation and made room for interest groups. The change would play a major role in subsequent attempts at constitutional reform.

The eight opposing premiers—known as the "Gang of Eight"—insisted that by flagrantly bypassing the provinces and proceeding alone, Trudeau was violating the basic principle of Canadian federalism that recognized two orders of government. When they challenged his right to proceed unilaterally, the Supreme Court ruled that he stood on firm legal grounds, but he had clearly violated constitutional convention, or the accepted but unwritten rules of constitutional practice, that substantial provincial consent was required before the federal government could amend the *British North America Act*.

Trudeau relented and invited the premiers to another round of negotiations in November 1981, where seven English-speaking premiers broke with Lévesque and agreed to a deal with the federal government on November 5. For some, such as Saskatchewan's Allan Blakeney and Manitoba's Sterling Lyon, it was evidence of Canada as a negotiated nation; for others, such as Lévesque, it was a clear indication of how Quebec remained outside the Canadian polity. Quebec saw the constitutional compromise as a betrayal—"the night of the long knives"—that isolated it from the constitutional process as the federal government and the English-speaking provincial politicians hammered out a deal in an Ottawa hotel suite. The provinces had been able to force a few amendments to Trudeau's constitutional package, including one on energy. A new clause (section 92A) was added to the BNA *Act*, granting the provinces legislative authority over natural resources, including the export of those resources, provided the producing province did not discriminate in prices or supplies available to other provinces. Even so, the constitution states that nothing in section 92A was to derogate "from the authority of Parliament to enact laws in relation to the matters referred to" in that clause, and when the law of Parliament conflicts with provincial laws, "the law of Parliament prevails to the extent of that conflict." The provinces celebrated that the Constitution recognized their control over natural resources, but some commentators have concluded that the amendments muddled the jurisdictional issue even further. Since Trudeau, no prime minister has attempted to assert Ottawa's control over natural resources and the matter remains a moot point until one does. Despite Trudeau's insistence on a people's constitution, in the end this round in Canada's constitutional odyssey was another example of elite accommodation and compromise, even if it resulted in a Charter of Rights and Freedoms and wins for both Ottawa and the provinces. Ottawa even offered two amendments to the package to lure Lévesque into signing the constitutional deal, but he refused. First Nations were

Figure 10.4 Her Majesty Queen Elizabeth II with Prime Minister The Rt. Hon. Pierre Elliott Trudeau signing the constitution, April 17, 1982.

also losers in the constitutional compromise: Indigenous rights were dropped from the constitutional package at the last minute and a new provision added, mandating several constitutional conferences to address matters affecting the Indigenous peoples of Canada.

Some prominent political scientists contend that Trudeau's constitution signified the end of the Canadian dream by destroying the duality of Canada. For many federalists in Quebec, their ideal of Canada was that of a compact between two peoples and nations, one Francophone and the other Anglophone, and as long as each nation respected the rights of the other, then there was good reason for the two to cooperate within Confederation. When Trudeau remade Canada with a different national philosophy—one based on liberal individualism and equality under the Charter of Rights and Freedoms—many in Quebec argued that he fundamentally altered the nature of Canada by destroying the duality that had been enshrined in 1867. Others have argued that Trudeau not only remade Canada, but with the Charter he hoped to undermine the nation-building project that had begun in Quebec with the Quiet Revolution by creating Canada's own nation-building project, based on new notions of political citizenship that left little room for the claims of historic minorities such as Quebec. Moreover, the Charter gave the courts considerably more power, giving them the authority to overrule any law from Parliament that contradicts the rights and freedoms that the Charter guarantees. Before 1982, Parliament was supreme and it could enact any law within its constitutional jurisdiction—even oppressive ones—but the Charter challenges the supremacy of Parliament and puts significantly more power in the hands of citizens to challenge the power of the state through the courts. The Quebec legislature later voted 70 to 38 to reject the constitutional proposals, but ratification did not depend on provincial consent. On April 17, 1982, Queen Elizabeth II gave royal assent in Ottawa to Trudeau's constitutional package, which became the *Constitution Act*. The ceremony was a federal affair, as was the constitutional process itself.

CONCLUSION

When Pierre Trudeau announced his resignation in February 1984, after 15 years as prime minister, it was the end of an era in Canadian politics. Although Trudeau became an elder statesman admired by many, he had divided Canadians and left office with an approval rating barely in the double digits. The Charter of Rights and Freedoms was his greatest legacy, and it transformed Canada, helping to make it the modern secular society it has become. His management of the economy was generally regarded as poor and he left Canada more divided than he had found it; he failed to improve French–English relations, even though he attempted to make Canada a bilingual and multicultural society where citizenship was based on rights, not on ethnicity. His task of national reconciliation was perhaps doomed to fail, as he did not see Canada as a negotiated nation as the Fathers of Confederation had in 1867.

Trudeau was a Canadian nationalist, even though, ironically, he was vehemently opposed to nationalism of all varieties. Throughout his tenure as prime minister, he constantly looked for ways to strengthen the national identity and to strengthen the power of the national government, often through constitutional litigation and constitutional change. He saw the necessity of a strong national state that could create both stability and durability by creating a political identity of pluralism that would transcend the competing identities within Canada and establish a cohesive national political community that could protect Canadian economic, social, and cultural interests. While many English Canadians embraced Trudeau's vision of Canada, others rebelled. Indigenous Canadians and Quebec nationalists insisted on their distinctiveness and refused to have their identities manipulated even in a society that promised to be pluralistic and liberal. The West and much of Atlantic Canada saw Trudeau's vision of a national economy as merely serving the interests of Central Canada at their expense, and women and other marginalized groups never realized the just society he promised.

11 COMPROMISE AND NEGOTIATION IN CRISIS, 1984–1993

INTRODUCTION

O n September 4, 1984, Canadians elected 211 Progressive Conservatives to Parliament, the largest number ever from a single party in a general election. When Brian Mulroney became the new prime minister a few days later, Canadians left little doubt that they had had enough of the Liberal Party, which had held office almost continuously since 1963. Mulroney saw his huge victory as a mandate for decisive and transformative change—and it was change that he delivered during the decade that followed. Canada adopted a new approach to social welfare, established closer relations with the United States—even negotiating a Canada–US free trade agreement—renewed its commitment to the military, changed the direction and nature of foreign policy, and made debt reduction and tax reform a priority. Crown corporations were privatized, and the government moved to constitutionally entrench self-determination for Indigenous peoples. Mulroney's government attempted to create a more decentralized federation through a new relationship between Ottawa and the provinces, and, albeit ultimately unsuccessfully, to have Quebec recognized as a distinct society. These policies transformed the nation, but they also inspired debate, mobilized citizens, reinvigorated Canada's social movement, generated much anger, and prompted Canadians to throw the Progressive Conservatives out of office nine years later—in spectacular fashion.

AN ANGRY NATION VOTES FOR CHANGE: NEW IDEAS AND NEW APPROACHES

The mood of Canadians was particularly foul at the end of the Trudeau era. Western Canada smarted over Trudeau's National Energy Policy and lingering disputes with Ottawa over ownership of the offshore oil reserves had alienated the Atlantic provinces. Quebec was bitter over the 1982 constitutional process that it claimed had left it isolated and marginalized. Ontario shared with the rest of Canada a genuine disgust with Trudeau's economic agenda. His appointment of more than 200 Liberals to patronage jobs as he left office roused widespread anger throughout the country. Although the Charter of Rights and Freedoms had guaranteed certain rights to Canada's Indigenous populations, there was a growing frustration and anger within First Nation communities over second-class economic and social status. Other groups, ranging from women's organizations to Japanese Canadians interned during World War II, were disappointed that their demands had not been met in Trudeau's just society.

In their hopes for a better country, Canadians turned to Mulroney, a neophyte in the combative world of electoral politics. Fluently bilingual, he had left Baie-Comeau on Quebec's North Shore for a private Catholic high school in New Brunswick in 1953, and then St. Francis Xavier University in Nova Scotia. After earning a law degree at l'Université Laval, he enjoyed success as a labour lawyer in Montreal and eventually in business. His first foray into formal politics came in 1976, when he challenged for the leadership of the Progressive Conservatives, a post he later won in 1983 on the promise of national reconciliation. Conservatives had finally come to believe that a leader with strong ties to French Canadians was essential to their winning Quebec and forming government.

Yet, in many ways, the Conservative Party that Mulroney inherited from Joe Clark was as fractious as the nation itself. The Western Canadian Tories, small "c" conservatives—meaning they were socially and fiscally conservative—and the left-leaning Conservatives under Premier William Davis in Ontario had little in common, except that they were usually out of power in Ottawa. Mulroney knew he could win only if all factions worked together to be a party of moderation. He was able to unite the "Red Tories," the name given to the progressive elements within the Conservative Party, with the Western Tories and the "Blue Tories," those who were economically and fiscally conservative and primarily from the business elites in Toronto and Montreal. He also attracted to his coalition many Quebec nationalists, as well as many disaffected Liberals who had turned away from Trudeau and disliked new Liberal Party leader

John Turner. The Conservatives became a powerful force in Canadian politics, but it was a coalition unable to withstand the rigours of governing.

Mulroney came to power at a time when many nations, notably the United Kingdom and the United States, had radically reformed the role of the state. There was a clear move away from Keynesian economics, which was predicated on the notion that governments can play a crucial role in creating economic stability and generating growth. Canada had embraced Keynesianism in World War II and had enjoyed economic prosperity. For more than a generation its citizens witnessed continuous social and economic improvement, as both the size of government and its scale of activities grew. When Canada and other countries encountered economic difficulties in the late 1970s and early 1980s, many wondered if Keynesianism had been taken too far and if there was a better way to promote prosperity and secure personal liberty. Perhaps too much government intervention was inefficient and wasteful, and people wondered if it had become part of the problem. A new ideology emerged in political discourse, and elements of it were evident in Canada as early as the mid-1970s when Trudeau became concerned about the rising deficit and slowing economic growth; he subsequently slashed government spending, introduced income-tested tax credits, and even pondered free trade with the United States. It was just a harbinger of things to come.

Although ideological labels such as neoconservatism and neoliberalism have been bantered around to explain the changes that came after the Conservatives were elected, Mulroney was never an ideologue in the tradition of British Prime Minister Margaret Thatcher or American President Ronald Reagan. Canada's fervent neoliberals came later, but elements of a neoliberal agenda that emphasized trade and financial liberalization, privatization of government-run industries, deregulation, and openness to foreign direct investment, fiscal responsibility (balanced budgets), lower taxes, and smaller government were evident from the late 1970s. Neoliberals sought welfare reform to make it more efficient, and they strived for greater equality in society by targeting benefits to those in greatest need. As well, they tied social assistance and unemployment benefits to retraining in order to encourage participation of all eligible citizens in the labour market. Neoliberalism ushered in an era where the rule of the market place would play a prominent role in all facets of Canadian life, and neoliberals also believed in a new international paradigm where international trade would spawn global growth. They believed that such organizations as the World Trade Organization, International Monetary Fund, the World Bank, and others would set rules for fair and efficient global trade that would benefit all nations.

While Mulroney embraced some neoliberal policies, particularly free trade and privatization, he maintained social spending and was ambiguous about deficits and taxation. As a labour lawyer skilled in the art of negotiation and compromise, he understood that in Canada compromise, reconciliation, and equity were the principles that had been the trademarks of successful prime ministers. Canada was a negotiated nation where the state had a role to play. Determined to find a new balance between the public and private sectors, he opted for a middle-of-the-road approach, one that followed some of the general tenets of the Thatcher-Reagan revolution to reduce the role of government and bring a more entrepreneurial spirit, which he believed was critical if the country was to improve its standard of living. He warned that refusing change was no longer an option for Canada.

Controlling the burgeoning public debt (the accumulated annual deficits, which are the difference between government revenue and expenditure) became one of the government's priorities and a preoccupation of opposition parties, think-tanks, the media, and Canadians generally. Beginning in the early 1980s and continuing for the next quarter century, debt-as-crisis became an ideology—a problem that had to be solved to avoid imminent financial disaster. In fiscal 1983, the federal government's expenditures exceeded revenue collected by more than 50 per cent. The federal deficit that year was $38.5 billion, up from slightly more than $1 billion in

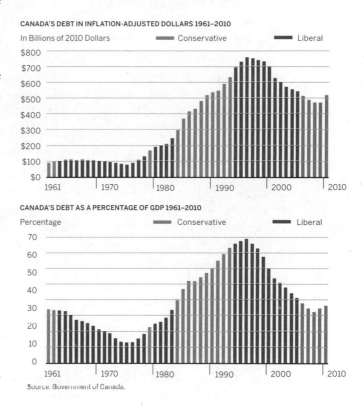

Figure 11.1 Canada's total debt and debt as a percentage of GDP, 1961–2010.

1970. In fiscal 1968, the federal debt was $18 billion, or 26 per cent of the gross domestic product (GDP), and in Trudeau's final year in office it was $206 billion, or 46 per cent of the GDP. Interest payments on the debt consumed nearly one-third of every dollar that Ottawa collected, and this rate was growing. The deteriorating fiscal situation threatened the level of services to which Canadians had grown accustomed.

The government attempted to solve the fiscal problem by aligning expenditure with revenues collected. It raised revenue through tax increases on personal incomes and introduced a Goods and Services Tax (GST), a national tax of 7 per cent, to replace the existing Manufacturers Sales Tax (MST) that had been levied at the wholesale level on manufactured goods. It also cut government programs and eliminated popular measures, such as the home-ownership savings plan, and began a partial de-indexing of some social programs. It substantially reduced grants and subsidies to business, sold a number of Crown corporations, and reduced employment at the federal level by about 90,000 employees.

The federal government also changed the fiscal relationship between Ottawa and the provinces as a part of its deficit reduction strategy. Ottawa had long transferred funds to the provinces through Established Program Financing (EPF), and the Mulroney government reduced the amount of the federal transfers even further than Trudeau had, effectively transferring some of the cost of fighting the deficit to provincial governments. The period was a difficult one in federal–provincial relations, and much of the confrontation stemmed from Ottawa unilaterally off-loading programs to the provinces and withdrawing federal monies from a variety of health and social services.

Many of these measures were unpopular, especially the new sales tax, even though they were welcomed by business leaders who believed that the MST was a bad tax, as it penalized exporters and producers of goods manufactured in Canada while favouring imported goods, which were not taxed in the same way. However, Canadians hated the GST: they regarded it as a new and direct tax on most goods and services and turned viciously on the Mulroney Conservatives for introducing it. All 10 provinces, the major opposition parties, and lobby groups, such as the Pro-Canada Network—a broad-based coalition of labour and social groups—joined the protest, claiming that the tax would harm lower-income Canadians and maintaining that it would add $15 per week to the budget for a family of four. One poll showed that 80 per cent of Canadians objected to the new tax measures. More than 1.7 million Canadians sent GST protest cards to their MPs, but after a noisy and acrimonious debate in the House of Commons, the GST came into effect on January 1, 1991. The province of Alberta, which had no provincial sales tax, challenged the constitutionality of the GST, but the Supreme Court of Canada ruled that the measure was constitutional under the federal taxing power as defined in section 91(3) of the *Constitution Act, 1867*. By the end of the 1990s, the GST accounted for slightly more than 15 per cent of all federal tax revenues, and it became a major weapon in the Liberal arsenal after 1993 to eliminate the deficit.

Although it had reduced the deficit to $19 billion in fiscal 1988, the Mulroney government backed away from its tough deficit reduction measures after cutting spending by $14 billion annually over the period. By fiscal 1993, the deficit reached $34 billion as the government borrowed heavily to service the national debt. By the time the Conservatives left office, the national debt had grown to nearly $300 billion.

SOCIAL POLICY IN A PERIOD OF RETRENCHMENT

This was also a period of shifting social policy regimes, not only in Canada but around the globe. Canadians had placed great faith in the state to provide a variety of social programs to help families raise their children; to provide protection against unemployment, ill health, and old age; and to solve most of the social ills that citizens faced. Social security played an important role in the national psyche, and the Conservatives maintained that Canada's social safety net was a "sacred trust." They reassured Canadians that the welfare state would not be dismantled, even if it were reformed. In fact, spending on social programs increased from 1984 to 1993, both as a percentage of total government expenditure and as a percentage of GDP, but there was a change in the approach to social security. The system moved from one based on universal access and financial entitlements for all to one that was decidedly neoliberal, based on financial need.

The shift from universality to selectivity in social programs came because the government believed that a well-managed program provided assistance to those most in need, not to those who already enjoyed sufficient income. Following such a strategy, the government moved to end the universal family allowance benefits that had been paid to all mothers for their children since 1945 in favour of increased benefits for lower-income Canadians. The government also abolished universality of the Old Age Security program in 1991. Directing funds to those most in need might explain why both poverty and income inequality declined during the Mulroney years. The period represented a shift in the approach to social welfare that continued throughout the coming decades.

FEMINISTS ON THE DEFENSIVE

Women's groups were hopeful going into the 1984 election campaign. More than 200 women stepped forward as candidates and all three party leaders participated in a debate on women's issues. Twenty-seven women won election, including 19 Conservatives, the most-ever for any party. Six women joined the Conservative cabinet. For many women, however, the period was a frustrating one as feminists were on the defensive. By the mid-1980s, the women's movement in Canada had moved beyond being concerned with such matters as the number of women in the federal cabinet— they were intent on addressing systematic discrimination and substantive inequalities. Organized women's groups moved away from what many had considered traditional women's issues to become involved in all aspects of the government's agenda.

At a time when the government was intent on reducing the role of the state, it was not surprising that many women's groups were disappointed with the lack of progress on

Figure 11.2 Emergency workers rush a victim out of the Polytechnique on Dec. 6, 1989, after a man walked into a classroom at the École Polytechnique and killed 14 women in Canada's worst mass murder.

their concerns. There was no greater disappointment than with the issue of violence against women. The magnitude of the problem was most evident in 1989 when a young man, embittered by his hatred of feminists, murdered 14 female engineering students at the École Polytechnique in Montreal. The "Montreal Massacre," as it became known, moved awareness of violence against women into mainstream society. In a response to a petition from women's groups across the country, the government promised in 1991 to appoint a blue-ribbon panel to undertake an inquiry into violence against women, even though many demanded a Royal Commission. As the Conservative tenure was coming to an end in 1993, the Canadian Panel on Violence Against Women issued its report, *Changing the Landscape: Ending Violence—Achieving Equality*. While it provided a comprehensive documentation of violence against women and concluded that violence could only be eliminated when women and men were fully equal, many women's groups were disappointed that the report did not provide either a timetable or a strategy for implementing its 400 recommendations.

Nevertheless, the period saw continued advances in women's contributions to the workplace. The dramatic growth in the share of women in the paid workforce continued to increase. In 1984, 47.7 per cent of women 15 and over worked outside the home, a number that grew to 51.6 per cent by 1993. Similarly, women continued to make gains as a percentage of the workforce, rising from 42 per cent in 1984 to 45 per cent in 1993. Women also saw a marked increase in their numbers in management and professional roles: in 1987, women occupied 28 per cent of managerial positions, but by 1993 held 35 per cent, although that number reflected the difficulty women had moving into traditional male roles. In the professions, women increased their share from 49.8 to 52 per cent, though women also continued overwhelmingly to occupy clerical and administrative roles. Increasing numbers of women with children continued to work outside the home: In 1983, 49.9 per cent of all women with children under 16 were in the labour force, and that number jumped to 62.8 per cent in 1993. Not all women enjoyed the same gains, though. The number of lone female parents in the labour force remained static at about 50 per cent, while the number of women with partners jumped from 51 per cent to 65 per cent. The numbers of women between 15 and 24 equalled that of men in paid labour, but those women between 55 and 64 had participation rates far behind those of men of similar age.[1]

The equality provisions of the Charter of Rights and Freedoms enacted in 1982 came into force in 1985, offering additional protection for women in Canadian society. The Royal Commission on Equality in Employment, headed by Judge Rosalie Abella, issued its report shortly after the Conservatives were elected. The report called for a massive policy intervention to solve the problem of women's inequality. The federal government responded with a new *Employment Equity Act* in 1986 to address inequalities of four target groups: women, disabled people, Indigenous peoples, and visible minorities. The legislation covered the federal civil service as well as federally regulated employers with more than 100 employees doing business with the government through the Federal Contractors Program. The Act required employers to produce an annual report showing how the target groups fared in terms of participation rates, occupational distribution, and salary comparisons, as well as a plan for the greater representation of the four groups in their organization.

Women also made important gains through the courts. The Supreme Court of Canada struck down certain restrictions with respect to abortion in section 251 of the Criminal Code, which it claimed violated women's rights to "life, liberty and security of the person" because of the lack of access and delays in the operation of the abortion system in Canada. The Court also offered a new interpretation of "maternity" benefits when it ruled that the 15-week benefit period at the birth of a child could not be denied to the father. The government subsequently introduced a 10-week parental benefit leave, available to either parent, in addition to the 15 weeks available to the mother.

One of the most important changes came for Indigenous women in 1985 when the Mulroney government removed the discriminatory provisions of the *Indian Act* that had stripped women of their legal status when they married outside their race. Although the Supreme Court had upheld the law in a divided decision in 1973, the ruling was controversial and certainly did not settle the issue. Sandra Lovelace, a Maliseet woman from the Tobique Reserve in New Brunswick, was instrumental in forcing

---

1 Statistics Canada, *Women in Canada. Work Chapter Updates.* August 2001. Catalogue No. 89F0133XIE.

the government to change the legislation. She had married an American soldier and moved to the United States in 1970, but when the marriage ended she returned home and discovered that she and her children were denied housing, education, health care, and other services provided to those with status under Canada's *Indian Act*. Under the 1869 legislation, the legal status of a woman was determined by the male head of the household. What this meant, in effect, was that women such as Lovelace who married non-status men lost their status at marriage. Two Indigenous women's organizations, the Indian Rights for Indian Women and the National Native Women's Association, were determined to change the law. With the support of the National Action Committee on the Status of Women (NAC) and the Voice of Women, they waged a vigorous campaign but with little success until 1977, when Lovelace joined the group. She took the matter to the Human Rights Committee of the United Nations, which ruled in 1981 that Canada was violating the International Covenant on Civil and Political Rights by insisting on the legislation. In 1985, the Mulroney government passed Bill C-31, an *Act to Amend the Indian Act*—despite opposition from some bands. As a result, First Nations women who married non-status men did not lose their status.

The organized women's movement, left wing in orientation, often found itself in conflict with a more right-wing federal government. Most feminist groups saw the state as being a positive force in society that could regulate the workplace, provide social and health benefits, and help ensure a greater measure of equality; the Conservative government believed in limited government and an important role for the market. It was a classic clash of ideologies, and the conflict was reflected in the clash over free trade with the US. The NAC had passed a resolution opposing free trade at its annual convention in 1984, after it became apparent that the Royal Commission on Canada's Economic Prospects (the *Macdonald Report*) would recommend a free trade agreement. The NAC was also a founding member of the Council of Canadians, one of the groups in the social movement that sprang up to oppose free trade. In fact, the first anti-free trade coalition held its inaugural meeting at the NAC offices in Toronto. Women's groups opposed free trade because they feared that the sectors of the economy where women predominated, such as clothing and textiles, would be most affected by the removal of tariffs, and because they feared that trade harmonization with the United States would adversely impact Canada's social programs. Women's groups were also at the forefront of bringing public attention to the implications on Canadian society of increased globalization and international agreements such as the North American Free Trade Agreement, which was being considered as Mulroney left office.

The relationship between women's groups and the government worsened in the Conservatives' second term as the government moved to deal more aggressively with the deteriorating economic situation and the growing debt. When Finance Minister

Michael Wilson announced major budgetary cuts in the early 1990s, few sectors escaped unscathed; funding was cut for women's centres, feminist organizations, and women's magazines. The NAC had relied on the federal government for nearly two-thirds of its funding, but that was reduced to about half as Ottawa supported other women's organizations, notably REAL (Realistic, Equal, Active, for Life) Women of Canada, which promised a different perspective from the established feminist organizations (the government had come to regard the NAC as a lobby group). For REAL Women, the family was the most important social unit in society and it believed that motherhood was a role that should be supported through taxation and government policies. In its effort to save more than $7 billion in spending, the government announced it would not proceed with retroactive pay settlements for pay equity, primarily for women in the civil service. Retrenchment within the civil service also had a profound impact on women, as in the preceding decade the civil service had provided an important model in advancing gender and wage equality. In the government's social reform package, there was a definite shift away from framing policy in terms of women and toward children, child development, and attachment to the labour force, which some groups saw as an attack on women and their demand for equality.

LEAP OF FAITH: FREE TRADE WITH THE AMERICANS

After Wilfrid Laurier was defeated in the 1911 election after negotiating a free trade agreement with the United States, Canada's prime ministers avoided the politically sensitive issue until Mulroney introduced legislation for a free trade deal in June 1988. In fact, the previous Liberal government had tapped into the anti-American rhetoric that generally plays well in Canada. It had embraced a decidedly nationalist economic policy with the creation of the Canada Development Corporation (1971), the Foreign Investment Review Agency (1973), and the National Energy Program (1980), as well as Trudeau's much-vaunted "Third Option" to reduce Canada's dependence on trade with the US in favour of enhanced economic links with the Asia-Pacific region and the European Community. Before Trudeau left office in 1984, however, he realized that his nationalist policies had failed; he even raised the prospects of sectoral free trade to avoid the growing American protectionism that threatened to jeopardize Canada's trading relations with its southern neighbour. In a review of Canada's trade policy on August 31, 1983, International Trade Minister Gerald Regan proclaimed "the death of the third option and the dawning of a new era in trade relations with the United States."[2]

---

2 Quoted in Bill Dymond and Colin Robertson, *Decision at Midnight: Inside the Canada–US Free-Trade Negotiations* (Vancouver: University of British Columbia Press, 1994), 18.

When Mulroney became prime minister, free trade with the US was already on the policy agenda. The Economic Council of Canada (ECC) in its 1975 report, *Looking Outward: A New Trade Strategy for Canada*, had linked free trade with increased productivity and economic prosperity.[3] Given Canada's low productivity, its small internal market, an inadequate industrial plant size, and high tariffs, the ECC warned that the key factors contributing to sustainable economic growth and improving the material living standards of Canadians were missing. Free trade would help improve Canadian productivity in manufacturing through improved economies of scale when producing for a larger market. It would also encourage greater specialization and more innovation in Canada's industrial sector, which more than anything else would improve the economic and social well-being of Canadians.

Senior government officials also recognized that Canada's economic circumstances were bleak and that improved economic relations with the United States offered one possibility for strengthening the economy. Moreover, the Trudeau-appointed Royal Commission—headed by Donald Macdonald, a former Liberal finance minister—recommended a bilateral Canada–US free trade agreement when it reported in 1985. The Canadian Manufacturers Association, long the major voice of Central Canadian protectionism and a strong opponent of free trade, changed its position. Public opinion polls showed that a majority of Canadians also favoured free trade.

There were several factors pushing Canada toward a renewed interest in some sort of trade agreement with the Americans. First, natural resource exports were finding new competition from developing nations, and Canada needed a secure market for those exports. Second, the Canadian economy, while becoming more diversified, was still dependent on the US market. Third, investment and growth in the non-resource sectors of the economy meant that Canadian firms had to be more competitive to compete outside the protected domestic market. Fourth, the American market was becoming increasingly protective, and Canada needed certainty in at least one export market, given the creation of trading blocs such as the European Union. The United States wanted guaranteed access to the vast oil reserves in Western Canada, as its own oil and gas reserves declined rapidly. After months of internal study and debate, public consultations, and media scrutiny of free trade, the government announced on September 26, 1985, that Canada would seek a bilateral trade agreement with the United States.

The regional cleavages in Canada were immediately evident in the free trade debate that followed. The West and Atlantic Canada generally supported free trade. Both regions had long resented the economic dominance of Central Canada, which had benefited

---

3   Economic Council of Canada, *Looking Outward: A New Trade Strategy for Canada* (Ottawa: Economic Council of Canada, 1975).

enormously under the protection provided by the National Policy; the Western and Atlantic provinces believed free trade would strengthen their economies. The West, especially the province of Alberta, also was predisposed, philosophically and ideologically, to closer economic relations with the United States. Although Ontario had benefited immensely from the Auto Pact, it worried that a general free trade agreement would have a detrimental impact on many of its manufacturing firms. Many of Canada's cultural industries were located in Ontario and they were fierce opponents of free trade. In Quebec, where many of the Canada's textile, footwear, and clothing manufacturers were established, there was some concern about the impact of free trade, but it did not share Ontario's level of opposition. In fact, there was considerable support for free trade in Quebec.

The opposition to free trade was determined and fierce, though it was based more on nationalist rhetoric than on economic rationale. Opponents to the Canada–US deal feared it would lead to the increasing Americanization of Canada and the further weakening of Canadian values, culture, and sovereignty. A social movement that shared a common left-leaning ideology and included a coalition of populist groups concerned with a variety of issues—culture, health care, environmental protection, gender equality, and other largely non-economic concerns—coalesced around their eagerness to stop the ratification of the deal and to defeat the Mulroney Conservatives. The free trade opposition offered a form of nationalism that believed Canada was threatened by greater continental integration, and it regarded the state as the primary defender against the continental forces led by the United States. Women, for example, led by the NAC, believed that their equality would be best promoted by the state and were worried that free trade would limit the ability of the federal government to address their issues. The social movement that emerged to fight free trade was traditional in the sense that it was on the left of the political spectrum and wedded to the existing economic system. However, a new social movement would emerge out of the free trade debate to challenge the globalization movement of the 1990s, and would call for direct citizen action to create a new civil society.[4]

Canada's two opposition parties—the Liberals and the New Democrats—also fought free trade. Liberal leader John Turner warned that free trade "will finish Canada as we know it and replace it with a Canada that will become nothing more than a colony of the United States."[5] For him, the issue was Canadian sovereignty, and in August 1988, Turner instructed the Liberal-dominated Senate to prevent ratification of the implementation legislation for free trade until the Canadian people had had the opportunity to consider the matter in a general election. Mulroney took the challenge and called an election, which became a referendum on free trade with the United States.

---

4 Rod Bantjes, *Social Movements in a Global Perspective: Canadian Perspectives* (Toronto: Canadian Scholars' Press, 2007), Chapter 11, "Coalition Politics."

5 House of Commons, *Debates*, June 29, 1988.

Figure 11.3 Brian Mulroney became prime minister promising to restore better relations with the United States. He and US President Ronald Reagan became very good friends while in office.

All three of the major political parties waged nationalist campaigns based largely on fear. The Liberals and New Democrats argued that free trade would destroy everything Canadians had worked to achieve in their country, if not the country itself. Both parties told voters that free trade with the United States would undermine Canada's social security system, destroy pensions and health care, and reduce Canada to being a ward of the United States. Turner accused Mulroney with "selling out" Canada to the United States and repeatedly warned that free trade would lead to the end of Canada as an independent, sovereign nation. For the Progressive Conservatives, the issue was also nation building but within a continental framework. Mulroney said: "Our view of Canada is confident and outward looking." He believed that free trade was an important step in nation building, and throughout the campaign, he argued repeatedly that the deal would permit Canada to end some of the lingering problems with regional disparity; protect Canada's progressive legislation in social welfare, culture, and foreign policy; and allow Canada to become a prosperous nation. During the election campaign, several prominent artists, including Mary Pratt, Christopher Pratt, Alex Colville, and Morley Callaghan, among others, signed a national advertisement that appeared as "Artists and Writers for Free Trade—We Are Not Fragile." The pro-free trade Canadian Alliance for Trade and Job Opportunities noted in a full-page advertisement in the nation's newspapers that Canadian culture would not only survive but would thrive under free trade. Many of the country's largest businesses also supported free trade.

The Conservatives won the debate and formed a second consecutive majority government, the first party in nearly three decades to do so. With 43 per cent of the popular vote, the Conservatives captured 169 seats, compared to 82 for the Liberals and 44 for the New Democrats; Atlantic Canada, Metropolitan Toronto, parts of

Manitoba, and Saskatchewan voted against the Conservatives.[6] The Liberal-dominated Senate had little choice but to pass the legislation implementing free trade, which came into effect on January 1, 1989. Its impact was staggering. In 1980, two-way bilateral trade in goods and services represented about 40 per cent of Canadian GDP. By 2000, that figure had reached nearly 75 per cent, and Canada–US trade was valued at $700 billion annually or $2 billion each day. About 30,000 trucks carrying a variety of goods crossed the border daily in 2000. Two-way flows of foreign direct investment reached new highs of about $10 billion annually. All this activity meant, however, that Canada had become dependent on the US market, which took about 85 per cent of all exported goods and services in 2000. The free trade agreement reoriented Canadian producers from an east–west to a north–south axis, integrating the Canadian economy with that of the United States. Yet, the Canada–US Free Trade Agreement did not eliminate trade disputes between Canada and the United States, although it did provide a means of resolving conflict over trade.

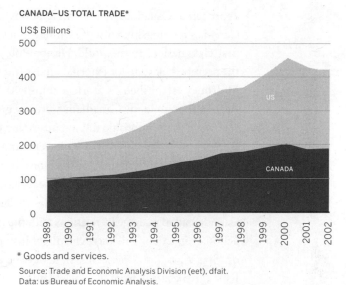

CANADA–US TOTAL TRADE*

US$ Billions

* Goods and services.

Source: Trade and Economic Analysis Division (eet), dfait.
Data: US Bureau of Economic Analysis.

Figure 11.4 Since the implementation of the Canada–US Free Trade Agreement in 1989 and the North American Free Trade Agreement in 1994, there has been a dramatic increase in two-way inter-dependence between the two economies. As can be seen from the adjacent chart, US exports bound for Canada increased from $US 93.4 billion in 1989 to $US 184.9 billion in 2002—an increase of almost 100 per cent. Similarly, US imports from Canada increased from $US 99.0 billion to $US 232.4 billion between 1989 and 2002.

DIPLOMATIC DEPARTURES: CANADIAN FOREIGN POLICY

It was not only in trade that Canada charted a new direction in foreign policy after 1984. Canada broke with a number of traditions in Canadian statecraft established under the Pearson and Trudeau Liberals. Most Canadians expected a different

6   Eighty-two per cent of the electorate saw the issue of free trade as the "most important election issue," although only about half of voters claimed to have made up their mind on how to vote mainly on the basis of the free trade issue. See Alan S. Frizzell, Jon H. Pammett, and Anthony Westell (eds.), *The Canadian General Election of 1993* (Ottawa: Carleton University Press, 1994), 122–25.

approach to Canadian–American relations, as Mulroney had promised to "refurbish" Canada's relationship with the United States, but he also promised to make Canada "a first-class nation" in the world. He appointed Joe Clark, the former prime minister, as the secretary of state for external affairs (foreign minister), as the post was then called. Mulroney established close friendships with both Ronald Reagan and George H.W. Bush, although many Canadians were uncomfortable with their cosiness.

The close relationship did not mean that Canadian–American relations were free from conflict. There were disputes over extraterritoriality on Cuba, American unilateralism toward international institutions, US policy on Central America, intrusions on Canadian sovereignty in the Arctic, defence policy, and acid rain originating in American states and falling in Canada. Through all these issues, there was a sense that Canada had to manage its relations with the US rather than simply react to American action or inaction. This was evident, for instance, in the Strategic Defense Initiative (SDI), or "Star Wars," an American plan to develop a space-based defence shield against ballistic missile attack from the Soviet Union. Canada rejected the SDI after a parliamentary committee recommended that it not participate, but despite that rejection, the US still allowed Canadian industries to bid on US military projects. Similarly, when the United States refused to recognize Canada's territorial sovereignty claims over the Northwest Passage through the Arctic, Mulroney intervened with President Reagan and was able to negotiate the Arctic Cooperation Agreement in January 1988. The United States insisted that the Arctic waters were international, but it agreed nonetheless to seek Canadian consent before sending US icebreakers through the region. Mulroney was also successful in convincing the United States that it was a major contributor to the acid rain killing Canadian forests and streams, and in 1991, the two countries negotiated the Acid Rain Accord that significantly reduced emissions from US factories. This level of cooperation was a significant change after the frosty relationship between the two countries that existed during the 1970s and demonstrated how the two countries could manage to find accommodation on the issues that divided them.

Another indication of the major new directions in Canadian foreign policy came when news broke of the famine in Ethiopia in October 1984, a few weeks after the Mulroney government took office. When the CBC broadcast images from war-ravaged Ethiopia, the Canadian government adopted a new approach to an international crisis. Instead of working through its Department of External Affairs or the Canadian International Development Agency, the government appointed a Canadian Emergency Co-ordinator for African Famine to organize the government's efforts. It also created a Special Fund for Africa and promised to match financial contributions from Canadians. It brought non-governmental organizations into the process of making program allocation decisions—a first for a Canadian government. The government held a series of community meetings across Canada and involved members of Parliament when the Standing Committee on External Affairs and National Defence held hearings on famine relief in early 1985. The response to the crisis in Ethiopia demonstrated the government's willingness to open up the policy process to a broader public.

During this time, human rights also emerged as an important imperative for Canada, particularly on apartheid in South Africa and state repression in China. Canada sought to isolate South Africa over its whites-only policy. This put Mulroney in direct confrontation with Thatcher and Reagan, who both opposed sanctions that other nations wanted. Mulroney was the only G-7 leader favouring a tough stand on South Africa and won strong support for his position. Similarly, Canada angrily denounced the Tiananmen Square massacre of June 1989 in China, in perhaps the harshest statements ever by a Canadian government on an internal matter in a foreign country. Canadians were offered a unique perspective into the events from Jan Wong, a third-generation Chinese Canadian and the *Globe and Mail*'s correspondent in China, who watched the crackdown from her hotel room overlooking Tiananmen Square. Canada subsequently imposed sanctions against China that prevented all trade in arms. In the fall of 1991, Mulroney announced that human rights and good governance would be a cornerstone of Canada's foreign policy. Hereafter, all Canadian foreign aid would be conditional on the satisfactory performance by recipients of these two factors. Mulroney was particularly interested in children's issues and as co-chair of the World Summit for Children in 1990, he promised to put children's issues at the top of the international agenda.

There were also new approaches to the thorny notions of national sovereignty and peacekeeping. The period saw a decline in wars between nations, but a rise in bloody internal conflicts. One of the most vicious occurred in the Balkans in the early 1990s. Barbara McDougall, who had replaced Clark as secretary of state for external affairs, said, "National sovereignty should offer no comfort to repressors, and no protection of those guilty of breaches of the common moral codes enshrined in the Universal Declaration of Human Rights."[7] In 1991, Mulroney was the first Western leader to call for United Nations intervention in the growing civil war in Yugoslavia to impose a peace on the region; he also promised Canadian participation in such a mission. Canada also dispatched a mechanized infantry battalion to Croatia in 1991 and subsequently moved it to Bosnia to secure Sarajevo International Airport. Canada deployed the Canadian Airborne Regiment to Somalia to stop the ethnic cleansing there, but the brutal 1993 beating death of a Somali teenager, Shidane Arone, by two

---

7 Cited in Tom Keating and Nicholas Grammer, "The 'New Look' in Canada's Foreign Policy," *International Journal* 48 (Autumn 1993): 727.

Canadian soldiers shocked Canadians and raised serious questions about the elite forces in Canada's military and the nature of peacekeeping.

Peacekeeping operations had clearly changed and, as Somalia demonstrated, the Canadian Forces had much to learn about planning, command and control, joint operations, and training in the post-Cold War world. In part because of Somalia, and the hope for a new world order that would see the international community join in the pursuit of justice and the quest for peace and prosperity after the end of hostilities with the Soviet Union, Canada hoped that large conventional forces would be less important. However, elite military units might still be required to keep Canada (and the world) free of terror. In 1985, Canada had its first encounter with "non-state actors" that would rise to international prominence in the 1990s, when terrorists placed a bomb on Air India Flight 182 departing from Vancouver on June 22, 1985, killing 329 people and making it Canada's worst case of mass murder. The army was also deployed as an Aid of the Civil Power to deal with what the media called the "Mohawk civil war" at Akwesasne, near Cornwall, Ontario, and at Kanesatake, south of Montreal, where a land dispute between the municipal authorities and the Kanesatake Mohawk nation escalated into a violent confrontation in 1991.

The government never promoted Canada as a pseudo-neutral in the Cold War, and even participated in several covert activities internationally during the 1980s. Canadian forces often lent support to groups fighting Communism in the Third World and were known to airlift seriously injured Afghan mujahideen, fighting the pro-Soviet Afghan government, to Canada for specialized medical treatment. However, the government's need to cut spending to deal with the massive debt, combined with the collapse of the Soviet Communist system, meant that many of the plans for spending on defence were not followed through. The planned purchases for the Canadian Patrol Frigates and the land forces, for instance, were either scaled back or cancelled. The fiscal crisis and the so-called peace dividend of the early 1990s meant that there were few new priorities in defence policy, and the Canadian forces were reduced in size from 86,000 to 76,000 between 1986 and 1993, even though military expenditure as a percentage of GDP remained unchanged at 2.1 per cent.

CONSTITUTIONAL RECONCILIATION: TRIUMPH AND FAILURE

Mulroney promised national reconciliation in 1984, and for him it was important to bring Quebec into the constitution to complete the business of 1982. Although a rejuvenated Robert Bourassa and his Liberal Party defeated the *Parti Québécois* in 1985, Bourassa made constitutional reform a top priority. Warning English-speaking

Canada that Quebec nationalism was thriving, he laid out five minimum conditions for Quebec's acceptance of the *Constitution Act, 1982*: explicit recognition of Quebec as a distinct society; increased powers over immigration; limitation of federal spending power; recognition of Quebec's traditional veto rights; and allowing Quebec's participation in the appointment of Supreme Court judges. The other premiers supported Quebec's position and, like Mulroney, they wanted to bring closure to the constitutional process. Mulroney also believed that it was incumbent upon the national government to create greater harmony in Canadian federalism.

However, what Canada's political leaders had forgotten when they began their discussion of the constitution was that the political culture of Canada had changed since 1982. First, the Canadian Charter of Rights and Freedom had created among Canadians the sense that all citizens had rights that could not be tampered with. Fundamental to this was the notion of equality of all citizens and no special status for anyone. Second, the constitution had committed Canada to the notion of equality of the provinces and no single province having a veto over proposed constitutional changes. The *Constitution Act, 1982* did not recognize the distinctiveness of Quebec or provide it with the right of veto over further constitutional change. The style of constitutional negotiations that had been in place between first ministers since Confederation was obsolete by the time Mulroney came to office. Moreover, after more than two decades of trying to meet Quebec's aspirations, many English-speaking Canadians were less than enthusiastic about restarting conversations regarding the constitution to accommodate Quebec.

When, in April 1987, Mulroney and the premiers began the process to secure Quebec's acceptance of the 1982 constitution, they reverted to the traditional method of intergovernmental negotiations of 11 men in suits negotiating behind closed doors. They were successful, however, in reaching an agreement, and on June 3, 1987, agreed to a constitutional package that became the Meech Lake Accord, promising "the full and active participation of Quebec in Canada's constitutional evolution." The Accord would fundamentally change Canadian federalism. First, it recognized Quebec as a distinct society, even as it emphasized the principle of equality of all provinces and the duality of Canada, acknowledging an English-speaking minority in Quebec and a French-speaking minority elsewhere. Second, it strengthened the relative powers of the provinces against those of the federal government. The provinces were to be provided with a role in the nomination of Supreme Court judges and Senate appointments. The power of the federal government to spend on national programs was to be limited and, in those cases where Ottawa did initiate programs, it would agree to provide financial compensation for provinces that opted out of any federal initiatives. Third, it called for an annual constitutional conference to discuss such issues as Senate reform (particularly important to Alberta) and the role and responsibility of the provinces in the fisheries (particularly important to Newfoundland); it also gave the provinces much greater power over immigration.

Many Canadians welcomed the announcement of the Meech Lake Accord. Even the Liberals and NDP in the House of Commons supported it. Most of the early criticism, largely from academics, was dismissed, but when Pierre Trudeau voiced his concerns, the opposition mushroomed. Critics argued that the "distinct society" clause was an assault on the equality principle that Canadians had come to see as basic to their liberal democracy. The fate of Meech was placed in further jeopardy when the government of Quebec used the constitution's "notwithstanding clause" (which was perfectly legal) to override the Supreme Court of Canada's decision against Quebec's repressive language legislation. The Court had ruled on December 15, 1988, that the 1977 Quebec legislation prohibiting the use of any language other than French on commercial signs in the province was unconstitutional. Using the notwithstanding clause (section 33(1) of the Charter of Rights and Freedoms) to override the Court's decision on language rights, Bourassa confirmed for many throughout Canada the illiberal nature of Quebec nationalism, which Meech Lake seemed to strengthen.

When Meech was negotiated, it seemed a mere formality that all provincial legislatures had to ratify the Accord, but within a few months some of the premiers who had forged the deal were replaced by determined critics of the Accord. New Brunswick, Manitoba, and Newfoundland and Labrador all elected premiers worried about the decentralizing intent of the Accord, as well as the much-debated distinct society clause. The most vociferous in his opposition was Clyde Wells, premier of Newfoundland and Labrador, who quickly became a national hero for his insistence on the equality of all Canadians. On April 6, 1990, the Newfoundland legislature rescinded its earlier approval of the Accord, throwing the ratification process into chaos. Bourassa called Wells an "extremist" and federal cabinet minister Lucien Bouchard said Canadians would have to choose between Quebec and Newfoundland. The opposition to the Accord mounted when Indigenous leaders and the territorial governments complained about their exclusion from both the process and the substance of the Meech Lake Accord. The West was particularly annoyed about the absence of Senate reform, an issue that gave the fledgling Reform Party the ammunition it needed to launch a major offensive against both the deal and the Mulroney government in Western Canada.

These were some of the most tumultuous and divisive times in Canada's history. Bouchard, a long-time Mulroney friend, resigned from Mulroney's cabinet and the Conservative Party, arguing that Meech Lake had been a bare minimum for Quebec and any changes or side deals to bring the opposing premiers on side were unacceptable. Several other Quebec Conservatives also resigned from their party, as did a few disgruntled Liberals, prompting Bourassa to warn that the country could fall apart if the Accord was not ratified. There followed a series of intergovernmental bargaining that almost saved the Accord, including a make-it-or-break-it First Ministers' Conference in Ottawa that lasted for a week that had all holdout premiers promising to bring the Accord to their provincial legislatures for a final ratification vote. However, on June 12, 1990, Elijah Harper, an Oji-Cree from Red Sucker Lake and the first treaty Indian elected as a provincial politician when he served in the Manitoba legislature from 1981 to 1992, refused to give his consent to a motion that would provide for the initiation of hearings on the Accord. Although Harper won the admiration of many, some Indigenous peoples, including the Métis National Council, had supported the Accord. Harper wanted to protest the exclusion

Figure 11.5 In June 1990, Elijah Harper repeatedly refused to stand to give consent to the passage of the Meech Lake Accord by the Manitoba legislature. He held an eagle feather for spiritual reasons.

of First Nations and Indigenous peoples from the constitutional process. Holding a single eagle feather, he refused to grant unanimity to waive the usual two-day period to debate a new motion that would have enabled a vote on Meech Lake. When Manitoba did not vote on the Accord, Wells decided it was futile to have another vote in the Newfoundland legislature. The Meech Lake Accord failed in the ratification process.

The reaction to the defeat of the Meech Lake Accord was severe. In Quebec, the failure was interpreted as another humiliation of the Québécois nation by English Canada. A month after the defeat of the Accord, Lucien Bouchard and six other MPs created the *Bloc Québécois* as a new separatist party in the House of Commons to protect Quebec's interests in Ottawa. Support for independence in Quebec reached an all-time high of 64 per cent in November 1990, and Bourassa announced there would either be radical reform of the federation or sovereignty for Quebec. Negotiations with other premiers were over, he said, but he would wait until October 26, 1992, for offers from the federal government on a state-to-state basis. After that, he would hold a referendum on either renewed federalism or sovereignty.

In the words of many, Bourassa had "put a knife to the throat of English Canada" and they were not happy. Many Canadians feared that their nation would not survive to the millennium, but they wanted the matter resolved once and for all. Several provinces created commissions or task forces to seek views on the future of Canada. The federal government appointed Keith Spicer to engage with Canadians in a Citizens' Forum on Canada's Future. Some 400,000 Canadians came forward either to vent their anger or offer solutions, telling the Commission they had little regard for their prime minister, their provincial premiers, and their opposition leaders. The Forum Report concluded that "The concept of equality applies both to individuals and to their provinces, territories and regions....Participants strongly disapprove of government policies which seem to promote the rights of groups over individuals, especially in comparison with citizens in other Canadian jurisdictions. [Canadians] would not accept any inequality among provinces or 'special privileges' for one or more provinces."[8]

Canada's First Ministers responded. If the Meech Lake Accord had been negotiated in private, the following round of constitution making became a virtual open house where everything was on the program and the guest list broadened. When the federal and provincial governments started to put together a package to offer Quebec, Ontario Premier Bob Rae insisted that representatives of Canada's First Nations join with federal, provincial, and territorial leaders. The leaders eventually hammered out a deal that was changed slightly in the negotiations with Quebec to give Bourassa what he thought he needed to win a referendum on keeping Quebec in Canada. The Charlottetown Accord, as the package was called, was put to Canadians in a fall national referendum in 1992. Before the vote was taken, Trudeau entered the fray once more, calling the Accord "a big mess." It was defeated by a vote of 54 per cent to 46 per cent. More than 56 per cent of those voting in Quebec (which held its own referendum) voted against the Accord. After several years of constitutional negotiations between Ottawa and the provinces from 1987 to 1992, the Quebec National Assembly had still not ratified the *Constitution Act, 1982*, and the country was more divided than it had been a decade earlier.

INDIGENOUS PEOPLES: SEEKING A NEW VOICE

The Mulroney government inherited a legacy of frustration among Indigenous peoples. Even though they had been guaranteed certain rights by the Charter of Rights and Freedoms, there had been little change in either their well-being or in Indigenous–state relations after Trudeau's White Paper. At the First Ministers' Conference on the

---

8 Government of Canada, *Citizens' Forum on Canada's Future. Report to the People of Canada* (Ottawa: Minister of Supply and Services Canada, 1991), 99.

Rights of Indigenous Peoples in 1985—one of four constitutionally mandated conferences under section 37 of the 1982 constitution to deal with Indigenous issues—the government promised to make space for Indigenous governments. However, at the end of the four meetings, no decisions had been reached on such critical issues as self-government and land claims. Moreover, the closed-door constitutional process that had led to the Meech Lake Accord represented for Indigenous peoples a reversal of what Mulroney had promised.

Indigenous–state relations reached a low point shortly after the collapse of Meech, when Mohawks from the Kanesatake near Oka, Quebec, erected a blockade to protest the construction of a golf course on sacred land and blocked one of the major routes into Montreal. The Mohawk Warrior Society, an armed militant group committed to defending Indigenous rights, and allegedly involved in the smuggling of cigarettes and liquor across the Canada–US border, joined the blockades. A police officer was killed in a subsequent armed standoff with the *Sûreté du Québec* (the provincial police force), and Quebec Premier Robert Bourassa asked that the Canadian Army be dispatched to the area in aid of the civil power.

The 78-day Oka Crisis focused Canadian attention on Indigenous issues, and after the crisis was resolved without further bloodshed, the government announced a new federal Indigenous agenda. It promised to establish a new working relationship between the Canadian state and Indigenous peoples, expedite land claims settlements, improve the social and economic well-being of Indigenous peoples, renew and reform Indigenous relations and processes with the government, and deal with accommodating self-government within the constitutional framework.[9] A Royal Commission on Aboriginal Peoples (RCAP) was appointed in August 1991 as part of the new arrangement with Indigenous peoples, though its primary purpose was to offer recommendations to solve the problems that had long-plagued Indigenous–state relations in Canada. The most comprehensive and inclusive study of the complex world of Indigenous policy in Canada, it would report in November 1996.

Indigenous leaders participated in the process that led to the Charlottetown Accord in 1992 and signalled the possibility of a new beginning. If the Accord had been successful, it would have represented major constitutional gains by entrenching Indigenous self-government as one of the three orders of government in Canada, recognizing the inherent right of self-government, and creating Indigenous seats in the Senate. The Accord was rejected by Canadians, including many First Nations reserve

---

9 B. Mulroney, CARC—*North Perspectives* 21, no. 3 (Fall 1993). See also A. Fleras and J.L. Elliott, *The Nations Within: Aboriginal-State Relations in Canada, the United States, and New Zealand* (Toronto: Oxford University Press, 1992), 97.

residents and the Native Women's Association of Canada, who claimed that it did not go far enough to meet their demands even though, for the first time, Ovide Mercredi, then grand chief of the Assembly of First Nations, had participated equally with other first ministers. Many Indigenous women feared that self-government would undermine women's rights, and many objected to the fact that they were excluded from the Indigenous national representation.

Several other developments were important, as they allowed First Nations peoples to assume greater responsibility and control over their own affairs. First, the Mulroney government transferred responsibility to First Nations for managing most federal programs on reserves. By 1991, more than 77 per cent of program spending was managed by First Nations. However, socio-economic evidence suggests that the level of Indigenous well-being was far below national averages. Second, important gains were made on the issue of land claims. When the Supreme Court ruled in the *Calder* case in 1973 that Indigenous title was recognized in common law, the federal government negotiated with Indigenous peoples to resolve some outstanding land claims and moved to settle breaches of treaty obligations. Section 35 of the *Constitution Act, 1982*, explicitly recognized and affirmed the existing Indigenous and treaty rights, including those that resulted from comprehensive land claims. The process for resolving this complex issue is still far from complete, but the Mulroney government realized that land claims and self-government issues had to be resolved together.

One significant accomplishment, in 1993, came when the Inuit of the Eastern Arctic reached an agreement with the federal government to create Nunavut as a third territory in Canada's North, giving them control of their collective future. However, with a small population, huge costs, and impending global warming, the North will face considerable challenges in the coming decades. Third, the *Indian Act* was amended in 1985 through Bill C-31 (as noted above) to give Registered Indian Status to women who had been removed from the Indian Register because they had married non-status Indians. Their children were also permitted to register under the Act. Individual First Nations were also given the authority to establish their own rules governing membership. Across Canada, the impact was enormous, as the incremental growth associated with Bill C-31 totalled about 174,500 individuals. For the first time, the federal government also recognized people who had been referred to as "non-status" Indians. This includes Métis, urban Indigenous peoples, and other Indigenous peoples not recognized in federal legislation and not included in the *Indian Act*. The government created the office of a federal interlocutor for Métis and Non-Status Indians, with a cabinet minister responsible for relations between the federal government and the representatives of these groups. In all, important progress was made, but the standard of living for many Indigenous peoples remained far below the national level.

THE PROVINCES: FRUSTRATION AND CHANGE

Many of the provincial governments shared some of the frustration felt by Indigenous and First Nations' communities. Achieving intergovernmental harmony is no easy task in Canada, but in the early years of the Mulroney government, it seemed possible. The first meetings between the premiers and the prime minister were positive affairs without the acrimony so evident during the Trudeau years. Moreover, longstanding grievances with the provinces were solved quickly. Newfoundland, a province that had struggled economically since joining Canada in 1949, finally secured an equal voice with Ottawa on development of the vast offshore oil reserves in the Canada–Newfoundland Atlantic Accord, signed in February 1985. A month later, Ottawa eliminated a series of federal taxes in the oil and gas sector with the Western Accord, an agreement between the governments of Canada, Saskatchewan, Alberta, and British Columbia on oil and gas pricing and taxation, ending the feud with the Western provinces that had marked much of the previous decade.

The new style of cooperation did not last long, however, as the fundamentally different interests among the provinces, which had always made intergovernmental harmony difficult, re-emerged. On the issue of free trade, for example, Alberta Premier Peter Lougheed and Premier Bourassa of Quebec were in favour because of their provinces' reliance on the export of raw and semi-processed materials. David Peterson, the premier of Ontario, on the other hand, was opposed. He feared for his province's vast manufacturing sector amid reports that Ontario might lose nearly 300,000 manufacturing jobs if the border was open to American producers. At a first ministers meeting to discuss how to proceed on free trade, Mulroney agreed to provincial participation in the trade talks. The premiers, especially Peterson, believed this to mean that the first ministers would have a voice in the negotiations. However, Ottawa had no intention of making the premiers partners in the process; they would be kept informed during the negotiations, but there was little of the intergovernmental collaboration that many had anticipated. It was clear during this period that Ottawa would act unilaterally when it felt necessary. In the case of the Atlantic and Western Accords, for example, there had been little consultation with the provinces, as both agreements resulted from unilateral federal action, even if the spirit and letter of the accords meet with provincial approval.

As a way of addressing the deficit, the federal government unilaterally decided to limit its contribution to the Canada Assistance Plan, a cost-shared program between the federal and provincial governments to provide comprehensive social services across Canada. While Ottawa's decision allowed it to address its deficit problem, it increased the disagreements between the two orders of government. In fact, the federal government came to realize that intergovernmental relations was one of the most difficult files to manage, as the various intergovernmental files could not be kept separate. For instance, the country was dealing with free trade and the constitution at the same time that Ontario and British Columbia were quarrelling with Ottawa over how best to deal with American duties on Canada's export of softwood lumber. Mulroney learned that free trade affected constitutional negotiations, and the equalization program had an impact on all others. With so many contentious issues, none could be dealt with in an entirely independent manner. Intergovernmental relations are complex in Canada, made doubly so by the extent of regional diversity in this country. This lesson was perhaps most apparent in Western Canada.

In 1986, the government awarded the billion-dollar maintenance contract for the CF-18 aircraft fighter jet used by the Canadian Forces to Montreal-based Canadair instead of Winnipeg-based Bristol Aerospace—even though the Western firm had a cheaper and technically superior bid. This decision sealed Mulroney's fate in the West. It had the same effect emotionally as Trudeau's National Energy Program and led in part to the creation of a new Western political party. In 1987, Preston Manning, son of former Alberta Premier Ernest Manning, created the Reform Party of Canada as an expression of Western discontent. The party was formed by Conservatives in the West who were disappointed with Mulroney. One of its primary objectives was to achieve what it termed a Triple-E Senate—elected, equal, and effective.

The Reform Party immediately became a threat to the Conservative base in Western Canada. The Mulroney coalition of the West and Quebec held in the 1988 election, but it showed signs of strain soon after. As Mackenzie King discovered much earlier, Mulroney had to choose between the two sections of Canada. In 1988, the government introduced Bill C-72 "to fulfill the bilingualization of Canada in general and the Canadian government in particular." The West saw this as another sign of pandering to Quebec. When Manitoba Tory Dan McKenzie refused to vote for the bill, he was fired as parliamentary secretary to the minister responsible for Veteran's Affairs. A Quebec MP, Charles Hamelin, who threatened to quit the party and join the *Parti Québécois* if Tory backbenchers blocked the legislation, replaced McKenzie. At the same time, a poll found that 71 per cent of those in the Prairies and British Columbia felt that the Mulroney government had done too much for Quebec, although only 60 per cent of all English-speaking Canadians felt that way.

In the 1988 election, the Reform Party failed to win a single seat but it captured 15 per cent of the vote in Alberta. In March 1989, Deborah Grey, singing the Reform's "the West wants in" message, won a by-election in east-central Alberta to become the first Reform member in the House of Commons. Henceforth, Mulroney continued to lose support in the West, as the region, and particularly Alberta, felt increasingly alienated from the party. In fact, in April 1991, the Alberta Progressive Conservative Party severed all ties with the national party. Much of the alienation came from a perception in the West that Mulroney was even more obsessed with Quebec than was the region's earlier nemesis, Pierre Trudeau. A public opinion gave the Conservatives 15 per cent of public support and the Reform Party 43 per cent. This came at a time when the West had 10 of the 30 seats in the federal cabinet, but the Conservative Party had clearly lost touch with the region, which had shifted to the ideological right and had become even more "small-c" conservative. At end of the Mulroney period, the Reform Party would replace the Conservatives as the dominant political force in Western Canada.

CONCLUSION: A CONSERVATIVE IS A CONSERVATIVE

On February 25, 1993, with the economy mired in a stubborn recession, unemployment rates at a 20-year high, the country deeply divided, and his own approval rate the lowest of any sitting prime minister, Mulroney resigned. The coalition he had forged among Quebec nationalists, Western conservatives, and Ontario Tories, which had resulted in two consecutives majorities, had come unravelled.

Not even Kim Campbell, the new energetic leader of the Progressive Conservatives and Canada's first woman prime minister, could save the party. In October 1993, Campbell led the Conservatives to one of the most disastrous defeats in Canadian political history: their popularity drop from 43 per cent of the popular vote and 169 seats in 1988 to 16 per cent and just 2 seats in 1993.

Many of Mulroney's policies—the GST, free trade, peacekeeping, reducing government spending, and a stated commitment to debt reduction—were embraced by the government that followed. Nevertheless, the Conservatives had clear failures as well, principally two unsuccessful attempts at constitutional reform to meet the needs of Quebec and First Nations peoples. Many English speaking Canadians had developed a visceral dislike of Mulroney and were delighted when he left the Prime Minister's Office. In his own defence he said, "I always tried to do what I thought would be right for Canada in the long term, not what would be politically popular in the short term."[10] Mulroney did not disappear from

Figure 11.6 The Honourable Kim Campbell, minister of justice and attorney general of Canada, and first female prime minister.

---

10 *Montreal Gazette*, February 25, 1993.

Canadian politics after he resigned, as rumours of corruption within his government and by those around him persisted after he left office, although he was never found guilty of any wrongdoing.

Compromise and negotiation that had been the hallmarks of national politics for much of the period since Confederation no longer seemed to work; the tensions long evident in the national polity, it seems, finally reached a breaking point. The 1993 election demonstrated that Quebec and the West, both with longstanding grievances with the centre, turned their backs on the traditional parties, opting instead to create new, regionally based parties to represent their interests in Parliament. That meant that the party that could win Ontario controlled the national government, which was a new phenomenon in Canada. Regardless, the decade was a momentous one in Canadian history, one that brought profound change, breathed new life into Canada's social movement, and destroyed one of the founding political parties that had created Canada. More than anything, however, the period demonstrated that Canada had become a nation with deep-rooted conflicts that would not easily be resolved through negotiation and compromise.

12 THE NEW MILLENNIUM: SEARCHING FOR NATIONAL PURPOSE

INTRODUCTION

Canada was in the midst of a stubborn and severe economic downturn in the final decade of the twentieth century. The fiscal crisis made it nearly impossible for governments to continue the level and quality of services to which Canadians had grown accustomed. Some advised deep cuts to government spending and a rethinking of the role of governments, but others cautioned that reductions in social spending were ideological, driven by Canada's political and economic elites that wanted to minimize the role of the state. The malaise was not just economic. More than 1,200 patients were infected with the deadly HIV virus through blood transfusions, prompting the federal government to launch a public inquiry into the safety of Canada's blood supply. The United Nations Committee on Economic, Social and Cultural Rights criticized Canada for its high level of poverty and homelessness, especially among Indigenous peoples, despite the fact that it was one of the world's richest countries. Quebec was poised for another vote on independence. Taken together, it is little wonder that many Canadians feared their country would break apart before they reached the new millennium.

In the federal election held on October 25, 1993, only 69.6 per cent of eligible voters bothered to mark a ballot, the lowest turnout since 1925. The coalition Brian Mulroney had assembled in 1984 collapsed in spectacular fashion, and the Conservatives, led by Kim Campbell, who became Canada's first female prime minister on June 25, captured a mere 16 per cent of the popular vote, winning only two seats. Led by the charismatic Lucien Bouchard, the *Bloc Québécois* won nearly 50 per cent of the vote and 54 of 75 seats in Quebec—enough to become Her Majesty's Official Opposition in the House of Commons, an ironic outcome that angered many in English-speaking Canada. The newly established, Western-based, populist Reform Party, led by Preston Manning, capitalized on Western discontent and captured 18.7 per cent of the popular vote and 52 of the 86 ridings west of the Ontario–Manitoba border. The rapid rise of Reform swamped the New Democrats, which, like the Conservatives, lost official party status in the House of Commons.

The Liberals won a majority with 177 seats, sweeping Ontario and Atlantic Canada. Politically, Canada was a fragmented nation, and its regional cleavages were exposed. Yet contemporary Canada had to deal with many of the same issues that had animated the country for decades: the role of the state, the nature of Canada's social programs, the relationships between the state and Indigenous peoples, the lack of gender equality, federal–provincial relations, foreign relations, and multiculturalism and diversity. Simply put, these issues were essentially a debate about the very nature of Canada and what type of nation citizens wanted. The decade was about negotiating differences and trying to find enough common ground to make the country work. In that search for a common ground, there were winners and losers as there had been throughout Canadian history.

With a few minor and perhaps symbolic changes, the Chrétien government embraced many of the policies of the Mulroney Conservatives, some, ironically, with greater exuberance and determination than had Mulroney. Ironically, too, Chrétien reaped the political benefits of some of Mulroney's most unpopular policies, notably the Goods and Services tax (GST), used by his Liberal government to control the deficit and the national debt, which had reached $423 billion by 1993. Chrétien and Finance Minister Paul Martin became convinced that they had to reduce public spending, and they were ruthless in cutting expenditures and transfers to the provinces. Their greatest legacy was improving Canada's fiscal position and returning government to annual surpluses. Unlike previous post-war Liberal governments, which had believed an activist government could solve any national problem, Chrétien's government pursued a neoliberal agenda.

Martin had initially been tentative in curtailing spending, but during a tour of the world's financial markets after his first budget, including a visit to the International Monetary Fund headquarters in Washington, he was lectured on how Canada had failed to eliminate its deficit after talking about it for more than 25 years. Canada was "going down the tubes," he was told. The influential *Wall Street Journal* described Canada as an honorary member of the Third World and warned that it was about to hit the "debt wall" and drop into the financial abyss if it failed to manage spending more effectively.[1] When Moody's Investors Services downgraded Canada's sovereign bond rating, borrowing money became more expensive for the government, something Canada could ill afford.

The federal deficit then stood at nearly $40 billion, while the national debt exceeded $500 billion and was growing by $85,000 a minute. About 34¢ of every dollar collected went to pay interest on the debt; that was $6 billion not available for new government spending. Confronting the deficit was not about ideology, but arithmetic, Martin told his officials. Polls showed most Canadians agreed, although few were prepared for the cuts that followed. In his 1995 Budget Speech Martin said, "There are times in the progress of a people when fundamental challenges must be faced, fundamental choices made—a new course charted. For Canada, this is one of those times."[2]

Expenditure cuts of $80 billion were outlined for the next four years. Government spending as a percentage of gross domestic product (GDP) dropped to levels not seen since 1951.[3] Martin abandoned the interventionist policies of earlier governments and tried to temper expectations. Every department in the federal government—with the exception of Indian and Northern Affairs Canada—suffered major cuts; the civil service was reduced by 45,000 jobs, or 14 per cent. Subsidies to businesses were eliminated or reduced, and many government services had to operate on a cost-recovery model. Crown corporations, including Canadian National and Petro-Canada, were privatized, as was air traffic control. The Crow's Nest Pass rate, the subsidy that assisted Western farmers in moving their grains to market, was eliminated. Expenditure on foreign aid decreased, and immigration fees were raised. The Liberal promise of a national childcare program, at about $360 million, was scrapped, and spending on social (low-income) housing ceased. Some said it was neoliberalism run amok. Still, nearly 70 per cent of those polled believed the government acted prudently. In fiscal 1997–98, Martin reported a surplus of $2.9 billion—the first since 1969—and after several years of surpluses, Moody's upgraded Canada's credit rating—a vindication, Martin said, of his handling of the fiscal crisis. Canadians saw him as a prime minister in waiting.

The fiscal crisis changed the relationship between Ottawa and the provinces. For more than a generation, the federal government had transferred funds through such programs as the Canada Assistance Plan (CAP) and the Established Programs Financing (EPF) to support health, social welfare, and post secondary education. Although the amount had been capped since 1991, Ottawa's contributions allowed it to set national

---

1 Quoted in John Gray, *Paul Martin In the Balance* (Toronto: Key Porter Books, 2003), 114.
2 Quoted in Canada, Department of Finance, *Budget Speech*, February 27, 1995.
3 *Maclean's*, March 18, 1996.

Figure 12.1 Prime Minister Jean Chretien and Finance Minister Paul Martin. Together, they tackled Canada's growing deficits and debt, cutting federal spending as a percentage of GDP to the lowest levels since the 1950s.

standards and to impose some consistency in social citizenship across Canada. That changed in 1996, when Chrétien announced transfer cuts to the provinces of more than $20 billion by fiscal 1998 and replaced existing programs with a new Canada Health and Social Transfer (CHST). Just before the 1997 general election, Ottawa restored $6 billion of the cuts, only to announce further cuts later. Between fiscal 1993–94 and fiscal 2002–03, federal transfers to the provinces decreased from 3.9 to 3.0 per cent of GDP. The introduction of the CHST did remove a source of irritation in federal–provincial relations, as Ottawa allowed the province to spend the federal transfers as they wished and without having to adhere to any national priorities or standards that it imposed.

Yet, it was a high price for provinces to pay for the removal of federal oversight. The new federal approach downloaded responsibility for much of the social spending for health, education, and social welfare to the provincial governments, which could ill afford it. The federal cuts represented about 3 per cent of all provincial revenues and left most of the provinces nearly broke. All had to implement their own austerity programs by restructuring school boards, hospitals, and municipalities to save money. In Saskatchewan, which had a brush with bankruptcy, NDP Premier Roy Romanow embraced deficit reduction through spending cuts and privatization. He even introduced balanced budget legislation—showing the extent of the fiscal crisis.

In Ontario, another NDP Premier, Bob Rae, cut spending to virtually every sector, including municipalities, universities, schools, hospitals, and social welfare—a difficult task for a socialist government. Rae's attempt to negotiate a social contract with the public sector and labour on how best to achieve the province's fiscal objectives was an abject failure. His attempts to balance the budget through wage freezes and rollbacks, early retirement, and unpaid days off (called "Rae days") earned Rae and the NDP nothing but contempt from his supporters and detractors alike. Although Rae had pursued a progressive social agenda, including recognizing the inherent right of Indigenous peoples to self-government and a bill to provide benefits to same-sex couples (which was defeated when his own party refused to support it), his party was decimated in the 1995 provincial election, going from 74 to 17 seats. Progressive Conservative

Mike Harris promised a "Common Sense Revolution" predicated on restoring fiscal responsibility to government through tax and spending cuts. He embraced a policy of restraint that diminished the role for the state as he cut spending on welfare, social programs, and the MUSH (municipalities, universities, schools, and hospitals) sector. He had little interest, however, in such issues as same-sex marriage and abortion. Alberta's Ralph Klein, premier from 1992 to 2006 and another Conservative, adopted a similar approach. Although dubbed the "Klein Revolution," it, too, became apparent that Klein was more interested in simply reducing spending than revolutionizing Alberta politics. Those on the right wing of his party were disappointed that he did not pursue more radical ideas, such as embracing private health clinics and a variety of other issues important to social conservatives. As Jason Kenney, then president of the Canadian Taxpayers' Federation and later a Conservative Member of Parliament, complained, "This isn't a revolution...we have just traded a Rolls-Royce for a Cadillac."[4]

Women's groups also felt the brunt of the neoliberal agenda that threatened the gains they had made in recent years. They braced for the worst when Chrétien refused to participate in a debate on women's issue during the 1993 campaign, dismissing women's organizations as a special interest group. He even mused that the government should get out of funding lobby groups. In 1995, the government closed the Canadian Advisory Council on the Status of Women, which had been established in 1973 to provide research and advice on women's issues within government.[5] Chrétien's government failed to understand that a reduction in social spending ignored the gendered dimension of such decisions and threatened women's struggle for equality. This was demonstrated in changes to the unemployment insurance program in 1996, which made it more difficult for part-time workers, most of whom were women, to qualify. In 1994, the federal government also closed its Family Violence Initiative (only to restore funding before the 1997 election) and shifted to the provinces responsibility for shelters for victims of domestic violence.

The Canadian government retreated generally on women's issues. It had earlier incorporated language and analyses developed by radical feminists and had become a leader in addressing violence against women, recognizing the problem in gender-specific terms such as wife battering, rape, and other forms of violent acts directed specifically against women. It saw violence against women as a symptom of sexual

4   Quoted in David Leyton-Brown (ed.), *Canadian Annual Review of Politics and Public Affairs: 1995* (Toronto: University of Toronto Press, 2002), 211.

5   S. Weldon, "Citizen, Victims, Deviants, Restructuring Government Response to Violence Against Women in Canada." Paper presented at the annual meeting of the American Political Science Association, Hilton Chicago and the Palmer House Hilton, Chicago, IL, September 02, 2004. http://citation.allacademic.com/meta/p_mla_apa_research_citation/0/6/1/8/2/p61822_index.html.

inequality, but during the Chrétien regime, government ceased seeing such violence as an issue of gender inequality and started using gender-neutral language to describe the problem. Violence against women became part of a "law and order" agenda that emphasized the need to protect citizens against criminal activity, rather than a discussion about traditional gender roles and social inequality.

REINVESTING IN CANADA

After several years of dramatic spending cuts, the federal government declared a budgetary surplus in 1997 and began to reinvest in the country. It introduced a series of new programs for children, post-secondary education, and health, all aimed at enhancing social solidarity and fostering a caring and sharing society that would be national in scope.[6] There would be no return, however, to a system of cost sharing with the provinces. Ottawa hoped to create a new social Canada through direct transfers to individuals and families, a new commitment to health care, and the creation of foundations to support post-secondary education and research.

The system existing in 1993 created significant financial disincentives for parents in low-income families to leave social assistance and enter the workforce. To do so, they lost health, dental, and prescription drug benefits for their children. They were often financially better off on welfare than in a low-paying job. In 1998, Ottawa, the provinces, and territorial and First Nations governments introduced a National Child Benefit (NCB), the first major national social program in more than three decades that would make parents better off financially when working. The goals were simple: reduce child poverty, allow parents to participate in the labour market without losing their child benefits, and reduce overlap and duplication in government programs.

The National Child Benefit had two components. The first was a monthly payment from the Government of Canada to families with children. The direct federal benefit, known as the Canada Child Tax Benefit (CCTB), assisted low- and middle-income families with the costs of raising their children. The level of benefits decreased as family incomes rose and was fully phased out at $99,128 (in 2007). Some 3.5 million families and 6 million children received the CCTB. The second component was the NCB Supplement, paid to an additional 1.6 million families with incomes less than $36,387, many of whom were on provincial social assistance. Provincial and territorial governments agreed that any savings earned from reduced payments to social assistance recipients with children would be reinvested through new or enhanced supports for

---

6 Privy Council Office, *Renewing the Canadian Federation: A Progress Report* (Ottawa: Government of Canada, 1996), 2.

low-income families, including childcare/daycare initiatives, additional child benefits and earned income supplements, special services for early childhood development and children-at-risk, and supplementary health benefits for children. By 2005–06, more than $870 million had been reinvested by the provinces.

The National Child Benefit, totalling $6 billion, provided considerable support to low-income families across Canada and was billed as an important national project.[7] The percentage of low-income families with children declined from 17.6 per cent to 11.6 per cent between 1996 and 2005. Quebec did not participate in the program, but still received the NCB supplements from Ottawa. It used the money saved from reducing its social assistance payments to finance other family programs, including $5-a-day childcare programs in regulated centres, a full-day kindergarten for all five-year-olds, and a half-day program for four-year-olds from low-income families whom the government considered at risk of encountering learning problems once they entered the school system.

Another initiative under the National Child Agenda was Early Childhood Development (ECD), designed to increase and expand provincial programs for children and their families. It added $2.2 billion to the Canadian Health and Social Transfer between 2001–02 and 2005–06, which the provinces had to direct to four general areas: the promotion of healthy pregnancy, birth, and infancy; improving parenting and family supports; strengthening early childhood development, learning, and care; and strengthening community supports. There were no conditions or performance measures attached to the new federal money: the federal government expected that each province would be held accountable by its citizens. Once again, Quebec opted out, claiming that the program infringed on its constitutional jurisdiction on social policy. Nonetheless, it insisted on its share of the ECD funding, which was paid to the provinces on a per capita basis.

At the end of Chrétien's mandate in 2003, Ottawa negotiated the Early Learning and Child Care Initiative (ELCCI) with the provinces and territories. This went some distance to fulfilling the 1993 promise of a national childcare program. The initiative, slated to cost nearly $1 billion, was designed to support provincial and territorial investment in early learning and childcare, especially for low-income families. A side agreement focused on children in First Nations communities. As prime minister, Paul Martin attempted to build on these childcare provisions initiated by Chrétien and signed separate agreements with all 10 provinces for more childcare spaces, but the national daycare program was replaced in 2006 by the Conservatives, who made a $1,200 cash payment to parents of children under six for help with childcare costs.

---

7 Department of Finance, *Working Together Towards a Child Benefit System* (Ottawa: Government of Canada, 1997), 1–2.

THE RISING COST OF HEALTH

Another priority was health care. It accounted for nearly 40 per cent of all provincial spending, making it the largest and fastest-growing segment of provincial expenditures. Total health expenditure as a percentage of provincial GDP ranged from 6.9 per cent in Alberta to 15.3 per cent in Prince Edward Island. Between 1975 and 2008, the total cost for health care had risen from 7.5 per cent ($12 billion) to 11 per cent ($172 billon) of Canada's GDP, but Ottawa's share had declined significantly as it dealt with its budgetary deficits. Total health care spending as a percentage of GDP fell each year between 1993 and 1997, to reach 8.9 per cent in 1997 even as costs soared and waiting lists for various medical procedures (such as hip replacement and cataract surgery) grew.

The crisis in health care prompted a heated debate that often pivoted on the issue of whether or not health care was a public good that should only be delivered through a publicly administered system or through private clinics, or a combination of both. All major political parties supported federal spending on health and a system governed by national principles, including public administration, comprehensiveness, universality, portability, and accessibility. They insisted, too, that medicare embodied the Canadian values of equity and solidarity.

In 1999, the federal government allocated $11.5 billion in new funding over the coming five years to deal with the growing crisis in health care. The 2000 budget added another $2.5 billion, and at a first ministers' conference on health later that same year, Ottawa announced two new health funds, one of $1 billion for equipment and another of $800 million for a health transition fund to test and evaluate innovative ways to deliver health care services. Ottawa only asked that the provinces report publicly on how the money was spent. In February 2003, the provincial and the federal governments reached a new health accord. The agreement separated the CHST into a Canada Health Transfer and a Canada Social Transfer, with Ottawa committing $34.8 billion more in new funding over the period 2003–04 to 2007–08. An additional $2 billion in funding followed in 2004, aimed at primary health care, home care—particularly for the mentally ill and end-of-life care—and catastrophic drug care, but it was still not enough. A year later, Ottawa negotiated a new 10-year plan with the provinces that saw it commit an additional $18 billion to the provinces and territories by 2010, with a promise to increase federal transfers by 6 per cent annually until 2015, bringing the total federal commitment to health to nearly $80 billion. Once again, separate deals were negotiated with Quebec. By 2014, spending on health care was $6,045 per capita (11 per cent of GDP), up from $599 or 7 per cent of GDP in 1976.

NEW WAYS OF FUNDING EDUCATION

The third area of federal reinvestment was in post-secondary education, and once again, Ottawa moved away from the federal–provincial transfers that had long been the norm. In the 2000 budget, Ottawa created the $900 million Canada Research Chairs program to fund salaries and research costs of university chairs across Canada. This was part of the government's commitment to innovation, which it believed was a necessary condition for economic prosperity. From 2006 to 2016, however, women filled only 31 per cent of the available Canada Research Chair positions.

Ottawa also funded post-secondary education through the creation of foundations, which transferred more than $10 billion to nine foundations after 1996. The Canada Foundation for Innovation (CFI), designed to make strategic infrastructure investments in science, engineering, health, and the environment, was one of the most important. The Canada Millennium Scholarship Foundation (CMSF) provided funds for students with financial need through the provincial student aid programs. The foundations, although creations of the federal government, operated at arm's length. Nevertheless, they were very much tied to the government's "competitiveness" agenda that placed an important role on research and education, especially in those sectors composing the new economy. These initiatives also demonstrated the government's belief that Canada's universities would promote innovation and increase productivity and economic development.

UNITY AND A SECOND REFERENDUM

Canada faced its greatest unity crisis in the 1990s, when many feared that it then had a leader with neither the vision nor the political smarts to handle the problem. Although Jean Chrétien claimed that national unity had been his primary goal during a lifetime in politics, he had presided over ministries in Ottawa that had exacerbated the unity crisis. He was minister of Indian affairs when Indigenous peoples rose up in anger against the White Paper in 1969, justice minister during the patriation process in 1982 that alienated Quebec, and minister of energy when the National Energy Policy spawned a generation of Western alienation. Two years after he became prime minister, vowing never to open the constitution to please Quebec, he nearly lost the country.

When the Meech Lake Accord failed in 1990, it signalled the inevitability of a second referendum on Quebec independence. After the *Parti Québécois* was elected in 1994, it promised a vote within a year. Jacques Parizeau, the new premier, aristocratic and distant, was never suited for the lead in such a dramatic event—that fell to Lucien Bouchard, who emerged as one of the most charismatic politicians in Canadian history in the months before the October 30, 1995, referendum. Passionate, brilliant, and determined, he had a brush with death just before Christmas 1994. Doctors amputated his leg to try and save him from the flesh-eating disease *necrotizing fasciitis*. The national media carried stories that he had died and that a state funeral was planned. During his ordeal he had scribbled "*Que l'on continue, merci*," on a scrap of paper, which many in Quebec interpreted as a political message that the battle for independence had to continue even if he died. He survived, his popularity soared, and Parizeau yielded centre stage to him. Bouchard brought Mario Dumont, the young, dynamic leader of the fledgling *Action démocratique du Québec*, into the sovereigntist camp and promised there would be no outright declaration of sovereignty but an attempted partnership with Canada if they won the referendum. The "Yes" side finally had momentum, while the "No" campaign faltered badly. With less than two weeks to go to referendum, the "Yes" side pulled ahead.

Federalists denounced the referendum question as misleading, largely because it made no reference to Quebec's independence. Chrétien was largely kept out of the campaign because of the antipathy toward him in Quebec, though he was confident that Quebeckers would vote as they had in 1980. Federalists warned of the immense costs of separation and constantly reminded Quebeckers that a "Yes" vote really meant Quebec's separation from Canada. Many of Quebec's business leaders, mostly federalists, were worried as support grew for the *oui* side in the final days of the campaign. They blamed federalist politicians for mishandling the situation. English-speaking Canadians, too, were shocked that their country might be plunged into chaos.

Many blamed Chrétien, questioning his abilities and judgment—not just ordinary citizens, but some in his cabinet as well. With little more than a week before the referendum and the polls indicating a "Yes" victory, some of his senior ministers realized that they had no idea what Chrétien might do in the event of a sovereigntist victory. Did he have the moral authority to remain as prime minister if Quebec voted "Yes"? Moreover, Chrétien was in New York from October 22 to 24 to participate in the United Nations' 50th anniversary celebrations and had left no instructions on how to prepare for the possible breakup of the country. Still, several fighter jets stationed at CFB Bagotville, in Quebec, were moved to US bases in Virginia and South America, and the army had made plans to secure major defence installations in Quebec and at key federal institutions like the Radio-Canada building in Montreal if Quebec voted for sovereignty.

On October 25—five days before the vote—a shaken and worried Chrétien addressed the nation for the first time, a clear indication of the gravity of the crisis. He asked Quebeckers if their lives and their families' lives would be better with Canada in tatters. He promised to recognize Quebec as a distinct society, move toward greater decentralization, and grant it a constitutional veto on matters that affected the powers of the provincial government if separation were rejected. Bouchard was given

Figure 12.2 A huge Canadian flag is passed along a crowd that gathered in Montreal on October 27, 1995, in support of Canadian unity during Quebec's second referendum on sovereignty and independence.

equal airtime, and he held up a 1981 newspaper showing Chrétien and former Prime Minister Pierre Trudeau smiling for the cameras after they patriated the Canadian constitution without the support of Premier René Lévesque. Bouchard's message was powerful: Chrétien was no friend of Quebec. He could not be trusted.

Brian Tobin, the federal minister of fisheries, organized for Friday, October 27—a mere three days before the vote—a rally dubbed "The Crusade for Canada" at Montreal's Place du Canada to allow Canadians to express their love for Quebec. More than a 100,000 Canadians converged on Montreal, aided by huge discounts offered by the major airlines and Via Rail, even if doing so violated Quebec electoral laws, which set strict limits on campaign spending.

Canadians sat on the edge of their seats as the referendum votes were counted. The "Yes" side led for much of the evening, though at one point the two sides were separated by a mere 29 votes. More than 93 per cent of eligible voters casted a ballot: 50.58 per cent voted against sovereignty, a mere 54,288-vote majority, less than the capacity crowd for a CFL game at Montreal's Olympic Stadium. Indigenous peoples in Northern Quebec refused to participate in the PQ referendum and held their own vote, rejecting sovereignty by 96.3 per cent. It was the second defeat for the sovereigntist movement in 15 years; six out of ten Francophones had voted for independence, and in Parizeau's mind the dream had been denied by "money and the ethnic vote." Bouchard, who replaced him as premier, promised supporters another chance, but he and most sovereigntist leaders knew that it would not be anytime soon.

Support for sovereignty dropped after the vote to traditional levels of about 40 per cent. Many English Canadians had had enough of the secessionists, and they were in no mood for their national government to make further constitutional concessions to a province that seemed intent on destroying their country. Nonetheless, Chrétien hoped to restore Canada's credibility in Quebec and passed a symbolic resolution in the House of Commons to recognize Quebec as a distinct society. He also transferred to Quebec (and the other provinces) greater jurisdiction over manpower, training, and immigration, and promised to limit federal spending in social policy without provincial consent. The Quebec government was not interested in any of this and refused to participate in federal–provincial meetings. In 1999, Ottawa negotiated the Social Union Framework Agreement (SUFA) with all the provinces except Quebec. SUFA was a set of principles governing social policy, including Ottawa's agreement not to introduce new national programs in a variety of social programs including post-secondary education, health, and social assistance without provincial agreement; federal recognition of the provinces' role in defining national priorities and objectives; and provincial authority to design social programs. These measures, referred to as Plan A, were designed to give Quebec greater powers and to show that federalism was flexible, and Quebec welcomed the new arrangement.

The second strategy, Plan B, was to play hardball with the sovereigntists, and it took two forms. First, Chrétien launched an advertising campaign run largely out of his office to increase the federal presence in Quebec and to encourage a positive perception of Canada there. The program, which lasted from 1997 to 2003 and cost $250 million, provided financial support to nearly 2,000 sports and cultural events in exchange for using the Canada word-mark and displaying the Canadian flag and other promotional materials. Most of the funds passed through Liberal-friendly advertising agencies in Quebec and resulted in the Sponsorship Scandal, which contributed to the defeat of the Liberal government in 2006.[8]

Second, Ottawa decided to set rules for future referenda in Quebec. It first asked the Supreme Court in September 1996 to rule on the legality of a unilateral provincial declaration of independence. The Court ruled that Canada is based on a set of shared values, including federalism, democracy, constitutionalism and the rule of law, and respect for minorities, and no province has the constitutional right to secede unilaterally. However, Canada has an obligation to negotiate separation if a clear majority in any province voted in favour on a clear referendum question. Following the Court's ruling, Ottawa passed the *Clarity Act*, establishing rules under which the Government of Canada would

---

8 Office of the Auditor General of Canada, *2003 November Report of the Auditor General of Canada*, Chapter 3, "The Sponsorship Program," http://www.oag-bvg.gc.ca/internet/English/parl_oag_200311_03_e_12925.html.

negotiate secession. Any referendum had to be clear on independence and the result had to have the support of more than 50 per cent of voters plus one. Parliament would decide if a referendum question and its results met the conditions set out in the *Clarity Act*. While Chrétien often claimed the Act as his greatest achievement, it should be noted that states rarely follow constitutional protocol when they break apart. Ottawa has not said how it would respond if Quebec unilaterally declared independence after Parliament declared a vote on a question unclear, or if the referendum passed with a majority of one.

STRUGGLES OF INDIGENOUS PEOPLES

Secessionists in Quebec were not the only Canadians disappointed that their priorities were not addressed during the Chrétien period. Indigenous peoples, too, struggled to resolve satisfactorily a series of lingering issues. Chrétien rejected constitutional negotiations on self-government, promising instead to negotiate "practical and work-able" self-government agreements that would adhere to four foundational principles. These were the right of Indigenous peoples to negotiate agreements affecting their communities in such areas as health care, education, child welfare, housing, and economic development; the recognition of differences within Indigenous communities across Canada; the sharing of the costs of self-government among federal, provincial, territorial, and First Nations governments; and the responsibility of Indigenous peoples to initiate negotiations on self-government.

The federal government regarded comprehensive claims settlements and the land claims process as important parts of the self-government agenda, but First Nations were frustrated about the slow pace of negotiations. More than a thousand outstanding claims had been registered with Indian and Northern Affairs Canada, only a fraction of which had been settled. One of the most important was the Nisga'a Treaty negotiated between Ottawa, British Columbia, and the Nisga'a in 2000, authorizing the Nisga'a government to make laws in many areas, giving it authority over its own administration, citizenship, language, and culture, and managing its lands and assets. The treaty imposed limits, requiring that all laws be consistent with the Canadian constitution. Ottawa transferred to the Nisga'a $487 million for lost revenue from the forestry sector and promised $462 million for a variety of social services and economic development over the first five years of the treaty, with additional supports to be negotiated later.

There was great hope around the appointment in 1991 of the Royal Commission on Aboriginal Peoples (RCAP) to investigate Indigenous–state relations in Canada, but much disappointment in the government's response to the five-volume report released in 1996. The report called for major changes to the relationship between Indigenous peoples, non-Indigenous people, and governments in Canada. It contended that the economic marginalization and social problems facing Indigenous communities could only be reversed through a new relationship with the Canadian state, one that recognized Indigenous peoples as self-governing nations and one that replaced the colonial relationship with one premised on the principles of equality, mutual respect and consent, and strict adherence to historical treaties.

The federal government's response in *Gathering Strength: Canada's Aboriginal Action Plan* in 1997 was tepid, including its apology for decades of mistreatment and abuse suffered at the hands of the Canadian government in its "Statement of Reconciliation." Indigenous leaders considered the apology, delivered by Indian and Northern Affairs minister Jane Stewart in a conference room in Ottawa—and not by the prime minister in Parliament, as insincere, even if Stewart singled out particularly the physical and mental abuse of children at government-run residential schools. The government created a $350 million "healing fund" to address the legacy of the residential school system. Other initiatives included policies to strengthen First Nations governance, to build a new fiscal relationship with Indigenous governments that emphasized financial stability, self-reliance, and accountability, and to work to improve their social conditions and build strong Indigenous communities. These all held promise of a new relationship, ending the assimilative policies that had existed as late as the 1960s, but were short on specifics.

Phil Fontaine, grand chief of the Assembly of First Nations, described the apology and the government's response as an important first step in forging a new relationship, but few Indigenous groups shared his enthusiasm. To Inuit, Métis leaders, and Indigenous women, the apology was weak and the measures proposed insufficient to overcome the tremendous difficulties confronting them. Both national and international human rights organizations agreed. Two UN agencies, including its Human Rights Committee, criticized Canada for ignoring the urgency of Indigenous issues, a criticism particularly stinging for Chrétien, who routinely pointed out that the UN had consistently ranked Canada as among the best countries in the world to live. The Canadian Human Rights Commission also criticized government for its tardiness on responding to the pressing needs of First Nations communities.

Chrétien never seemed to understand the persistence of colonialism that angered many Indigenous leaders, even as violence between the state and Indigenous peoples continued. In 1995, a crisis occurred on land in and around Ontario's Ipperwash Provincial Park, which was claimed by the Kettle and Stony Point First Nations. During World War II the federal government had appropriated Stony Point Reserve under the *War Measures Act* for use as a military camp. The Stony Point First Nation had opposed the action, but the federal government relocated them to the nearby Kettle Point Reserve. When Stony Point members occupied the camp in 1993, Ottawa

promised to return the land, but in 1995, with the military still occupying it, the protesters returned. Tension between the protesters and the heavily armed Ontario Provincial Police (OPP), which had been dispatched to keep the peace, increased, resulting in an armed confrontation with protesters

Figure 12.3 Two protesters stand by a barricade near the entrance to Ipperwash Provincial Park, near Ipperwash Beach, Ont., on September 7, 1995.

on September 6, 1995, after Premier Mike Harris reportedly said "I want the f—ing Indians out of the park."[9] Anthony O'Brien Dudley George, a Stony Point Ojibway, was killed in the mêlée; Acting Sergeant Ken Deane claimed that George had pointed a firearm at police officers, but he was convicted of criminal negligence causing death on April 28, 1997. A public inquiry later found that the OPP had failed to educate its officers on Indigenous rights and issues, and that the federal government had delayed too long in returning the land to the Stony Point First Nation. The episode was not settled until 2015, when the land was finally returned to the Stony Point First Nation; even then protests continued, as some members of Stony Point were angry that the Chippewa of Kettle Point Reserve shared in the compensation package that included $20 million for band members and $70 million for future development of the land.

---

9 "Exoneration of Mike Harris? Not in the Least," *Toronto Star*, June 1, 2007, http://www.thestar.com/opinion/2007/06/01/exoneration_of_mike_harris_not_in_the_least.html.

In Parliament in 2001, Chrétien expressed concern that Canada "may be spending too much time, too much energy, and too much money on the past, and not nearly enough on what is necessary to ensure a bright future for the children of today and tomorrow....Our approach will be to focus on the future."[10] He did not see the redress of historical grievances as part of the process of reconciliation and moving forward. The government ceased negotiating approximately 30 land claims and self-government negotiations that had stalled, claiming that the "Indigenous industry" of lawyers and consultants was more interested in the negotiations than reaching agreement. The problems often stemmed, however, from the government's insistence on dominating the process and extinguishing Indigenous rights in any negotiated settlement.

Chrétien's approach to Indigenous issues was reflected in the introduction of Bill C-7, the *First Nations Governance Act*, designed to strengthen governance in First Nations communities and Indian Bands. It established governance codes and procedures in matters of leadership selection, the administration of government, and financial accountability in an attempt to modernize First Nations' governance and foster economic independence and autonomous decision-making powers. The federal government hoped to reduce its involvement with First Nations' government. The legislation was introduced following consultation but not negotiations with Indigenous communities, which claimed that such a process reinforced paternalism in Indigenous–state relations rather than the equality that the Liberals had promised. The emphasis on governance ignored the longstanding and urgent social and economic issues in First Nations communities. When he became prime minister, Paul Martin scrapped the legislation amid allegations that it was just another attempt to change the *Indian Act* without the consent of First Nations.

While the social and economic conditions for Indigenous peoples improved only marginally, some progress was made on clarifying treaty rights in the courts. One of the most important came in December 1997, when the Supreme Court provided its first interpretation on Aboriginal title in *Delgamuukw v. British Columbia*. In *Calder v. The Attorney General of British Columbia* (1973), the Supreme Court had ruled that Aboriginal title had indeed existed in 1763 at the time of the Royal Proclamation, and that Indigenous peoples had legal right to use lands other than those provided for later by treaty or statute since 1867. In 1984, the Gitxsan and 13 Wet'suwet'en peoples of British Columbia took the province to court to secure title to 58,000 square kilometres in northern British Columbia. The Court

---

10 Quoted in Michael Murphy, "Looking Forward Without Looking Back: Jean Chretien's Legacy for Aboriginal-State Relations," in Lois Harder and Steve Patten (eds.), *The Chretien Legacy: Politics and Public Policy in Canada* (Montreal and Kingston: McGill-Queen's University Press, 2006), 169.

this is a comma

did not rule on the merits of the Gitxsan and Wet'suwet'en title claim and ordered a new trial in 1996, but Chief Justice Lamer clarified that Aboriginal title bestows a property right and is much more extensive than the right to traditional usage of the land for hunting, fishing, or gathering. The Court—which accepted oral history as evidence for the first time in any proceeding—recognized Aboriginal title as a communal right (not an individual right) and ruled that the lands could be sold only to the government. The Court also said in the Tsilhqot'in decision in 2014 that Aboriginal title is not absolute and there can be "infringement" if there is "a compelling and substantial public purpose." The Court recommended against further litigation and urged the parties to negotiate a solution to the thorny land claims issue and the extent of Aboriginal title. Going forward, the tricky part will be to balance Aboriginal title with Crown sovereignty.

A great opportunity had been missed in British Columbia to resolve a number of outstanding issues with Indigenous peoples. In 2009, Premier Gordon Campbell surprised many when he proclaimed a new relationship with the province's First Nations. He changed the provincial Department of Aboriginal Affairs to the Ministry of Aboriginal Relations and Reconciliation and promised to recognize immediately Aboriginal title to the land. Although his promise was vague, he had made it after negotiating with Indigenous leaders, who later rejected his offer of reconciliation as not going far enough after taking it to their communities for discussion.

THE PECULIAR WAYS OF FOREIGN POLICY

Foreign aid, the military, and the nation's diplomatic corps—many of the items usually associated with foreign policy—were all victims of government cuts in the 1990s. Foreign policy was never an important issue for the Chrétien government, and when the prime minister turned his attention to such matters, he was driven primarily by domestic political considerations. Still, during this period, Canada broke with two traditions in foreign policy. First, it took military action against one of its North Atlantic Treaty Organization (NATO) allies; and second, it refused to participate with its two major allies, the United States and Britain, in military action against Iraq. Many Canadians cheered both developments.

One trend was undisputable, however: Canada was becoming more inextricably tied to the North American economy. Although Chrétien had vowed during the 1993 campaign to cancel the North American Free Trade Agreement (NAFTA) between Canada, the US, and Mexico that had been negotiated by the outgoing Conservative government, he did not. That agreement, and the earlier Canada-US pact, transformed Canada's economy from an east–west axis to a north–south one. All provinces, with the exception of Manitoba, traded more with the United States than with the rest of Canada by 2000.[11] More than 80 per cent of Canada's exports went to the United States, and Canadians seemed quite comfortable with this, as opinion polls showed that 70 per cent of Canadians supported NAFTA by 2003. Canada needed access to the North American market, but as a skilled politician, Chrétien knew that anti-Americanism played well in domestic politics. He rejected the close personal relationship that Mulroney had with Presidents Ronald Reagan and George H. Bush and was determined to distance Canada from this type of relationship. By the time Chrétien became prime minister in 1993, Canadians did not seem overly concerned about the United States, although they wanted some indication that their country had not become a weakling among the nations of the world. Canadians briefly found their cause when environmentalism, economics, and foreign policy converged and Canada fired at a NATO ally.

Canada experienced an environmental and economic catastrophe in the early 1990s when fish stocks off the east coast declined dramatically and the federal government imposed a ban, or moratorium, on catching ground fish on the east coast in 1993. The closure displaced 36,000 workers, the vast majority in Newfoundland and Labrador, and created havoc in one of Canada's most economically challenged regions. The resource was so overfished that nothing short of a miracle could save the industry.

In March 1995, after a tough federal budget, a federal report acknowledging the rapid depletion of west coast salmon stocks and the collapse of much of the east coast fishery, an impending showdown with sovereigntist forces in Quebec, and amid a growing environmental lobby, the Chrétien government considered it an opportune time to take action on foreign overfishing on the famed Grand Banks and assert Canada's strength on the international stage. The object of Canada's concern was the turbot, a slimy, spineless flatfish that straddled Canada's 200-mile (320-kilometre) exclusive economic zone. Canada claimed that Spanish and other European trawlers were catching the turbot without any consideration for sustainability, and if not stopped, the turbot would become extinct. After repeated attempts to have European Union fishing vessels adhere to Canada's catch limit for turbot, on March 9, 1995, Chrétien put Canada on a war footing and authorized the deployment of submarines and patrol ships to enforce Canada's ban on foreign overfishing against Spain and Portugal, its NATO allies. Canada subsequently chased down the *Estai*, a Spanish fishing vessel, for illegal fishing. When it refused to stop, one of Canada's patrol vessels fired a volley of shots across its bow, warning that the next ones would be into the

---

11 Tom Courchene, *The Changing Nature of Canada-Quebec Relations: From the 1980 Referendum to the Summit of the Canadas* (Montreal: Institute for Research on Public Policy, 2004), 15.

ship. Canadian sailors clambered over the sides of the *Estai* in international waters and arrested its captain for overfishing. Spain dispatched two naval patrol vessels to the Grand Banks, each armed with 76-mm guns and two machine guns. Chrétien ordered the deployment of a Canadian frigate and a destroyer to support the six armed fisheries patrol vessels and a submarine already in the area.[12] A compromise was reached a few days later, but more than 90 per cent of Canadians supported the government's action. Canadians are flag-waving patriots, too, who want the national interest defended.

When the Government of Canada completed its foreign policy review in 1995, it said foreign policy would be based on three related aims, or pillars. These were the protection of Canada's security within a stable global framework, the promotion of prosperity and employment, and the promotion of the values and culture that Canadians cherish—although those values were absent during the Turbot War. Despite its insistence on multilateralism, the rule of law, and the promotion of Canadian values, Canada's response to the overfishing of turbot in the international waters outside Canada's exclusive economic zone had nothing to do with what Canadians like to think of as their "values" and everything to do with the desire to enhance their prosperity.[13]

9/11: A NEW IMPERATIVE IN FOREIGN AFFAIRS AND DOMESTIC SECURITY

The terrorist attacks on the World Trade Center in New York and the Pentagon in Washington, DC, on September 11, 2001, killing 3,000, including 26 Canadians, made "Al-Qaeda," "war on terror," and "security" household words across Canada. Suddenly, Canadians felt vulnerable. Chrétien reorganized his cabinet, creating the Cabinet Committee on Public Security and Anti-terrorism (a counterpart to the US Homeland Security Office), responsible for protecting Canada. Given the volume of goods that crossed the Canada–US border daily, by September 2002 Canada and the United States had put in place a series of electronic programs dubbed the Smart Border Declaration to facilitate the movement of traffic and frequent travellers across the border. More than $8 billion were spent to enhance security by 2006.

Canada also enacted new and controversial legislation in its *Anti-Terrorism Act*. The legislation defined a terrorist act as one committed "for a political, religious

---

12 *Toronto Globe and Mail*, March 29, 1995.

13 See Denis Smith, "Myths, Morals, and Reality in Canadian Foreign Policy," *International Journal* 58, no. 2 (Spring 2003).

or ideological purpose, objective or cause," and gave security forces new powers to monitor, investigate, prosecute, and prevent terrorist activities both within Canada and abroad. Even as the legislation was being debated in Parliament, concerns were raised that it trampled civil liberties, as it gave police sweeping new powers, including the authority to arrest people and hold them without charge for up to 72 hours if suspected of terrorist acts. The legislation passed quickly and without amendment.

The 9/11 attack led to the American–British decision to invade Iraq in March 2003. By mid-2008, the war, widely accepted by then as misguided, had resulted in the deaths of more than 4,000 US and British soldiers and more than 40,000 civilians. Chrétien had refused to participate, insisting that Canada was committed to multi-lateralism in foreign policy. It was not Canada's role to bring about regime change in Iraq, nor anywhere around the world. Canada would not participate without a UN resolution sanctioning military action, even though it had dispatched troops to US-led missions in Kosovo and Afghanistan. Chretien's critics, who had earlier heaped scorn on him for not following through on his pledge to renegotiate NAFTA, now hailed him as a great Canadian nationalist for not participating in the "coalition of the willing," as those nations that supported the Iraq War were called. Ironically, Chrétien had been ready to join with US President Bill Clinton in 1998 to strike Iraq militarily without a UN mandate to enforce Security Council Resolution 6878, which required Iraq to destroy all chemical, nuclear, and biological weapons, as well as all ballistic missiles with a range greater than 150 kilometres. Consistency was not a strong point in Canada's foreign policy, but the prime minister gauged public opinion accurately. Seventy-one per cent supported his decision to stay out of Iraq.

Canada never had a clear sense of its role in the world when Chrétien was prime minister. Under Foreign Minister Lloyd Axworthy, Canada was at the forefront of a successful campaign for a human security agenda that included a landmine treaty, an international criminal court, and a campaign against child soldiers. These objectives reflected what Chrétien called Canadian values, but he used foreign policy—as other prime ministers had—to drum up business for domestic enterprises through "Team Canada" missions around the world. Such trade promotion created a measure of cynicism. Noting the decline of Canada's influence in the world, *Time* magazine asked in May 2003, "Would anyone notice if Canada disappeared?" Andrew Cohen's 2003 bestseller *While Canada Slept: How We Lost Our Place in the World* also captured the public's sentiment about foreign policy, and historian Norman Hillmer termed Canada the Walter Mitty of foreign policy: Canada dreams of much more than it can deliver but it followed "its interests directly, ruthlessly, relentlessly."[14] Michael Ignatieff,

14 Norman Hillmer, "The Secret Life of Canadian Foreign Policy," *Policy Options* (February 2005): 32.

a noted Canadian scholar and later leader of the Liberal Party, said Canada was living off a Pearsonian reputation that it no longer deserved.[15]

Canada participated in the NATO-led mission in Afghanistan, although Chrétien had great difficulty explaining why. While the Taliban, a fundamentalist Islamic organization, had long attracted international condemnation for its repressive human rights record, particularly its oppressive treatment of women, it was the Taliban's support for Al-Qaeda militants led by Osama bin Laden, who had master-minded the 9/11 attacks, that had precipitated the US attack on the Taliban government in October 2001. Canada supported the American-led invasion, secretly sending Joint Task Force Two (JTF2) elite troops in late 2001, followed by a formal deployment of troops with other NATO forces in February 2002 and a third in 2003. Intervening in Afghanistan allowed Canada to participate in the American War on Terror without committing to Iraq. When the Taliban troops retreated in 2005 to the mountains in southern Afghanistan and deployed improvised explosive devices (IEDs), better known as roadside bombs, Canadian troops and other coalition forces faced considerable resistance. Afghanistan became a quagmire, and some contended that Canada's involvement ran counter to its traditional peacekeeping tradition and it had no business being there in an offensive role.

SOCIAL AND CULTURAL CANADA

Debates over foreign policy, the government's fiscal woes, and a host of other issues after 1993 were essentially debates about trying to define the type of community Canada should be. A variety of social issues such as gun control, the right to abortion, same-sex marriages, new trade agreements, public spending for health care, and immigration policy all animated the public agenda at different times. Whatever the issue, the political right argued for greater individual responsibility and a less intrusive state, and the political left and small-l liberals maintained Canada was a caring and sharing society that demanded an activist state willing to invest to achieve a greater measure of equality among Canadians.

Some observers believed the Canadian state was in perpetual crisis, divided by a collection of rival rights groups (gays versus straights, Indigenous peoples versus non-Indigenous, French speakers versus English speakers, immigrants versus native-born, rural versus urban). This trend was accentuated by the rejection of traditions and national history and the failure of the state to defend historical institutions and values necessary to provide stability and create a national community. The focus on

---

15 Michael Ignatieff, "Canada in an Age of Terror—Multilateralism Meets a Moment of Truth," *Policy Options* 24, no. 2 (2003): 14–19.

rights, some argued, led to a clear imbalance between rights and responsibilities with a resultant "civic deficit," whereby particular groups sought to defend their individual interests without much concern for democratic values, civic responsibility, and the general responsibilities of citizenship. The right's revolution had failed to eliminate the social and political fragmentation and construct within Canada a strong national community and a stronger sense of belonging. Canadian citizenship had become contested terrain.[16] The national traits of deference and respect for authority and a sense of collective security were replaced by a belief in individualism and a culture of self-interest. This new national philosophy was manifested in various ways, including the decriminalization of the possession of small amounts of marijuana and the legalization of same-sex marriages.[17]

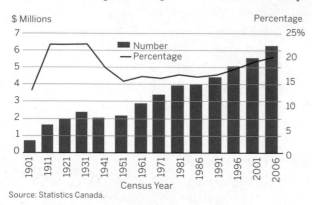

Source: Statistics Canada.

Figure 12.4 Immigration in Canada: a portrait of the foreign-born population, 1901 to 2006.

Canada was changing in other ways too, as the 2006 Census revealed. More than 90 per cent of the 31.6 million Canadians lived in large metropolitan areas, compared to less than 20 per cent at the time of Confederation. Ontario and Quebec had the largest share of the population, but Alberta had the greatest growth—10.6 per cent since the 2001 Census, compared with a 5.4 per cent increase for the country as a whole. Newfoundland and Labrador and Saskatchewan registered the largest declines. Toronto, Vancouver, and Montreal remained the largest cities and together with Ottawa-Gatineau, Calgary, and Edmonton accounted for 68 per cent of all Canadians.

The face of Canada had changed too. Those with Indigenous identity surpassed the 1 million mark, or 3.8 per cent of the population, a 44.9 per cent increase, making Indigenous peoples the fastest-growing group in Canada. Visible minorities numbered 5 million, or 16.2 per cent of the population, compared with 11.2 per cent in 1996. More than 200 ethnic groups were identified in the Census, and more than 41 per cent reported more than one ethnic origin; South Asians surpassed Chinese as the largest visible minority, and the vast majority of visible minorities lived in large metropolitan

---

16 Andrew Nurse, "'A Necessary Precondition': Michael Ignatieff and the Dilemmas of 'Civic Nationalism'," in Andrew Nurse and Raymond Blake (eds.), *Beyond National Dreams: Essays on Canadian Citizenship and Nationalism* (Toronto: Fitzhenry & Whiteside, 2009), 31.

17 This idea comes from Andrew Nurse, Director of the Centre for Canada Studies at Mount Allison University in Sackville, New Brunswick.

areas. Canada continued to have one of the most liberal immigration policies in the world, and in 1993, it became the first country formally to recognize people facing gender persecution as refugees. Even so, the Chrétien government prioritized self-sufficient immigrants and those with investment dollars.

Canada's policy of multiculturalism also came under scrutiny. First introduced in 1971, official multiculturalism not only recognized the reality of pluralism in Canada but also made it clear that long-held policies of assimilation would cease. For nearly two decades, multiculturalism held a place of pride in Canada, a reality strengthened in the equality provisions in the Charter of Rights and Freedoms. After September 11, 2001, there was considerable discussion, however, about how far Canada should go to accommodate its immigrant communities and newcomers. This discussion gave rise to questions of "reasonable accommodation." Polling data suggested that more than 53 per cent of Canadians believed immigrants should fully adapt to Canadian culture.[18]

The matter reached a crisis in the 2007 Quebec election. Premier Jean Charest appointed Gérard Bouchard and Charles Taylor, two well-respected university professors, to chair the Consultation Commission on Accommodation Practices Related to Cultural Differences to investigate the cultural and social accommodation of religious and ethnic minorities in the province. They acknowledged that Quebec was no longer a uniquely French-Canadian society but an increasingly pluralistic one that embodied the concept of interculturalism (rather than multiculturalism). The government had to recognize and promote a secular society in Quebec. As a first step, they recommended that the Quebec legislature remove the crucifix from the *Assemblée nationale du Québec* to show the government's secular nature and function, but the legislature voted unanimously to keep the crucifix. This issue of reasonable accommodation is not limited to Quebec, and it is certain—as it has been since before Confederation—that the debate about Canadian identity, citizenship, and nationalism will continue.

FROM CHEERS TO DITHERS

Although he won three consecutive majority governments, by 2003, Chrétien was dogged by persistent rumours of scandal and financial mismanagement in his government. An internal audit of the Department of Human Resources Development found that the Liberal government had failed to account for employment program grants worth more than $1 billion, creating what the media called "the billion-dollar boondoggle." The RCMP launched more than a dozen investigations for misuse of public

18 Institute for Research of Public Policy. News Release, "Canadians Overwhelmingly Support Limits to Accommodation," September 25, 2007. http://www.irpp.org/newsroom/archive/2007/092507e.pdf.

funds. The most noteworthy was the Sponsorship Scandal, which Auditor General Sheila Fraser said "broke just about every rule in the book."[19]

On December 12, 2003, Paul Martin succeeded Jean Chrétien as prime minister. On his first day, Martin cancelled the sponsorship program and fired several of Chrétien's high-profile former ministers who had been given lucrative patronage appointments. Martin also appointed Mr. Justice John Gomery to head a Commission of Inquiry to investigate the program. Even though Gomery later exonerated him from any wrongdoing, many Canadians felt that Martin, as minister of finance and a senior Quebec minister, had to know what was going on in the government—and if he did not, he should have. The Gomery Commission sealed Martin's fate.

It was not the popularity of the Conservatives but the unpopularity of the Martin government that led to the Liberal defeat. Although the right-wing populist Reform Party had formed the Official Opposition in 1997, its prospects appeared dim, even after Stephen Harper became leader and united the Conservatives within a single party in 2004. The *Bloc Québécois* continued to hold half the seats in Quebec. Martin managed to hang on to a minority in the 2004 election by scaring many voters into believing that a government under Harper threatened the things that Canadians valued, such as medicare, individual freedoms and liberties, and social justice. Throughout 2005, however, the Gomery Commission heard allegations of criminal corruption in the Liberal Party, and the Commission's report, released on November 1, found a "culture of entitlement" within the government. Martin lost a confidence vote in the House, and the January 2006 election that followed became a referendum on the Liberal government. The Conservatives under Stephen Harper ran a flawless campaign with a tightly controlled message and Martin's fear mongering failed to work a second time. The Conservatives won a minority government with 37 per cent of the popular vote.

A DECADE-LONG CONSERVATIVE INTERLUDE

Harper was an unlikely prime minister. He had become involved in politics first with the Liberals and then with the Progressive Conservatives, whom he left to become a founding member of the Reform Party. He ran successfully for the leadership of the Canadian Alliance and then created a new Conservative Party by merging Reform with the remnants of the venerable Progressive Conservative Party. He presented a moderate set of proposals as party leader and, despite his lack of charisma and charm, began to appear prime ministerial. In October 2008, he won a second minority before winning a majority in 2011 with 40 per cent of votes cast.

---

19 Quoted in "Something Rotten," *Time Magazine*, February 23, 2004.

The Liberals' warnings about social conservatism under Harper were not borne out. He allowed a free-vote to repeal same-sex marriages in Parliament, but it was defeated, as he knew it would be. He prevented his backbenchers from putting any limits on abortion rights and renewed Canada's commitment to a continued military presence in Afghanistan, promising as well to improve the capacity of Canada's military. He extended Canada's mission in Afghanistan, but when Canadians began to wonder if it was a wise policy, he ended it in 2011. The war cost $18 billion, and more than 40,000 Canadians served, of whom 1,800 were injured and 158 killed. Canadians took pride in a more active military, but they were not always sure what they wanted their armed forces to do. However, they did support the deployment of Canada's warplanes joining a US-led coalition in Iraq and Syria in 2014 to degrade and destroy the extremist black-clad *jihadists* in the Islamic State. Another of the government's defence priorities was protecting Arctic sovereignty. Throughout his mandates, Harper was criticized for promoting a greater remembrance of Canada's military history and its embrace of the military mission in Afghanistan. Canada's commemoration of the bicentennial of the War of 1812 was particularly galling for many academics, as Harper insisted—as Laurier had in 1908 with the 300th anniversary celebration of Champlain's founding of Quebec City—that the event marked the founding of Canada.

Despite Harper's ideological commitment to smaller and less intrusive government, public spending increased in each of the Conservative budgets from 12.6 per cent of GDP in 2005–06 to 13 per cent in 2014–15. When the international financial crisis hit Canada in 2008, Harper, after some hesitation, announced a $29 billion economic stimulus package, or deficit spending, which many thought inconceivable under the Conservatives. General Motors and Chrysler received a $9-billion bailout in 2009, and the government directed more than $1 billion to regional development during the period. The government also created a new agency to subsidize development in southern Ontario and invested $51 billion in infrastructure in the New Building Canada Plan, policies oddly reminiscent of 1970s-style industrial policy and what was then called corporate welfare. While the government insisted that it would not allow a return to "structural deficits"—the term used to describe borrowing over the long-term to fund expenditures—Harper was never able to deliver on that promise. However, he kept interest charges on the debt to less than the 9 per cent of government revenues it had been when he became prime minister.

The Harper government was also aggressive in its tax policy for Canadian families, which significantly reduced the revenue coming to the federal government as more earned income remained with workers. The Parliamentary Budget Office concluded that all tax reforms, including the Child Tax Credit and Working Income Tax Benefit, among others, from 2006 to 2013 have been progressive overall, as they most greatly impacted low- and middle-income earners. Those earning between $12,200 and $23,000 saw an increase of 4 per cent in after-tax incomes, while the highest 10 per cent of earners pocketed tax savings of 1.4 per cent more income during Harper's years in office. Income splitting for families, which allowed couples to transfer up to $50,000 from the higher-income earner to the lower-earning spouse, cost Ottawa $7.2 billion in lost revenue, but 69 per cent of those dollars went to families with combined incomes of less than $120,000. The median family income for Canadians rose 14 per cent, from $45,800 to $53,500, during the Harper years, and Statistics Canada reported that the top 1 per cent's share of income peaked at 12.1 per cent in 2006 and had declined to 10.3 per cent in 2012. The government also invested heavily in infrastructure spending, health and Indigenous programs, and it became a champion of maternal health around the globe, even if it refused to fund abortions as part of that agenda.

By 2016, women had made remarkable gains from just two decades earlier. The gender gap had been reversed for middle-class women, especially those in post-secondary education and in many professions. More than 60 per cent of Canadian undergraduates are now women, when 20 years ago they were underrepresented in post-secondary institutions of all types. Challenges continue in engineering, mathematics, and computer science, which remain dominated by male students, but other areas have seen spectacular change. For the past decade women have held 80 per cent of spots in veterinary schools and 56 per cent of the seats in medical schools. More than half of the all law graduates are female, and slightly more than 50 per cent of auditors, accountants, and investment professionals in Canada are women. Even so, the Conference Board of Canada notes that "men still dominate many of the fields with superior employment and income prospects for graduates." Women are changing the dynamic of the workplace. Violence toward women remains a major problem in Canadian society, however, and no more so than on university campuses, where attempts to eliminate a "rape culture" remains a pressing concern.[20] Because of the persistence of violence against women, especially among Indigenous women and girls, and the nearly 14 per cent of women who live in poverty, some commentators maintain that gender equality in Canada has stalled. The World Economic Forum's Global Gender Gap Index ranked Canada first in international measures of gender equality in 1994, but by 2014 it had fallen to nineteenth place.

Harper practised a more open and flexible federalism than his predecessors, believing that greater autonomy had to be given to the provinces and that they should not all be treated the same. Harper believed a more decentralized federation was necessary, not only to avoid the continual bickering with the provinces, but as a way to deal with

---

20 *Toronto Globe and Mail*, October 22, 2016.

cleavages within the country. He dispensed with formal first ministers' conferences and opted instead for bilateral meetings with premiers. Federal transfers to provinces went from $40 to $60 billion under Harper, but there were some notable disputes, particularly with Danny Williams of Newfoundland and Labrador and Kathleen Wynne of Ontario.

Although the Conservatives had embraced multiculturalism and Canada's immigrant communities throughout their mandate, and had promoted a shared sense of Canadian values, by the time of the 2015 federal election it was difficult for many Canadians to recall the early years of Harper's government. Through a motion in the House of Commons, he acknowledged that "the Québécois form a nation within a united Canada," even though he had earlier denounced the appeasement of ethnic nationalists. He apologized to several groups in Canada, including Indigenous peoples and Ukrainians, for past injustices inflicted by the Canadian government. For his apology to First Nations and Indigenous peoples in 2008, he invited Indigenous leaders and residential school survivors to the floor of the House of Commons, telling them: "Today, we recognize that this policy of assimilation was wrong, has caused great harm and has no place in our country. The government of Canada sincerely apologizes and asks the forgiveness of the Aboriginal Peoples of this country for failing them so profoundly. We are sorry."[21]

On the important matter of Indigenous education, little progress had been made, although in 2014, Harper and Shawn Atleo, then grand chief of the Assembly of First Nations, had negotiated the *First Nations Control of First Nations Education Act* that would have provided $1.9 billion in new funding to increase graduation levels on reserves. The proposed legislation agreed to respect First Nations treaty rights and jurisdiction and recognized languages and culture as central to Indigenous education, but many chiefs and First Nations communities, who had terrible memories of residential schools, refused to accept federal involvement in their educational outcomes. They opposed the deal that insisted on minimum education standards consistent with provincial standards, minimum attendance requirements, and proper certification for teachers. Atleo was forced to resign when the deal collapsed. That the two sides failed to reach a deal was a terrible setback for the 330,000 First Nations peoples living on 617 reserves across Canada. Many of the First Nations reserves face considerable challenges associated with limited populations and isolation and need better educational outcomes.

Earlier, in 2007, Harper implemented the Indian Residential School Settlement Agreement that provided a Common Experience Payment (CEP) to all surviving former students of federally administered residential schools and an Independent Assessment

---

21 "A Long-Awaited Apology," CBC News, June 11, 2008. http://www.cbc.ca/archives/
entry/a-long-awaited-apology-for-residential-schools.

Figure 12.5 Harper shakes hands with Indigenous leaders on June 11, 2008, the day he formally apologized on behalf of the Canadian government for the residential school system. He also appointed the Truth and Reconciliation Commission.

Process (IAP) to address compensation for physical and sexual abuse. It also provided funds for commemoration projects and a victim-centred Truth and Reconciliation Commission (TRC) chaired by Justice Murray Sinclair. These initiatives were implemented to address the longstanding and destructive legacy of the Indian residential school system, which includes lateral violence, suicide, poverty, alcoholism, lack of parenting skills, weakening or destruction of cultures and languages, and lack of capacity to build and sustain healthy families and communities. Equally important, the TRC was established with a mandate to inform all Canadians about what happened in residential schools and begin the process of reconciliation with Indigenous peoples to renew the relationship between the state and Indigenous peoples on the basis of mutual understanding and respect. Inter-societal relations needed to be managed better going forward.

A week before the TRC reported in 2015, Supreme Court Chief Justice Beverley McLachlin told a gathering that Canada had attempted to create "cultural genocide" against Indigenous peoples in its attempt to deal with what John A. Macdonald referred to as the "Indian problem." In its desire to "take the Indian out of the child," the federal government had outlawed Indigenous religious and social traditions and forced children into residential schools. "Indianness" was not to be tolerated in Canada, she lamented. Some 150,000 children—more than a third of all Indigenous children—were torn from their families and sent to church-run residential schools established by the federal government over seven generations since the late nineteenth century. Despite the years of colonization and a terrible legacy of dispossession of Indigenous lands and culture, however, First Nations and other Indigenous peoples have shown remarkable resilience and determination. Today, Canada's Indigenous peoples, at more than 1.5 million, account for nearly 5 per cent of the country's population and are projected to be the fastest growing demographic in the next three decades. In 1871, the Indigenous population was about 102,000. In 2016, after a long legal battle, the Supreme Court of Canada ruled that the Métis and non-status Indians are "Indians," according to the meaning of term in Canada's 1867 constitution. This decision gives the federal government a fiduciary relationship with nearly 700,000 people who now have the same rights as status Indians around land claims and enhanced social benefits, and the right to be consulted and negotiate on matters affecting them.

The TRC also saw state policy after Confederation as resulting in cultural genocide. It made 94 recommendations to right the wrongs of Canada's treatment of Indigenous peoples. It blamed political leaders for the government's approach to Indigenous policies, noting that "the beliefs and attitudes that were used to justify the establishment of residential schools are not things of the past: they continue to animate much of what passes for Aboriginal policy today." The hurtful legacy of residential schools continues to "disfigure" Canadian life, the Commission concluded, and it called for radical change, especially in greater Indigenous control over child welfare, education, language and culture, health, and justice. It recommended the adoption of the UN Declaration on the Rights of Indigenous Peoples, passed in 2007—which Canada has accepted as an "aspirational document," but not as a treaty enforceable in Canada's courts. The Canadian government was worried about certain aspects of the Declaration, including the right of Indigenous peoples to self-determination, a right not granted any of the provinces under the Canadian constitution. Yet, for the TRC, the UN Declaration provides an opportunity to reconcile the sovereignty of the Crown and the sovereignty of Indigenous peoples so that they are not simply another minority group in Canada but have original rights that must be respected. Liberal leader Justin Trudeau promised to implement all 94 recommendations, including the UN Declaration, if elected.

At the time, opinion polls showed Trudeau had little chance of becoming prime minister in the upcoming federal election campaign, mandated by Parliament for fall 2015. When the election was called in late August, it became one of the longest campaigns in Canadian history, and one where *niqabs* and barbaric cultural practices

Figure 12.6 The lifeless body of Alan Kurdi was found on a beach in Turkey, after the boat in which his family was trying to get to Greece capsized. It changed the tone of the 2015 federal election in Canada.

became a sideshow. Support for Stephen Harper and the Conservatives dropped considerably in the final days before the vote. The image of drowned Syrian toddler, Alan Kurdi, whose lifeless body washed up on the shores of the Mediterranean, and whose family was fleeing the civil war in Syria, appeared in the Canadian media and pushed the Syrian refugee crisis to the centre of the campaign. It also raised questions not only about Harper's commitment to the humanitarian crisis in Syria, which had been ravaged by civil war, but his approach to governing in general. Questions were raised about what had happened to the caring and passionate Canada Canadians had long known.

The Conservative government wanted an election about the economy in a troubled period. Instead, it became a referendum on Harper's style of government—his apparent secretiveness, his tendency to demonize opponents and divide Canadians with wedge issues, his identity politics and targeting of Muslims, his attack on parliamentary democracy, his battles with the Supreme Court, his determined stance on foreign policy issues—notably the refusal to engage on climate change and his underfunding of the military—and the kind of country Canadians wanted (though, like most prime ministers, he had generally compromised and governed with pragmatism). A decade earlier Harper had capitalized on Liberal fear-mongering to become prime minister, but in 2015 Conservative fear-mongering backfired, just as it had for the Liberals in 2006. Justin Trudeau, idealistic, wealthy, handsome, and charming, ran an effective campaign that convinced 39.5 per cent of voters that Canada must be an optimistic, inclusive, and forward-looking country. His "sunny ways" and the promise of a more virtuous government resulted in 184 Liberal seats compared to 99 for the Conservatives (32 per cent of the popular vote). The New Democrats were relegated to third place with 44 seats and 20 per cent of the vote. With the return of the Liberals, political power shifted from the Canadian West back to Quebec and Ontario.

In 2015, the Liberal Party under Justin Trudeau understood the Canadian electorate better than either the Conservatives or the New Democrats. Canadians believed that Trudeau reflected the type of country they desired: accommodating and hopeful. He promised a progressive and inclusive Canada and delivered immediately: his cabinet became the first to have gender parity. He created ministerial portfolios, such as Families, Children and Social Development and Environment and Climate Change, to reflect new priorities. At the same time, he raised expectations. There was a vast array of promises in health care, tax cuts for the middle class, environmental policy, the legalization of cannabis, a new relationship with First Nations and Indigenous peoples, democratic reform, and massive infrastructure spending—all to be accomplished with just a few years of modest deficits.

Trudeau also promised to transform Canada abroad as well as at home. *The Economist,* the influential international magazine, praised Canada as an example to the world in October 2016, noting in particular how it welcomed 33,000 Syrian refugees and remains committed to free trade and globalization. "Canada has long seemed to outsiders to be a citadel of decency, tolerance and good sense," it wrote, adding, "Today, in its lonely defence of liberal values, Canada seems downright heroic. In an age of seductive extremes, it remains reassuringly level-headed."[22] Such a view of Canada took on added meaning after the divisive Donald Trump was sworn in as the 45th president of the United States on January 20, 2017. Canada has its problems and challenges, too, as all nations certainly do, but many in Canada are hopeful that their country can be an example to the world. Many of the 60 per cent of Canadians who did not vote for Justin Trudeau and the Liberal party in the 2015 federal election agreed, nonetheless, with their new prime minister when he remarked that Canada mattered in the world and that diversity was Canada's greatest strength. The optimism and excitement that Trudeau initially created is all oddly reminiscent of the early years after Confederation when John A. Macdonald, George-Étienne Cartier, and, later, Wilfrid Laurier, harnessed the exuberance of a youthful nation and saw the great potential that lay ahead for Canada.

22 "Liberty Moves North: Canada's Example to the World," *The Economist,* October, 29, 2016.

INDEX

Entries about a specific government are found under the prime minister's name (e.g. Chrétien, Jean) or the topic. For provinces, topics that cover several provinces are found under "provinces" whereas topics about a single province is found under that province's name.

SOURCES

Page 8 Library and Archives Canada/George P. Roberts/C-000733. Page 12 Library and Archives Canada/Notman & Son/C 02162. Page 15 Library and Archives Canada/C-001855. Page 19 Library and Archives Canada/Topley Studio/PA-025486. Page 21 Library and Archives Canada/Notman Studio, Acc. No. 1957-049, C-002048. Page 30 Library and Archives Canada/C-006513. Page 33 Library and Archives Canada/C-010460. Page 37 National Archives of Canada/C-017233. Page 42 © McCord Museum, II-88120.0. Page 44 © McCord Museum, MP-0000.25.532. Page 50 Library